Urban Social Segregation

Edited by

Ceri Peach

Lecturer in Geography, University of Oxford
and Fellow of St. Catherine's College

Longman London and New York

41893

Longman Group Ltd.

Longman Group Limited
London and New York
Associated companies, branches and
representatives throughout the world
Published in the United States by
Longman Inc., New York

This edition
© Longman Group Limited 1975

 his edition first published 1975

Library of Congress Cataloging in Publication Data
Main entry under title:

Urban social segregation.

Includes index.
1. Sociology, Urban – Addresses, essays, lectures.
2. Social distance – Addresses, essays, lectures.
3. Social classes – Addresses, essays, lectures.
4. Minorities – Addresses, essays, lectures.
I. Peach, Ceri.
HT151.U68   301.1'09173'2   74–80434
ISBN 0–582–48088–4
ISBN 0–582–48089–2 pbk.

Printed in Great Britain by
Lowe & Brydone (Printers) Ltd, Thetford, Norfolk

Contents

Acknowledgements

We are grateful to the following for permission to reproduce copyright material:

The American Geographical Society for an article 'Residential Segregation and Intermarriage in San Fernando, Trinidad' by Colin G. Clarke. Reprinted by courtesy of the *Geographical Review*, Vol. 61, 1971, copyrighted by the American Geographical Society of New York; The American Sociological Association and respective authors for an article 'The Interaction of Social and Physical Space' by Arnold S. Feldman and Charles Tilly in *American Sociological Review*, Vol. 25, No. 6, December 1960, an article 'A Methodological Analysis of Segregation Indexes' by Otis Dudley Duncan and Beverly Duncan in *American Sociological Review*, Vol. 20, April 1955, an article 'Assortative Mating and the Structure of Cities' by Natalie Rogoff Ramsøy in *American Sociological Review*, Vol. 31, No. 6, 1966; an extract from an article 'A Comparison of Mathematical Models for the Effect of Residential Propinquity on Mate Selection' by William R. Catton Jnr. and R. J. Smircich in *American Sociological Review*, Vol. 29, No. 6, 1964, and an extract from an article 'Residential Propinquity of White Mates at Marriage in Relation to Age and Occupation of Males, Columbus, Ohio, 1938 and 1946' by Marvin R. Koller in *American Sociological Review*, Vol. 13, 1948; The Association of American Geographers for an extract from an article by H. Rose in *Annals of the Association of American Geographers*, Vol. 60, No. 1, March 1970; *Australian Geographical Studies* for an article by I. H. Burnley in *Australian Geographical Studies*, No. 10, 1972; Colston Research Society for an extract from Colston Papers No. 22, 'Regional Forecasting', by B. J. Berry edited by M. Chisholm, A. Frey and P. Haggett; The Clarendon Press for an article 'Immigrants and Residence' by Peter Collison from *Sociology*, Vol. 1, 1967 (c), 1967 Oxford University Press, by permission of The Clarendon Press, Oxford; The *Geographical Review* for an extract from an article 'The Negro Ghetto: Problems and Alternatives' by Richard

L. Morrill in *Geographical Review*, July 1965, Vol. 55. Copyrighted by the American Geographical Society of New York; The New Zealand Geographical Society for an article by D. Rowland in *New Zealand Geographer*, Vol. 27, No. 1, April 1971; The Queen's University of Belfast for an extract from *Irish Geographical Studies* by F. W. Boal; Royal Dutch Geographical Society for an extract from *Tijschrift voor Economische en Sociale Geografie* 1970 by R. J. Stimson, Vol. 61; The *Sociological Review* for the paper 'The Distribution and Segregation of Roman Catholics in Belfast' (1956) by Prof. Emrys Jones; University of North Carolina Press for an extract from an article by S. Lieberson in *Social Forces*, Vol. 40, 1961, and for an extract from an article by F. Lancaster Jones in *Social Forces*, Vol. 45, No. 3, March 1967; University of Southern California for an extract from an article by D. Timms in *Sociology and Social Research*, Vol. 53, No. 3, April 1969; The University of Chicago Press and respective authors for an extract from *The Urban Community* by R. E. Park edited by E. W. Burgess, an extract from an article by Otis Dudley Duncan and Beverly Duncan in *American Journal of Sociology*, Vol. 60, No. 5, March 1955, an extract from an article by Eugene S. Uyeki in *American Journal of Sociology*, Vol. 69, No. 5, March 1964, an extract from an article by P. F. Cressey in *American Journal of Sociology*, Vol. 44, No. 1, July 1938, an extract from an article by Otis Dudley Duncan and S. Lieberson in *American Journal of Sociology*, Vol. 64, January 1959, an extract from an article by Karl E. Taeuber and A. E. Taeuber in *American Journal of Sociology*, Vol. 69, No. 4, January 1964, an extract from an article by N. Kantrowitz in *American Journal of Sociology*, Vol. 74, May 1969, and for an extract from an article by Ruby J. R. Kennedy in *American Journal of Sociology*, Vol. 48, 1943.

Abbreviations used in the notes

Am. J. Sociol.	*American Journal of Sociology*
Am. Sociol. Rev.	*American Sociological Review*
Geogrl. J.	*Geographical Journal*
Geogrl. Rev.	*Geographical Review*
J. Am. Stat. Ass.	*Journal of the American Statistical Association*

Note. In reprinting these papers, many of them from American sources, the spelling of the original has been retained.

Ceri Peach

Introduction
The spatial analysis of ethnicity and class

The theme of this book is the relationship between social distance and geographical space. Its basic hypothesis is that the greater the degree of difference between the spatial distributions of groups within an urban area, the greater their social distance from each other. It argues that degrees of spatial similarity between socially defined groups are correlates and symbiotes of the degree of social interaction between those groups; that there is a spectrum of spatial association varying from complete similarity between groups, at one end, to complete segregation at the other; that the correlate of complete spatial similarity is complete social interaction, with high rates of intermarriage, while the correlate of segregation is the rejection, by the higher group, of social interaction with the lower group.

> Social distance . . . may be used to describe the relationships among social classes, occupational groups, or any other grouping. Social distance may be measured behaviorally – who marries whom, who lives near whom, and so forth; or it may be measured psychologically by the traditional social-distance scale in which persons are asked to rank various ethnic and racial groups according to a series of hypothetical social relationships – would you marry an X, eat meals with an X, have an X in your neighborhood, in your school, at your job, and so forth (Beshers, 1962, p. 50).

Three principles have guided the selection of readings: the first was to present a clear statement of the conceptual relationship between social distance and spatial association; the second was to explain the methodology of social spatial analysis; the third was to present substantive contributions to the theory.

The paper which presents the clearest statement of the conceptual relationship between social distance and spatial association was published by Park in 1926 [1]*. This paper is the fountainhead from which all else

* Numbers in square brackets refer to essays in this symposium.

1

flows. Not only does it phrase the arguments forcefully, but after fifty years their clarity, strength and inspiration remain. The paper also has an historical importance, tracing in its first footnote, the divergent paths of ideographic geography and nomothetic sociology. It seems a fitting point from which to start a book which attempts to channel the two divergent flows within the same course. In this latter respect, the present book may be regarded as an extension of Theodorson's attempt at synthesis (Theodorson, 1961).

The second guiding principle has been that of methodology. If social and spatial associations are so intimately related, then statistical measures of that association are fundamental to analysis of the relationship. A number of indices of segregation are shown in this book, but the demonstration by Duncan and Duncan [2] of the superiority of the index of dissimilarity over the other indices has done more for the advance of social geography than any other methodological innovation. This does not mean that no significant work was produced before this measure was available, but the full importance of the Duncans' methodological advance can be seen when one compares the attack of the problem of the analysis of segregation and assimilation made by Cressey [6] in 1938 with that made by Duncan and Lieberson in 1959 [7]. Cressey was limited to linear distance from the centre of the city in his measurement of dispersion: it is a blunt tool since some groups moved outward without dispersing. Duncan and Lieberson, using indices of dissimilarity, were able to gauge dispersion through measures of spatial mixing rather than distance from a single pole. Cressey offered only evidence: Duncan and Lieberson produced proof.

The use of the index of dissimilarity allows us to distinguish between the residential similarity of groups and the residential proximity of individuals. Clearly, high degrees of residential dissimilarity between groups are not incompatible with high degrees of residential proximity between individuals belonging to those different groups. Working-class Roman Catholics and Protestants in Belfast, for example, are highly segregated, although the segregated areas often abut each other. Individuals on either side of a segregated interface belong to dissimilar distributions, but are physically close to one another. Nor should one expect all areal parts of socially defined groups in a city to be contiguous, although one might expect higher degrees of social interaction between discontiguous parts of the same social group than between socially dissimilar but adjacent groups (see Boal, 1970 [15]). In terms of indices of dissimilarity, what bonds a social group together is not contiguity, but its spatial dissimilarity from, and lack of penetration by, other groups. Thus it is possible to view, for example, the middle class in an urban area as a community, even though it may be split into several separated parts. Similarly, adjacent parts of highly segregated groups may be viewed as being distinct despite their proximity. Thus, the use of indices of dissimilarity allow us to consider community independently of the contiguity of the group and shows us that proximity is not necessarily productive of community.

The attempt to produce a satisfactory index that would measure the spatial mix of populations is thus an important part of the development of social spatial analysis and for this reason it was tempting to include the main papers of the 'index war' that was waged between 1947 and 1955. However, for practical purposes, the Duncans' (1955b) paper [3] is the most important and the others are excluded. As the Duncans themselves remark [3, p. 42], it is unlikely that any single index can adequately measure all forms of segregation. The index represents degrees of spatial mix and contains no information about distributional patterns. It is subject to the disadvantages of all average measures. However, the index of dissimilarity has a large number of positive attributes. It is independent of the relative sizes of the two groups that are being compared – a fundamental advantage over most indices, which are influenced by the size of minority groups. It is, moreover, an index which is simple to compute, (unlike the Gini index, which otherwise shares many of its good characteristics) and one which has direct verbal meaning.

The index of dissimilarity represents the percentage of a population group which would have to shift its residence in order to reproduce a spatial distribution identical with that of the group with which it is being compared. The index thus has a theoretical minimum of 0 (complete similarity) and a maximum of 100 (complete segregation). Since the fundamental thesis of this book is that the greater the degree of spatial dissimilarity between groups, the greater their degree of social distance, the practical value of the index of dissimilarity, which measures this distance in percentage terms, can be appreciated. For readers who wish to pursue the subject further, a clear discussion is given by Timms (1965) and an excellent overview of the literature is given by the Taeubers (1965, Appendix A). However, since the index is of such fundamental importance to understanding much of what follows, and since some readers may be frightened of it in the form $Id = \frac{1}{2} \sum_{i=1}^{k} |x_i - y_i|$ the following explanation is included. The index of dissimilarity is equal to half the sum of the differences of the x and y populations contained in each of the i units which comprise the k universe.

An example of the calculation is given below (see table). The difference is calculated by subtracting the smaller of the x and y (black and white) figures from the larger in each of the i units (regions) of the k universe (the coterminous United States). The sum of the resulting differences is then halved to give the index of dissimilarity, which in this example would be 25. Thus, at the regional scale 25 per cent of the black population of the United States in 1970 would have to change its region of residence in order to replicate the regional distribution of the white population. In

3

	USA 1970		
Region	Per cent of the black population	Per cent of the white population	Difference
South	53	28	25
North East	19	25	6
North Central	20	29	9
West	8	18	10
Total	100	100	50

the present book, the index is applied to much smaller units than regions (to census tracts and block data) within much smaller universes (cities) but the principle remains the same. However, the smaller the areal units used for measurement, the higher the index and at the city level the degrees of dissimilarity for black and white are strikingly different from the regional figures.

The third principle of choice was to select papers in which substantive contributions were made to the understanding of the relationship of social distance to physical space. Assimilation and integration are difficult terms to define and to measure (Gordon, 1964; Price, 1969). However, the association between spatial and social separation on the one hand and dispersal and assimilation on the other evidenced by the papers collected here is strong. Duncan and Lieberson's paper (1959 [7]) is perhaps the most important of the papers on the ethnic theme, but the Taeubers (1964 [9]) paper in which they demonstrate a continuing pattern of ethnic hierarchy in Chicago and in which they demonstrate the small contribution of economic factors to the sharp separation of the Afro-Americans at the bottom of that hierarchy, is of major importance. The general pattern of class segregation demonstrated by the Duncans (1955a [2]) may not have been surprising, but the demonstration of the financial sacrifices of those at the bottom of the white-collar ladder, to leapfrog the richer group at the top end of the blue-collar section, in order to remain spatially associated with the rest of the white-collar group is clearly of significance ([2] p. 64). Inevitably, American material predominates here. This is a reflection of the excellence of American work as well as its quantitative dominance in the field. This is in turn a reflection both of the heterogeneity of American society and the availability, from a comparatively early date, of small area census statistics (Robson, 1969, pp. 39–45). Enumeration district material was first made available in the United Kingdom in 1951 (and then for only a few areas). However, out of this first release came Emrys Jones's (1956 [14]) classic analysis of the segregation of Roman Catholics and Protestants in Belfast. In Britain, since that time, as ethnic differentiation has increased

4

and the data have become more widely available, studies have multiplied. Work has been done by Collison and Mogey (1959), Collison (1967 [16]), P. N. Jones (1967) and Peach (1968). Significantly, Australia and New Zealand whose societies have also become more ethnically differentiated since the last war, are now areas where considerable research is being pursued on spatial differentiation. Prominent among the workers are Zubrzycki (1960), Lancaster Jones (1967 [17]), Stimson (1970 [18]), Burnley (1972 [19]) and Rowland (1972 [21]). Yet, while this collection contains a preponderance of American material, it does not, even so, do justice to the research effort of that country in this field since it does not include work from three indispensable books in this field: Duncan and Duncan's *The Negro Population of Chicago* (1957), Lieberson's *Ethnic Patterns in American Cities* (1963) and Taeuber and Taeuber's *Negroes in Cities* (1965).

Spatial sociology may seem to some to be unfortunate neologism but if the term is found inelegant it may, nevertheless, be found useful. It is used here to define that part of sociology which employs spatial analysis to elucidate social structures. Within this general field, four main subgroups may be defined and it is with only one of these subgroups that this collection is predominantly concerned.

The four main groups that may be distinguished are: the human ecologists, the social area analysts, the factorial ecologists and what, for want of a better term, I call the dissimilarists. All of these groups are connected to some degree, but the dissimilarists are distinct in being concerned more with space than place. The classical ecologists, on the other hand, show great concern with the relationship of groups to urban morphology and distance from city centres. Included in such a group would be work by Burgess himself, Frazier (1937), Cressey (1938), Ford (1950) and Kiang (1968). The social area analysts are concerned with problems of regionalization and of grouping of social characteristics defined by *a priori* deductive reasoning (or by *post facto* inductive rationalization, according to its opponents). Shevky, Bell and Williams (Shevky and Williams, 1949; Shevky and Bell, 1955) are among the originators and proponents of this approach. The factorial ecologists (and, allowing for differences of techniques, the principal components analysts and cluster analysts) are concerned with the same kind of regionalization problems as the social area analysts, but allow computers to collapse their large number of variables into more manageable factors rather than deciding, *a priori* what variables are most highly correlated. Geographers such as Berry and Rees have been particularly active in this field. It is thought a more objective technique than social area anlysis, though the eventual factors depend completely on the original selection of variables. It is therefore subject to the computers' caveat: garbage in; garbage out.

Thus, in contrast to the ecologists, the social area analysts and the factorial ecologists, who can express many of their results in maps, the results of the dissimilarists analysis are not easily susceptible to cartographic representation. Lieberson's *Ethnic Patterns in American Cities* contains no maps. The Taeubers include maps in *Negroes in Cities* but they are contained in an appendix and are not central to their analysis. Similarly, there is an enormous difference between Kantrowitz's (1969a[10]) cartographic analysis of Negroes and Puerto Ricans in New York written as geography and his dissimilarist analysis of ethnicity in New York which contains no maps (1969b); the first is about place, the second about space. The dissimilarists are concerned with the total degree of spatial mixing of groups rather than where those groups are placed on the ground. They are concerned with an almost topological concept of interrelationship and mix rather than with the Euclidean geometry of location. They are concerned with the representation of the analysis of the aggregate rather than with the representation of the individual areal components of that aggregate. The main impetus for their work has come from the Duncans and their successors in the use of their method include Lieberson and the Taeubers. This is not to say that those workers who use the index of dissimilarity are unconcerned with the spatial pattern of the location of groups; the Duncans, for example, stressed the importance of pattern [3, p. 42].

If one were to reduce the number of subgroups of spatial sociology from four to two, then, despite their apparent contrasts, the social area analysts and the factorial ecologists would form one group and the human ecologists and the dissimilarists would form the other. The 'deductive' social area analysts and the 'inductive' factorial ecologists are distinguished more by technique than by aim; indeed, one might say more by technology than by technique. Factorial analysis could be seen as a more sophisticated social area analysis. The union of the ecologists, with their concern for the concrete morphology and pattern, with the abstract dissimilarists may seem a more curious pairing and require greater explanation, yet the abstract idea of spatial mix has developed essentially out of the analysis of the concrete patterns of the ecologists. It is implicit in the initial statement of Park [1, p. 28] about the relationship of social and geographical distance that measures of mixing other than the crude linear measure of the distance between groups would be necessary for the analysis of such relationship; in other words, that a degree of mathematical abstractions would be required. Indeed, not only did the dissimilarist approach develop out of the classical ecological method but in some of the key works both methods are utilised. The Duncans' *The Negro Population of Chicago* (1957) combines both the ecological and dissimilarist approaches; indeed, their earlier fundamental paper on residential distribution and occupational stratification [3] produced the same fusion by developing the index of centralization (thus quantifying the Burgessian distance-from-the-centre interest of the human ecologists) and applying their own index of dissimilarity (the associational space, not place) to occupational groups.

The human ecologists, the social area analysts and the factorial ecologists have all been extensively reported to geographers; the human ecologists by Theodorson (1961), Robson (1969), Timms (1971) and Johnston (1971); the social area analysts by Herbert (1967) and Timms (1971); the factorial analysts by Berry and Rees (1971). The dissimilarist works, however, have been rather neglected, though reported by Timms (1965) and Johnston (1971). The aim of this book is to bring them more into the mainstream of geographical literature.

In very broad terms, there are two major approaches to the study of society, the first through the study of the behaviour and psychology of individuals, the second through the study of the actions of groups. It might be thought that these two approaches are part of a continuum; that by breaking down the actions of groups into their component parts one might arrive at an understanding of individual behaviour or that, conversely, by aggregating the actions of individuals, one might arrive at an understanding of the action of groups. Such an argument sounds seductive but there is enormous difficulty in meshing together the two approaches: at different scales of investigation different parameters control; what is true at the macro scale is not necessarily true at the micro scale; while at the macro level the distribution of black and white has been becoming more similar in the United States, at the micro level it has become more dissimilar. However, to give a hypothetical example, at the macro level, a person's choice of town to live in may be controlled by economic factors such as the location of jobs; within the town, the decision as to which area to live in may be controlled by social rather than by purely economic decisions, while at the very smallest scale the decision as to which house to occupy within the selected area may be controlled by very minor or even apparently random factors. Thus the parameters of control vary with the scale of investigation. We may say with truth that we live in a particular house because we like the size of the kitchen (true at the micro level) or that we like social atmosphere of the neighbourhood (true at the meso level) or because our job is in this town (true at the macro level). We may not even be aware of the major parameters that control our location. The essential paradox is that of Heisenberg's 'uncertainty principle' (Haggett, 1965, p. 25): at the subatomic level individual particles behave randomly, yet the masses which comprise the unpredictable particles are themselves predictable. One may predict with a high degree of accuracy the action of large aggregate groups without being able to predict the action of particular individual components of that group. Gravity models, for example, may be accurate predictors of aggregate movement for large populations although they may not be able to specify which individuals will compose their aggregates. History faces the same philosophical problem; what is the relative importance of individual action and general

7

conditions to the moulding of events?

Two of the major controversies within geography have revolved round related topics: first, should geography be a study of the unique or the general; second, are distributions in geography the result of random, free will probabilities or of deterministic factors? Some methodological, if not philosophical, resolution of the second problem has been yielded by the use of stochastic simulation models which allow probabilities to be randomly distributed within deterministic bounds or constraints. Chance, within Morrill's model of ghetto expansion (Morrill, 1965 [11]), for instance, is not totally random. From the determinist's point of view, the use of randomness within the deterministic constraints of the system can be taken as representing those small-scale determining factors which are unknown; for the possibilist, the random element can be interpreted as true randomness or free will. The first problem, the ideographic versus the nomothetic, is similar to the difference between the study of individuals and groups. If individuals can appear to operate randomly while groups that comprise those individuals act predictably, it seems that one may not achieve a full understanding of the group simply through aggregating individuals; there are truths about aggregate behaviour which are different from truths about individual behaviour; the study of the mass and the study of individuals are not simply differences of scale along a continuum, they are qualitatively different. This present study is concerned with group behaviour and attitudes measured by degrees of spatial mixture rather than with the study of the behaviour or individuals.

The social importance of this spatial approach to the study of society is this: from the overall, spatial, residential matrix of social groups within urban areas, one can deduce the strengths of social divisions between those groups. Such deductions may not be informative about the relationship of individual members of groups, but will nevertheless be instructive about the group relationships. From infrared photographs of the earth, taken from satellites, it is possible to detect the disease of potato blight before the disease can be detected in individual plants on the ground; viewing the plants as a mass evidently cumulates over the whole what is not visible for the individual. By examining the spatial mix of population groups in urban areas, it is possible to discover the strength of attitudes that may be difficult to assess from a study of individuals. The examination of residential patterns of social groups is *one* path to an understanding of society.

However, if we accept the general proposition about the significance of spatial mix to measuring social differences, there remains the problem of interpreting the *process* of separation from the *pattern* of distributional dissimilarity (Duncan and Duncan, 1955a [2, p. 42]; Taeuber and Taeuber, 1965, p. 28). The pattern is the net effect of two gross forces; the first is the positive self-ascriptive force which makes a group want to segregate itself; the second is the negative proscriptive force of outside society which prevents the segregated group from dispersing. From the pattern one can determine the net effect of both forces, but one cannot immediately distinguish the *relative* strengths of the positive and negative forces. It is even possible, as the Duncans argue, for decreases in the degree of segregation (and thus an apparent decrease in net hostility) to be brought about by conditions which represent exactly the opposite social situation. The analogy which comes to mind, in relation to their explanation of the increase in 'mixed areas' in Chicago between 1940 and 1950 (Duncan and Duncan, 1957, pp. 97–9), is that of the forward wave of black expansion at the edge of the ghetto moving outward at a faster rate, under pressure from within the ghetto, than the white tide in that same fringing area could retreat. The degree of overlap thus produced reduces the degree of dissimilarity between the two groups, but does not represent a situation of stable integrated residence.

A further problem is that the analysis of spatial mixture of groups tells us about the effects of social tension; it does not tell us how to cure the causes, the tensions of which the distributions are symptoms. We may accept the proposition that from the liberal point of view the ghetto is the geographical manifestation of social failure, yet doubt that the tensions would be cured by enforced distributions that ensure the identical (even after allowing for standardization of group characteristics) distribution of all groups. We do not know whether manipulation of the pattern will have a beneficial effect on that process. Sociospatial analysis may have come a long way but sociospatial engineering for integration has hardly begun. Sociospatial engineering for the negative, segregationist model, has reached near perfection in South Africa, but positive thinking about alternatives in less authoritarian societies seems to date back only to Downs (1968).

At this stage we arrive at a discussion of the geographical contribution to the spatial analysis of society, for in its most recent developments we may see the beginnings of an approach to sociospatial engineering.

There have been four main stages in the geographers' contribution to the spatial analysis of ethnicity. The first is the macro scale studies such as [1] those by Hartshorne (1938) on all major racial groups in the United States and those by Calef and Nelson (1956) and Hart (1960) of the distribution of the black population of the United States; Peach on the distribution of West Indians in Great Britain (1966). The second is the descriptive approach to urban distributions, Hodder on the Chinese in Singapore (1953), Novak on the Puerto Rican distribution in Manhattan (1956), Rose on the black population of Miami (1964), Clarke on Kingston, Jamaica (1966), Peach on West Indians in British Cities (1968), Kantrowitz on New York (1969a). The third is the use of the dissimilarist approach, for example by [3] Burnley (1972) on the immigrant groups of Sydney, Stimson on Melbourne (1970[18]) and Kantrowitz on New York (1969b[10]), Rowland on the

Maoris in Auckland (1972 [21]), Winchester on coloured immigrants in Coventry (1973). The fourth is the application of predictive models to ethnic distributions, beginning with Morrill (1965 [11]), Rose (1970 [12]), Hansell and Clark (1970), Berry (1971 [13]) and continuing with Woods on Birmingham (1973).

It is in this last group that some interesting developments are taking place from the viewpoint of social policy. Morrill's technique was to apply Monte Carlo simulation techniques to the spatial expansion of the ghetto, while Berry's technique was to apply Markov chains to the black school population of Chicago to predict the change in racial mix over time. Projections, of course, depend very strongly on historical experience so that the outcomes of such exercises are likely to be 'more of the same' rather than any revolutionary departure from the existing situation. Interest thus centres on the accuracy of the simulated distributions, when compared with the actual outcome, as a reflection of the accuracy of the assessment of original inputs and constraints built into the system. Even if the simulated and real outcomes coincide quite well, there may still be doubt as to whether the co-equal finality was simulated by the correct process (see for example, Rose's 1970 comments on Morrill's 1965 work). The predictive geographical models, however, do have a very important role to play in social engineering. They present a picture of the probable distributions that will arise if *laissez-faire* policies continue in the allocation of housing.

Finally, two questions about residential distributions have to be considered: first, are they more significant than workplace or any other spatial distribution in measuring social interaction; second, is intermarriage a more significant measure of assimilation and integration than spatial distribution? Conclusions on those points in the absence of data must be speculative. Residence, in terms of the census population, refers to the night-time distribution. If a daytime census were taken, it is possible that sex and age segregation would be more important than ethnic or class segregation, with women in their homes, men in their workplaces and children at school. It is possible that with daytime data, ethnic groups might achieve a higher degree of spatial similarity. From night-time censuses, it would seem that men and women are socially integrated while their economic segregation is not as obvious. Thus, residential similarity is not the only kind; workplaces and places of entertainment, for example, offer opportunities for social interaction. The locations of these activities may be only indirectly related to the residential places of the interacting populations. Considerations such as these have led to a growing interest in time/space budgets, pioneered by Engle-Frisch (1943) and Hawley (1950) and taken up by Hagerstrand (1969). Thus one should not expect all social interaction to be related directly to degrees of residential similarity. There is an asymmetry to be expected in the relationship of residential space and social interaction. The spatial similarity of social groups is socially significant, but not all socially significant relationships are related to residential similarity.

In the traditional social-distance scale, residential similarity ranks lower than intermarriage or eating together (Beshers 1962, p. 50). However, the conclusions to be drawn from the literature as to the relative importance of residence and other measures of segregation or integration is that residence is the highest explanatory, available measure, but that intermarriage is, perhaps, the most significant measure. Intermarriage rates have been calculated for foreign-born persons in countries such as the USA (Kennedy 1943, 1944, 1952) and Australia (Price and Zubrzycki 1962a, 1962b) where they are available, but for Britain, for example, they are not available.

Marriage rates, however, are preconditioned by both residential proximity of individuals (Kennedy 1943 [23]; Koller 1948 [24]) and by spatial similarity of groups (Timms 1969 [20]). Beshers argues that intermarriage is not simply a consequence of residential segregation, but a prime causal factor in bringing residential segregation about (Beshers 1962, pp. 105–6 and 151–2). Beshers argues, in fact, that residential segregation is not only a reflection of the social stratification system, but that part of the process by which that system is perpetuated is by the intermarriage of physically proximate social peers (Beshers 1962, pp. 111–21). He also argues (p. 135) that if his analysis is correct, it should be possible to predict the degree of residential segregation between any two groups in Northern American cities from a knowledge of the intermarriage rates between those two groups. Beshers does not produce such evidence, but the study by Lancaster Jones (1967 [17]) suggests complementary evidence in a high degree of correlation between the degree of in-marriage and the degree of residential concentration of ethnic groups in Melbourne. A study by Timms (1969 and 1971, pp. 103–4) on intermarriage, residential dissimilarity and other measures of social distance in Queensland, supports this hypothesis. Work by Peach (1974a) has demonstrated that there is a high and significant correlation of indices of residential dissimilarity and marital dissimilarity for nine birthplace groups in Sydney. Koller's evidence from Columbus, Ohio, demonstrates that men of lower occupational status had shorter median distances between themselves and their future wives than men with higher occupational status (Koller, 1948). This underlines the importance of using measures of dissimilarity as well as linear distance in such studies. Given the Duncans' demonstration (1955a[3]) and the replication of their findings by Feldman and Tilly (1960 [5]) that, in North American cities, the lower the occupational status the greater the degree of concentration of the group near the city centre, it could be argued that, the more dispersed upper occupational groups would have to travel greater distances in order to generate a social peer group with numbers equivalent to that available to the lower class groups in their more centralized

11

and therefore more confined space. Thus we may conclude that residential distributions and indices of residential dissimilarity are significant not only as correlates of the most important social interactions, but in their own right.

There is, however, one major piece of work which argues against the ecological conditioning of the selection of marriage partners. Ramsøy, in an analysis of marriage partners in Oslo in 1962 (Ramsøy 1966 [26]) was able to demonstrate that the two tendencies to marry people who were occupationally similar and who were geographically proximate were independent of each other. She also argued that segregation was not a phenomenon that linked these tendencies. Further work has argued against this latter conclusion (Peach 1974b), demonstrating that it arose out of her method of categorizing marriages. Likeness and nearness were more intimately associated than Ramsøy had concluded and residential segregation of grooms by occupation was highly and significantly correlated with indices of dissimilarity of choices of brides classified by occupation.

The situation we postulate therefore, is one in which indices of residential dissimilarity are more important than simple measures of proximity. They are more important because they allow us to predict the discounting of social interaction between adjacent parts of dissimilar groups. Proximity continues to operate within the group. Thus one would predict higher degrees of interaction within contiguous parts of a group than between discontiguous parts of that group. However, group perception should ensure that discontiguous parts of its peer group, within a city, are perceived as being closer than adjacent parts of a different group.

Although social interaction is highly correlated with spatial similarity, the behavioural connection that unites these spatial correlates is not precisely known. It is thought to be a function of opportunity to meet, and distance decay. Distance decay means simply that, other things being equal, there will be greater amounts of interaction (measured in such terms as visits, telephone calls, etc.) between people and places close to one another than those further apart. Zipf (1949) has made the most general application of this concept, but small-scale studies such as those by Festinger, Schachter and Back (1950), Catton and Smircich (1964 [25]) and Timms (1971, pp. 11–12), are perhaps more relevant here. Timms' study of a new housing development showed that women living within 100 yards of a respondent were more than ten times as likely to be chosen as friends as those living 400 yards away.

Proximity is necessary but insufficient to produce positive interaction. At their edges, highly segregated communities are very close to one another, but this interface is often one of instability and hostility. Residents are often conditioned to perceive the social border as a barrier. Thus activity and interaction of people is constrained not only by a general distance decay factor but among other factors by a subjective appraisal of distance. Everyone carries a personal metric which differs from the objective, linear metric. Hagerstrand's migration studies in Sweden (cited by Haggett, 1965, pp. 38–9) suggested that his subjects had a logarithmic view of space – great detail of the area close to them and an exaggeration of the size of this area in relation to the rest of the world which was bunched together, with little differentiation, at the edge of their local area. The most striking example of this kind of study is that by J. Ross MacKay (1958) on areal interaction in Canada. By collapsing the two variables of distance and size of interacting centres into a single measure (by dividing the size of the centre by a measure of distance, since activity between places, other things being equal, would decrease with distance while activity between places, other things being equal, would increase with the size of interacting centres) MacKay was able to measure interaction (for example by the number of telephone calls) in relation to the single distance/ size measure. There was regularity in this relationship – the bigger the size/distance (gravity) measure, the greater the interaction. However, there were three parallel courses of the plots for this interaction, depending upon the political units in which the interacting centres were located. Towns in the rest of Quebec behaved in relation to Montreal as if they were five to ten times closer than towns of the same size and separation in the rest of Canada; towns in the United States behaved as if they were fifty times as far away. Thus, while it is not possible to attribute this effect precisely among the contributing causes, interactions seem to depend not only on the true size and distance relationship, but on perception values as well.

At a smaller scale of investigation, the subjective value of place has been known for a long time; Firey's (1945) Boston example is the most widely quoted example of the effect of the attachment of symbolic, social values to place on the development of urban morphology. However, in terms of the effect of perception on the segregation of activity, Boal's work on Belfast (1969, 1970 [15] and 1971) is the most interesting and relevant. In these studies, in which he controls for the effects of religion and social class, he demonstrates, first, how even the choice of bus stop may be made with regard to the religion of the area within which it is situated rather than by absolute distance from the traveller's point of origin. He also shows the segregation of shopping and visiting activities by religion. In his study of adjacent areas of similar religion, but different social class, he again demonstrates the segregation of activities of the two groups and the lack of interaction between the adjacent areas.

Thus, to sum up, it is hoped that this book will do four things. First, it shows the relevance of spatial pattern to social behaviour by showing how the degree of spatial differentiation of groups is a reflection of the attitudes of groups towards each other; that the greater the degree of spatial dissimilarity, the greater the social gulf. Secondly, it shows that spatial patterns can be comprehended at a number of different levels and that perhaps the most significant patterns are represented by mathematical indices of spatial mix rather than by cartographic representation. Thirdly, it is hoped that this collection will show how ideas have developed over time, and finally, that it will show the relevance of sociology to social geography and vice versa.

Bibliography

BERRY, B. J. L. (1971) 'Monitoring trends, forcasting change and evaluating goal achievements: the ghetto v. desegregation issue in Chicago as a case study,' *Colston, Papers No. 22, Regional Forecasting*, ed. M. Chisholm, A. E. Frey and P. Haggett, London, Butterworth. [13]

BERRY, B. J. L. and REES, P. H. (1971)

BESHERS, J. M. (1962) *Urban Social Structure*, New York, Free Press.

BOAL, F. (1970) 'Social space in the Belfast urban area,' in *Irish Geographical Studies*, ed. N. Stephens and R. E. Glasscock, 373–393, Queens University of Belfast. [15]

BURGESS, E. W. (1924) 'The Growth of the City: an Introduction to a Research Project', *Publications, American Sociological Society*, **21**, 178–84.

BURNLEY, I. H. (1972) 'European immigration and settlement patterns in metropolitan Sydney, 1947–66', *Australian Geographical Studies*, **10**, 61–78. [19]

CALEF, W. C. and NELSON, H. J. (1956) 'Distribution of Negro population in the United States', *Geogrl. Rev.*, **46**, 82–97.

CATTON, W. R. and SMIRCICH, R. J. (1964) 'A comparison of mathematical models for the effect of residential propinquity of mate selection', *Am. Sociol. Rev.*, **29**, 522–9. [25]

CLARKE, C. G. (1969) 'Population Pressure in Kingston, Jamaica, A Study of Unemployment and Overcrowding,' *Transactions of the Institute of British Geographers*, **38**, 165–82.

CLARKE, C. G. (1971) 'Residential segregation and intermarriage in San Fernando, Trinidad', *Geogrl. Rev.*, **61**, No. 2. 198–218. [227]

COLLISON, P. (1967) 'Immigrants and residence', *Sociology*, **1**, No. 3, 277–292. [16]

COLLISON, P. and MOGEY, J. M. (1959) 'Residence and Social Class in Oxford', *Am. J. Sociol.*, **64**, 599–605.

CRESSEY, P. F. (1938) 'Population succession in Chicago', *Am. J. Sociol.*, **44**, 56–9. [6]

DOWNS, A. (1968) 'The Future of American Ghettos', *Daedalus*, **97**, 1331–78.

DUNCAN, O. D. and DUNCAN, B. (1955a) 'A methodological analysis of segregation Indexes', *Am. Sociol. Rev.*, **20**, 210–17. [2]

DUNCAN, O. D. and DUNCAN, B. (1955b) 'Residential distribution and occupational stratification', *Am. J. Sociol.*, **60**, No. 5, 493–503. [3]

DUNCAN O. D. and DUNCAN, B. (1957) *The Negro Population of Chicago*, Chicago University Press.

DUNCAN, O. D. and LIEBERSON, F. (1959) 'Ethnic segregation and assimilation', *Am. J. Sociol.*, **64**, 364–74. [7]

ENGLE-FRISCH, G. (1943) 'Some neglected temporal aspects of human ecology', *Social Forces*, **22**, 43–7.

FELDMAN, A. S. and TILLY, C. (1960) 'The interaction of physical and social space', *Am. Sociol. Rev.*, **25**, 877–84. [5]

FESTINGER, L., SCHACHATER, S. and BACK, K. (1950) *Social Pressures in Informal Groups*, New York, Harper.

FORD, R. G. (1950) 'Population Succession in Chicago', *Am. J. Sociol.*, **56**, 151–60.

FRAZIER, E. F. (1937) 'Negro Harlem: An Ecological Study', *Am. J. of Sociol.*, **43**,72–88.

GORDON, M. M. (1964) *Assimilation in American Life*, New York, Oxford University Press.

HAGERSTRAND, T. (1969) 'What about people in regional science?', *Regional Science Association Papers*, 1–21.

HAGGETT, P. (1965) *Locational Analysis in Human Geography* London, Edward Arnold.

HANSELL, C. R. and CLARK, W. A. V. (1970) 'The expansion of the Negro Ghetto in Milwaukee: a descriptive and simulation model,' *Tijdschrift voor Econ. en Soc. Geog.*, **61**, 267–77.

HART, J. F. (1960) 'The Changing Distribution of the American Negro', *Annals of the Association of American Geographers*, **50**.

HARTSHORNE, R. (1938) 'Racial Maps of the United States', *Geogrl. Rev.*, **28**, 276–88.

HAWLEY, A. H. (1950) '*Human Ecology: a theory of community structure*, New York, Ronald Press.

HERBERT, D. T. (1967) 'Social Area Analysis: A British Study', *Urban Studies*, **4**, 41–60.

JOHNSTON, R. J. (1971) *Urban Residential Patterns*, London, Bell & Sons.

JONES, EMRYS (1956) 'The distribution and segregation of Roman Catholics and Protestants in Belfast', *Sociological Review*, **4**, 167–89. [14]

JONES, F. LANCASTER (1967) 'Ethnic concentration and assimilation: An Australian case study', *Social Forces*, **45**, no. 3. 412–23. [17]

JONES, P. N. (1967) *The Segregation of Immigrant Communities in the City of Birmingham*, Hull, Department of Geography, University of Hull.

KANTROWITZ, N. (1969a) *Negro and Puerto Rican Population of New York City in the Twentieth Century*, New York, American Geographical Society.

KANTROWITZ, N. (1969b) 'Ethnic and racial segregation in the New York Metropolis, 1960', *Am. J. Sociol.*, **74**, 685–95. [10]

KENNEDY, R. J. R. (1943) 'Premarital residential propinquity and ethnic endogamy', *Am. J. Sociol.*, **48**, no. 5. 580–4. [23]

KENNEDY, R. J. R. (1944) 'Single or triple melting pot? Intermarriage trends in New

15

Haven, 1870–1940', *Am. J. Sociol.*, **49**, 331–9.

KENNEDY, R. J. R. (1952) 'Single or triple melting pot? Intermarriage in New Haven, 1870–1950', *Am. J. Sociol.*, **58**, 56–9.

KIANG, Y-C. (1968) 'The distribution of ethnic groups in Chicago', *Am. J. Sociol.*, **74**, 292–5.

KOLLER, M. R. (1948) 'Residential propinquity of white mates at marriage in relation to age and occupation of males, Columbus, Ohio, 1938 and 1946', *Am. Sociol. Rev.*, **13**, 613–16. [24]

LIEBERSON, S. (1961) 'The impact of residential segregation on ethnic assimilation', *Social Forces*, **40**, 52–7. [8]

LIEBERSON, S. (1963) *Ethnic Patterns in American Cities*, New York, The Free Press of Glencoe.

MACKAY, J. ROSS (1958) 'The interactance hypothesis and boundaries in Canada: A preliminary Study', *The Canadian Geographer*, **11**, 1–8.

MORRILL, R. L. (1965) 'The Negro Ghetto: problems and alternatives', *Geol. Rev.*, **55**, 339–61. [11]

NOVAK, R. T. (1956) 'Distribution of Puerto-Ricans on Manhattan Island', *Geogl. Rev.*, **46**, 182–6.

PARK, R. E. (1926) 'The urban community as a spatial pattern and a moral order', in *The Urban Community*, ed. E. W. Burgess, Chicago University Press. [1]

PEACH, G. C. K. (1966) 'Factors Affecting the Distribution of West Indians in Great Britain', *Transactions of the Institute of British Geographers*, **38**, 151–63.

PEACH, G. C. K. (1968) *West Indian Migration to Britain: A Social Geography*, Oxford University Press, for the Institute of Race Relations.

PEACH, G. C. K. (1974a) 'Ethnic segregation and intermarriage patterns in Sydney', *Australian Geographical Studies*, October, 1974.

PEACH, G. C. K. (1974b) 'Homogamy, Propinquity and Segregation: a Re-evaluation', *Am. Sociol. Rev.*

PRICE, C. A. (1969) 'The study of assimilation', in *Migration*, ed. J. A. Jackson, Cambridge, Cambridge University Press.

PRICE, C. A. and ZUBRZYCKI, J. (1962a) 'The use of inter-marriage statistics as an index of assimilation', *Population Studies*, **16**, 58–69.

PRICE, C. A. and ZUBRZYCKI, J. (1962b) 'Immigrant marriage patterns in Australia', *Population Studies*, **16**, 123–33.

RAMSØY, N. R. (1966) 'Assortative mating and the structure of cities', *Am. Sociol. Rev.*, **31**, no. 6, 713–86. [26]

ROBSON, B. T. (1969) *Urban Analysis*, Cambridge, Cambridge University Press.

ROSE, H. M. (1964) 'Metropolitan Miami's Changing Negro Population, 1950–1960', *Economic Geography*, **40**, 221–38.

ROSE, H. M. (1970) 'The development of an urban sub-system: The case of the Negro ghetto', *Annals of the Association of American Geographers*, **60**, 1–17. [12]

ROWLAND, D. T. (1972) 'Maori migration to Auckland', *New Zealand Geographer*, **27**, no. 1. 21–37. [21]

SHEVKY, E. and BELL, W. (1955) *Social Area Analysis*, Stanford, Stanford University Press.

SHEVKY, E. and WILLIAMS, M. (1949) *The Social Areas of Los Angeles*, Berkeley, University of California Press.

STIMSON, R. J. (1970) 'Patterns of immigrant settlement in Melbourne, 1947–61', *Tijdschrift voor Econ. en. Soc. Geog.* [18]

TAEUBER, K. E. and TAEUBER, A. F. (1964) 'The negro as an immigrant group: recent trends in racial and ethnic segregation in Chicago', *Am. J. Sociol.*, **69**, 374–82. [9]

TAEUBER, K. E. and TAEUBER, A. F. (1965) '*Negroes in Cities*, Chicago, Aldine Publishing Co.

THEODORSON, G. A. (ed.) (1961) *Studies in Human Ecology*, Evanston Illinois Row, Peterson and Co.

TIMMS, D. W. C. (1965) 'Quantitative Techniques in Urban Social Geography', in *Frontiers in Geographical Teaching*, ed. R. J. Chorley and P. Haggett, London, Methuen.

TIMMS, D. W. G. (1969) 'The dissimilarity between overseas-born and Australian-born in Queensland: dimensions of assimilation', *Sociology and Social Research*, **53**, 363–74. [20]

TIMMS, D. W. G. (1971) *The Urban Mosaic: towards a theory of residential differentiation*, Cambridge University Press.

UYEKI, E. S. (1964) 'Residential distribution and stratification, 1950–1960', *Am. J. Sociol.*, **59**, no. 5, 491–8 [4]

WINCHESTER, S. W. C. (1973) 'Immigration and the Immigrant in Coventry: A Study in Segregation', unpublished paper delivered at the annual conference of the Institute of British Geographers, Birmingham, January, 1973.

WOODS, R. I. (1973) 'The Role of Simulation in the Modelling of Immigrant Spatial Sub-systems: An Application to Birmingham', an unpublished paper delivered at the annual conference of the Institute of British Geographers, Birmingham, January, 1973.

ZIPF, G. K. (1949) *Human behaviour and the principle of least effort*, Cambridge, Cambridge University Press.

ZUBRZYCKI, J. (1960) *Immigrants in Australia*, Melbourne, Melbourne University Press.

Part I

General

R. E. Park

1 The urban community as a spatial pattern and moral order*

Some thirty years ago Professor Eugenius Warming, of Copenhagen, published a little volume entitled *Plant Communities (Plantesamfund)*. Warming's observations called attention to the fact that different species of plants tend to form permanent groups, which he called communities. Plant communities, it turned out, exhibit a good many of the traits of living organisms. They come into existence gradually, pass through certain characteristic changes, and eventually are broken up and succeeded by other communities of a very different sort. These observations later become the point of departure for a series of investigations which have since become familiar under the title 'Ecology'.

Ecology, in so far as it seeks to describe the actual distribution of plants and animals over the earth's surface, is in some very real sense a geographical science. Human ecology, as the sociologists would like to use the term is, however, not identical with geography, nor even with human geography. It is not man, but the community; not man's relation to the earth which he inhabits, but his relations to other men, that concerns us most.

Within the limits of every natural area the distribution of population tends to assume definite and typical patterns. Every local group exhibits a more or less definite constellation of the individual units that compose it. The form which this constellation takes, the position, in other words, of every individual in the community with reference to every other, so far as it can be described in general terms, constitutes what Durkheim and his school call the morphological aspect of society.[1]

Human ecology, as sociologists conceive it, seeks to emphasize not so much geography as space. In society we not only live together, but at the same time we live apart, and human relations can always be reckoned, with

* Reprinted from *The Urban Community*, ed. Ernest W. Burgess, University of Chicago Press, 1926.

21

more or less accuracy, in terms of distance. In so far as social structure can be defined in terms of position, social changes may be described in terms of movement; and society exhibits, in one of its aspects, characters that can be measured and described in mathematical formulas.

Local communities may be compared with reference to the areas which they occupy and with reference to the relative density of population distribution within those areas. Communities are not, however, mere population aggregates. Cities, particularly great cities, where the selection and segregation of the populations has gone farthest, display certain morphological characteristics which are not found in smaller population aggregates.

One of the incidents of size is diversity. Other things being equal, the larger community will have the wider division of labor. An examination a few years ago of the names of eminent persons listed in *Who's Who* indicated that in one large city (Chicago) there were, in addition to the 509 occupations listed by the census, 116 other occupations classed as professions. The number of professions requiring special and scientific training for their practice is an index and a measure of the intellectual life of the community. For the intellectual life of a community is measured not merely by the scholastic attainments of the average citizen, nor even by the communal intelligence-quotient, but by the extent to which rational methods have been applied to the solution of communal problems – health, industry, and social control, for example.

One reason why cities have always been the centers of intellectual life is that they have not only made possible, but have enforced, an individualization and a diversification of tasks. Only as every individual is permitted and compelled to focus his attention upon some small area of the common human experience, only as he learns to concentrate his efforts upon some small segment of the common task, can the vast co-operation which civilization demands be maintained.

In an interesting and suggestive paper read before the American Sociological Society at its meeting in Washington in 1922, Professor Burgess sketched the processes involved in the growth of cities. The growth of cities has usually been described in terms of extensions of territory and increase in numbers. The city itself has been identified with an administrative area, the municipality; but the city, with which we are here concerned, is not a formal and administrative entity. It is rather a product of natural forces, extending its own boundaries more or less independently of the limits imposed upon it for political and administrative purposes. This has become to such an extent a recognized fact that in any thoroughgoing study of the city, either as an economic or a social unit, it has been found necessary to take account of natural, rather than official, city boundaries. Thus, in the city-planning studies of New York City, under the direction of the Russell Sage Foundation, New York City includes a territory of 5,500 square miles, including in that area something like one hundred minor administrative units, cities, and villages, with a total population of 9,000,000.

We have thought of the growth of cities as taking place by a mere aggregation. But an increase in population at any point within the urban area is inevitably reflected and felt in every other part of the city. The extent to which such an increase of population in one part of the city is reflected in every other depends very largely upon the character of the local transportation system. Every extension and multiplication of the means of transportation connecting the periphery of the city with the center tends to bring more people to the central business district, and to bring them there oftener. This increases the congestion at the center; it increases, eventually, the height of office buildings and the values of the land on which these buildings stand. The influence of land values at the business center radiates from that point to every part of the city. If the growth at the center is rapid it increases the diameter of the area held for speculative purposes just outside the center. Property held for speculation is usually allowed to deteriorate. It easily assumes the character of a slum; that is to say, an area of casual and transient population, an area of dirt and disorder, 'of missions and of lost souls'. These neglected and sometimes abandoned regions become the points of first settlement of immigrants. Here are located our ghettos, and sometimes our bohemias, our Greenwich Villages, where artists and radicals seek refuge from the fundamentalism and the Rotarianism, and, in general, the limitations and restrictions of a Philistine World. Every large city tends to have its Greenwich Village just as it has its Wall Street.

The growth of the city involves not merely the addition of numbers, but all the incidental changes and movements that are inevitably associated with the efforts of every individual to find his place in the vast complexities of urban life. The growth of new regions, the multiplication of professions and occupations, the incidental increase in land values which urban expansion brings – all are involved in the processes of city growth, and can be measured in terms of changes of position of individuals with reference to other individuals, and to the community as a whole. Land values can be reckoned, for example, in terms of mobility of population. The highest land values exist at points where the largest number of people pass in the course of twenty-four hours.

The community, as distinguished from the individuals who compose it, has an indefinite life-span. We know that communities come into existence, expand and flourish for a time, and then decline. This is as true of human societies as it is of plant communities. We do not know with any precision as yet the rhythm of these changes. We do know that the community outlives the individuals who compose it. And this is one reason for the seemingly inevitable and perennial conflict between the interests of the individual and the community. This is one reason why it costs more to police a growing city than one which is stationary or declining.

Every new generation has to learn to accommodate itself to an order which is defined and maintained mainly by the older. Every society imposes some sort of discipline upon its members. Individuals grow up, are incorporated into the life of the community, and eventually drop out and disappear. But the community, with the moral order which it embodies, lives on. The life of the community therefore involves a kind of metabolism. It is constantly assimilating new individuals, and just as steadily, by death or otherwise, eliminating older ones. But assimilation is not a simple process, and, above all else, takes time.

The problem of assimilating the native-born is a very real one; it is the problem of the education of children in the homes and of adolescents in the schools. But the assimilation of adult migrants, finding for them places in the communal organization, is a more serious problem: it is the problem of adult education, which we have just in recent years begun to consider with any real sense of its importance.

There is another aspect of the situation which we have hardly considered. Communities whose population increase is due to the excess of births over deaths and communities whose increase is due to immigration exhibit important differences. Where growth is due to immigration, social change is of necessity more rapid and more profound. Land values, for one thing, increase more rapidly; the replacement of buildings and machinery, the movement of population, changes in occupation, increase in wealth, and reversals in social position proceed at a more rapid tempo. In general, society tends to approach conditions which are now recognized as characteristic of the frontier.

In a society in which great and rapid changes are in progress there is a greater need for public education of the sort that we ordinarily gain through the public press, through discussion and conversation. On the other hand, since personal observation and tradition, upon which common sense, as well as the more systematic investigations of science, is finally based, are not able to keep pace with changes in conditions, there occurs what has been described by Ogburn as the phenomenon of 'cultural lag'. Our political knowledge and our common sense do not keep up with the actual changes that are taking place in our common life. The result is, perhaps, that as the public feels itself drifting, legislative enactments are multiplied, but actual control is decreased. Then, as the public realizes the futility of legislative enactments, there is a demand for more drastic action, which expresses itself in ill-defined mass movements and, often, in mere mob violence. For example, the lynchings in the southern states and the race riots in the North.

So far as these disorders are in any sense related to movements of population – and recent studies of race riots and lynchings indicate that they are – the study of what we have described as social metabolism may furnish an index, if not an explanation, of the phenomenon of race riots.

One of the incidents of the growth of the community is the social selection and segregation of the population, and the creation, on the one hand, of natural social groups, and on the other, of natural social areas. We have become aware of this process of segregation in the case of the immigrants, and particularly in the case of the so-called historical races, peoples who, whether immigrants or not, are distinguished by racial marks. The Chinatowns, the Little Sicilies, and the other so-called 'ghettos' with which students of urban life are familiar are special types of a more general species of natural area which the conditions and tendencies of city life inevitably produce.

Such segregations of populations as these take place, first, upon the basis of language and of culture, and second, upon the basis of race. Within these immigrant colonies and racial ghettos, however, other processes of selection inevitably take place which bring about segregation based upon vocational interests, upon intelligence, and personal ambition. The result is that the keener, the more energetic, and the more ambitious very soon emerge from their ghettos and immigrant colonies and move into an area of second immigrant settlement, or perhaps into a cosmopolitan area in which the members of several immigrant and racial groups meet and live side by side. More and more, as the ties of race, of language, and of culture are weakened, successful individuals move out and eventually find their places in business and in the professions, among the older population group which has ceased to be identified with any language or racial group. The point is that change of occupation, personal success or failure – changes of economic and social status, in short – tend to be registered in changes of location. The physical or ecological organization of the community, in the long run, responds to and reflects the occupational and the cultural. Social selection and segregation, which create the natural groups, determine at the same time the natural areas of the city.

The modern city differs from the ancient in one important respect. The ancient city grew up around a fortress; the modern city has grown up around a market. The ancient city was the center of a region which was relatively self-sufficing. The goods that were produced were mainly for home consumption, and not for trade beyond the limits of the local community. The modern city, on the other hand, is likely to be the center of a region of very highly specialized production, with a corresponding widely extended trade area. Under these circumstances the main outlines of the modern city will be determined (1) by local geography and (2) by routes of transportation.

Local geography, modified by railways and other major means of transportation, all connecting, as they invariably do, with the larger industries, furnish the broad lines of the city plan. But these broad outlines are likely to be overlaid and modified by another and a different distribution of

25

population and of institutions, of which the central retail shopping area is the center. Within this central downtown area itself certain forms of business, the shops, the hotels, theaters, wholesale houses, office buildings, and banks, all tend to fall into definite and characteristic patterns, as if the position of every form of business and building in the area were somehow fixed and determined by its relation to every other.

Out on the periphery of the city, again, industrial and residential suburbs, dormitory towns, and satellite cities seem to find, in some natural and inevitable manner, their predetermined places. Within the area bounded on the one hand by the central business district and on the other by the suburbs, the city tends to take the form of a series of concentric circles. These different regions, located at different relative distances from the center, are characterized by different degrees of mobility of the population.

The area of greatest mobility, i.e. of movement and change of population, is naturally the business center itself. Here are the hotels, the dwelling-places of the transients. Except for the few permanent dwellers in these hotels, the business center, which is the city *par excellence*, empties itself every night and fills itself every morning. Outside the city, in this narrower sense of the term, are the slums, the dwelling-places of the casuals. On the edge of the slums there are likely to be regions, already in process of being submerged, characterized as the 'rooming-house areas', the dwelling-places of bohemians, transient adventurers of all sorts, and the unsettled young folk of both sexes. Beyond these are the apartment-house areas, the region of small families and delicatessen shops. Finally, out beyond all else, are the regions of duplex apartments and of single dwellings, where people still own their homes and raise children, as they do, to be sure, in the slums.

The typical urban community is actually much more complicated than this description indicates, and there are characteristic variations for different types and sizes of cities. The main point, however, is that everywhere the community tends to conform to some pattern, and this pattern invariably turns out to be a constellation of typical urban areas, all of which can be geographically located and spatially defined.

Natural areas are the habitats of natural groups. Every typical urban area is likely to contain a characteristic selection of the community as a whole. In great cities the divergence in manners, in standards of living, and in general outlook on life in different urban areas is often astonishing. The difference in sex and age groups, perhaps the most significant indexes of social life, are strikingly divergent for different natural areas. There are regions in the city in which there are almost no children, areas occupied by the residential hotels, for example. There are regions where the number of children is relatively very high: in the slums, in the middle-class residential suburbs, to which the newly married usually graduate from their first honeymoon apartments in the city. There are other areas occupied almost wholly by young unmarried people, boy and girl bachelors. There are regions where people almost never vote, except at national elections; regions where the divorce rate is higher than it is for any state in the Union, and other regions in the same city where there are almost no divorces. There are areas infested by boy gangs and the athletic and political clubs into which the members of these gangs or the gangs themselves frequently graduate. There are regions in which the suicide rate is excessive; regions in which there is, as recorded by statistics, an excessive amount of juvenile delinquency, and other regions in which there is almost none.

All this emphasizes the importance of location, position, and mobility as indexes for measuring, describing, and eventually explaining, social phenomena. Bergson has defined mobility as 'just the idea of motion which we form when we think of it by itself, when, so to speak, from motion we abstract mobility'. Mobility measures social change and social disorganization, because social change almost always involves some incidental change of position in space, and all social change, even that which we describe as progress, involves some social disorganization. In the paper already referred to, Professor Burgess points out that various forms of social disorganizaation seem to be roughly correlated with changes in city life that can be measured in terms of mobility. All this suggests a further speculation. Since so much that students of society are ordinarily interested in seems to be intimately related to position, distribution, and movements in space, it is not impossible that all we ordinarily conceive as social may eventually be construed and described in terms of space and the changes of position of the individuals within the limits of a natural area; that is to say, within the limits of an area of competitive co-operation. Under such interesting conditions as these all social phenomena might eventually become subject to measurement, and sociology would become actually what some persons have sought to make it, a branch of statistics.

Such a scheme of description and explanation of social phenomena, if it could be carried out without too great a simplification of the facts, would certainly be a happy solution of some of the fundamental logical and epistemological problems of sociology. Reduce all social relations to relations of space and it would be possible to apply to human relations the fundamental logic of the physical sciences. Social phenomena would be reduced to the elementary movements of individuals, just as physical phenomena, chemical action, and the qualities of matter, heat, sound, and electricity are reduced to the elementary movements of molecules and atoms.

The difficulty is that in kinetic theories of matter, elements are assumed to remain unchanged. That is, of course, what we mean by element and elementary. Since the only changes that physical science reckons with are changes in space, all qualitative differences are reduced to quantitative differences, and so made subject to description in mathematical terms. In the case of human and social relations, on the other hand, the elementary units – that is to say, the individual men and women who enter into these different combinations – are notoriously subject to change. They are so far from representing homogeneous units that any thoroughgoing mathematical treatment of them seems impossible.

Society, as John Dewey has remarked, exists in and through communication, and communication involves not a translation of energies, such as seems to take place between individual social units, for example, in suggestion or imitation, two of the terms to which sociologists have at various times sought to reduce all social phenomena; but rather communication involves a transformation in the individuals who thus communicate. And this transformation goes on unceasingly with the accumulation of individual experiences in individual minds.

If human behavior could be reduced again, as some psychologists have sought to reduce it, to a few elementary instincts, the application of the kinetic theories of the physical sciences to the explanation of social life would be less difficult. But these instincts, even if they may be said to exist, are in constant process of change through the accumulation of memories and habits. And these changes are so great and continuous that to treat individual men and women as constant and homogeneous social units involves too great an abstraction. That is the reason why we are driven finally, in the explanation of human conduct and society, to psychology. In order to make comprehensible the changes which take place in society it is necessary to reckon with the changes which take place in the individual units of which society seems to be composed. The consequence is that the social element ceases to be the individual and becomes an attitude, the individual's tendency to act. Not individuals, but attitudes, interact to maintain social organizations and to produce social changes.

This conception means that geographical barriers and physical distances are significant for sociology only when and where they define the conditions under which communication and social life are actually maintained. But human geography has been profoundly modified by human invention. The telegraph, telephone, newspaper, and radio, by converting the world into one vast whispering-gallery, have dissolved the distances and broken through the isolation which once separated races and people. New devices of communication are steadily multiplying, and incidentally complicating, social relations. The history of communication is, in a very real sense, the history of civilization. Language, writing, the printing press, the telegraph, telephone, and radio mark epochs in the history of mankind. But these, it needs to be said, would have lost most of their present significance if they had not been accompanied by an increasingly wider division of labor.

I have said that society exists in and through communication. By means of communication individuals share in a common experience and maintain a common life. It is because communication is fundamental to the existence of society that geography and all the other factors that limit or facilitate communication may be said to enter into its structure and organization at all. Under these circumstances the concept of position, of distance, and of mobility have come to have a new significance. Mobility is important as a sociological concept only in so far as it insures new social contact, and physical distance is significant for social relations only when it is possible to interpret it in terms of social distance.

The social organism – and that is one of the most fundamental and disconcerting things about it – is made up of units capable of locomotion. The fact that every individual is capable of movement in space insures him an experience that is private and peculiar to himself, and this experience, which the individual acquires in the course of his adventures in space, affords him, in so far as it is unique, a point of view for independent and individual action. It is the individual's possession and consciousness of a unique experience, and his disposition to think and act in terms of it, that constitutes him finally a person.

The child, whose actions are determined mainly by its reflexes, has at first no such independence and no such individuality, and is, as a matter of fact, not a person.

It is this diversity in the experiences of individual men that makes communication necessary and consensus possible. If we always responded in like manner to like stimulation there would not be, as far as I can see, any necessity for communication, nor any possibility of abstract and reflective thought. The demand for knowledge arises from the very necessity of checking up and funding these divergent individual experiences, and of reducing them to terms which make them intelligible to all of us. A rational mind is simply one that is capable of making its private impulses public and intelligible. It is the business of science to reduce the inarticulate expression of our personal feelings to a common universe of discourse, and to create out of our private experiences an objective and intelligible world.

We not only have, each of us, our private experience, but we are acutely conscious of them, and much concerned to protect them from invasion and misinterpretation. Our self-consciousness is just our consciousness of these individual differences of experience, together with a sense of their ultimate incommunicability. This is the basis of all our reserves, personal and racial; the basis, also, of our opinions, attitudes, and prejudices. If we were quite certain that everyone was capable of taking us, and all that we regard as personal to us, at our own valuation; if, in other words, we were as naïve as children, or if, on the other hand, we were all as suggestible and lacking in reserve as some hysterics, we should probably have neither persons nor society. For a certain isolation and a certain resistance to social influences and social suggestion is just as much a condition of sound personal existence as of a wholesome society. It is just as inconceivable that we should have persons without privacy as it is that we should have society without persons.

It is evident, then, that space is not the only obstacle to communication, and that social distances cannot always be adequately measured in purely physical terms. The final obstacle to communication is self-consciousness.

What is the meaning of this self-consciousness, this reserve, this shyness, which we so frequently feel in the presence of strangers? It is certainly not always fear of physical violence. It is the fear that we will not make a good impression; the fear that we are not looking our best; that we shall not be able to live up to our conception of ourselves, and particularly, that we shall not be able to live up to the conception which we should like other persons to have of us. We experience this shyness in the presence of our own children. It is only before our most intimate friends that we are able to relax wholly, and so be utterly undignified and at ease. It is only under such circumstances, if ever, that communication is complete and that the distances which separate individuals are entirely dissolved.

This world of communication and of 'distances', in which we all seek to maintain some sort of privacy, personal dignity, and poise, is a dynamic world, and has an order and a character quite its own. In this social and moral order the conception which each of us has of himself is limited by the conception which every other individual, in the same limited world of communication, has of himself, and of every other individual. The consequence is – and this is true of any society – every individual finds himself in a struggle for status: a struggle to preserve his personal prestige, his point of view, and his self-respect. He is able to maintain them, however, only to the extent that he can gain for himself the recognition of everyone else whose estimate seems important; that is to say, the estimate of everyone else who is in his set or in his society. From this struggle for status no philosophy of life has yet discovered a refuge. The individual who is not concerned about his status in some society is a hermit, even when his seclusion is a city crowd. The individual whose conception of himself is not at all determined by the conceptions that other persons have of him is probably insane.

Ultimately the society in which we live invariably turns out to be a moral order in which the individual's position, as well as his conception of himself – which is the core of his personality – is determined by the attitudes of other individuals and by the standards which the group uphold. In such a society the individual becomes a person. A person is simply an individual who has somewhere, in some society, social status; but status turns out finally to be a matter of distance – social distance.

It is because geography, occupation, and all the other factors which determine the distribution of population determine so irresistibly and fatally the place, the group, and the associates with whom each one of us is bound to live that spatial relations come to have, for the study of society and human nature, the importance which they do.

It is because social relations are so frequently and so inevitably correlated with spatial relations; because physical distances, so frequently are, or

seem to be, the indexes of social distances, that statistics have any significance whatever for sociology. And this is true, finally, because it is only as
social and physical facts can be reduced to, or correlated with, spatial facts
that they can be measured at all.

Note

1. Geographers are probably not greatly interested in social morphology as such.
   On the other hand, sociologists are. Geographers, like historians, have been
   traditionally interested in the actual rather than the typical. Where are things
   actually located? What did actually happen? These are the questions that
   geography and history have sought to answer. See *A Geographical Introduction
   to History*, by M. Lucien Febvre and Lionel Bataillon, 1966.

Part II

Methodological

O. D. Duncan and B. Duncan

2 A methodological analysis of segregation indexes[*]

There have been proposed in the literature several alternative indexes of the degree of residential segregation of the nonwhite population of a city.[1] This paper shows that all of these can be regarded as functions of a single geometrical construct, the 'segregation curve'. From this there are developed several important implications: 1. The proposed indexes of segregation have a number of hitherto unnoticed inter-relationships which can be mathematically demonstrated. 2. Some of them have mathematical properties of which their proponents were unaware, and which lead to difficulties of interpretation. 3. As a consequence, the status of the empirical work already done with segregation indexes is questionable, and their validity for further research is undetermined.

This paper consists of a summary of the mathematical analysis made of segregation indexes and of a documentation of the conclusions listed. The problem of validating segregation indexes is viewed as one of some importance, not only in its own right, but also as an illustration of the difficulties in finding an adequate rationale for much sociological research using index numbers.

The segregation curve

Consider the k census tracts of a city. The ith tract contains N_i nonwhites and W_i whites, totalling to $N_i + W_i = T_i$. Summing over i, $\sum_1^k N_i = N$, $\sum_1^k W_i = W$, and $\sum_1^k T_i = T$. For each tract compute the nonwhite proportion, $q_i = N_i/T_i$, and array the tracts in ranks 1 to k in order of magnitude of q_i. With this ordering compute tract by tract the cumulative proportions

* Reprinted from *American Sociological Review*, **20** (1955), 210–17.

of nonwhites and whites, letting the cumulative proportion of nonwhites through the ith tract be X_i and the cumulative proportion of whites be Y_i, e.g., $X_2 = (N_1 + N_2)/N$, $Y_2 = (W_1 + W_2)/W$. The segregation curve is the function $Y_i = f(X_i)$, as graphed in Fig. 2.1. The observed segregation curve, together with the nonwhite proportion in the entire city, $q = N/T$, contains all the information involved in the calculation of any of the segregation indexes suggested in the literature. As is suggested below, research on segregation is not likely to progress far with the research problem limited to the study of this information alone.

Definition of indexes

We here define, with reference to the segregation curve, the several indexes proposed in the literature, omitting the proofs of the equivalence of our definitions and those originally given. In all cases these proofs involve only elementary algebra and geometry.

The 'Gini Index', Gi,[2] is the area between the segregation curve and the diagonal of Fig. 2.1, expressed as a proportion of the total area under the diagonal. It can also be defined as the 'mean cost rating' of the cost-utility curve with $Y = $ cost and $X = $ utility;[3] or as the weighted mean difference with repetition,[4] of the tract nonwhite proportions, q_i, divided by the mean difference, $2pq$, of the binomial variable of color, for the total city population, scoring each white person unity and each nonwhite zero (where $q = N/T$, $p = 1 - q$). The simplest formula for computing Gi is $\sum_1^k X_{i-1} Y_i - \sum_1^k X_i Y_{i-1}$, keeping the tracts in the order established for constructing the segregation curve.

The 'Nonwhite Section Index',[5] here denoted D, for dissimilarity or displacement,[6] is the maximum vertical distance between the diagonal and the curve in Figure 1, i.e., the maximum of the k differences $(X_i - Y_i)$. Alternatively, suppose there are s tracts for which $qi \geq q$; then $D = X_8 - Y_8$. If x_i and y_i are the *uncumulated* proportions of the city's nonwhites and whites, i.e., $x_i = N_i/N$, $y_i = W_i/W$, then $D = \frac{1}{2} \sum_1^k |x_i - y_i|$. Furthermore, D is the weighted mean deviation from q of the tract proportions, q_i, divided by the mean deviation, $2pq$, for the total population. It may be interpreted as the proportion of nonwhites who would have to change their tract of residence to make $q_i = q$ for all i (hence the term, displacement).

Our interest in the Cowgills' index[7] is confined to the mathematical form of the index, without regard to the important but logical distinct issue of the appropriate size of area units. The general form of the index is the ratio of the number of areas occupied exclusively by whites to the maximum number of areas which could be so occupied. To obtain a relationship to the segregation curve we have considered a slight further generalization: the ratio of the number of *persons* living in exclusively white areas to the total whites in the city. The generalized Cowgill Index (*Co*) is then the length of that segment of the curve, if any, which coincides with the vertical drawn from (1,0) to (1,1) (see Fig. 2.2).

It may be noted that the foregoing indexes can be described as measuring directly the degree of departure of the segregation curve from the diagonal, which is the norm of even distribution. Other such indexes of 'unevenness' could doubtless be suggested.[8] The remaining indexes proposed in the literature can be related to the segregation curve only by explicitly introducing the city nonwhite proportion, q. We assume throughout that $q \leqslant 5$.

The 'Nonwhite Ghetto Index', Gh,[9] is found graphically by plotting the line $Y = q(1 - X)/p$. The index value is then $(X_g - Y_g)$, denoting by (X_g, Y_g) the point where this line intersects the segregation curve (see Fig.2.3).

The 'Reproducibility Index', Rep,[10] is formally identical with the index of efficiency used in prediction work.[11] To obtain Rep graphically construct the line parallel to $Y = qX/p$ which is 'tangent' to the segregation curve, i.e., which intersects but one point of the curve or which coincides with that segment (if any) which has a slope q/p. Then the value of Rep is the X-intercept of the auxiliary line (see Fig. 2.4).

The correlation ratio of the binomial variable, color, on tract is by definition the square root of the variance between tract proportions divided by the total variance of the population; i.e.

$$eta = \sqrt{\dfrac{\sum\limits_{1}^{k} T_i q_i^2}{Tpq} - \dfrac{q}{p}}.$$

In the case of a binomial variable, eta is identical with the mean square contingency coefficient, phi,[12] and is equal within a very close approximation to the intraclass correlation.[13] It is, therefore, a well known statistic, appearing, *e.g.* in Robinson's formula for ecological correlation as a measure of 'clustering by area'.[14] The 'revised index of isolation' recently suggested by Bell[15] is identical with the square of eta. This term, as well as the term 'segregation score' used by Jahn *et al.*,[16] seems somewhat superfluous. It also seems undesirable to restrict the use of eta to the case of tracts of equal size, as the latter authors do. Unlike the other indexes, eta involves a squared term, and no simple geometric relationship of eta to the segregation curve has been found. That a relationship exists is, however, indicated below.

Interrelations of indexes

Previous work has made it clear that the foregoing indexes are not independent. Jahn *et al.*[17] found moderate to high empirical correlations

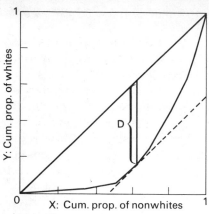

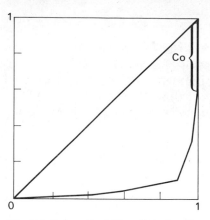

Fig. 2.1 Section index in relation to segregation curve (curve for Macon, Ga, 1940 D = 0·47).

Fig. 2.2 Generalized Cowgill index (Syracuse, NY, Co = 0·42).

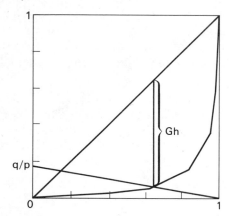

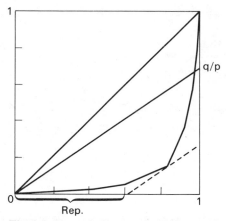

Fig. 2.4 Reproducibility index (Birmingham, Ala, Rep. = 0·62).

Fig. 2.3 Ghetto index (Louisville, Ky., Gh = 0·60).

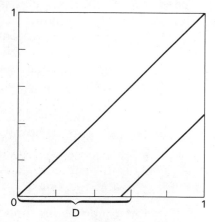

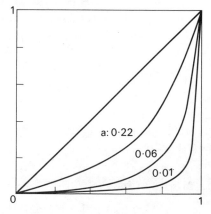

Fig. 2.6 Hyperbola model, $Y = aX/(1-bX)$, for selected values of a.

Fig. 2.5 Williams' model of the segregation curve, with D = 0·56.

among four of them. Hornseth[18] demonstrated that the same four could all be expressed in formulas of one general type. Williams found relationships among them for a segregation curve of a specified type.[19]

In fact, there are definite relationships among the several indexes which hold irrespective of the form of the segregation curve, and which can be derived formally without reference to data. For example, the minimum value of Gi is D, and the maximum is $2D - D^2$. Some of the other relationships which have been found are the following:

1. $qD/(1-pD) \leq Gh \leq D$
2. $1 - p(1-D)/q \leq Rep \leq D$, unless the term on the left is negative, in which case $Rep = 0$.
3. $Gh \leq eta \leq \sqrt{Gh}$
4. $1 - 2p(1-Gh) \leq Rep \leq Gh/(p+qGh)$
5. Co is the minimum value of Gi and D; $qCo/(1-pCo)$ is the minimum of Gh; and if $Co > 1 - q/p$, then $Rep \geq 1 - p(1-Co)/q$.

(Some values of eta and Gh reported by Jahn *et al.* which are inconsistent with the third relationship are to be attributed to their use of a formula for eta not weighted for tract size, or to computational errors.)

From the above it is clear that there is almost necessarily a high correlation between D and Gi, as well as between eta and Gh. On the other hand the correlation between D and Gh need not be high if there is considerable variation in q. These mathematical relationships, therefore, appear to account satisfactorily for the empirical intercorrelations of the index values reported by Jahn *et al.*

A model for the segregation curve

Williams' model of the segregation curve, referred to above, is represented geometrically by the line parallel to the diagonal of the graph which includes the points $(D,0)$ and $(1, 1-D)$ (see Fig. 2.5). For such a curve Williams showed that $Gi = 2D - D^2$, $Gh = D$, and $eta = \sqrt{D}$. It can also be shown that $Co = D$ and $Rep = D$.

The Williams model, although a useful analytical construct, does not serve well to describe empirical segregation curves. We have worked with an alternative model which assumes that the segregation curve has the form of a hyperbola, $Y = aX/(1-bX)$, where a and b are both non-negative, and $a+b = 1$. Fig. 2.6 shows selected curves of this form. It can be seen that the smaller the value of a, the greater is the degree of segregation, as measured by Gi or D. For a segregation curve of the form described, it can be shown that the segregation indexes have the following formulas:

1. $Gi = 1 + 2a(b + \log_0 a)/b^2$.
2. $D = (1 - \sqrt{a})/(1 + \sqrt{a})$

3. $Co = 0$

4. $Rep = (\sqrt{ap} - \sqrt{q})^2/bq$, when $q/p \geqq a$, and $Rep = 0$, when $q/p < a$.

5.
$$Gh = 1 - \frac{\sqrt{4abpq - a^2} - a}{2bpq}$$

No exact formula for *eta* has been found, but in view of the relationship between *eta* and *Gh* stated in the preceding section, the following is suggested as a close approximation:

6. $eta = (Gh + \sqrt{Gh})/2$, where the value of *Gh* is taken from the formula just given.

To fit the hyperbola to census tract data for a city, *D* was calculated from the data, and the parameters of the curve were computed from the formulas $b = 1 - a$, and $a = (1 - D)^2/(1 + D)^2$, the latter being the solution for *a* of the second formula in this section.

A hyperbola was fitted to the census tract data for each of the sixty tracted cities of the United States in 1940. Then, predicted values of each

Table 2.1 Selected measures or closeness of fit of actual segregation index values to values calculated from the hyperbola, for sixty tracted cities: 1940

Segregation index	Mean arithmetic error	Mean absolute error	Root-mean-square error	Correlation index*
D	0·0	0·0	0·0	1·0
Gi	−0·006	0·015	0·019	0·980
Gh	−0·003	0·044	0·066	0·945
Rep	0·028	0·065	0·102	0·908
Eta	−0·016	0·039	0·054	0·958
Co	0·078	0·078	·124	—

* Correlation index $= \sqrt{1 - (\sum d^2)/k \cdot Var\,(I)}$, where the *d*'s are differences between corresponding actual and calculated values of a segregation index, and $Var\,(I)$ is the variance of the actual values. The correlation indexes for this problem are slightly lower than the Pearsonian correlations between actual and observed values.

of the indexes were computed, entering these parameters and the corresponding observed *q*'s in the foregoing formulas. The results summarized in Table 2.1 make it clear that most of the segregation indexes can be predicted rather closely, given *D*, *q*, and the assumption that the segregation curve conforms to the hyperbola model. The largest errors occur for *Co*, since the hyperbola model requires this index to be zero. Even so, the model does not sacrifice a great deal of information. There are eighteen cities whose *Co* index is actually zero, and another thirteen have values of *Co* under 0·05. An index of this type is evidently of little use in comparing cities on the basis of census tract data.

Two important conclusions may be drawn from the experience with the hyperbola model. First, there appears to be a characteristic form for the segregation curves of most large American cities, despite the considerable variation among them in degree of segregation. Second, for this universe of cities, there is little information in any of the indexes beyond that contained in the index, D, and the city nonwhite proportion, q. Each of the other indexes can be obtained to a close approximation given D, q, and the assumption of the hyperbolic form of the segregation curve. This conclusion might require modification if area units other than tracts were employed; and it has not been checked for any date except 1940.

Empirical consequences of the choice of an index

A number of criteria have been offered for the choice of an index formula,[20] with no consensus on the matter having been reached. In our judgment it has been insufficiently emphasized that the empirical results obtained with an index may be strongly affected by its mathematical properties.

For example, Jahn *et al.* report several correlations between Gh and other variables,[21] of which three are large enough to be statistically significant and possibly of theoretical importance. We have reworked these correlations with a somewhat different sample of forty-six cities, calculating segregation indexes for the nonwhite, rather than the Negro, population.

The correlation of Gh with the 1939–40 crude death rate from tuberculosis for these cities was 0·58. A much higher correlation, 0·83, was found between the city nonwhite proportion, q, and the tuberculosis death rate. Further, since q and Gh correlated 0·51, the partial correlation between Gh and the tuberculosis death rate, with q held constant, dropped to 0·32, which is on the borderline of statistical significance at the 0·05 level. Or, when the tuberculosis death rate was standardized for color, the correlation with Gh dropped to 0·29, which is of doubtful significance. In addition it was found that Gi correlated only $-0·02$ and 0·06, respectively, with the crude and standardized tuberculosis death rates. It appears, therefore, that the tuberculosis death rate responds primarily to the proportion nonwhite, rather than to the degree of nonwhite segregation, and that the correlation obtained with Gh reflects primarily the correlation of Gh with q. The difference between the results obtained with Gh and Gi follows from the fact that Gi depends only on the segregation curve, while Gh involves not only the curve but also the nonwhite proportion, q.

It was also found that the correlation between Gh and the per cent of overcrowded housing, 0·40, dropped to 0·02 with q partialled out, and that the correlation with Gi was a nonsignificant $-0·13$, with q being a better predictor than either Gh or Gi, correlating 0·76 with per cent of overcrowding. Similarly the r of $-0·39$, between Gh and Thorndike's 'G' was clearly attributable to the high correlation, $-0·87$, between q and 'G', and even changed in sign to an r of $0·11$ when q was partialled out. The correlation of Gi with 'G' was a nonsignificant $0·18$.

These results indicate that the ability of a segregation index to predict other variables is an insufficient criterion of its worth. If we wished to predict the tuberculosis death rate, the percentage of overcrowding, or Thorndike's 'G', we would use none of the segregation indexes, but instead, q, as the predictor. Yet the theoretically interesting question would remain, e.g. is the tuberculosis death rate associated with the segregation of non-whites? To investigate this question we require a measure of segregation whose validity is established independently of its correlation with the death rate.

Inadequacies of segregation indexes

The literature on segregation indexes contains references to a number of difficulties in their use and interpretation. Some of these require additional comment.

All of the segregation indexes have in common the assumption that segregation can be measured without regard to the spatial patterns of white and nonwhite residence in a city. Yet it is common knowledge that in some cities – e.g. Chicago – the nonwhite population is predominantly clustered in a 'Black Belt', whereas in other cities nonwhite occupancy takes the form of scattered 'islands' or 'pockets'. Surely whatever variables of ecological organization and change are related to the degree of segregation must also be affected by the spatial pattern of segregation. We have found that in 1940, in fifty of the fifty-one non-suburban tracted cities studied, the non-white population was more concentrated toward the ecological center of the city than the white population. (This study involved the use of an 'index of centralization', which has not yet been described in published work, but which is in some respects similar to the Gini segregation index.) Other aspects of the spatial pattern of segregation need to be studied as well. It seems unlikely that any single index of segregation will be found sufficient for the purposes of such research.

In none of the literature on segregation indexes is there a suggestion about how to use them to study the *process* of segregation or change in the segregation pattern. As a first step in this direction we have experimented with an adaptation of the method of expected cases to determine (1) how much of the segregation of nonwhites can be attributed to differences between whites and nonwhites in income, occupational status, and rentals paid, and (2) whether changes in degree of segregation over a ten-year period are related to changes in these variables. It has been found, for example, that there is a marked difference between southern and northern cities in the influence on residential segregation of white-nonwhite differentials in labor force and occupational status. When this variable is held constant, the

Gini index of segregation is reduced by 12 to 22 per cent in most southern cities, but by only 2 to 9 per cent in most of the cities of the North. Such preliminary findings indicate the advisability of taking account of socio-economic factors in analyzing differences in residential segregation. There is, further, a need for research to develop mathematical and empirical bases for anticipating the effects on measures of segregation of such changes as a marked increase in the nonwhite proportion, an improvement of the nonwhite's relative socio-economic status, or an invasion-succession sequence.

The problem of the appropriate areal unit for research on segregation has been forcefully stated by the Cowgills.[22] As they imply, it is easy to gerrymander tract boundaries to increase or decrease the apparent degree of segregation. However, the problem cannot be solved merely by reducing the size of areal units, e.g. to blocks. The objections made to the census tract basis apply also, *mutatis mutandis*, to blocks. For example, if all nonwhites resided on alleyways and all whites in street-front structures, then even a block index would fail to reveal the high degree of segregation. The most complete discussion of the problem of area unit has been given by Wright,[23] who has indicated the formidable difficulties in the way of finding segregation measures which are not relative to the system of area units used.

Implications for index theory

In this paper we have not sought to formulate a comprehensive set of criteria for determining the validity of a segregation index. Probably such an attempt would be premature in the present stage of empirical investigation and conceptualization of the phenomenon of segregation. In our judgment the criteria thus far suggested in the literature fall short of comprehensiveness, and not all of them are likely to be generally accepted. However, we feel that the work reported here is relevant to the problem of validating segregation indexes, and possibly suggestive for the general problem of index development in social research.

Specifically, we have established the following:

1. There was a lack of clarity and consistency in the specifications for a segregation index originally proposed. Jahn *et al.* suggested that 'a satisfactory measure of ecological segregation should . . . not be distorted by . . . the proportion of Negroes'.[24] Though it has never been made clear what would constitute 'distortion' in this respect, it is apparent from our analysis that the nonwhite proportion, q, does enter into the formulas for such indexes as Gi, D, Gh, and Rep, and that q is involved in different ways in the several formulas. For example, if the segregation curve remains constant, but q changes, then the values of Gh, Rep, and eta will be affected, but not those of Gi, D, and Co. As yet there is no criterion to determine which of these is the more desirable property for an index number. Lacking

such a criterion it is perhaps doubtful whether a meaningful comparison can be made of the degrees of segregation of two cities with greatly different q's.

2. The empirical correlations among alternative indexes are clarified by determining the mathematical relationships holding among them – either in general, or under the assumption of a particular model of the segregation curve. Thus the assessment of segregation indexes is carried a step beyond the speculation of Jahn *et al.* that their four indexes comprise 'two sets of independently discriminative measures', [25] and Hornseth's erroneous judgment that these four indexes 'are for practical purposes identical measures'.[26]

3. The mathematical analysis of segregation index formulas discloses the areas of redundancy and ambiguity among them, i.e. it permits a conclusion as to the circumstances in which two indexes will give interchangeable results and in which they will give incompatible results. Hence it goes beyond the truism that the empirical results obtained with an index are in part a function of the mathematical form of the index, to indicate what specific property of the index is responsible for the kind of results obtained. Thus, for example, the finding that Southern cities are more segregated than Northern can be properly qualified if it is known that the index being used responds in a certain way to variations in q, and that Southern cities generally have higher nonwhite proportions than Northern.

A difficult problem of validation is faced by the proponent of a segregation index formula. The concept of 'segregation' in the literature of human ecology is complex and somewhat fuzzy, i.e. the concept involves a number of analytically distinguishable elements, none of which is yet capable of completely operational description. Yet it is a concept rich in theoretical suggestiveness and of unquestionable heuristic value. Clearly we would not wish to sacrifice the capital of theorization and observation already invested in the concept. Yet this is what is involved in the solution offered by naive operationism, in more or less arbitrarily matching some convenient numerical procedure with the verbal concept of segregation. The problem must be faced of considering a variety of possible selections of data and operations on these data in an effort to capture methodologically what is valuable in the work done with the concept prior to the formulation of an index. As we have suggested, it may be that no single index will be sufficient, because of the complexity of the notion of segregation, involving as it does considerations of spatial pattern, unevenness of distribution, relative size of the segregated group, and homogeneity of sub-areas, among others. In short, we are emphasizing the distinction between the problems of (*a*) working from a limited set of data to a mathematically convenient summary index, and (*b*) working from a theoretically problematic situation to a rationale for selecting and manipulating data.

Lazarsfeld and his co-workers[27] have taken the lead in a much needed effort to codify the procedures by which concepts are so specified that index construction may profitably be undertaken and to rationalize the decisions involved in formulating an index for research use. Sociologists will learn, as economists have, that there is no way to devise adequate indexes which avoids dealing with theoretical issues. Incidentally, one lesson to be learned from the relatively unproductive experience with segregation indexes to date is that similar problems are often dealt with under different headings. Most of the issues which have come up in the literature on segregation indexes since 1947 had already been encountered in the methodological work on measures of inequality, spatial distribution, and localization in geography and economics.[28]

Notes and References

Revision of paper read at a meeting of the Midwest Sociological Society, April 1954. The clerical assistance of Florence Sugeno, Richard W. Redick and Robert Glassburg is gratefully acknowledged, as is the financial assistance of the Social Science Research Committee of the University of Chicago. This research was supported in part by the US Air Force under Contract Number AF 33 (038)–25630, monitored by the Human Resources Research Institute. Permission is granted for reproduction, translation, publication and disposal in whole and in part by or for the US Government.

1. Donald O. Cowgill and Mary S. Cowgill, 'An index of segregation based on block statistics', *Am. Sociol. Rev.*, **16**, (Dec. 1951), 825–31; Julius A. Kahn 'The measurement of ecological segregation: derivation of an index based on the criterion of reproducibility', *Am. Sociol. Rev.*, **15**, (Feb. 1950), 100–4; J. A. Kahn, Calvin F. Schmid and Clarence Schrag, 'The measurement of ecological segregation', *Am. Sociol. Rev.*, **12**, (June 1947), 293–303.
2. Jahn, Schmid and Schrag, *op. cit.*, Index #3.
3. O. D. Duncan, 'Urbanization and retail specialization', *Social Forces*, **30**, (March 1952), 267–71; O. D. Duncan, Lloyd E. Ohlin, A. J. Reiss, Jr., and H. R. Stanton, 'Formal devices for making selection decisions', *Am. J. Sociol.*, **58**, (May 1953), 573–84.
4. M. G. Kendall, *The Advanced Theory of Statistics*, 3rd edn., London, Griffin 1947, vol. i, ch. 2.
5. Jahn, Schmid, and Schrag, *op. cit.*, Index #4; Josephine J. Williams, 'Another commentary on so-called segregation indices', *Am. Sociol. Rev.*, **13**, (June 1948), 298–303.
6. D. J. Bogue, *The Structure of the Metropolitan Community*, University of Michigan Press, 1949; Edgar M. Hoover, Jr, 'Interstate redistribution of population, 1850–1940', *J. Econ. Hist.*, **1**, (November 1941), 199–205.

7. Cowgill and Cowgill, *op. cit.*
8. Leo A. Goodman, 'On urbanization indices', *Social Forces*, **31**, (May 1953), 360–2.
9. Jahn, Schmid and Schrag, *op. cit.*, Index #1; Williams, *op. cit.*, 301.
10. Jahn, *op. cit.*
11. Lloyd E. Ohlin and O. D. Duncan, 'The efficiency of prediction in criminology', *Am. J. Sociol.*, **54**, (March 1949), 441–51.
12. Williams, *op. cit.*
13. Leslie Kish, 'On the differentiation of ecological units', Ph.D. dissertation, University of Michigan, 1952.
14. W. S. Robinson, 'Ecological correlations and the behavior of individuals', *Am. Sociol. Rev.*, **15**, (June 1950), 351–7.
15. Wendell Bell, 'A probability model for the measurement of ecological segregation', *Social Forces*, **32**, (May 1954), 357–64.
16. Jahn, Schmid, and Schrag, *op. cit.*, Index #2.
17. Jahn, Schmid, and Schrag, *op. cit.*
18. R. A. Hornseth, 'A note on 'The measurement of ecological segregation' by Julius Jahn, Calvin F. Schmid, and Clarence Schrag', *Am. Sociol. Rev.*, **12**, (October 1947), 603–4.
19. Williams, *op. cit.*, 302.
20. Cowgill and Cowgill, *op. cit.*; Hornseth, *op. cit.*; Jahn, *op. cit.*; Jahn, Schmid, and Schrag, *op. cit.*; Julius A. Jahn, Calvin F. Schmid, and Clarence Schrag, 'Rejoinder to Dr Hornseth's note on "The measurement of ecological segregation"', *Am. Sociol. Rev.*, **13**, (April 1948), 216–17; Kish, *op. cit.*; and Williams, *op. cit.*
21. 'The measurement of ecological segregation', *op. cit.*, 302–3.
22. Cowgill and Cowgill, *op. cit.*
23. John K. Wright, 'Some measures of distribution', *Ann. Ass. Am. Geogr.*, **27**, (December 1937), 177–211.
24. 'The measurement of ecological segregation', *loc. cit.*, 294.
25. *Ibid.*, 299.
26. Hornseth, *op. cit.*, 604.
27. Paul F. Lazarsfeld and Allen H. Barton, 'Qualitative measurement in the social sciences: classification, typologies, and indices', in *The Policy Sciences*, edited by Daniel Lerner and Harold D. Lasswell, Stanford University Press, 1951.
28. P. Sargant Florence, W. G. Fritz, and R. C. Gilles, 'Measures of industrial distribution', ch. 5 in National Resources Planning Board, *Industrial Location and National Resources*, Washington: Government Printing Office, 1943; Edgar M. Hoover, Jr, 'The measurement of industrial localization', *Review of Economic Statistics*, **18**, (November 1936), 162–71; Wright, *op. cit.*; John K. Wright, 'Certain changes in population distribution in the United States', *Geogrl. Rev.*, **31**, (July 1941), 488–90; Dwight B. Yntema, 'Measures of the inequality in the personal distribution of wealth or income', *J. Am. stat. Ass.*

28, (December 1933), 423–33. See also Federal Housing Administration, *The Structure and Growth of Residential Neighborhoods in American Cities*, by Homer Hoyt, Washington: Government Printing Office, 1939, ch. 5; P. Sargant Florence, *Investment, Location, and Size of Plant*, Cambridge University Press, 1948; and George C. Smith, Jr, 'Lorenz curve analysis of industrial decentralization', *J. Am. Stat. Ass.*, **42** (December 1947), 591–6.

Part III

USA social and ethnic

O. D. Duncan and B. Duncan

3 Residential distribution and occupational stratification *

The idea behind this paper was forcibly stated – in fact, somewhat over-stated – by Robert E. Park:

> It is because social relations are so frequently and so inevitably cor-related with spatial relations; because physical distances so frequently are, or seem to be, the indexes of social distances, that statistics have any significance whatever for sociology. And this is true, finally, because it is only as social and psychical facts can be reduced to, or correlated with, spatial facts that they can be measured at all.[1]

This study finds a close relationship between spatial and social distances in a metropolitan community. It suggests that a systematic consideration of the spatial aspect of stratification phenomena, though relatively neglected by students of the subject,[2] should be a primary focus of urban stratification studies. Aside from demonstrating the relevance of human ecology to the theory of social organization, the study offers further evidence for the suitability of a particular set of methodological techniques for research in comparative urban ecology.[3] These techniques are adaptable to a wide variety of problems in urban ecological structure, permit economical and objective comparisons among communities, and thus overcome some of the indeterminacy of a strictly cartographic approach. The techniques are here applied to only one metropolitan community, Chicago; however, com-parative studies, conducted on an exploratory basis, indicate their ability to produce significant results.

Data and method

The sources of data for this study, except as noted otherwise, were the

* *American Journal of Sociology*, **60** No. 5 (March 1955), 493–503.

...ished volume of 1950 census tract statistics for Chicago and adjacent areas[4] (coextensive with the Chicago Metropolitan District, as delineated in 1940), and the census-tract summary punch cards for this area obtained from the Bureau of the Census. The ecological analysis pertains to employed males fourteen years old and over, classified into the eight major occupation groups listed in the tables below. The occupation groups disregarded in this analysis (farmers and farm managers, farm laborers, private household workers, and occupation not reported) include only twenty-one thousand of the one and a half million employed males in the Metropolitan District.

A portion of the analysis is carried through with the census tract as the area unit. There are 1,178 census tracts in the Metropolitan District, of which 935 are in the city of Chicago and 243 in the adjacent area. The remainder of the analysis rests on a scheme of zones and sectors, delineated rather arbitrarily. Tracts were assigned to circular zones, concentric to the center of the city at State and Madison streets, with one-mile intervals up to fourteen miles, two-mile intervals up to twenty-eight miles, and with residual categories of tracts more than twenty-eight miles from the city center and tracts in the adjacent area too large to be classified by zones. The latter category contains only 1·4 per cent of the employed males. Five sectors were established, with boundaries approximating radial lines drawn from the city center. The North Shore sector runs along Lake Michigan through such suburbs as Skokie, Evanston, Lake Forest, and Waukegan; the Northwest sector extends through Park Ridge and Des Plaines to Arlington Heights; the West sector includes the suburbs of Cicero, Oak Park, and Berwyn, running out as far as Wheaton and Naperville; the Southwest sector is approximately bisected by a line running through Blue Island, Harvey, and Chicago Heights to Park Forest; and the South Shore sector runs along Lake Michigan through the Indiana suburbs of East Chicago, Hammond, Gary, and East Gary. Combining the zone and sector schemes yielded a set of 104 zone-sector segments; that is, area units averaging about ten times the size of a census tract, though with considerable variation in area and population.

The spatial 'distance' between occupation groups, or more precisely the difference between their areal distributions, is measured by the *index of dissimilarity*.[5] To compute this index, one calculates for each occupation group the percentage of all workers in that group residing in each area unit (tract or zone-sector segment). The index of dissimilarity between two occupation groups is then one-half the sum of the absolute values of the differences between the respective distributions, taken area by area. In the accompanying hypothetical example the index of dissimilarity between occupations *A* and *B* is 20 per cent (i.e. 40/2). This may be interpreted as a measure of displacement: 20 per cent of the workers in occupation *A* would have to move to a different area in order to make their distribution identical with that of occupation *B*.

Area	A	B	Diff.
1	10%	15%	5%
2	20	15	5
3	40	25	15
4	30	45	15
Total	100%	100%	40%

When the index of dissimilarity is computed between one occupation group and all other occupations combined (i.e. total employed males except those in the given occupation group), it is referred to as an *index of segregation*.[6] An equivalent and more convenient means of computing the segregation index is to compute the index of dissimilarity between the given occupation group and total employed males (i.e. all occupations), 'adjusting' the result by dividing by one minus the proportion of the total male employed labor force included in that occupation group.

The indexes of segregation and dissimilarity were computed on both a tract basis and a zone-sector segment basis to determine the effect of the size of the area unit on the results. While the indexes for tracts are uniformly higher than for zone-sector segments, this effect can be disregarded for purposes of determining the relative positions of the occupation groups. The product-moment correlation between the two sets of segregation indexes in Table 3.2 is 0·96. The correlation between the two sets of dissimilarity indexes in Table 3.3 is 0·98, with the segment-based index (s) related to the tract-based index (t) by the regression equation, $s = 0·8t - 1·3$. These results indicate that for the kind of problem dealt with here the larger, and hence less homogeneous, unit is as serviceable as the smaller one. This suggests that some of the recent concern about census-tract homogeneity may be misplaced.[7]

The *index of low-rent concentration* is obtained by 1. classifying tracts into intervals according to the median monthly rental of tenant-occupied dwelling units; 2. computing the percentage distribution by rent intervals for each occupation group and for all occupations combined; 3. cumulating the distributions, from low to high rent; 4. calculating the quantity $\Sigma X_{i-1} Y_i - \Sigma X_i Y_{i-1}$, where X_i is the cumulated percentage of the given occupation through the ith rent interval, Y_i is the cumulated percentage of all occupations combined, and the summation is over all rent intervals; and finally, 5. 'adjusting' the result (as for the segregation index) to obtain an index equivalent to the one obtained by comparing the given occupation group with all other occupations combined. This index varies between 100 and -100, with positive values indicating a tendency for residences of the given occupation group to be in areas of relatively low rent and with negative values indicating relative concentration in high-rent areas.

The *index of centralization* is computed in the same fashion, except that

53

tracts are ordered by distance from the center of the city, that is, are classified according to the zonal scheme. A negative index of centralization signifies that the given occupation group tends to be 'decentralized', or on the average located farther away from the city center than all other occupations, while a positive index is obtained for a relatively 'centralized' occupation.[8]

Occupation and socioeconomic status

Selected nonecological indicators of the relative socioeconomic status of the major occupation groups are shown in Table 3.1. The professional and managerial groups clearly have the highest socioeconomic rank, while operatives, service workers, and laborers are clearly lowest in socioeconomic status. The ranking by socioeconomic level would probably be agreed on by most social scientists. The major occupation groups correspond roughly with the Alba Edwards scheme of 'social-economic groups'. Edwards does not separate sales workers and clerical workers by 'social-economic group', and the group of service workers, except private household, contains individual occupations variously classified by Edwards as skilled, semiskilled, and unskilled, predominantly the latter two.

A ranking in terms of median income results in two reversals in rank. The 1949 median income of male managerial workers in the Chicago Standard Metropolitan Area was about $500 greater than that of professional workers, although both were substantially above that for sales workers. The median income for the craftsmen-foremen group was about $500 higher than that for clerical workers. In fact, the median income for the craftsmen-foremen group was only slightly below that for sales workers, whereas the median income for clerical workers was only slightly above that for operatives.

However, in median school years completed, professional workers clearly rank first, while there is little difference in the medians for the managerial, sales, and clerical groups. The median drops sharply, over 2·5 years, for the craftsmen-foremen group and declines further for each group in the order of the initial listing.

In the Chicago Metropolitan District the proportion of nonwhites in an occupation group appears to be closely related to its socioeconomic status. The proportion is very low in the professional, managerial, and sales groups, but it is somewhat higher for clerical workers than for the craftsmen-foremen group. Increasing proportions are observed for operatives, service workers, and laborers, in order.

The suggested ranking is in general conformity with the National Opinion Research Center's data on popular attitudes toward occupations, except that sales occupations appear to rank below clerical and craft oc-

Table 3.1   Selected indicators of socioeconomic status of the major occupation groups

Major occupation group*	Median income in 1949†	Median school years completed‡	Edwards' socio- economic groups #	Per cent nonwhite □
Professional, technical, and kindred workers	$4,387	16+	1	2·7
Managers, officials, and proprietors, except farm	4,831	12·2	2	2·2
Sales workers	3,698	12·4 ⎱		⎰ 2·8
Clerical and kindred workers	3,132	12·2 ⎰	3	⎱ 7·4
Craftsmen, foremen, and kindred workers	3,648	9·5	4	4·9
Operatives and kindred workers	3,115	8·9	5	12·4
Service workers, except private household	2,635	8·8	5–6	23·0
Labourers, except farm and mine	2,580	8·4	6	27·4

* Does not include farmers and farm managers, private household workers, farm laborers, and occupation not reported.

† For males in the experienced labor force of the Chicago Standard Metropolitan Area, 1950. *Source: 1950 US Census of Population*, Bulletin P-C13, Table 78.

‡ For employed males twenty-five years old and over, in the North and West, 1950. *Source: 1950 US Census of Population*, Special Report P-E no. 5B, Table 11.

\# Approximate equivalents. *Source:* Alba M. Edwards, *Comparative Occupation Statistics for the United States, 1870 to 1940* (Washington, DC: Government Printing Office, 1943).

□ For employed males in the Chicago Metropolitan District, 1950. Based on nonwhites residing in census tracts containing 250 or more nonwhite population in 1950. These tracts include 95·8 per cent of all nonwhite males in the Metropolitan District.

cupations in the NORC results.[9] An inadequate sampling of occupational titles within the sales group may account in part for the low prestige rating of sales workers obtained by the NORC. Furthermore, their data do not differentiate prestige ratings by sex. Particularly in a metropolitan area, the male sales worker group is more heavily weighted with such occupations as advertising, insurance, and real estate agents and sales representatives of wholesale and manufacturing concerns than is the case for female sales workers, among whom retail sales clerks are the large majority.

The failure of different bases of ranking to give identical results has been discussed by writers on stratification in terms of 'disaffinity of strata' and 'status disequilibrium'.[10] The reversals in rank between the professional and managerial groups and the clerical and crafts workers are most frequent. The upshot seems to be that no one ranking can be accepted as sufficient for all purposes. The examination of residential patterns discloses other instances of disequilibrium, which are of interest both in themselves and as clues to the interpretation of those already noted.

Residential patterns

Four aspects of the residential patterning of occupation groups are considered. The first is the degree of residential segregation of each major occupation group with respect to all others, that is, the extent to which an occupation group is separated residentially from the remainder of the employed labor force. The second is the degree of dissimilarity in residential distribution among major occupation groups, that is, the extent to which pairs of occupation groups isolate themselves from one another. The third aspect is the degree of residential concentration of each occupation group in areas characterized by relatively low rents. Finally, the degree of centralization of each major occupation group (i.e. the extent to which an occupation group is concentrated toward the center of the metropolitan community) is examined. In each case the spatial patterning of the residences is considered in relation to socioeconomic level.

⊂ A clear relationship of the ranking of major occupation groups by socioeconomic status and by degree of residential segregation is shown in Table 3.2. Listed in the order given there, the indexes of residential segregation form a U-shaped pattern. The highest values are observed for the professionals and the laborers and the lowest value for the clerical workers. The degree of residential segregation varies only slightly among the professional, managerial, and sales groups; however, it declines markedly for the clerical workers and then increases regularly for each successive group.

⬭ This finding suggests that residential segregation is greater for those occupation groups with clearly defined status than for those groups whose status is ambiguous. The latter groups are necessarily subject to cross-pressures from the determinants of residential selection; for example, the clerical group has an income equivalent to that of operatives but the educational level of managerial workers.

To check the hypothesis that spatial distances among occupation groups parallel their social distances, the indexes of dissimilarity in residential distribution among major occupation groups are shown in Table 3.3. As

Table 3.2 Index of residential segregation of each major occupation group, for employed males in the Chicago Metropolitan District, 1950

Major occupation group*	By census tracts	By zone-sector segments
Professional, technical, and kindred workers	30	21
Managers, officials, and proprietors, except farm	29	20
Sales workers	29	20
Clerical and kindred workers	13	9
Craftsmen, foremen, and kindred workers	19	14
Operatives and kindred workers	22	16
Service workers, except private household	24	20
Labourers, except farm and mine	35	29

* Does not include farmers and farm managers, private household workers, farm laborers, and occupation not reported.

previously indicated, a listing of major occupation groups by socioeconomic level can at best only roughly approximate a social distance scale. Similarly, a measure of dissimilarity in residential distribution can only approximate the spatial distance between groups – the index measures only the dissimilarity of the residential distributions with respect to a particular set of areas and is insensitive to other important aspects of the spatial pattern such as proximity of areas of concentration.

Nonetheless, the data in Table 3.3 indicate the essential correspondence of social and spatial distance among occupation groups. If it is assumed that the ordering of major occupation groups corresponds with increasing social distance (e.g. the social distance between professional and sales workers is greater than that between professional and managerial workers), and if it is assumed that the index of residential dissimilarity approximates the spatial distance between the two groups, the expected pattern would be the following: Starting at any point on the diagonal, the indexes would increase reading up or to the right (down or to the left, in the case of the indexes below the diagonal, based on zone-sector segments). It is clear that the expected pattern, though not perfectly reproduced, essentially describes the observed pattern. The exceptions are few and for the most part can be explained hypothetically; such hypotheses provide clues for additional research.

The least dissimilarity is observed between professional and managerial workers, managerial and sales workers, and professional and sales workers. Furthermore, the dissimilarity of each of these groups with each other occupation group is of approximately the same degree. In fact, three of the inversions of the expected pattern concern the comparison between the managerial group and sales workers; that is, the residential dissimilarity of sales workers with craftsmen-foremen, operatives, and laborers is slightly greater than that of the managerial group, although their difference in terms of socioeconomic level is presumably less.

The residential distribution of clerical workers is more dissimilar to the distribution of sales workers, professional, and managerial workers than to that of the craftsmen or the operatives. Hence, although clerical workers are often grouped with professional, managerial, and sales workers as 'white-collar', in terms of residential distribution they are more similar to the craftsmen and operatives than to the other white-collar groups.

The remaining inversions of the expected pattern involve service workers, except private household. One-fifth of these are 'janitors and sextons'. Presumably a substantial proportion of the janitors live at their place of work in apartment buildings housing workers in the higher status occupation groups.[11] It is hypothesized that this special circumstance accounts for the tendency of service workers to be less dissimilar to the higher status groups than expected on the basis of socioeconomic status.[12] At the same time the color composition of the service group presumably acts in the opposite direction. In so far as residential segregation on basis of color, cutting across occupational lines, exists within the metropolitan community, occupational status is rendered at least partially ineffective as a

Table 3.3 Indexes of dissimilarity in residential distribution among major occupation groups, for employed males in the Chicago Metropolitan District, 1950

(Above diagonal, by census tracts; below diagonal, by zone-sector segments)

Major occupation group*	Major Occupation Group*							
	Professional, technical, kindred	Managers, officials, Proprietors	Sales workers	Clerical, kindred	Craftsmen, foremen	Operatives, kindred	Service, except private household	Laborers, except farm and mine
Professional, technical, kindred workers	—	13	15	28	35	44	41	54
Managers, officials, and proprietors, except farm	8	—	13	28	33	41	40	52
Sales workers	11	7	—	27	35	42	38	54
Clerical and kindred workers	20	18	17	—	16	21	24	38
Craftsmen, foremen, kindred workers	26	23	25	12	—	17	35	35
Operatives, kindred workers	31	29	30	16	14	—	26	25
Service workers, except private household	31	31	30	19	25	19	—	28
Laborers, except farm and mine	42	41	42	32	30	21	24	—

* Does not include farmers and farm managers, private household workers, farm laborers, and occupation not reported.

determinant of residential location. These factors, however, probably do not wholly explain the largest single deviation from the expected pattern, the much larger index of dissimilarity between craftsmen-foremen and service workers than between clerical and service workers.

The first column of Table 3.4 shows the indexes of low-rent concentration of the occupation groups. Some caution must be exercised in interpreting them, since the tabulation on which they are based did not distinguish between male and female workers, and the indexes had to be computed for total employed persons rather than males. It is clear, nonetheless, that the degree of low-rent concentration is inversely related to the socioeconomic status of the occupation groups. All four of the white-collar occupation groups have negative indexes, signifying relative concentration in high-rent areas, whereas all four of the blue-collar groups have positive indexes. Again, there is a relatively sharp break between the clerical and the other

Table 3.4 Indexes of low-rent concentration and of centralization for major occupation groups, Chicago Metropolitan District, 1950

	Index of low-rent concentration (total employed persons)	Index of centralization (employed males)					
				Sector			
Major occupation group*		Metropolitan District	North Shore	North-west	West	South-west	South Shore
Professional, technical, and kindred workers	−32	−14	−15	−20	—29	−20	5
Managers, officials, and proprietors, except farm	−30	−12	−20	−16	−19	−15	1
Sales workers	−25	−5	−15	−12	−12	−9	8
Clerical and kindred workers	−9	5	7	2	1	5	9
Craftsmen, foremen, and kindred workers	11	−8	6	−6	−7	−5	−26
Operatives, kindred workers	29	10	21	16	18	8	−4
Service workers, except private household	7	21	16	18	20	16	36
Laborers, except farm and mine	32	7	9	21	30	16	—1

* Does not include farmers and farm managers, private household workers, farm laborers, and occupation not reported.

three white-collar groups. The managerial group has a slightly greater index of low-rent concentration than the professional group, despite the higher income level of the former. It is even more striking that the low-rent concentration of craftsmen-foremen is substantially higher than for clerical workers, again the reverse of the relative positions on income. It can be shown that in 1940 the combined clerical and sales group tended to spend a larger proportion of its income for rent than did the group of craftsmen, foremen, and kindred workers. For example, for tenant families with wage and salary incomes between $2,000 and $3,000 in 1939, and without other income, 63 per cent of the families headed by a clerical or sales worker paid $40 per month or more rent, as compared with only 38 per cent of families whose heads were craftsmen, foremen, or kindred workers.[13]

The index of low-rent concentration for service workers, although positive, is low compared to the other blue-collar groups. This exception to the expected pattern no doubt has the same explanation as advanced above; that is, that a substantial proportion of service workers live in comparatively high status areas in connection with their place of employment.

The indexes of centralization of the occupation groups are given in Table 3.4, both for the Metropolitan District as a whole and within each of the five sectors. According to the Burgess zonal hypothesis, there is an upward gradient in the socioeconomic status of the population as one proceeds from the center to the periphery of the city. Hence one would expect the degree of residential centralization of an occupation group to be inversely related to its socioeconomic status. The data provide general support for this hypothesis, although there are some significant exceptions. Thus, for the Metropolitan District as a whole, three of the four white-collar indexes are negative (indicating relative decentralization), and three of the four blue-collar indexes are positive (indicating relative centralization). The exceptional cases are again the clerical and craftsmen-foremen groups.

In three of the five sectors (Northwest, West, and Southwest), the hypothesized pattern of centralization indexes is perfectly reproduced, except for the inversion between clerical workers and the craftsmen-foremen group, which appears in all sectors. For the North Shore sector the principal deviation from the pattern is the comparatively low degree of centralization of service workers and laborers. In this sector the managerial group is somewhat more decentralized than the professional group, as is also true in the South Shore sector. The latter sector exhibits a quite marked departure from the expected pattern, in that the only decentralized occupations are those in the blue-collar category. There is a small measure of confirmation for the hypothesized pattern, in that within the white-collar category the least centralized groups are the professional and managerial, and within the blue-collar category the most decentralized is the craftsmen-foremen group. The high index for service workers is doubtless due to the relatively high proportion of nonwhites in this occupation, and the relatively central location of the South Side 'Black Belt', a large portion of which falls in the South Shore sector. The decentralization of the other blue-collar groups is attributable to the presence of the Indiana industrial suburbs on the periphery of the South Shore sector. A similar effect of some industrial suburbs at the northern end of the North Shore sector is observable in the low centralization index for laborers in that sector. It is apparent that expectations based on the zonal hypothesis must be qualified by recognizing distortions of the zonal pattern produced by peripheral industrial concentrations. Such concentrations appear only in certain sectors, and, where they are absent, the zonal hypothesis leads to a realistic expectation concerning the pattern of residential centralization by socioeconomic status.

Residential separation and dissimilarity of occupational origins

There are good reasons for supposing that residential patterns are related to occupational mobility. For example, ecologists have noted a tendency for advances in socioeconomic status to be accompanied by migration toward the city's periphery. Residential segregation is doubtless one of the barriers to upward mobility, in so far as such mobility is affected by the opportunity to observe and imitate the way of life of higher social strata. Among the findings reported above, at least one may have an explanation that involves mobility. It is surprising that the residential patterns of sales workers do not differ more than they do from those of professional and managerial workers; since the income of sales workers is well below that of either, they rank lower in prestige, and their educational attainment is substantially less than that of professional workers. But there are data which suggest that a sizable proportion of sales workers are moving to a higher occupational level, or aspire to such a move, anticipating it by following the residential pattern of the higher group. The Occupational Mobility Survey found that for males employed in both 1940 and 1950 there was a movement of 23 per cent of the men employed as sales workers in 1940 into the group of managers, proprietors, and officials by 1950. This is the largest single interoccupational movement in the mobility table, except that 23 per cent of laborers moved into the group of operatives and kindred workers.[14]

Another aspect of occupational mobility is illuminated by the data in Table 3.5, which shows indexes of dissimilarity among the major occupation groups with respect to the distribution of each group by major occupation group of the employed male's father.[15] These indexes, therefore, pertain to differences among the major occupation groups in background, origin, or recruitment. The hypothesis to be tested is that, the greater the dissimilarity between a pair of occupation groups in occupational origins, the greater is their dissimilarity in residential distribution.

The pattern of Table 3.5 is clearly like that of Table 3.3. The indexes of dissimilarity with respect to residence, computed on the zone-sector segment basis, correlate 0.91 with the indexes for occupational origin. The correlation is 0.94 for the residential indexes based on census tracts, with the regression of the tract-based index (t) on the index of dissimilarity in occupational origin (u) being $t = 1.2u - 1.8$. The hypothesis is thereby definitely substantiated.

In Table 3.5 all but one of the inversions of the pattern expected on the assumption of an unequivocal ranking of the occupation groups involve the sales and service workers. Sales workers are closer to professional workers

Table 3.5* Indexes of dissimilarity in distribution by father's occupation among major occupation groups, for employed males in six cities in the United States, 1950

Major occupation group†	Major occupation group†						
	Managers, officials, Proprietors	Sales workers	Clerical, Kindred	Craftsmen, foremen	Operatives, kindred	Service, including private household	Laborers, excluding mine
Professional, technical, and kindred workers	20	16	27	38	39	34	46
Managers, officials, and proprietors, except farm	—	11	28	31	34	30	42
Sales workers	—	—	26	35	37	35	47
Clerical and kindred workers	—	—	—	18	20	28	39
Craftsmen, foremen, kindred workers	—	—	—	—	14	25	31
Operatives, kindred workers	—	—	—	—	—	22	23
Service workers, including private household	—	—	—	—	—	—	20

Source: Unpublished data from Occupational Mobility Survey, Table W-9. For description of sampling and enumeration procedures see Gladys L. Palmer, *Labor Mobility in Six Cities* (New York: Social Science Research Council, 1954).
† Does not include farmers and farm managers and occupation not reported. A small number of private household workers are included with service workers, and a small number of farm laborers with laborers, except mine.

with respect to occupational background than are the managerial workers and farther from each of the blue-collar groups. Actually, a more consistent pattern would be produced by ranking sales workers second in place of the managerial group. In this respect the data on occupational origins are more consistent with the ecological data than are the data on socioeconomic status in Table 3.1. In terms of the indexes of dissimilarity in occupational origins, service workers are closer to the first three white-collar groups than are any of the other blue-collar groups. However, in comparisons among the clerical and blue-collar groups, service workers clearly rank next to last, or between operatives and laborers. Again, the factor of occupational origins is more closely related to residential separation than are the indicators of socioeconomic status.

The last point deserves emphasis. Not only do the indexes of dissimilarity on an area basis have the same general pattern as those on an occupational origin basis but also the deviations from that pattern occur at the same points and in the same direction. This cannot be said regarding the several indicators of socioeconomic status. If income determined residential separation, managers would outrank professionals, and clerical workers would be virtually identical with operatives in their separation from other groups. If education determined residential separation, there would be substantial differences between the indexes for professional workers and managerial workers. Neither of these hypotheses is borne out by the data, whereas differences in occupational background lead to accurate, specific predictions of the pattern of differences in residential distribution.

The ecological analysis has provided strong support for the proposition that spatial distances between occupation groups are closely related to their social distances, measured either in terms of conventional indicators of socioeconomic status or in terms of differences in occupational origins; that the most segregated occupation groups are those at the extremes of the socioeconomic scale; that concentration of residence in low-rent areas is inversely related to socioeconomic status; and that centralization of residence is likewise inversely related to socioeconomic status. These results are in accord with accepted ecological theory, provide support for it, and demonstrate the relevance of ecological research to the theory of social stratification.

These generalizations, however, are perhaps no more significant to the advancement of knowledge than are the instances in which they do not hold and the additional hypotheses advanced to account for the exceptions. Conventional measures of socioeconomic status do not agree perfectly as to the rank order of the major occupation groups, nor do the several ecological indexes. The prime case in point occurs at the middle of the socioeconomic scale, at the conventional juncture of white-collar and blue-collar occupations. Clerical and kindred workers have substantially more education than craftsmen, foremen, and kindred workers, and the clerical occupations are usually considered of greater prestige than the craft and related occupations. However, craftsmen-foremen have considerably higher incomes on the average, and, among males, their nonwhite proportion is smaller. The pattern of the indexes of dissimilarity in residential distribution clearly places the clerical group closer to the other white-collar groups than the craftsmen-foremen are, and the clerical workers' index of low-rent concentration is less than that of the craftsmen and foremen. But in terms of residential centralization the clerical group tends to fall with the lower blue-collar groups, and the craftsmen-foremen group with the other white-collar groups. In general, it would appear that 'social status' or prestige is more important in determining the residential association of clerical with other white-collar groups than is income, although the latter sets up a powerful cross-pressure, as evidenced by the comparatively high rent-income ratio of clerical families. To account fully for the failure of clerical workers to be residentially decentralized like the other white-collar groups, one would have to consider work-residence relationships. Data on work-residence separation for a 1951 Chicago sample show that clerical workers resemble craftsmen, foremen, and kindred workers in the degree of separation much more than they do sales, managerial, or professional workers.[16]

Perhaps the most suggestive finding of the study is that dissimilarity in occupational origins is more closely associated with dissimilarity in residential distribution than is any of the usual indicators of socioeconomic status. This result can only be interpreted speculatively. But one may suppose that preferences and aspirations concerning housing and residential patterns are largely formed by childhood and adolescent experiences in a milieu of which the father's occupation is an important aspect.

The discovery that 'status disequilibria' are reflected in inconsistencies in the ordering of occupation groups according to their residential patterns provides a further reason for distinguishing 'class' from 'social status' elements[17] within the complex conventionally designated as 'socioeconomic status'. Apparently, attempts to compound these two can at best produce a partially ordered scale; at worst, they may obscure significant differences in life-style, consumption patterns, and social mobility.

There is one important qualification of the results reported. Like census tracts, broad occupation groups are not perfectly homogeneous. The managerial group includes proprietors of peanut stands as well as corporation executives, and night-club singers are classified as professional workers along with surgeons. One would therefore expect to find a much sharper differentiation of residential patterns if more detailed occupational classifications were available. In particular, the points at which cross-pressures on residential location develop should be more clearly identified.

Further research should seek other forces producing residential segregation. Ethnic categorizations other than race are doubtless relevant though difficult to study directly for lack of data. In general, the patterns described here would be expected to hold for females, but significant deviations might also occur, in part because the residence of married females is probably determined more by their husbands' occupation than by their own, and in part because the occupations that compose each of the major occupation groups are different for females from those for males (as mentioned above in regard to sales workers). Both race and sex would bear upon residential patterns of private household workers, who are predominantly female and nonwhite. A final class of especially important factors is the effect of the location of workplaces on residence. There is evidence that residences are not distributed randomly with respect to places of work. If location of work is controlled, an even sharper differentiation of residential patterns than that described here may be revealed.

Notes and References

The authors wish to acknowledge the financial support of the Social Science Research Committee and the Population Research and Training Center of the University of Chicago, the clerical assistance of David A. Lane and Gerald S. Newman, and the helpful suggestions of Evelyn M. Kitagawa and Philip M. Hauser.

1. 'The urban community as a spatial pattern and a moral order', in *The Urban Community*, ed. E. W. Burgess, University of Chicago Press, 1926, p. 18.
2. See, however, the discussion of 'dwelling area' by W. Lloyd Warner *et al.*, *Social Class in America*, Chicago: Science Research Associates, 1949, pp. 151–4.
3. Otis Dudley Duncan and Beverly Duncan, 'A methodological analysis of segregation indexes', *Am. Sociol. Rev.*, **20** (1955), 210–17. Donald J. Bogue, *The Structure of the Metropolitan Community*, University of Michigan Press, 1949, p. 72; Richard W. Redick, 'A study of differential rates of population growth and patterns of population distribution in central cities in the United States: 1940–1950', paper presented at the 1954 annual meeting of the American Sociological Society, Urbana, Illinois.
4. *1950 United States Census of Population*, Bulletin P-D10.
5. For the use of the index of dissimilarity as a 'coefficient of geographic association', see National Resources Planning Board, *Industrial Location and National Resources*, Washington, DC; Government Printing Office, 1943, p. 118.
6. For discussion of the index of dissimilarity as a segregation index see Duncan and Duncan, *op. cit.*, and the literature there cited.

7. Jerome K. Myers, 'Note on the homogeneity of census tracts: a methodological problem in Urban Ecological Research', *Social Forces*, **32** (May 1954), 364–6; Joel Smith, 'A method for the classification of areas on the basis of demographically homogeneous populations', *Am. Sociol. Rev.*, **19** (April 1954), 201–7.

8. The indexes of low-rent concentration and of centralization are formally identical with the index of urbanization proposed in Otis D. Duncan, 'Urbanization and retail specialization', *Social Forces*, **30** (March 1952), 267–71. The formula given here is a simplification of the one presented there; and the area units and principle of ordering are, of course, different.

9. National Opinion Research Center, 'Jobs and occupations: a popular evaluation', *Opinion News*, **9** (1 September, 1947), 3–13.

10. Cf. Pitirim A. Sorokin, *Society, Culture, and Personality*, Harper, 1947), pp. 289–94, on disaffinity of strata. On status disequilibrium cf. Émile Benoit-Smullyan, 'Status, status types, and status interrelations', *Am. Sociol. Rev.* **9** (April 1944), 154–61; Harold K. Kaufman, *Defining Prestige in a Rural Community* (Sociometry Monograph, no. 10) New York, Beacon House, 1946.

11. Cf. Ray Gold, 'Janitors versus tenants: a status-income dilemma', *Am. J. Sociol.*, **57** (March 1952), 486–93.

12. This effect has been definitely noted in data, not shown here, for female private household workers, about one-fourth of whom 'live in'.

13. Data for the Chicago Metropolitan District, 1940, from Table 11, *Families: Income and Rent, Population and Housing, 16th Census of the United States: 1940*.

14. Based on unpublished Table W-56 of the Occupational Mobility Survey, taken in six cities in 1951. For description of the sampling and enumeration procedures see Gladys L. Palmer, *Labor Mobility in Six Cities*, New York: Social Science Research Council, 1954, chap. 1 and Appendix B.

15. These indexes are based on the aggregated results of sample surveys in six cities in 1951. Although separate data are available for Chicago, these were not used here, because the sample was too small to produce reliable frequencies in most of the cells of the 8×9 table from which the dissimilarity indexes were computed. (In the intergeneration mobility table the classification of fathers' occupations included the group 'farmers and farm managers' as well as the eight major occupation groups listed in Table 3.5. This was desirable, since a significant proportion of fathers – though very few of the sons in this urban sample – were farmers.)

16. Beverly Duncan, 'Factors in work-residence separation: wage and salary workers, Chicago, 1951', paper presented at the annual institute of the Society for Social Research, Chicago, 5 June, 1953.

17. See 'Class, status, party', in *From Max Weber: essays in sociology*, ed. H. H. Gerth and C. W. Mills, New York: Oxford University Press, 1946.

E. S. Uyeki

4 Residential distribution and stratification*

Introduction

This article reports on a replication in space and extension in time of the Duncans' study of residential distribution and occupational stratification,[1] which was undertaken for Chicago for 1950. The results reported below are for what is essentially the Cleveland Standard Metropolitan Area (SMA) for 1950 and 1960.[2] The Duncans have demonstrated the close relationship between social distance and spatial distance for one large American metropolis. Wilkins has shown this relationship, though differing at certain points, for eight medium-sized American cities.[3] Cleveland, although about one-fourth the size of Chicago, shows many similarities with the latter on several characteristics which are considered to have some effect on residential distribution of the population in urban areas. A confirmation in Cleveland of the findings for Chicago will support the applicability of this general approach to comparative urban social patterns of large American cities.

Cleveland and Chicago are both cities fronting on the Great Lakes. Each is built up on flat land with a river merging with the lake near the city center. Both began their period of rapid growth during the 1850s with decreasing growth around the turn of the century and actual population decline in the central city in the last decade. The industrial breakdowns for the two cities are similar: both have diverse manufacturing, including heavy industry such as primary metals, professional services, and public administration. Both cities have large areas of older housing and have urban renewal projects finished or under way (Table 4.1).

In 1950 Cleveland and Chicago had quite similar proportions of their populations in the various categories of racial and ethnic status (Table 4.2).[4] Moreover, as may be seen in Table 4.1, in 1950 the occupational

* *American Journal of Sociology*, **69** No. 5 (March 1964), 491–98.

Table 4.1 Selected characteristics of male experienced civilian labor force by major occupation groups in Cleveland Metropolitan Area, 1950 and 1960, and Chicago Metropolitan Area, 1950

	Cleveland 1950			Difference, Chicago 1950 minus Cleveland 1950			Change, Cleveland 1960 minus Cleveland 1950		
	Per cent distribution	Per cent non-white	Median income	Per cent distribution	Per cent non-white	Median income	Per cent distribution	Per cent non-white	Median income
All	100·00	9·0	$3,281	0·0	0·3	$43	0·0	2·2	$2,290
Professional, technical, kindred workers	9·6	2·0	4,363	−0·2	0·7	24	2·7	1·5	2,999
Managers, officials, and proprietors, except farm	11·1	2·4	4,712	0·4	−0·2	119	−0·6	−0·2	3,538
Sales workers	7·4	2·3	3,395	−0·3	0·5	303	0·8	0·7	2,430
Clerical and kindred workers	8·9	6·4	3,148	1·2	1·0	−16	0·0	4·1	2,055
Craftsmen, foremen, kindred workers	24·0	5·0	3,514	−1·3	−0·1	134	−0·8	1·8	2,516
Operatives and kindred workers	24·3	11·5	3,101	−1·9	0·9	14	−0·1	4·8	2,118
Service workers, except private household	6·4	22·4	2,486	1·8	0·6	149	−0·5	3·2	1,500
Laborers, except farm and mine	8·3	31·1	2,484	0·2	−3·7	96	−1·5	3·2	1,462

Source: 1950 Census of Population, Characteristics of the Population, State Tables 35 and 78; 1960 Census of Population, General Characteristics, State Table 74, and Detailed Characteristics, Table 124.

68

Table 4.2   Racial and ethnic status of populations
of Cleveland and Chicago

	Per cent	
	Cleveland	*Chicago*
White	89·5	89·0
Negro	10·4	10·7
Other races	0·1	0·3
Foreign-born white	13·0	12·8

composition of the male work force in the two metropolitan centers was virtually identical; only 3·6 per cent of the Chicago work force would have to shift major occupation group for the Chicago and Cleveland occupational distributions to correspond perfectly.

Finally, the socioeconomic status of the several occupation groups, as indexed by the proportion non-white and median income, is much the same in the two cities. Laborers are the only group in which the percentage of non-white workers differs by as much as 1 percentage point; the proportion non-white is 3·7 points higher in Cleveland than in Chicago. Sales workers are the only group for which median income differs by as much as $150; the median income for Chicago sales workers was $303 greater than for Cleveland sales workers. There is one inversion in rank order; craftsmen-foremen in Cleveland had a higher median income than did sales workers whereas the reverse is true for Chicago.

Given these striking similarities, then, in Cleveland we should expect to find not only a fairly close relationship between social distance and spatial distance, but also a pattern the details of which resemble closely those of the Chicago pattern. Otherwise, some factor other than topography, growth history, racial-ethnic and occupational composition, industrial breakdown, and relative status of socioeconomic groups must have a powerful influence on socioeconomic differentiation.

Comparison of Cleveland and Chicago in 1950

The computational procedures for the various indexes describing the spatial distribution of occupational groups have been described in Duncan and Duncan and therefore are not detailed here.[5] The nature of the indexes will be briefly indicated. The index of dissimilarity measures the difference in areal distribution between two occupation groups. The index of segregation measures the difference in areal distribution between one occupation group and all the remaining occupation groups. The index of low-rent concentration measures the extent to which one occupation group compared with the remaining occupation groups is concentrated in areas with a low median monthly rent of tenant-occupied dwelling units. The index of centralization measures the extent to which one occupation group compared with all the remaining occupation groups is concentrated in areas located near the center of the city.

There are some differences between this study and the Duncans' which relate primarily to size and number of zone sectors. The Chicago study had five sectors and zones radiating out and varying in size from 1-mile intervals for the first fourteen miles to two-mile intervals after that, for a total of 104 zone-sector segments. The Cleveland analysis is based on five sectors also, but the zones radiate out from the central business district at intervals of approximately $2\frac{3}{4}$ miles for the first four zones and the last zone includes all of the remaining tracted areas for the 1950 Census. There are twenty-one zone-sector segments for Cleveland.[6]

The index of residential segregation for each occupation group relative to all other groups appears in Table 4.3. The rank-order correlation coefficients for the indexes for Cleveland and Chicago for 1950 are as follows: (1) by zone-sector segment, 0·88; and (2) by census tracts, 0·96. Both are significant at the 0·01 level or greater.[7] The difference in index value is no more than 3 points by tract and no more than 5 points by zone-sector segment. The only index which is out of line is that for service workers for Cleveland, which is less than that for operatives – its immediately preceding category. Except for this, however, the Cleveland data show the U-shaped distribution hypothesized by the Duncans, that is, with the upper and lower parts of the occupational categories being more segregated than those in the middle ranges.

The index of residential dissimilarity between each occupation group and every other occupation group appears in Table 4.4.[8] The rank-order correlation coefficients between the twenty-eight index values for Cleveland and Chicago, 1950, are 0·97 based on census tracts and 0·93 by zone-sector segments.[9] A closer analysis of the spatial patterns between the two cities is possible by rank-ordering the indexes for each of the major occupation groups in its comparison with all the other groups.[10] Of the possible fifty-six comparisons between the cities (ignoring a difference of 0·5 which indicates a tied rank), there are fifteen comparisons which are out of line, with only six involving differences of more than one rank. All six occur in comparisons involving a 'blue-collar' group: craftsmen, operatives, or laborers. The pattern for the clerical group is marred by a single inversion of one rank; and the rank-ordering of dissimilarity for the top three white-collar groups is duplicated perfectly between the two cities. Moreover, the numerical differences between the Cleveland and Chicago indexes of dissimilarity for pairs of occupations are small. For twenty-four of these twenty-eight comparisons, the difference is less than 3 percentage points. In three cases, the difference is in the 5–7 point range; and in the intercity comparison for craftsmen versus service workers, a difference of 11 points is observed. The lesser dissimilarity in residential distri-

Table 4.3 Index of residential segregation of each major occupation group for employed males: Cleveland 1950 and 1960, and Chicago 1950

	Cleveland 1950		Difference, Chicago 1950 minus Cleveland 1950		Change, Cleveland 1960 minus Cleveland 1950 (by
	By census tracts	By zone-sector segments	By census tracts	By zone-sector segments	zone-sector segments)
Professional, technical, kindred workers	33	22	−3	−1	−1
Managers, officials, and proprietors, except farm	31	21	−2	−1	2
Sales workers	27	18	2	2	2
Clerical and kindred workers	12	8	1	1	−1
Craftsmen, foremen, and kindred workers	18	9	1	5	1
Operatives and kindred workers	23	19	−1	−3	−1
Service workers, except private household	21	16	3	4	−1
Laborers, except farm and mine	33	25	2	4	6

Source: Chicago data from Duncan and Duncan, 'Residential distribution and occupational stratification,' *op. cit.*, Table 2.

Table 4.4 Indexes of dissimilarity in residential distribution among major occupation groups, for employed males, based on census-tract grid, Cleveland and Chicago, 1950*

	Major occupation group							
Major occupation group	A	B	C	D	E	F	G	H
A. Professional, technical, kindred workers	—	0	2	−1	−2	−2	2	2
B. Managers, officials, and proprietors, except farm	13	.—	0	−7	−2	−2	1	2
C. Sales workers	13	13	—	3	3	2	1	5
D. Clerical and kindred workers	29	35	24	—	3	0	1	3
E. Craftsmen, foremen, kindred workers	37	35	32	13	—	0	11	2
F. Operatives, kindred workers	46	43	40	21	17	—	5	1
G. Service workers, except private household	39	39	37	23	24	21	—	3
H. Laborers, except farm and mine	52	50	49	35	33	24	25	—

* Above the diagonal: difference, Chicago 1950 minus Cleveland 1950; below the diagonal: Cleveland 1950.
Source: Chicago data are from Duncan and Duncan, 'Residential distribution and occupational stratification,' *op. cit.*, Table 3.

bution between craftsmen and service workers in Cleveland may reflect the fact that only one-eighth of the male service workers in Cleveland are janitors and sextons as compared with one-fifth in Chicago.

The ρ for the relation between the indexes of centralization for Cleveland and Chicago in 1950 is 0·90 (Table 4.5). As in the Chicago distribution, the clerical group is out of line with the other white-collar groups and the crafts-men-foremen group is the most decentralized of the blue-collar occupational categories. The largest discrepancy between the two cities is the greater centralization of laborers in Cleveland. Cleveland does not lack industrial suburbs which ought to be a decentralizing factor in Chicago in 1950.

Table 4.5   **Indexes of centralization and of low-rent concentration of each major occupation group for employed males, Cleveland 1950 and 1960, and Chicago 1950**

Major occupation group	Centralization			Low-rent concentration*		
	Cleveland 1950	Chicago 1950 minus Cleveland 1950	Cleveland 1960 minus Cleveland 1950	Cleveland 1950	Chicago 1950 minus Cleveland 1950	Cleveland 1960 minus Cleveland 1950
Professional, technical, kindred workers	−22	8	−2	−74	42	41
Managers, officials, and proprietors, except farm	−21	9	−4	−53	23	13
Sales workers	−15	10	−4	−25	0	−8
Clerical and kindred workers	1	4	2	−2	−7	3
Craftsmen, foremen, and kindred workers	−2	−6	−1	7	4	−1
Operatives and kindred workers	14	−4	6	20	9	6
Service workers, except private household	17	4	−2	8	−1	5
Laborers, except farm and mine	25	−18	8	14	18	18

* The Chicago index for low-rent concentration includes employed females.
Source: Chicago data are from Duncan and Duncan, 'Residential distribution and occupational stratification,' *op. cit.*, Table 4.

There are some minor inversions in rank order among the indexes. A majority of the inversions involve comparisons of craftsmen with another occupation. Interestingly enough, the sole inversion in the ranking of occupational groups by income also involves the craftsmen group. In sum, not only are the patterns and the differences in the two cities similar, but the magnitude of the intergroup differences are also similar.

The other important finding demonstrates the great stability of residential patterns of the major occupation groups in Cleveland from 1950 to 1960. We cannot account in any systematic way for the small changes that have occurred. With respect to nearly every index of residential distribution, laborers have become more differentiated from the other groups; in both absolute and relative terms, the increase in income for laborers over the decade was less than for any other group.

These results demonstrate that the details of socioeconomic residential differentiation in Chicago are almost perfectly reproduced in Cleveland, a smaller city but one whose growth history, industrial structure, and socioeconomic stratification are similar; and that there is strong persistence in the pattern of socioeconomic differentiation within a city over the span of a decade. Finally, the results suggest that changes in residential pattern tend to occur for groups whose relative socioeconomic status is changing.

Notes and References

I would like to thank the Case Research Fund for a grant which made part of this analysis possible and D. Atkins, L. Saban, and C. Applebaum for their statistical assistance. Acknowledgement is also made for the assistance of the staff and the use of the facilities of the Andrew R. Jennings Computing Center.

1. Otis Dudley Duncan and Beverly Duncan, 'Residential distribution and occupational stratification', *Am. J. Sociol.*, **60** (March, 1955), 493–503. For other applications of the same method see Otis Dudley Duncan and Stanley Lieberson, 'Ethnic segregation and assimilation', *Am. J. Sociol.* **64** (January, 1955), 364–74; Arthur H. Wilkins, 'The residential distribution of occupation groups in eight middle-sized cities of the United States in 1950', unpublished PhD dissertation, University of Chicago, 1956; and Otis Dudley Duncan and Beverly Duncan, *The Negro Population of Chicago: a study of residential succession* (University of Chicago Press, 1957). Also see Arnold S. Feldman and Charles Tilly, 'The interaction of social and physical space', *Am. Sociol. Rev.* **25** (December 1960), 877–84 [5].
2. The 1950 census tracts are all those listed for Cleveland and Adjacent Area, 1950. This tracted area encompasses 96·7 per cent of the population in the Cleveland SMA for 1950.
3. The study by Wilkins, *op. cit.*, e.g. shows a greater regularity in the predicted directions for dissimilarity of occupational distribution for an average of eight middle-sized American cities (Hartford, Syracuse, Columbus, Indianapolis, Richmond, Atlanta, Memphis, and Forth Worth) in 1950. The patterns of dissimilarity for Cleveland and Chicago, as will be noted below, are more similar to each other than to the pattern for the eight medium-sized cities. This is suggestive of differences in residential patterns of the various occupation groups between medium-sized (340,000–675,000) and large (1,500,000) cities.
4. US Bureau of the Census, *US Census of the Population: 1950, Vol. II, Characteristics of the Population*, Part 35, *Ohio*, and Part 33, *Illinois* (Washington, DC: Government Printing Office 1952), Table 34.
5. See Duncan and Duncan, 'Residential distribution and occupational stratification', *op. cit.*, and Otis Dudley Duncan, 'Urbanization and retail specialization', *Social Forces*, **30** (March 1951), 267–71.
6. Because of low population densities, the west and southwest sectors have four zones and the southern sector has three. In each case, all of the remaining census tracts were added to the last zone in the sector.
7. For a one-tailed test, a ρ of ·83 or larger is significant at the 0·01 level and a ρ of ·64 or larger is significant at the 0·05 level for an N of 8.
8. The indexes of segregation and dissimilarity for Cleveland in 1950 were computed by census tracts and also by zone sector segments. The numerical values may be seen in Tables 4.3, 4.4, and 4.6. Like the Chicago indexes, the values

are larger by census tracts than by zone sectors, though the ordering remains the same.

The product-moment correlation coefficient between the two sets of indexes of segregation for Cleveland in 1950 is 0·93 and the regression equation is $s = 0.74\,t - 1.1$, where s stands for zone-sector segment and t for census tract. The coefficient for the two sets of dissimilarity indexes is 0·95 and the regression equation is $s = 0.79\,t - 2.26$. The comparable Chicago coefficients relating the indexes computed by zone-sector segments and by census tracts are 0·96 for the segregation indexes and 0·98 for the dissimilarity indexes. The difference of 0·03 in the coefficients of the two cities is probably a result of the grosser grid utilized in the Cleveland analysis, which averaged 17·5 census tracts to each zone-sector segment compared with 10 for Chicago. These results tend to confirm the Duncans' conclusion that for these purposes using a larger area may be an efficient way of ordering data.

9. For a one-tail test, a ρ of 0·45 or larger is significant at the 0·01 level and a ρ of 0·32 or larger is significant at the 0·05 level for an N of 28.

10. For example, in Cleveland in 1950 the professional group is most similar in residential pattern to the managerial and sales group, so its comparison with each is assigned rank 1·5; it is least similar to laborers, so the professional-laborer comparison is assigned rank 7·0. In Chicago in 1950 the professional-managerial comparison is ranked 1·0, the professional-sales comparison 2·0, and the professional-laborer comparison 7·0.

A. S. Feldman and C. Tilly

5 The inter-action of social and physical space*

The rationale for studies that examine the consonance of social and physical space was stated most aptly by Park, who stressed both the static correspondence between cultural and territorial organization and the dynamic proposition that 'most if not all cultural changes in society will be correlated with changes in its territorial organization and *every change in the territorial and occupational distribution of the population will effect changes in the existing culture*'.[1] The city's spatial order, in this view, reflects and affects its social order; social changes can be located by accurately tracing their spoor. Park's formulation posits not only a correspondence between physical and social distance, but also the converse: the near-identity of residential proximity and social equality.

Widespread agreement on the intimate character of the relationship between physical and social distance is accompanied by equally widespread disagreement on the factors that give rise to such intimacy. The crucial question is: how does social equality become transformed into physical proximity, and *vice versa*? With some imprecision, two positions may be distinguished.

First, there are those who view the spatial distribution of human activities as an orderly phenomenon in itself, governed by an impersonal, economic process of competition for locations with fixed differential value, a competition in which all units seek similar ends, but differ in costs and available resources. This is a competition that is essentially and profoundly economic.[2]

The alternative position, secondly, deals with space as a reflection or indicator of social values, governed in part by 'sentimental' or 'non-economic' or 'cultural' factors. The desire for and achievement of spatial location, in this view, involves the conscious choice of actors who vary in

* Reprinted from *American Sociological Review*, **25** (1960), 877–84.

their ends and values. This is a choice that is essentially and profoundly social.[3]

In various forms, these two types of analysis confront each other in most of the problems of urban ecology. Each has had a part to play, for example, in recent discussions of suburban growth in the United States. In this field, the 'economic competition' approach leads to a concern with transportation changes, land values, and competition between residential and non-residential uses of the land, as well as to the proposition that ability to pay is the primary factor in distance of residences from the center of the city or in the type and location of housing that different sorts of suburban families occupy.[4] To exaggerate the simplicity of the argument: market competition forces accessible central city land out of residential use; transportation improvements reduce the time and money costs of peripheral locations; families with essentially similar schedules of housing preference compete for desirable locations; differences in family income therefore determine differences in housing quality and location within the metropolitan area.

The 'social choice' approach, on the other hand, leads to a concern with personal motives for residential change, with styles of life, and with the status significance of suburban housing.[5] This approach is particularly hospitable to the propositions, first, that some kind of normative change is responsible for mass migration to the suburbs and, second, that each section of a metropolis tends to recruit residents of relatively similar values and aspirations.

The fact that their proponents have generally applied these two types of analysis to somewhat different problems has hidden some of their discontinuity and possible inconsistency. Nevertheless, the sociological literature concerning suburbanization contains the germ of the same strident debate over the relationship of social and physical space that has broken out periodically in other fields of urban sociology. The controversy is not exclusively about the extent to which order in physical space reflects order in human behavior. It is also a controversy about the specific factors that are the bases of significant social divisions. Occupation is the case in point. We may identify two ways of explaining the fact that people with different occupations tend to live in different sections of cities. These two types of explanation rest on divergent conceptions of occupational categories.

For some analysts, occupation is a measure of position *vis-à-vis* the labor and commodity markets and, by the same token, the market for housing. Differential association of occupations is therefore a consequence of economic competition – one of the effects of the classical economists' 'invisible hand'.[6] We may infer the magnitude of this component from the differential income levels of occupational categories. For others, the most salient feature of occupational categories is their shared norms. This position insists upon a sharp analytical distinction between the body of norms that constitute what is often loosely called an occupational sub-culture and the income or market position that accrues to an occupation. Rather than viewing occupational categories as resource or market units, these categories are viewed as indicative of different value systems or styles of life. Since these shared normative elements are presumably con-sequences of a shared socialization process, we may infer the magnitude of this component from the differential educational levels of occupational categories.[7]

Some methodological problems

Despite a welcome increase in the proportion of studies that employ personal interviews, aggregate social data for areal units remain the prin-cipal source of information about urban social structures. The problems that result from the combined use of areal units and fairly crude socio-logical measures may be grouped into three rough categories.

1. While areal units *per se* have intrinsic interest for sociologists, many analysts are at least equally interested in drawing behavioral inferences from ecological data. Of course, the direct extension of the characteristics of areal units to the characteristics of individuals residing in such units, involves the researcher in the familiar ecological fallacy.[8] Nevertheless, the residential area is one important *context* within which personal be-havior takes place. Thus, the fact of living in an area with certain character-istics, in income, education, race, and so on, is sociologically relevant, whether or not the personal traits of residents are similar to the averages of the areal units in which they reside.[9] If one carefully observes the restrictions on the kinds of inferences that may be based on ecological data, areal units of observation have considerable analytical utility for the sociologist.

2. The ecological fallacy is not limited to areal units. Lack of precision in the measurement of social space,[10] more often than not, matches the imprecise definition of units of physical space. The social variables being measured in ecological research are often as gross as the physical units of observation. This problem might be called that of aggregate social units, that is, the use of sociological measures that combine in unknown pro-portions the substantive content of a number of different, though allied, variables.

The problem of the aggregate social unit is central to this paper. The broad occupational categories normally employed in urban research conglomerate the effects of a number of variables, and thereby leave unde-termined what part such elements of occupational status as income, shared socialization, power, and job activity itself play in the process of differential association, residential segregation, and the like. We have attempted to distinguish the effects of two such elements.

3. The validity of this kind of analysis rests upon the shaky assumption that processes of change may be inferred from static, cross-sectional relationships. One of the great attractions of the language of human ecology is that it incorporates a vocabulary of *process* – invasion, succession, concentration, dispersion, segregation. One of the principal purposes of studies of urban occupational segregation is to discover the nature of the *processes* that lead to observed residential patterns. But much of the time investigators have only a set of simultaneous observations from which to infer the nature of those processes. This is certainly the case in the present study.

We are in the position, in fact, of wishing to discern the operation of the several components of occupation in the process of residential segregation, and even to make some inferences about the elements of occupational mobility, while having only summary data for areal units in terms of crude occupational categories for a single point in time. Our conclusions are therefore, at best, tentative.

The study's design and data

A rough test of the salience of the two components of occupation is possible through the use of partial correlations. Using data from the 1950 census for Hartford, Connecticut, a rank correlation coefficient, Kendall's *tau*, was computed over all census tracts for the proportion of employed males in each occupational category with (1) the proportion of employed males in every other occupational category, (2) income levels, and (3) educational levels.[11] Table 5.1 reports these correlations along with the *tau* between education and income.

The correlations presented in Table 5.1 are an expression of the similarity or dissimilarity of the residential distributions of the occupational categories. Table 5.2 presents the partial *tau*'s between each occupational category and every other one with income controlled. In this case, the mean difference between zero-order and partial *tau*'s for each occupation represents a measure of the importance of income for the differential association of occupational categories in physical space. Table 5.3 repeats this analysis, but with education rather than income controlled or 'partialled out'. Again, the mean difference between these figures and the simple *tau*'s represents a measure of the importance of education. Table 5.4 summarizes the effects of partialling for income and education. The differences between the mean reductions of *tau* when income is controlled and when education is controlled provide one rough measure of the relative importance of these two components. The Z at the bottom of Table 5.4 is a simple sign test, which provides an additional measure of relative salience.[12]

Table 5.1 Rank correlation coefficients for occupational groups with other occupational groups and with median income and median school years, Hartford, 1950

Occupational group	Professional, technical	Managers, proprietors	Sales	Clerical	Craftsmen, foremen	Operatives	Service	Laborers	Median income
Professionals	—								
Managers	0·5638	—							
Sales	0·6221	0·6479	—						
Clerical	0·3279	0·0594	0·2584	—					
Craftsmen	−0·2575	−0·2903	−0·2586	0·0596	—				
Operatives	−0·6198	−0·7457	−0·6606	−0·1485	0·3291	—			
Service	−0·5694	−0·6132	−0·5459	−0·0798	0·1178	0·4708	—		
Laborers	−0·6855	−0·4913	−0·6333	−0·4183	0·1768	0·5189	0·4619	—	
Median income	0·5038	0·5593	0·4991	0·1427	0·0287	−0·4354	−0·6171	−0·5491	—
Median school years	0·8154	0·6021	0·6477	0·2782	−0·2418	−0·6301	−0·5982	−0·6698	0·5447

Table 5.2 Partial rank correlation, coefficients for occupational groups with other occupational groups, median income controlled, Hartford, 1950

Occupational group	Professional, technical	Managers, proprietors	Sales	Clerical	Craftsmen, foremen	Operatives	Service
Professionals	—						
Managers	0·3935	—					
Sales	0·4952	0·5133	—				
Clerical	0·2994	−0·0249	0·2182	—			
Craftsmen	−0·3147	−0·3697	−0·3151	0·0561	—		
Operatives	−0·5150	−0·6729	−0·5682	−0·0969	0·3796	—	
Service	−0·3803	−0·4109	−0·3487	0·0142	0·1723	0·3322	—
Laborers	−05663	−0·2659	−0·4960	−0·4109	0·2305	0·3717	0·1871

Table 5.3 Partial rank correlation coefficients for occupational groups, median school years controlled, Hartford, 1950

Occupational group	Professional, technical	Managers, proprietors	Sales	Clerical	Craftsmen, foremen	Operatives	Service
Professionals	—						
Managers	0·1576	—					
Sales	0·2131	0·4240	—				
Clerical	0·1818	-0·1410	0·1069	—			
Craftsmen	-0·1456	-0·2064	-0·1610	0·1272	—		
Operatives	-0·2358	-0·5908	-0·4267	0·0359	0·2966	—	
Service	-0·1760	-0·3954	-0·2595	0·1125	-0·0137	0·1509	—
Laborers	-0·4224	-0·1485	-0·3012	-0·3252	0·0454	0·1680	0·1028

Table 5.4 Summary of differences between zero-order correlations and partial correlations for income and education, Hartford, 1950

Occupational group	(1) Mean correlation*	(2) Mean partial Correlation for income*	(3) Effect of income (1)−(2)	(4) Mean partial Correlation for education*	(5) Effect of education (1)−(4)	(6) Difference in effects (5)−(3)
Professionals	0·5209	0·4235	0·0974	0·2189	0·3020	0·2046
Managers	0·4874	0·3787	0·1087	0·2948	0·1926	0·0839
Sales	0·5181	0·4221	0·0960	0·2703	0·2478	0·1518
Clerical	0·1931	0·1601	0·0330	0·1472	0·0459	0·0129
Craftsmen	0·2128	0·2626	-0·0498	0·1423	0·0705	0·0321
Operatives	0·4991	0·4195	0·0796	0·2721	0·2270	0·1474
Service	0·4084	0·2637	0·1447	0·1730	0·2354	0·0907
Laborers	0·4837	0·3612	0·1225	0·2162	0·2675	0·1450

Sign test for relative magnitude of differences in *tau* for income and for education:
$Z = 3·97$, $P < 0·01$ (two-tailed test).

* Mean of absolute values of *tau*'s for specified occupation with each other occupational group.

The results

(*a*) Table 5.1 shows the expected and often-found systematic differences in the residential distribution of the eight occupational categories in Hartford. In general, the differences conform to the rank order in which these occupations are traditionally arrayed, that is, the order in which they appear in the tables. Thus, 'adjacent' occupations have relatively high *tau*'s while 'distant' occupations have relatively low *tau*'s.[13]

There is one noteworthy exception to the general pattern: the service occupational category is more similar to the white-collar occupations in residential distribution than the next 'highest' occupational category – the operatives. Five of the seven *tau*'s between the service category and other categories are thus 'anomalous'. The interpretation of this departure from the expected rank order that first comes to mind is the exceedingly heterogeneous character of the service category. However, this is hardly a characteristic that distinguishes the service category from the other seven.

An alternative interpretation may be tentatively suggested. The numbers of this category may be quite mobile occupationally, particularly in regard both to entry into and exits from the small-business owner classification.[14] If the frequency of such entries and exits is high, occupational mobility may not lead to corresponding residential mobility, a discontinuity that would account for the anomalous pattern discovered here. These findings may therefore identify one instance in which social mobility is not reflected in physical mobility.

(*b*) Table 5.2 reports the partial *tau*'s with income controlled, and shows that the removal of this variable generally reduces the size of *tau*, the mean reduction (reported in Table 5.4) being 0·0804. It appears that although its effect is fairly consistent, income is *not* a powerful determinant of differential residential association.

There is one illuminating exception – the craftsmen and foremen. They are, of course, the elite of blue-collar workers. In their case, partialling for income shifts all of the *tau*'s with the white-collar categories toward the negative extreme, and all of the correlations with the remaining blue-collar categories toward the positive end of the scale. Thus, when income is controlled, the craftsmen appear more similar to the other blue-collar categories. In this particular instance, income seems to be quite important. It is noteworthy that the *tau*'s between the craftsman and education and income (Table 5.1) indicate that the difference between this elite blue-collar group and the lowest white-collar group (clericals) is much sharper with respect to education than to income. Thus, they differ more from white-collar categories in regard to education than they do as to income, while exactly the reverse holds when craftsmen are compared with the blue-collar groups.

(*c*) Partialling for education (Table 5.3) results in a mean reduction in the *tau*'s of 0·1986, which is almost two and one-half times as great as the corresponding reduction for income. Thus education appears to exert considerably greater influence than income on the ordering of these occupational categories in physical space.[15]

(*d*) Table 5.4 reinforces this finding. The sign test based upon the twenty-eight comparisons between Tables 5.2 and 5.3 is quite significant. In all cases but one (the craftsmen), the mean reduction associated with controlling for education is greater than that associated with controlling for income.

Discussion and conclusions

In general, these findings lead to the conclusion that while both income and education contribute to the differences between the residential distributions of the various occupational categories, education is the more important. Or – to the extent that education and income are adequate measures – shared values are more important than economic resources.

The findings also raise some important questions, however, concerning the meaning of 'social choice' and 'economic competition', and the differences between them. The surface distinction between the will to live in desirable residential areas and the ability to do so when desirable areas are scarce and therefore costly, is inadequate. Both depend upon the definition of desirability. One might conclude from this study that the main element in the desirability of a residential area to members of any occupation is its inhabitation by other people with similar occupations, and that this relationship holds at all levels of the occupational hierarchy. This deduction, we suggest, neither fits all the facts nor takes into account the manner in which shared values and resources operate together.

The seemingly deviant case of craftsmen and foremen provides a partial test of the 'like attracts like' interpretation. Recall that this category was similar to white-collar groups as to income, but similar to blue-collar groups as to education. Thus the reasoning that 'like attracts like' would lead to the prediction that craftsmen will seek housing in the same localities inhabited by other blue-collar workers. But the reverse seems to be the case: craftsmen and foremen apparently use their increased resources to dissociate themselves from other members of the blue-collar occupational group. This one case may be more significant than it seems, for it is precisely the ability of craftsmen, with their higher incomes, to pay more for housing that may differentiate them from other blue-collar workers.[16] To some extent, they use this advantage to seek housing in higher-ranking, white-collar areas.

We suggest, then, that 'style of life' as used here is less a matter of occupational subcultures than of a general tendency of workers to identify themselves with others of similar or higher rank and to differentiate themselves from others of lower rank. For high-ranking occupations, this is evidently a matter of excluding others, while for low-ranking occupations, it is a matter of including themselves.

These findings may permit some inferences about the interaction among the three socioeconomic status variables – education, income, and occupation – with respect to their influence upon patterns of residential association and mobility. It seems likely that the level of education of lower-ranking white-collar workers is chiefly responsible for their residence in high-status residential areas. Conversely, income levels appear to be more important in accounting for the location of high-ranking blue-collar workers in higher-status areas. This suggests the more general conclusion that the effects of education and income are partially concentrated in different and separate levels of the occupational hierarchy. As to residential mobility, it would appear that educational changes are more potent among white-collar employees, and that income changes are more potent among blue-collar workers.

The relationship between physical and social space, and by inference mobility, eludes easy and excessively broad generalization. Our findings indicate that it is misleading to conceive of occupation, when used as a measure of social space, as either a single or a scalar dimension. We suggest that future research might usefully employ the following hypothesis as an efficient point of departure. The relationship between occupation and residential area varies jointly with: (*a*) the particular half of the occupational hierarchy to which a category belongs; and (*b*) the component of occupation, whether education or income, that is being investigated.

Notes and References

This is a revision of a paper read at the annual meeting of the American Sociological Association, September 1959. Feldman is indebted to the Committee on Economic Growth of the Social Science Research Council, and to the Center of International Studies, Princeton University, and Tilly to the Faculty Research Committee of the University of Delaware, for research aid on this study.

1. Robert E. Park, *Human Communities*, Glencoe, Ill.: Free Press, 1952, p. 231 (italics added).
2. See, e.g. R. M. Hurd, *Principles of City Land Values*, New York: The Record, 1903; Ernest W. Burgess, 'The growth of the city: an introduction to a research project', *Pub. Am. Sociol. Soc.*, **18**, (1923), 85–97; R. D. McKenzie, 'Spatial distance and community organization pattern', *Social Forces*, **5**, (June 1927), 623–7; James A. Quinn, *Human Ecology*, New York: Prentice-Hall, 1950. Of course, any such classification of the basis of emphasis does

violence to the subtlety and variety of views presented by these authors. We
have no desire to elect either a villain or a hero from these approaches. For a
more partisan view, see Otis Dudley Duncan and Leo F. Schnore (with comment by Peter Rossi), 'Cultural, behavioral, and ecological perspectives in
the study of social organization', *Am. J. Sociol.*, **65**, (Sept. 1959), 132–53.

3. See, e.g. Walter Firey, 'Sentiment and symbolism as ecological variables',
Am. Sociol. Rev., **10**, (April 1945), 140–8; Milla A. Alihan, *Social Ecology*,
New York: Columbia University Press, 1938; A. B. Hollingshead, 'A re-
examination of ecological theory', *Sociology and Social Research*, **31**, (Jan.–
Feb. 1947), 194–204; Paul K. Hatt, 'The concept of natural areas', *Am. Sociol.
Rev.*, **11**, (Oct. 1946), 423–7.

4. *Cf.* Donald J. Bogue, *Metropolitan Growth and the Conversion of Land to
Nonagricultural Uses*, Oxford, Ohio: Scripps Foundation for Research in
Population Problems, 1956; Beverly Duncan, 'Intra-urban population movement', in P. K. Hatt and A. J. Reiss, Jr, eds, *Cities and Society*, Glencoe: Free
Press, 1957, pp. 297–309; Philip M. Hauser, 'The changing population pattern
of the modern city', in Hatt and Reiss, *op. cit.*, pp. 157–74; Leo F. Schnore, 'The
growth of metropolitan suburbs', *Am. Sociol. Rev.*, **22**, (April 1957), 165–73.
It is rather more difficult to classify the analysts than it is to classify their
analyses; as Schnore remarks, even investigators firmly set in the tradition of
human ecology often shift to 'social psychological' or 'social choice' explanations in dealing with suburbanization.

5. Cf. Wendell Bell, 'Social choice, life styles, and suburban residence', in W. M.
Dobriner, ed., *The Suburban Community*, New York: Putnam, 1958, pp. 225–
47; Sylvia Fleis Fava, 'Suburbanism as a Way of Life', *Am. Sociol. Rev.*, **21**,
(Feb. 1956), 34–7; Ernest R. Mowrer, 'The family in suburbia', in Dobriner,
op. cit., 147–64; Richard Dewey, 'Peripheral expansion in Milwaukee County',
Am. J. Sociol., **53**, (May 1948), 417–22; Walter T. Martin, *The Rural-Urban
Fringe*, University of Oregon Press, 1953.

6. It is instructive to note the correspondence between the classical economists'
concept of the 'invisible hand' as the guiding principle for economic change and
the human ecologists' concepts of such processes as invasion, centralization,
and segregation. Both invoke 'natural' laws which have little to do with
behavior. Both also are descriptions of the differences in time between static
situations, rather than descriptions of observed processes. In their crude form,
the ecological processes may be considered subcategories of the theory of
market changes – invisible fingers of the invisible hand.

7. Lest the reader judge us to be incredibly naïve, we hasten to state our uncom-
fortable awareness of the dubious validity of inferring other 'life styles' solely
from educational levels. We may ruefully remark that most studies of this
kind based on census data suffer similar imperfections.

8. Cf. Otis Dudley Duncan and Beverly Davis, 'An alternative to ecological correlation', *Am. Sociol. Rev.*, **18**, (Dec. 1953), 665–6; Leslie Kish, 'Differentiation in metropolitan areas', *Am. Sociol. Rev.*, **19**, (Aug. 1954), 388–98;

Jerome K. Myers, 'Note on the homogeneity of census tracts; a methodological problem in urban ecological research', *Social Forces*, **32**, (May 1954), 364–6; W. S. Robinson, 'Ecological correlations and the behavior of individuals', *Am. Sociol. Rev.*, **15**, (June 1950), 351–6.

9. Cf. Paul F. Lazarsfeld and Allen H. Barton, 'Qualitative measurement in the social sciences: classification, typologies, and indices', in D. Lerner and H. D. Lasswell, eds, *The Policy Sciences*, Stanford University Press, 1951, pp. 187–92; Hanan C. Selvin, 'Durkheim's *Suicide* and Problems of Empirical Research', *Am. J. Sociol.*, **63**, (May 1958), 615–19.

10. The term 'social space', unfortunately, may convey a pretentious note. Our understanding of the term generally conforms to the usage of Pitirim A. Sorokin, *Social Mobility*, New York: Harper, 1927, chapter 1, as well as to the operational description in Allen H. Barton, 'The concept of property-space in social research', in P. F. Lazarsfeld and M. Rosenberg, eds, *The Language of Social Research*, Glencoe: Free Press, 1955, 40–53.

11. M. G. Kendall, *Rank Correlation Methods*, London: Griffin, 1948. The data were taken from *US Census of Population: 1950, Vol. III, Census Tract Statistics*, chapter 23. We wish to thank Charlotte Connor, Ralph Cyphers, Isabelle Fisch, William Grace, Mary Masland, and Earl Stout for research assistance. We have omitted private household workers from consideration here because of the frequency with which they live in their employers' homes. The *income level* is the median 1949 income of families and unrelated individuals for the tract; the *educational level* is the median of school years completed by all persons over twenty-five in the tract. The use of these Census measures implies the following assumptions: (1) in general, a household contains one employed male, and his occupation is more significant than those of female members of the household in determining its status; (2) the income figure is a good estimate of the relative income of the households in each tract; (3) the education figure is a good estimate of the relative educational level of the heads of households in each tract. None of these assumptions seems to be unreasonable.

12. Frederick Mosteller and Robert R. Bush, 'Selected quantitative techniques', in G. Lindzey, ed., *Handbook of Social Psychology*, Cambridge, Mass: Addison-Wesley, 1954, vol. I, pp. 312–14. The sign test applies, not to the *mean* reductions in *tau* reported in Table 5.4, but to the relative magnitude of the reductions for income and for education of the individual *tau*'s in Table 5.1. In twenty-five of the twenty-eight cases, the reduction for education was greater than the reduction for income.

13. In this regard, our findings are consistent with those of Otis Dudley Duncan and Beverly Duncan, 'Residential distribution and occupational stratification', *Am. J. Sociol.*, **60**, (Mar. 1955), 493–503 [3]; and with those of Arthur H. Wilkins, 'The Residential Distribution of Occupation Groups in Eight Middle-Sized Cities of the United States in 1950' (unpublished PhD thesis, University of Chicago, 1956). Cf. Beverly Davis, 'Spatial distribution of

occupational groups: Chicago, 1940', Urban Analysis Report no. 4, Chicago Community Inventory, February, 1952, ditto.

14. Cf. Seymour M. Lipset and Reinhard Bendix, *Social Mobility in Industrial Society*, University of California Press, 1959, pp. 172–81. The correlations between the service category and both education and income may represent an additional, though minor, bit of supportive evidence. Although the *tau* with education is third lowest, the *tau* with income is the lowest. This category may at any one time be a repository for downwardly mobile people, who nevertheless expect to and may move up again in the near future, for example, the barber who, having failed in one attempt to own his own shop, expects to make another attempt. This interpretation was initially suggested by Albert J. Reiss, Jr, in his discussion of the original paper presented to the American Sociological Association, 1959.

15. See Calvin F. Schmid, 'Generalizations concerning the ecology of the American city', *Am. Sociol. Rev.*, **15**, (Feb. 1950), 280; and Schmid, Earle H. McCannell, and Maurice D. Van Arsdol, Jr, 'The ecology of the American city: further comparison and validation of generalizations', *Am. Sociol. Rev.*, **23**, (Aug. 1958), 395, for conclusions (in a considerably different idiom) concerning the importance of education in residential differentiation.

16. For the Hartford Standard Metropolitan Area as a whole, reported 1949 median incomes for the male experienced civilian labor force were: professionals 4,254, managers and proprietors 4,204, sales workers 3,198, clerical workers 2,940, craftsmen and foremen 3,225, operatives 2,825, service workers 2,374, and laborers 2,182 dollars. *US Census of Population: 1950, Vol. II, Characteristics of the Population*, Part 7, Table 78.

P. F. Cressey

6 Population succession in Chicago 1898–1930 *

The population of Chicago doubled from 1898 to 1930, amounting at the latter date to more than three million people. This rapid growth was accompanied by marked changes in the distribution of the city's population. Not simply did the population expand over a larger area, but certain sections of the city grew more rapidly than others and various cultural groups moved at different rates of speed.

In order to measure these movements, data for census tracts in 1910, 1920, and 1930 were used, as well as material from an 1898 census taken by the Chicago School Board. These census tracts and the precincts of the 1898 census were grouped into a series of ten concentric mile-zones radiating from the center of the city. The last, or tenth zone, is not directly comparable with the other zones, since it includes all the area from the ninth zone to the city limits and is quite irregular in shape. The large industrial community of South Chicago lies within this tenth zone.

In 1898 Chicago was relatively compact, half of its population living within a radius of 3·2 miles from the center of the city. In subsequent years this median point has steadily moved outward, being located at 4·1 miles in 1910, 5·0 miles in 1920, and 5·8 miles in 1930.[1] One of the most striking aspects of this general expansion has been the loss of population in the areas near the center of the city. In 1898, 45 per cent of the city's population – a total of 824,000 people – lived within the first three mile-zones; but in 1930 this area housed only 14 per cent of Chicago's population, or 474,000 people.[2] This region includes most of the slum area of the city and corresponds roughly to what E. W. Burgess has designated as the 'zone in transition'.[3] During the years from 1898 to 1930 the population of the fourth to sixth mile-zones, inclusive, increased at approximately the same rate as that of the city as a whole. The greatest increase occurred in the

* *American Journal of Sociology*, **44**, No. 1 (July 1938) 56–9.

outlying zones. In 1898 the seventh, eighth, and ninth zones included but 10 per cent of the population, whereas in 1930, 33 per cent of the population lived in this area. The population of the tenth zone increased from 5 to 14 per cent of the city's total during this general period, a considerable part of this increase being due to the rapid growth of industry in South Chicago.

This outward movement of population has continued beyond the limits of the city into a large number of suburbs. Between 1900 and 1930 the population of Chicago increased 99 per cent, whereas the population of fifteen of the larger suburbs, for which data are available, increased 329 per cent.

A more detailed picture of these movements may be had by studying the figures for specific cultural groups. This is particularly revealing because of the heterogeneous character of Chicago's population. Chicago is, in fact, one of the most European cities in America. Persons of native-white parentage constituted but 21 per cent of the population in 1900 and 28 per cent in 1930, the latter figure, according to available records, representing the highest percentage of American stock in the city's history. In 1930 one-quarter of the people were of foreign birth, and an additional 40 per cent were the children of foreign parents. Only two cities in Poland have more Poles, and but two cities in Ireland have more Irish than are to be found in Chicago.[4] In addition Chicago is the third largest Swedish city in the world, the third largest Bohemian, the third largest Jewish, and the second largest Negro. There are seven immigrant groups in Chicago, each composed of over 100,000 people, in addition to which there are nearly a quarter of a million Negroes. This great diversity of population is one of the reasons why succession has been so conspicuous a phenomenon in the city's history.

The distribution of these various groups reflects a definite process of succession. Immigrant stocks follow a regular sequence of settlement in successive areas of increasing stability and status. This pattern of distribution represents the ecological setting within which the assimilation of the foreign population takes place. An immigrant group on its arrival settles in a compact colony in a low-rent industrial area usually located in the transitional zone near the center of the city. If the group is of large size several different areas of initial settlement may develop in various industrial sections. These congested areas of first settlement are characterized by the perpetuation of many European cultural traits. After some years of residence in such an area, the group, as it improves its economic and social standing, moves outward to some more desirable residential district, creating an area of second settlement. In such an area the group is not so closely concentrated physically, there is less cultural solidarity, and more American standards of living are adopted. Subsequent areas of settlement may develop in some cases, but the last stage in this series of movements is one of gradual dispersion through cosmopolitan residential districts. This diffusion marks the disintegration of the group and the absorption of the individuals into the general American population. The relative concentration or dispersion of various immigrant groups furnishes an excellent indication of the length of residence in the city and the general degree of assimilation which has taken place.

The distribution of the American groups has also followed a rather definite pattern, though their movements are more difficult to trace since they lack the conspicuous cultural traits of the various immigrant groups. The American groups have tended to locate in the areas having direct access to the Loop, the business center of Chicago. The most desirable American residential districts have always been located along the main avenues running north, south, and west from the Loop. As the wealthier Americans have moved out along these main axes of transportation, other American groups of lower economic and social standing have generally followed in their wake. Along these main thoroughfares, near the Loop, is the rendezvous of the hobo – and the hobo is always always an American. A little further out are the rooming-house areas whose population is predominantly of native parentage, and then follow apartment-house areas with their cosmopolitan American population.

The immigrant and American groups follow rather different patterns of distribution, but behind these differences there is a striking similarity in the way in which these changes take place. This common process of succession involves a cycle of invasion, conflict, recession, and reorganization. These successive stages are interrelated, and they recur in the movement of all groups in the city.

The first stage in this cycle, that of invasion, usually begins with a few pioneers whose entrance into a new area may be unnoticed by the older residents. These pioneers tend to be individuals who have achieved a little greater economic success than their neighbors and who desire to improve their social status by moving into an area of greater prestige. Mass invasions set in after the initial invaders have established themselves in the new area. Such movement may involve merely a gradual transition which slowly replaces the older population, or it may take place with such rapidity as to be thought of in terms of a stampede. The area invaded may either be contiguous, or considerable distance may intervene. The direction of such movement is influenced by ecological barriers and by the main arteries of transportation which connect the two communities. The relative importance of various streets in Chicago in effecting group movement was determined statistically by comparing the population of specific groups in the census tracts adjacent to these streets with the total population of these groups in the sectors through which the streets ran. Once a mass movement is under way individuals are caught up in its spirit and often move with no other apparent reason than that everybody else is moving.

Conflict may accompany invasion, varying in intensity with the cultural differences and prejudices of the groups involved. Where the groups are of a similar social and economic level with no particular dislike for each other, the supplanting of one group by another usually involves only a minimum of friction. But where marked prejudices exist and there is a fear that the invading group will cause a serious loss in real estate values, violent opposition may develop. This situation has arisen particularly in the expansion of the Negro population into white communities and has been the reason for numerous bombings and other types of violence. Less extreme forms of hostility have developed over the entrance of Jews into gentile areas, and the movement of immigrants into American neighborhoods.

The correlative of invasion is recession, or the departure of the older population. The entrance of unwanted 'outsiders' lowers the desirability of the area in the eyes of the older inhabitants. Community life begins to deteriorate and sooner or later there is a search for a newer and more respectable place to live. Recession, however, may sometimes precede invasion, for as an area grows old the housing accommodations become obsolete, street-paving and other public improvements may deteriorate, or there may be encroachments from trade or industry. Under such circumstances, as the area becomes less attractive, the older residents depart leaving unoccupied houses behind them, and this encourages the entrance of some new group into the area. Thus in some cases the normal sequence may be reversed and recession may precede rather than follow invasion. In such circumstances there is usually little or no conflict between the two groups.

The final stage of the cycle involves the reorganization of the social life of the invading group as it acquires dominance in the new area. It usually takes considerable time to transfer the institutions of the group, such as its churches, lodges, and other social organizations. Movement into a new community often creates a crisis in the life of a group. The established routine is interrupted, the 'cake of custom' is broken, and opportunities are presented for the adoption of new ways of life. Immigrants frequently take advantage of entrance into a new area to change their names to more American forms, changes such as the following being not uncommon: Garskovitz to Groves, Smallovitz to Small, Abrahamson to Abrams, Weinstein to Weston. The organization of the family seems to change with movement from one area to another, especially in the case of the newer immigrant groups. Patriarchal patterns of authority and control which often characterize the area of first settlement give way to greater equality in family relations in secondary areas of settlement. This modification in family organization is illustrated in the case of a family, of which it was said, 'After Mr F. moved into this more American community he even allowed his daughter to marry the man she fell in love with.' The adoption of more liberal forms of worship by the older synagogues in Chicago has always coincided with their movement and the construction of new houses of worship. Even after the invading group has established its dominance, a few of the older residents may still remain in the area. Such marooned families, surviving from earlier groups of inhabitants, may be found in many communities in Chicago and often furnish a clue to the past history of the area.

In time the invaders will become old residents. Another cycle may set in, with a new group of invaders entering the area and the older residents or their descendants moving on to other parts of the city. This cyclical process, with minor variations, has occurred repeatedly in the life of various cultural groups and in the history of different sections of the city.

Among the various groups in Chicago, the old American stock, because of its superior wealth and prestige, has been in the forefront in the outward movement of the city's population. In 1910 persons of native-white parentage were distributed at a median distance of 4·7 miles from the center of the city, and in the 1930 at 6·6 miles, nearly a mile farther out than the median for the total population of the city.

The two most American sections of Chicago are the North and South sides. On the North Side in 1920, 25 per cent of the population was of native stock. This rose to 38 per cent in 1930, making this section the most American part of the city. The 'Gold Coast', the wealthiest and most fashionable area of the city, is located along the lake shore in this sector. North of the city limits and adjacent to the lake there stretch a series of well-to-do American suburbs, five of the most important having quadrupled in size between 1900 and 1930, at which time 52 per cent of their total population was of native stock. The South Side in 1900 was more American than the North Side, but by 1930 it had lost this leadership, at which time its native white stock amounted to but 28 per cent. On the West Side the American population has moved outward in large numbers to suburbs beyond the city limits, eight of which communities had a total population of 154,000 in 1930, 50 per cent of which was of American ancestry.

European immigrants first arrived in Chicago in large numbers during the decade following 1850. The Germans were the most important group in this early movement and by 1860 they constituted approximately one-fifth of the city's population. They settled in a compact colony on the North Side, where today two small concentrations still remain, located several miles north of the original area of settlement.[5] The outward movement of the German population is shown by the shift in the median point of their distribution from 3·2 miles in 1898 to 5·7 miles in 1930.[6] On the North Side this movement has been directed primarily along the main arteries of travel. In 1930, 36 per cent of the Germans in Chicago were located on the North Side, and an additional 31 per cent lived in the adjacent Northwest Side. The great majority of the group has ceased to live in specific German communities and is scattered through more or less cosmopolitan residential areas. This widespread dispersion is an index of the decline of social unity among the Germans and of their gradual absorption into the general life of the city.

The Irish began to arrive in Chicago about the same time as the Germans settling primarily in the general vicinity of the Stock Yards on the Southwest Side of the city. At the present time only a very small settlement remains in this area of initial concentration and the group as a whole is widely scattered through more desirable residential districts farther from the center of the city. This outward movement of the Irish is indicated by the change in the median of their distribution from 3·2 miles in 1898 to 6·4 miles in 1930, a point over half a mile farther from the Loop than the median for the total population of the city. On the Southwest Side, where 36 per cent of the Irish still reside, the main axis of movement has also been along a main transportation artery. The Irish are even more widely dispersed through the city than the Germans, a fact which reflects the more complete disintegration of their group life and a greater degree of cultural assimilation.

The third large group of early immigrants was composed of Swedes who began arriving in considerable numbers during the 1860's. Their main center of settlement developed on the North Side where they became close neighbors of the Germans. In 1930, 37 per cent of the Swedish population lived in this section where two small colonies still remain from their original settlement. The great majority of the Swedish population has reached the final phase in the pattern of succession, that of widespread dispersion and assimilation. This is seen in the fact that for some years the Swedes have been located farther from the center of the city than any other specific group, the median of their distribution being 3·9 miles in 1898 and 7 miles in 1930.

The newer immigrant groups, from eastern and southern Europe, began to arrive in Chicago during the last decade of the nineteenth century. As they increased in numbers they displaced the older immigrant groups from their original areas of settlement. Most of these newer groups, despite considerable movement in recent years, still remain concentrated in distinct settlements relatively close to the center of the city.

The Czechoslovaks in Chicago are largely of Bohemian or Czech stock, there being only a relatively small number of Slovaks in the city. Their center of settlement has always been on the West Side, where in 1930, 50 per cent of the group resided. The median for the distribution of the Czechoslovaks has shifted from 2·7 miles in 1898 to 5·3 miles in 1930. Their movement on the West Side has followed the transportation lines into various suburbs west of the city limits. Cicero and Berwyn, the two most important of these suburbs, had a combined population of 114,000 in 1930, 34 per cent of this total being persons who were born in Czechoslovakia. The dispersion of this group has taken place more rapidly than that of any other group of recent immigrants. In part this may be due to their slightly longer residence in the city, but probably it also reflects their somewhat more rapid economic and cultural adjustment to urban American life.

The largest immigrant group in Chicago at the present time is composed of Poles. They have settled primarily on the Northwest Side, where in both 1898 and 1930, 48 per cent of the Poles lived. In addition to this main colony several minor areas of first settlement have developed in other parts of the city. As the group has grown in size there has been some outward movement, with the development of a few areas of secondary settlement. In 1898 the persons born in Poland were located at a median distance of 2·8 miles from the center of the city, and in 1930 at 4·6 miles. This latter figure is over a mile nearer the center of the city than the average for the total population, and represents the smallest amount of movement of any important group in the city during this period. The Poles still remain, on the whole, closely concentrated in areas of first settlement and they have not as yet made great progress in economic advancement or cultural assimilation.

The chief center of Italian settlement has been on the West Side, although there are a few small concentrations near industrial areas in other sections of the city. Until 1920 the Italians were even more compact and immobile than the Poles, the median of their distribution being 1·5 miles in 1898 and 2 miles in 1920. In the decade following 1920 there was considerable movement out to areas of secondary settlement, these new areas being connected with the old settlements by important through-streets. As a result of these movements the Italians in 1930 distributed at a median distance of 3·3 miles from the city's center. In spite of this recent expansion the majority of the Italians still live in areas of first settlement and the group as a whole is located closer to the center of the city than any other large immigrant population.

The Russians who have come to Chicago are almost entirely Russian Jews. They settled originally in a compact ghetto on the West Side, just south of the main Italian colony and far removed from the older group of German Jews living on the South Side. The decade from 1910 to 1920 witnessed a mass movement into an area of secondary settlement several miles west of the original ghetto area.[7] From 1898 to 1930 the median for the distribution of this group shifted from 1·6 to 4·8 miles, a movement covering a greater distance than that of any other group of recent immigrants. This mobility reflects a considerable amount of economic success, but the group as a whole, nevertheless, remains concentrated in rather definite settlements. The bonds of a common religion and culture and the external pressure of gentile prejudice have tended to give cohesion to the group and thus, despite its rapid movement, to retard the general dispersion and assimilation of its members.

Negroes have resided in Chicago since the earliest days of its history, but until the period of the World War they were relatively few in number and were widely scattered through the city. During the past twenty years, however, they have come to Chicago in such numbers that they now constitute one of the largest distinct groups in the city. Their chief area of settlement has been on the South Side where they now occupy an area approximately four miles long and a mile wide. This 'Black Belt' of Negro population increased from 17,000 in 1898 to 91,000 in 1920, and in 1930 amounted to 189,000, a figure which approaches that of New York's Harlem.[8] Negro settlements are also found in the abandoned Jewish ghetto area on the West Side, and in a few additional localities. Like other groups in the city the Negro population in recent years has moved out from the center of the city, the median for its distribution changing from 2·5 miles in 1898 to 4·5 miles in 1930. The unusual aspect of their history is that as they have moved and as their numbers have increased they have not become more widely dispersed through the city, but rather have come to be more highly concentrated in a few specific areas. There has, in fact, been an actual decrease in the number of Negroes in many sections of the city. As a result of their poverty and the pressure of white prejudice, the Negroes, particularly on the South Side, have come to live in a more compact community than any other important group in the city. One of the effects of this growing concentration has been to increase the racial consciousness and intensify the social and political solidarity of the Negroes in Chicago.[9]

The phenomena of succession have been so striking an aspect of Chicago's history largely because of the rapidity with which the city has grown and the great diversity of its cultural groups. These groups have moved through the city at varying rates of speed, reflecting different stages of economic and cultural advance. This process of succession has provided the framework for the distribution of the city's population and represents the way in which immigrant groups have escaped from their slum settlements and become assimilated into the general life of the city.

Notes and References

1. The medians for each year were calculated from the distribution of the population in the ten mile-zones into which the city was divided, and rested on the assumption that the population was evenly distributed within each zone. The medians for the specific cultural groups in the city were calculated on a similar basis.
2. For the sake of simplicity these and subsequent population figures are expressed in terms of the nearest whole thousand.
3. R. E. Park and E. W. Burgess, *The City*, Chicago, 1925, 51.

4. The statements in this paragraph referring to nationality groups in Chi̶ include those born in a specific country, together with the children of foreig̶ born parents.
5. H. W. Zorbaugh, *Gold Coast and Slum*, Chicago, 1929, 18–20, 149–50.
6. These medians and other statistical data in the remainder of this article referring to immigrant groups are calculated only for individuals of foreign birth, as no detailed data were available, prior to 1930, for the distribution of native-born persons of foreign parentage.
7. Louis Wirth, *The Ghetto*, Chicago 1928, 241–6.
8. In 1930 Harlem had a Negro population of 202,000. The total Negro population of Manhattan was 224,670.
9. Harold F. Gosnell, *Negro Politicians: the rise of Negro politics in Chicago*, Chicago, 1933, chap. 2.

7 Ethnic segregation and assimilation*

This study of residential patterns of ethnic groups in Chicago provides further evidence for R. E. Park's contention that 'social relations are . . . frequently and . . . inevitably correlated with spatial relations'.[1] It summarizes more recent data to supplement earlier studies of ethnic residential patterns in Chicago[2] and illustrates the use of certain methods adapted to comparative analyses which are needed to establish more general propositions than those emerging from case studies of individual ethnic groups.[3] Our leading hypotheses are, first, that the degree of residential segregation of a group of foreign stock at any given time is inversely related to appropriate indicators of its socioeconomic status and degree of assimilation and directly related to indicators of its 'social distance' from the population of native stock and, second, that ethnic segregation patterns are relatively stable over time but change in directions to be anticipated on the basis of the positive correlation between assimilation and length of time that the immigrant group has been established in the United States.

Data and methods

Except as noted otherwise, the data for the study are from official census publications or special compilations of unpublished census data. Such a special compilation of the 1930 data[4] provides what is certainly an unusual, if not a unique, body of information on intracity residential distributions of both the first and the second generation of foreign stock by country of origin. Because these statistics have not been analyzed adequately hitherto and because their detail cannot be duplicated for other

* Reprinted from *American Journal of Sociology*, **64** (January, 1959) 364–74.

periods, the emphasis of the paper is on the 1930 material. However, we also include comparative data for 1950.[5]

All our measures of residential distributions are based on statistics compiled for the seventy-five community areas of the city of Chicago. While it is certain that the results would have differed somewhat had census tracts or some other areal unit been employed, we believe that the grosser unit is adequate, particularly since we do not attempt to reach highly specific or refined conclusions.

In respect to analytical methods we follow closely the pattern of an earlier paper.[6] The index of dissimilarity between residential distributions is used to measure the segregation of a group of foreign stock from the native population or the separation of one such group from another. The same index serves for comparing residential distributions at two points in time. The index of centralization, computed as described in the earlier paper, measures relative concentration of residences toward the center of the city. Correlations between two characteristics of several ethnic groups are computed by the Spearman rank formula. For a ranking of ten groups a correlation with an absolute value of 0·62 is significant at the 5 per cent level by the appropriate t-test.

Except for a few remarks about Negroes and Jews at the end of the paper, we limit the study to the foreign-born and the second generation from Europe. In some places we employ a classification of them as 'old' immigrants – those from northern and western Europe – and 'new' immigrants – those from central and eastern Europe. This conventional classification is subject to criticism; in particular, it does not characterize them very precisely with respect to time of arrival.[7] However, it provides a gross classification in terms of the similarity of their national origins to those of the native population in the United States.

To simplify the exposition, we use the abbreviations N for native; W, white; F, foreign; B, born; M, mixed (one parent native, one foreign-born); and P, parentage. Thus the 'second generation' is identified as NWFMP, that is, native whites of foreign or mixed parentage. According to census rules, the nationality of a NWFP is that of the father and the nationality of a NWMP is that of the foreign parent.

In 1930 the FBW population made up 25 per cent of Chicago's total population; the percentage had declined to 14·5 by 1950. The country-of-origin groups of FBWs listed in Table 7.1 were the ten largest in both years. In 1930 they ranged in size from 25,000 (Austria) to 150,000 (Poland); in 1950, from 15,000 (England and Wales) to 94,000 (Poland). A good deal of our analysis of the 1930 data employed information on thirteen smaller groups, ranging down to as few as 2,000 FBWs. The results are quite consistent with those reported here and need not be summarized in detail, particularly since there are some reservations about the meaning of segregation indexes for such small categories.

97

O. D. Duncan and S. Lieberson

Segregation

There is considerable variation among the FBW groups in the extent to which they are residentially segregated from the total NW population. To make the proportional distribution by community areas for FBWs from England and Wales the same as that for all NWs, only 19 per cent of them would have had to move to other areas in either 1930 or 1950. By contrast, the segregation index for Lithuanian FBWs was 57 per cent in 1930 and 51·5 per cent in 1950 (cols 1 and 2, Table 7.1). For all ten countries shown in Table 7.1, the mean of the segregation indexes with respect to NWs was 39·4 per cent in 1930 and 35·9 per cent in 1950, indicating a small decline in degree of segregation. This decline, however, was confined to the FBW groups from the 'new' countries of immigration. The mean for the four 'old' countries was 27·7 in 1930 and 27·8 in 1950, whereas the mean for the six 'new' countries dropped from 47·1 in 1930 to 41·4 in 1950. Despite this differential change, the 'new' groups remained much more highly segregated in 1950 than the 'old', Austria being the only exception among the larger groups, as it is also in respect to several other comparisons between 'old' and 'new'.

For 1930 we can calculate the segregation of FBW groups against the NWNP population, as well as against the total NW population. The former basis (col. 3, Table 7.1) yields somewhat lower segregation indexes for the 'old' countries but rather higher indexes for the 'new'. Nevertheless, the two bases of computation rank the countries in much the same way; *rho* is 0·90 between columns 2 and 3 of Table 7.1.

A comparison of cols 3 and 4, Table 7.1, shows that the pattern of differ-

Table 7.1 Indexes of residential segregation and net redistribution of selected ethnic groups, Chicago, 1950 and 1930

Country of origin	FBW v. NW 1950 (1)	FBW v. NW 1930 (2)	FBW v. NWNP 1930 (3)	NWFMP v. NWNP 1930 (4)	FBW v. NWFMP* 1930 (5)	FBW, 1930 v. FBW, 1950 (6)
England and Wales	18·9	19·1	12·5	9·4	9·9	9·4
Irish Free State (Eire)	31·8	31·8	26·3	22·4	10·5	13·3
Sweden	33·2	34·0	28·1	24·0	11·6	10·2
Germany	27·2	26·0	28·0	19·6	12·8	14·0
Poland	45·2	50·8	62·5	63·7	8·5	11·2
Czechoslovakia	48·8	51·9	60·5	58·9	7·4	10·2
Austria	18·1	25·0	32·9	28·6	9·1	15·5
USSR	44·0	49·8	55·7	46·9	11·3	26·0
Lithuania	51·5	57·0	63·9	61·4	5·2	14·5
Italy	40·5	48·3	53·7	51·4	5·0	21·7
Unweighted means:						
4 'old' countries	27·8	27·7	23·7	18·8	11·2	11·7
6 'new' countries	41·4	47·1	54·9	51·8	7·8	16·5

* First *v.* second generation from the same country.

98

ential segregation is much the same for the second as for the first generation, as indicated by the *rho* of 0·96. However, on the average and for most individual countries, the second generation is somewhat less segregated from the NWNP population than is the first; this is especially true of the 'old' countries. As shown by the figures in col 5, the second generation from 'old' countries was farther removed from the first generation in terms of residential distributions than was the case for the 'new' countries. On the whole, not only were the FBWs from 'old' countries less segregated from the NWNP population than were either the FBWs or NWFMPs from the 'new' but also their offspring had moved away from a segregated residential pattern at a faster rate than had the second generation from 'new' countries.

The interannual rank correlation between cols 1 and 2 of Table 7.1 (0·99) indicates high stability of the pattern of differences in degree of segregation. This stability of areal pattern is in contrast to the well-known instability of individual residential units. Although we have no figures on particular ethnic groups, we know that 79 per cent of all Chicago families in 1934 lived in homes different from those they had ten years earlier and that 76 per cent of the dwelling units in Chicago in 1939 were occupied by households different from those residing there a decade previously.[8] Much of the dwelling-unit turnover occurs within local areas, of course, as is suggested by the fact that the index of *net* residential redistribution of the ten FBW groups, 1930–50 (col. 6, Table 7.1), averaged only 14·6 per cent. The fact that the net redistribution of the 'new' groups (mean 16·5) was somewhat greater than that of the 'old' groups (mean 11·7) is no doubt related to the fact that the average degree of segregation declined for the former though not for the latter.

Table 7.2 shows the index of dissimilarity between residential distri-

Table 7.2   **Indexes of dissimilarity among residential distributions of selected groups of foreign stock and Negroes, Chicago, 1930**
(Above diagonal, FBW; below diagonal, NWFMP)

| Country of origin | Country of origin (see Stub) | | | | | | | | | | |
	1	2	3	4	5	6	7	8	9	10	11
1. England and Wales	—	24·7	30·7	35·0	64·6	60·0	34·3	50·1	62·5	53·4	83·6
2. Irish Free State	20·3	—	42·4	44·1	68·3	63·7	43·9	59·5	62·2	56·6	84·3
3. Sweden	24·0	35·6	—	35·1	73·5	68·8	45·3	65·5	72·8	66·9	90·1
4. Germany	27·2	34·3	25·3	—	57·7	58·6	22·3	56·4	65·5	57·4	88·6
5. Poland	68·8	68·6	70·7	58·4	—	47·2	49·4	56·7	51·2	58·8	93·2
6. Czechoslovakia	61·9	61·4	66·0	56·2	49·8	—	49·1	62·5	49·9	63·6	92·7
7. Austria	34·8	38·3	37·3	19·9	49·9	47·1	—	48·2	57·1	52·2	88·4
8. USSR	47·0	50·2	55·4	47·9	63·7	62·2	42·1	—	68·6	56·7	89·8
9. Lithuania	63·2	60·0	68·0	61·0	52·0	45·9	52·2	66·1	—	66·4	90·9
10. Italy	53·9	54·6	63·4	54·0	60·9	64·0	50·5	56·3	66·1	—	79·2
11. Negro*	84·4	84·7	90·0	88·2	94·1	92·9	89·5	90·1	91·4	79·2	—

* Almost all born in the United States.

butions of specific country-of-origin groups in 1930. (The figures for Negroes are referred to subsequently.) Although there is considerable variation in these intercountry indexes of residential separation, the indexes by no means fall into any perfect hierarchical pattern. In particular, the separation of one FBW or NWFMP group from another cannot be predicted closely from their respective indexes of segregation from the NW or NWNP populations (shown in Table 7.1). The figures do reveal certain significant patterns, however. On the whole the intercountry indexes run as high as or higher than the segregation indexes with respect to NWs or NWNPs. For example, the mean of the six segregation indexes with respect to NWNPs for NWFMPs from 'new' countries (col. 4, Table 7.1) is 51·8, whereas the mean of the fifteen intercountry indexes for the NWFMPs from the six 'new' countries in Table 7.2 is 55·3. The situation revealed by these data, therefore, is one of a multiplicity of ethnic colonies scattered among the residential areas occupied by the native population rather than of a single 'ghetto' for all foreign groups. The persistence of such colonies over generations is indicated by the rank correlation of 0·94 for the forty-five pairs of observations for corresponding countries in Table 7·2. The correlation is 0·89 for the six pairs of indexes of dissimilarity among 'old' countries, 0·93 for the fifteen pairs of indexes among 'new' countries, and 0·92 for the twenty-four pairs of indexes for 'old' versus 'new' countries.

Table 7.3 (upper right half) presents similar intercountry indexes for 1950, for FBWs only, since information on the second generation is lacking. This table gives much the same picture as the preceding one. In fact, the inter-annual correlation is 0·93 between the forty-five pairs of corresponding

Table 7.3 Indexes of dissimilarity among residential and occupational distributions of selected foreign-born white groups and Negroes, Chicago, 1950

(Above diagonal, residential distributions, city of Chicago; below diagonal, occupational distributions, employed males, Chicago Standard Metropolitan Area)

| Country of origin | Country of origin (see Stub) | | | | | | | | | | |
	1	2	3	4	5	6	7	8	9	10	11
1. England and Wales	—	28·5	29·7	29·5	58·4	55·9	26·3	38·3	56·8	45·7	77·8
2. Ireland (Eire)	30·2	—	40·2	43·9	66·7	63·2	38·3	54·2	59·8	52·0	81·4
3. Sweden	28·1	32·5	—	32·3	67·8	66·0	38·8	54·0	66·2	60·9	85·5
4. Germany	16·0	23·8	17·9	—	55·9	47·2	21·3	47·2	54·3	54·3	85·4
5. Poland	28·4	15·5	26·4	21·0	—	43·5	47·3	58·3	50·8	52·6	90·8
6. Czechoslovakia	29·0	19·3	16·6	14·9	13·3	—	47·8	61·4	50·5	55·9	89·2
7. Austria	20·3	18·5	20·7	9·2	15·0	14·3	—	45·6	53·8	45·6	82·5
8. USSR	17·7	33·4	38·7	23·8	35·2	36·1	27·3	—	67·5	57·5	87·1
9. Lithuania*	—	—	—	—	—	—	—	—	—	61·6	84·7
10. Italy	30·4	10·4	29·6	23·0	10·3	18·6	14·4	34·1	—	—	69·6
11. Negro†	48·4	18·7	48·7	41·0	24·0	32·5	34·9	46·7	—	21·1	—

* Occupation data not available.

† Almost all born in the United States.

indexes in Tables 7.2 and 7.3; the correlations are 0·94 for the 'old' countries, 0·88 for the 'new' countries, and 0·92 for the 'old' versus 'new' countries. Both the intergeneration and the interannual correlations support the previous observation as to the stability of segregation patterns.

Averages (Table 7.4) summarizing the data in the two preceding tables reveal markedly lower intercountry indexes for the 'old' countries. Moreover, the 'new' country groups of both generations were as much separated from each other, on the average, as they were from the 'old' country groups. The intergeneration decline in mean inter-country indexes was rather greater for the 'old' than for the 'new' countries, but the difference between the 1930 and 1950 means for FBWs was greater for 'new' than for 'old' countries. Although ethnic colonies were becoming less distinct during the period 1930–50, they still remained quite visible at the end of the period, especially those of the 'new' immigrants.

Table 7.4   Mean indexes of dissimilarity among occupational and residential distributions of selected groups of foreign stock, Chicago, 1950 and 1930

Groups of countries* compared	No. of Comparisons†	1950, FBW Occupational	Residential	1930, Residential FBW	NWFMP
'Old' v. 'old'	6	24·8	34·0	35·3	27·8
'New' v. 'new'	15 (10)	21·9	53·3	55·8	55·3
'Old' v. 'new'	24 (20)	22·3	52·1	57·9	55·0

* See Table 7.1 for identification of countries and Tables 7.2 and 7.3 for data from which means were computed.
† Figures in parentheses pertain to occupational comparisons; data not available for Lithuania.

Centralization

Centralization, or zonal pattern, was emphasized in earlier research on residential distributions of ethnic groups (see the papers of Cressey and Ford cited in note 3). From our point of view, centralization is an aspect of segregation. A group highly concentrated toward the center of the city, as compared with the general or native population, is necessarily segregated; but the converse is not necessarily true: a group may be highly segregated without being centralized. It is even possible for a segregated group to be decentralized, that is, to have its major concentrations located toward the periphery of the city. The classic hypothesis, of course, is that immigrants initially tend to locate near the center of the city and, in the course of time and with the progress of assimilation, to disperse toward the periphery until they are no more centralized than the native population. Cross-sectional and longitudinal comparisons of indexes of centralization afford a somewhat more precise test of this hypothesis.

The indexes of centralization presented in Table 7.5 largely confirm expectations based on observations of previous students. In both 1950 and

1930 the 'old' immigrant groups were considerably less centralized than the 'new'; the Swedes, in fact, were rather decentralized in comparison with the native population. All ten FBW groups were relatively less centralized in 1950 than in 1930 (compare cols 1 and 2 of Table 7.5), although they maintained their relative positions with respect to each other,

Table 7.5 Indexes of centralization for selected groups of foreign stock Chicago, 1950 and 1930

Country of origin	FBW v. NW 1950 (1)	FBW v. NW 1930 (2)	FBW v. NWNP 1930 (3)	NWFMP v. NWNP 1930 (4)
England and Wales	−0·05	−0·04	0·03	−0·06
Irish Free State (Eire)	−0·05	0·00	0·07	0·00
Sweden	−0·19	−0·18	−0·11	−0·18
Germany	0·04	0·09	0·17	0·04
Poland	0·22	0·27	0·33	0·29
Czechoslovakia	0·19	0·23	0·31	0·27
Austria	0·03	0·13	0·20	0·13
USSR	0·10	0·24	0·33	0·25
Lithuania	0·08	0·15	0·21	0·18
Italy	0·25	0·38	0·43	0·42
Unweighted means:				
4 'old' countries	−0·06	−0·03	0·04	−0·05
6 'new' countries	0·14	0·23	0·30	0·26

as indicated by the interannual rank correlation of 0·96. Similarly, the intergenerational shift, as indicated by a comparison of cols 3 and 4 in Table 7·5, was uniformly in the direction of less centralization of the second generation, again with a high stability of the pattern of differential degrees of centralization summarized by a *rho* of 0·98. The difference between generations was, however, somewhat greater for those from the 'old' than from the 'new' countries. It is important to note that these interannual and intergenerational shifts do not refer merely to a centrifugal movement of the foreign stock but to a net centrifugal shift relative to the native population, which was itself increasing more rapidly toward the periphery than toward the center of the city. (The index of centralization of the 1950 with respect to the 1930 NW population was −0·05.)

That the classic hypothesis, though seemingly applicable to the countries discussed above, may not fit all instances is indicated by an interesting extreme case. With respect to total NWNPs, the Netherlands FBWs had a centralization index of −0·28, and the Netherlands NWFMPs had an index of −0·34 in 1930; they were, therefore, even more decentralized than the Swedes. The Dutch are a relatively small group consisting of 9,000 FBWs and 16,000 NWFMPs in 1930; 28 per cent of the former and 27 per cent of the latter lived in one community, 'Roseland', about twelve miles

south of the center of the city. The Dutch settled in this nei
farmers and railroad construction workers in the latter hal
teenth century, long before it became a part of the built-up urb
area.[9] Their present decentralization, therefore, is not the
process of dispersal from an initial settlement near the cen
This shows the need for caution in interpreting strictly cross-sectional
comparisons of centralization indexes.

Assimilation and socioeconomic status

The process by which immigrants adjust to conditions in the country of
destination include *naturalization*, the acquisition of legal citizenship;
absorption, or entry into productive economic activity; *assimilation*, or
integration into the social structure more or less on terms of socioeconomic
equality; and *acculturation*, or the adoption of the local customs and the
relinquishing of such cultural characteristics as would identify the immigrants as a distinct ethnic group. For our purposes it is unnecessary to
make an issue of the distinctions among these processes, since the available
data do not permit their independent measurement. Moreover, we feel
justified in treating conventional measures of socioeconomic status along
with other indicators of immigrant adjustment on the grounds that ethnic
differentials in socioeconomic status are indicative of incomplete absorption and assimilation.

The significance of the various indicators itemized in Table 7.6 is more or
less obvious. First of all, it should be noted that the classification of
countries on the basis of several of these indicators (with appropriate
choice of cutting points) is the same as the 'old-new' categorization. However, these indicators serve to specify certain major aspects of the differential
assimilation of the two categories. For example, the proportion arriving in
the United States in 1900 or earlier (col 1) is based on a classification of
individuals, in contrast to the characterization of country-of-origin groups
in historical terms according to the period in which they began to come to
this country in large numbers. The variable in col 5, 'NWMP as per cent of
NWFMP', is a rough indication of intermarriage as an aspect of assimilation. Other things being equal, the higher the percentage of the second
generation with one native parent, the greater the amount of intermarriage
between the first generation and the native population. It should not be
overlooked that in many cases the native parent is a second-generation
member of the same stock as the foreign parent, but the census data do not
permit us to distinguish such cases from those involving intermarriage in a
stricter sense. The available data on rentals and homeownership are somewhat unusual in that they rest on a classification of individuals rather than
dwelling units. This means, for example, that many NWFMP individuals
are classified by the rental of the dwelling unit occupied by a household with

103

head. It should also be observed that the rental and homeownership
data pertain to 1940, although there is no reason to believe that the ranks of
the several countries changed greatly between 1930 and 1940.

The lower panel of Table 7.6 shows correlations of the indicators of
assimilation and socioeconomic status with the indexes of segregation of
the foreign stock groups. For the most part, the correlations indicate that
segregation is inversely related to assimilation, confirming the hypothesis
stated by Halbwachs, who suggested that 'plus une population d'immigrants est concentrée, moins elle est assimilée',[10] and Hawley, who concluded that 'redistribution of a minority group in the same territorial pattern as that of the majority group results in a dissipation of subordinate
status and an assimilation of the subjugated group into the social structure'.[11] It may be noted that the correlations of the indexes of centralization (not shown) with the indicators of assimilation and socioeconomic
status were much like those for the indexes of segregation, though generally
slightly lower in absolute value.

Despite the confirmation of our general hypothesis, attention must also
be given to the negative findings. Unfortunately, the only indicator
available for both 1930 and 1950 is percentage of naturalized citizens
among the FBWs. Whereas in 1930 this variable was clearly correlated with
assimilation and exhibited higher values for the 'old' immigrants, by 1950 all
country-of-origin groups had moved so far toward complete naturalization
that the variable no longer correlated with segregation or discriminated
between 'old' and 'new' groups. The correlation between income and
segregation in 1950, though in the expected direction, was too low to be
statistically significant. The low correlation may be partly due to the use of
an income figure for all individuals with income rather than median
family income, which is not available. But the major finding which is
contrary to expectations is the positive correlation of homeownership with
segregation. Although the correlation is of doubtful significance, it is
certainly not in the direction anticipated on the basis of the usual positive
association of homeownership with other indicators of socioeconomic
status. That homeownership does not behave exactly like an indicator of
assimilation is indicated by the fact that it poorly discriminates between
'old' and 'new' countries and is consistently lower for the second generation than for the foreign-born. The contrast between generations is
magnified when a family, rather than individual, basis of classification is
employed. In 1930, 41·8 per cent of the families in Chicago headed by a
FBW person lived in homes they owned, as compared with 29·6 per cent
of families with NWFMP head and only 18·6 per cent of those with NWNP
head.[12] Although the high proportion of homeownership among the
FBWs may be related to their high average age, it is unlikely that age
differences account for the difference in homeownership between NWFMPs
and NWNPs. Quite similar differences in homeownership between nativity

Table 7.8 Indicators of assimilation and socioeconomic status and their rank correlations with segregation indexes, for selected groups of foreign stock, Chicago, 1930–50

Country of origin and variables correlated	Per cent of FBW arriving in 1900 or earlier 1930 (1)	Per cent of FBW naturalized citizens 1930 (2)	Per cent of FBW naturalized citizens 1950 (3)	Per cent of FBW able to speak English 1930 (4)	NWMP as per cent of NWFMP 1930 (5)	Median equivalent monthly rental, 1940 ($) FBW (6)	Median equivalent monthly rental, 1940 ($) NWFMP (7)	Per cent living in owner-occupied units, 1940 FBW (8)	Per cent living in owner-occupied units, 1940 NWFMP (9)	FBW median school years completed 1950 (10)	FBW median income in 1949 (dollars) (11)	Occupational dissimilarity, FBW v. NW 1950 (12)
England and Wales	38·8	71·7	84·0	(100)	52·6	40	41	27·9	25·1	9·0	2,601	11·7
Irish Free State (Eire)	44·2	75·2	89·8	(100)	30·0	37	40	43·1	35·8	8·5	2,432	22·8
Sweden	41·2	67·1	92·4	98·7	20·8	38	39	36·2	33·3	8·6	2,713	32·3
Germany	54·3	71·0	89·1	97·2	30·9	34	36	40·3	37·2	8·6	2,538	18·3
Poland	19·6	59·1	83·0	86·0	13·5	25	24	42·2	36·0	5·9	2,374	24·3
Czechoslovakia	28·2	68·7	90·7	88·6	17·0	26	25	55·1	42·3	8·2	2,356	25·2
Austria	18·7	67·9	91·0	96·3	21·0	31	32	41·8	33·5	8·3	2,695	19·1
USSR	17·3	67·5	90·7	95·4	13·2	42	43	13·5	11·3	8·1	2,892	18·7
Lithuania	14·1	51·5	—	89·1	8·5	29	29	43·5	35·1	—	—	—
Italy	17·3	58·1	88·5	84·8	16·4	24	25	39·1	32·5	5·2	2,630	23·4
Unweighted means:												
'Old' countries	44·6	71·2	88·8	99·0	33·6	37	39	36·9	32·8	8·7	2,571	21·3
'New' countries	19·2	62·1	88·8	90·0	14·9	30	30	39·2	31·8	7·1	2,589	22·1
Correlation with segregation index:												
FBW v. NW	—0·72	—0·65	—0·10	—0·83	—0·92	—0·56	—	0·44	—	—0·65	—0·33	0·62
FBW v. NWNP	—0·77	—0·77	—	—0·87	—0·88	—	—	—	—	—	—	—
NWFMP v. NWP	—0·69	—0·76	—	—	—	—	—0·74	—	0·25	—	—	—

Sources: Cols. 1, 2, 4, 5: *Fifteenth Census of the United States, 1930: Population, Vol. II: General. Report, Statistics by Subject* (Washington: Government Printing Office, 1933); cols. 6–9: *Sixteenth Census of the United States, 1940: Population Country of Origin of the Foreign Stock* (Washington: Government Printing Office, 1943); cols. 3, 10, 11, 12: *United States Census of Population, 1950, Vol. IV: Special Reports*, Part 3, Chapter A. 'Nativity and parentage' (Washington: Government Printing Office, 1954); data not given for Lithuania; data are for Chicago Standard Metropolitan Area.

Notes: Col. 4: persons ten years old and over; data in parentheses surmised; cols. 6–9: correlated with 1930 segregation indexes; individuals classified by unit lived in, excluding unrelated individuals; rental of owned units taken as 1 per cent of estimated value; col. 10: persons twenty-five years old and over; col. 11: persons fourteen years old and over with income; col. 12: employed males fourteen years old and over.

categories were observed in Detroit, Los Angeles, and Philadelphia in 1930, although they failed to appear in New York. Moreover, there was some consistency in the ranking of the various country-of-origin groups from one large city to another. This suggests a connection between 'propensity to homeownership' and factors such as previous urban or rural residence differentiating the backgrounds of the respective ethnic groups, although it is difficult to specify what these factors may be. It may be, too, that a high propensity to homeownership, whatever its explanation, retards the residential mobility required for lessening of segregation.

Whereas the residential segregation of FBWs with respect to NWs was significantly correlated with their occupational segregation (col 12, Table 7.6), the residential separation of one ethnic group from another had little to do with the dissimilarity of their distributions by major occupation groups. The rank correlation between the thirty-six corresponding indexes in Table 7.3 is only 0.26 – too low to be significant. Moreover, there is little difference between the average indexes of occupational dissimilarity among 'old' and 'new' countries (Table 7.4) or between their average indexes of occupational dissimilarity with respect to NWs (col 12, Table 7.6). Apparently the existence and perpetuation of ethnic colonies are not to be explained primarily by occupational differentiation, although our measure of the latter is rather crude owing to the use of only eleven broad occupational categories.

Social distance

Although 'psychological distance' may be a more appropriate term, the concept of 'social distance' has been applied to feelings of acceptance or rejection of minority ethnic groups by the general population. To indicate the close association between the ranking of ethnic groups in this respect and their ranking in terms of residential segregation, reference is made to the studies of Bogardus,[13] who asked subjects in various parts of the United States to endorse or reject such statements as the following with respect to specified ethnic categories: 'Would admit to my street as neighbors' and 'Would admit to close kinship by marriage.'

For sixteen European groups, the ranking on the 'neighbors' question obtained by Bogardus in 1926 correlated 0.73 with the ranking of our segregation indexes for FBWs versus NWNPs and 0.80 with the ranking of the segregation indexes for NWFMPs versus NWNPs. These correlations differ but slightly from that of 0.83 between rankings based on the 'marriage' question and our indicator of intermarriage – NWMP as percentage of NWFMP. Bogardus found that the social distance rankings of ethnic groups have been relatively stable over time, as were our segregation indexes. Consequently, it is difficult to detect any significant change in the relationship between the two.

Negroes

With the restriction of immigration, Negro migrants to the city had been said to have taken over many of the former roles of immigrants. Our data point to one limitation of the analogy: Negroes are much more segregated than any immigrant group. On a community-area basis, the index of segregation of Negroes with respect to NWs was 85·2 in 1930 and 79·7 in 1950. The indexes of dissimilarity between the Negro residential distribution and those of the several FBW groups were, for the most part, even higher; and they were uniformly higher than the intercountry indexes of dissimilarity (see col 11, Tables 7.2 and 7.3).

One of the early papers on segregation patterns called attention to 'the importance of further study of the relative resistance of different immigrant groups in determining the direction of the movement of Negro population in northern cities', in connection with its presentation of the following informal observations: 'No instance has been noted . . . where a Negro invasion succeeded in displacing the Irish in possession of a community. Yet, frequently . . . Negroes have pushed forward in the wake of retreating Jews. . . . It is rather significant to point out in passing the frequent propinquity of Negroes and Italian settlements in our larger cities.'[14] The hypothesis of differential 'resistance of different immigrant groups' is supported indirectly by the variation among groups in their indexes of dissimilarity to Negroes and especially by the persistence of its pattern as indicated by the inter-annual rank correlation of 0·92 between col 11 of Table 7.2 and col 11 of Table 7.3. The net redistribution of Negro population over the twenty-year period is indicated by an index of dissimilarity of 22·3 per cent between Negro residential distributions in 1930 and 1950; this net shift, together with those shown in col 6 of Table 7.1, was quite sufficient to have produced substantial modification of the pattern had forces not been at work to maintain it.

The comparatively low index of dissimilarity between Negroes and Italian FBWs in both years accords with Burgess' observation. On the other hand, on the basis of his remark about the Irish, one might well anticipate that their residential dissimilarity to Negroes would be greater than the data show it to be. The suggestion that there is an especially noteworthy tendency for Negroes to succeed Jews is not supported by the observation that the index of dissimilarity between Negroes and the predominantly Jewish USSR FBWs was close to the median of such indexes for the ten FBW groups in both 1930 and 1950. Estimates of the distribution of the total Jewish population for 1931 and 1951[15] indicate an index of residential dissimilarity between Jews and Negroes of 85·9 in 1930–31 and 80·9 in 1950–51. As compared with the other indexes given here, however, these are understated, inasmuch as the Jewish estimates are available for only fourteen individual community areas and seven combinations of community areas. Even so, they are approximately equal to the indexes of dissimilarity between Negroes and NWs and are higher than several of the indexes between Negroes and FBW groups.

A close check on the foregoing hypotheses would require the use of data with greater areal detail than we employ here, and one would, of course, have to turn to sources other than the Census to get evidence of any organized 'resistance' of immigrant groups to Negroes. No doubt the present interrelations of residential patterns of immigrants and Negroes reflect in large measure the historical accidents of the locations of areas of first settlement and access to areas for expansion and dispersion. To isolate any specific 'ethnic' factor in the variation of Negro-immigrant indexes of dissimilarity, one would doubtless have to compare a considerable number of cities.

On the evidence of this study we believe that much can be learned about processes of migrant adjustment from kinds of data which are readily available and amenable to comparative analysis. Even if an investigator makes a case study of a particular ethnic group, comparisons of the kind presented here can be illuminating, if only in identifying extreme or deviant cases. No doubt there is some connection, for example, among the high mobility of the USSR FBWs between 1930 and 1950 (col 6, Table 7.1), their relatively rapid decentralization over the same period (col 1 and 2, Table 7.5), their low proportions of homeownership (col 8, Table 7.6), and their relatively high incomes (col 11, Table 7.6).

Moreover, we believe that the coherence of our findings and their consistency with our major hypotheses afford support for the conceptualization of assimilation in ecological terms. It is not only that readily computed indexes based on areal data are closely related to indicators reflecting cultural characteristics and even subjective evaluations – though this finding is highly significant. Equally important are the implications of using indicators based on attributes of aggregates in intercorrelations with other aggregate characteristics. There is, of course, no necessary contradiction between findings based on comparisons of individuals and those derived from groups, critics of 'ecological correlation' to the contrary notwithstanding. In some cases the transition from one level of analysis to the other is made directly: we would tend to classify an individual as 'unassimilated' if he had not learned to speak English and a group as relatively 'unassimilated' if a high proportion of its members spoke only a foreign tongue. But there is no individual characteristic which strictly parallels the degree of occupational differentiation or residential segregation of an ethnic group. It would be unreasonable, for example, to characterize an individual as 'unassimilated' solely on the grounds that he followed a semiskilled occupation; but, if a disproportionately large number of members of an ethnic category are semiskilled workers, one has presumptive evidence of incomplete assimilation. Finally, such a correlation as that between an index of residential segregation and an index of occupational differentiation cannot even be conceptualized on the individual level.

Notes and References

We wish to acknowledge the financial assistance of the Social Science Research Committee, University of Chicago.

1. See Otis Dudley Duncan and Beverly Duncan, 'Residential Distribution and Occupational Stratification', *Am. J. Sociol.*, **60**, (Mar. 1955), 493–503 [3].
2. Ernest W. Burgess, 'Residential segregation in American cities', *Annals of the American Academy of Political and Social Science*, **140**, (Nov. 1928), 105–15; Maurice Halbwachs, 'Chicago, expérience ethnique', *Annales d'histoire économique et sociale*, **4**, (Jan. 1932), 11–49; Paul Frederick Cressey, 'Population succession in Chicago: 1898–1930', *Am. J. Sociol.*, **44**, (July 1938), 59–69 [6]; and Richard G. Ford, 'Population succession in Chicago', *Am. J. Sociol.*, **56**, (Sept. 1950), 156–60.
3. As represented by such studies as Christen T. Jonassen, 'Cultural variables in the ecology of an ethnic group', *Am. Sociol Rev.*, **14**, (Feb. 1949), 32–41; Jerome K. Myers, 'Assimilation to the ecological and social systems of a community', *Am. Sociol. Rev.*, **15**, (June 1950), 367–72; and Francis A. J. Ianni, 'Residential and occupational mobility as indices of the acculturation of an ethnic group', *Social Forces*, **36**, (Oct. 1957), 65–72.
4. Ernest W. Burgess and Charles Newcomb eds, *Census Data of the City of Chicago, 1930*: University of Chicago Press, 1933.
5. Tabulated from census tract summary cards supplied by the Bureau of the Census; these data are partially reported in Philip M. Hauser and Evelyn M. Kitagawa, eds, *Local Community Fact Book for Chicago 1950* (Chicago Community Inventory, 1953).
6. Duncan and Duncan, *op. cit.*
7. Niles Carpenter, *Immigrants and Their Children 1920*, Washington: Government Printing Office, 1927, chaps 4 and 5.
8. Charles S. Newcomb and Richard O. Lang, eds, *Census Data of the City of Chicago, 1934*: University of Chicago Press, 1934 (supplementary tables for Chicago total); Chicago Plan Commission, *Residential Chicago* (City of Chicago, 1942), Summary Table xxi, Appendix, 70.
9. Hauser and Kitagawa, *op. cit.*, 202.
10. Halbwachs, *op. cit.*, 39.
11. Amos H. Hawley, 'Dispersion versus segregation: apropos of a solution of race problems', *Papers of the Michigan Academy of Science, Arts, and Letters*, **30**, (1944), 674.

12. *Fifteenth Census of the United States, 1930: Population, vol. VI: Families* (Washington: Government Printing Office, 1933), State Table 4.
13. Emory S. Bogardus, 'The measurement of social distance', in *Readings in Social Psychology*, ed. T. M. Newcomb and E. L. Hartley (New York: Holt 1947); 'Changes in racial distances', *International Journal of Opinion and Attitude Research*, **1**, (Dec. 1947), 55–62.
14. Burgess, *op. cit.*, 11.
15 Beverly Duncan, 'Estimated Jewish population of Chicago and selected characteristics, 1951', Chicago Community Inventory Report, University of Chicago, 1954 (hectographed).

S. Lieberson

8 The impact of residential segregation on ethnic assimilation*

The importance human ecologists attribute to the spatial distributions of human populations and social institutions is not only widely known but, if anything, misunderstood by many of their fellow social scientists. The ecologist's interest in space is often taken as evidence either of a pre-occupation with the 'subsocial' or of an esthetic satisfaction derived from locating social events in terms of gradients, 'natural areas', multicolored maps, and the like. That this monolithic pursuit is to be found in the works of human ecologists – both present and past – ignores the far less constricted rationale which may be offered for this concern.

For example, during the heyday of European immigration to the United States, the propensity of immigrants to first locate in ghettos and their later movements out of these areas of first settlement were frequently utilized as a measure or index of an ethnic group's assimilation. Studies of such diverse urban centers as Chicago,[1] Durban,[2] Montreal,[3] Paris,[4] and the major cities of Australia[5] attest to the widespread existence of residential segregation and its usefulness as an indicator of ethnic assimilation. Indeed, during the twenties and thirties, ethnic residential patterns were a major research interest of sociologists and others.

However, another dimension to the residential segregation of ethnic and racial groups is frequently overlooked. That is, not only can the residential patterns of ethnic groups be viewed as a significant element in the study of their assimilation and as an indicator of other elements of assimilation but, further, residential segregation has an effect on other aspects of ethnic assimilation. Hawley has hypothesized that physical isolation is a necessary condition for the maintenance of subordinate ethnic group status and, further, that 'Redistribution of a minority group in the same territorial pattern as that of the majority group results in a dissipation of subordinate

* Reprinted from *Social Forces*, **40** (1961), 52–7.

111

status and an assimilation of the subjugated group into the social structure."[6] Hawley's reasoning is based on the dual effect of residential segregation, that is, both as a factor accenting the differences between groups by
heightening their visibility and, secondly, as a factor enabling the population
to keep its peculiar traits and group structure. Evidence exists to support
both of Hawley's contentions. For example, after finding that the greater
the number of Negroes arrested in a district in Philadelphia, the greater the
overestimation by policemen of the Negro rate in the district, Kephart has
concluded that visibility increases at a more rapid rate than sheer number.[7]
And Lieberson has shown close associations exist between the spatial
distributions of ethnic populations in Chicago and the location of ethnic
physicians' offices.[8]

This paper examines the impact of ethnic residential patterns on other
aspects of their assimilation. Roughly ten ethnic groups in each of ten
United States cities in 1930 were studied in terms of the relationships
between their spatial distribution and citizenship, intermarriage, and ability
to speak English. In addition, for a more limited number of groups and
cities, the impact of residential segregation on occupational composition of
ethnic groups was considered for 1950.

Data and methods

With one exception, published and unpublished United States census
reports for 1930 and 1950 were the sources for all analyses made below.
Because census tract data were available for only a limited number of
cities in 1930, the ten cities under investigation were not selected randomly.[9]
Since the 1930 census gives an unusually extensive array of data on various
aspects of immigrant and second generation behavior, it was all the more
necessary to include cities for which segregation indexes could be computed.
The larger immigrant and second generation groups were studied in each
city.

Residential segregation was computed by using indexes of dissimilarity
in a manner similar to that utilized in several recent studies.[10] With the
exception of Chicago where Community Areas were used, segregation of
immigrant groups from the native white population of each city was
determined on the basis of their degree of similarity in their intracity census
tract distributions. Indexes of dissimilarity were also used to compare
the degree of similarity in occupational composition between groups.
These indexes range from 0 (complete similarity) to 100 (complete dissimilarity).

Kendall's rank order correlation, *tau*, is the only measure of association
used in this study. This type of nonparametric correlation is of particular
value in this study since it permits the use of partial correlations.

112

Findings

Citizenship status

Naturalization is by no means a perfect indicator of an individual's assimilation. Thus some naturalized immigrants later return to their country of origin whereas not all immigrants remaining in the United States for 20 or more years adopt American citizenship. Nevertheless, it seems reasonable to use citizenship status 'as an indication that the assimilative process has proceeded to a moderate extent at least. The fact of naturalization is

Table 8.1 Rank order correlations (*tau*) between naturalization status, year of arrival, and segregation of selected immigrant groups from native whites, 1930

| City | Per cent of foreign born who are aliens and: | | Segregation foreign born from native whites and: | |
	Segregation foreign born from native whites (1)	Median year of arrival (2)	Median year of arrival (3)	Per cent of foreign born who are aliens (holding median year of arrival constant) (4)
Boston	0·47	0·62	0·18	0·46
Buffalo	0·29	0·64	0·29	0·14
Chicago	0·42	0·73	0·24	0·37
Cincinnati	0·44	0·76	0·42	0·17
Cleveland	0·64	0·78	0·69	0·22
Columbus	0·24	0·71	0·31	0·03
Philadelphia	0·42	0·58	0·47	0·20
Pittsburgh	0·56	0·44	0·47	0·45
St Louis	0·56	0·49	0·56	0·40
Syracuse	0·50	0·86	0·50	0·16

Note: Citizenship data for foreign born groups in Columbus, Cincinnati, and Syracuse based on all immigrants twenty-one years of age and older in 1930. Citizenship data for other cities based on immigrants of all ages except those not reporting their status.

indicative of an attitude towards the country very different from that of the immigrant who shows no desire to take out naturalization papers.'[11]

In 1930, there was a persistent association in all ten cities between the variations between immigrant groups in their segregation from native whites and their propensity to remain aliens, that is, groups highly segregated from native whites also have proportionately large numbers of adult males who are aliens (Table 8.1, col 1). These high rank order correlations between segregation and per cent alien indicate nothing more than that the spatial distributions of immigrant groups may be used as an indicator of at least one additional dimension of assimilation. In order to infer that the residential segregation of immigrant groups affects the propensities of immigrants to change their citizenship, it is necessary to consider whether this association would exist independently of other major factors influencing the acquisition of American citizenship such as length of residence in the United States and ability to read and write in the English language.

Since literacy in English was not a prerequisite to obtaining first papers,[12] we have at least partially eliminated this factor by considering only the proportions of immigrants who have remained aliens, that is, who had obtained neither first nor second papers. However, if we view acquisition of American citizenship as largely a unilateral and irreversible process, then it is reasonable to assume that length of residence in the United States would be a major influence, that is, immigrants living in the country for a longer period would be less likely to be aliens than more recent migrants. Consequently, the positive associations between immigrant group differences in length of residence and their proportions alien (Table 8.1, col 2) are not surprising. Since length of residence is also associated with the degree of immigrant segregation (col 3), the fact that the partial *tau* between segregation and citizenship status remains positive (although lower) in all ten cities (col 4) indicates that immigrant residential segregation decreases the proportion of a group taking at least minimal steps towards obtaining United States citizenship. Thus the magnitude of an immigrant group's isolation from the native white population appears to play a role in influencing the extent to which members of the group are prone to give up ties with their country of birth.

Intermarriage

In terms of theories with probability types of analysis, the examination of simply the number of exogamous and endogamous marriages for members of different ethnic groups is an inadequate indicator of group differentials in the propensity to intermarry. That is, the larger a group is in a given city, the greater the proportion of intra-group marriages we would expect for the group even if members of all groups chose their mates randomly.[13] Due to the limited data available, a rather crude indicator of intermarriage must be used; namely, the per cent of the second generation whose parents are of mixed nativity, that is, one parent foreign born and one parent native. The second generation of a given nationality was categorized by the Census Bureau into those who had both parents born in a foreign country and those who had one foreign parent and one native parent. As was noted in an earlier study using similar data, 'It should not be overlooked that in many cases the native parent is a second-generation member of the same stock as the foreign parent, but the census data do not permit us to distinguish such cases from those involving intermarriage in a stricter sense'.[14] It should also be added that we have no information about the number of cases in which there was intermarriage between persons who were born in different foreign countries and that all of the intermarriage material is based on the nativity classifications of offspring, that is, the second generation. Differential fertility and migration, to name but two factors, tend to reduce the usefulness of such data.

Nevertheless, the relationship between segregation from native whites and intermarriage (as measured by the crude indicator discussed above) is a very strong one. In each city, the proportion of the second generation

Table 8.2   Rank order correlations (*tau*) between residential segregation and intermarriage, 1930

City	*Foreign born segregation from native white and per cent of second generation with both parents foreign born*
Boston	0·60
Buffalo	0·69
Chicago	0·73
Cincinnati	0·53
Cleveland	0·78
Columbus	0·71
Philadelphia	0·67
Pittsburgh	0·78
St Louis	0·64
Syracuse	0·83

having 'mixed' parents is inversely related to the magnitude of the foreign born group's segregation from the native white population (Table 8.2). And, regardless of methodological shortcomings, these results are consistent with the assumption that residential propinquity is a factor in choice of mate.[15] Thus the more segregated a foreign born group, the more likely marriages are to occur between members of the same group.

Ability to speak English
Turning to the problem of language spoken by immigrants, one would expect to find an interaction between ability to speak English and segregation from native whites. Assuming that all native whites are able to speak English but no other language, then the larger the proportion of a given immigrant group able to speak English, the smaller the proportion of the immigrant group who would be hampered or handicapped by language differences in their location near native whites. Such would also be the case for native whites if we continue our somewhat arbitrary assumption that they all speak English but no other additional language. From this point of view, ability to speak English can be used as an independent variable in considering the fluctuations between immigrant groups in their segregation from native whites in a city. On the other hand, one could easily enough reverse the line of reasoning and assume that isolated foreign born groups

would have less reason and opportunity to learn English than a group widely dispersed among the native white population. Thus, in the latter case, ability to speak English would be the dependent variable and immigrant segregation from native whites the independent variable. At any rate, not only would we expect an interaction between the magnitude of an immigrant group's segregation from native whites and their ability to speak English but, further, it would be necessary to take into account the effect of length of residence in the United States on the ability of immigrants to speak English. That is, length of residence would presumably affect the ability of immigrants to speak English.

The *tau* correlations presented in Table 8.3 indicate that ability to speak English and segregation are correlated in the direction expected, that is, the more highly segregated an immigrant group is from native whites, the larger the proportion unable to speak English (col 1). Similarly, median length of residence for the immigrant groups in each city is positively related to their ability to speak English (col 2). There is but one exception, Buffalo, where the correlation is nil. Column 3 indicates the correlations

Table 8.3   Rank order correlations (*tau*) between ability to speak English, year of arrival, and segregation of selected immigrant groups from native whites, 1930

City	Per cent of foreign born able to speak English and:		Segregation foreign born from native whites and:	
	Segregation foreign born from native whites (1)	Median year of arrival (2)	Median year of arrival (3)	Ability to speak English (holding median year of arrival constant) (4)
Boston	0·71	0·42	0·18	0·71
Buffalo	0·53	0·00	0·29	0·55
Chicago	0·44	0·44	0·24	0·38
Cincinnati	0·29	0·47	0·42	0·11
Cleveland	0·40	0·49	0·69	0·10
Columbus	0·40	0·40	0·31	0·32
Philadelphia	0·84	0·49	0·47	0·79
Pittsburgh	0·49	0·44	0·47	0·35
St Louis	0·51	0·47	0·56	0·34
Syracuse	0·64	0·75	0·50	0·47

considered earlier which show some relationship between length of residence and degree of segregation. Taking into account the findings that both segregation and ability to speak English are in part functions of length of residence in the United States, the partial *tau* correlations between segregation and ability to speak English are computed (col 4). Although these partial correlations are generally lower than the correlations found without taking into account length of residence (compare cols 1 and 4), they are nevertheless all positive and indicate an association between ability to speak English and segregation from native whites even after length of residence is taken into account.

Occupational composition

Although the use of ethnic occupational composition as an indicator of assimilation is a moot procedure, there is little doubt that the nature of an ethnic group's participation in the economy of a city is an extremely significant dimension of its adaptation to the new society. Hawley has suggested that residential segregation – regardless of its causes – 'is a restriction of opportunity; it hampers the flow of knowledge and experience and thus impedes diversification of interests and occupations'.[16] One would therefore expect the occupational composition of highly segregated ethnic groups to be more sharply differentiated from native whites than the occupational composition of those groups less spatially isolated from the native white population. This association is found in four of the five cities for which both occupational and residential data were computed. That is, with the exception of Boston, immigrant occupational segregation from native whites varies with the magnitude of their residential segregation from the native whites in their city (Table 8.4, col 2).

Notwithstanding the importance of these descriptive associations, the critical problem involves determining whether the magnitude of residential segregation influences the occupational composition of ethnic groups. Clearly, there are a number of general social forces operating to influence an individual's choice of occupation, for example, sex, educational attainment, father's occupation, age, and the like. If ethnic groups differ in these attributes, then we would expect the groups to vary in their degree of occupational similarity to that of the native white population. The influence

Table 8.4   Rank order correlations (*tau*) between residential segregation of selected foreign born groups from native whites and: foreign born occupational segregation from native whites; deviation of second generation males, ages 25–44, from 'expected' occupational composition, 1950

City*	Number of groups (1)	Occupational and residential segregation (2)	Deviation from expected occupational composition and residential segregation (3)
Boston	7	−0·05	0·14
Chicago	9	0·50	0·50
Cleveland	8	0·29	0·36
Philadelphia	7	0·52	0·24
Pittsburgh	8	0·64	0·29

* Occupational data based on Standard Metropolitan Areas; residential data based on central cities.

of segregation on one such general social pattern is considered below.

Intergenerational occupational mobility

It is fairly evident that father's occupation influences the occupations his sons select. For example, one would hardly expect the sons of laborers to have the same occupational distribution as the sons of professionals in a community. Using unpublished data gathered by Gladys L. Palmer for 1950,[17] male intergenerational occupational mobility rates were determined on the basis of data for four combined cities; Chicago, Los Angeles, Philadelphia, and San Francisco. This intergenerational mobility table yielded rates that were largely in the direction one would expect. For example, 29 per cent of the sons of professional workers were professionals themselves, whereas only 4 per cent of the sons of laborers were professionals. By contrast, 3 per cent of the sons of professionals were laborers, whereas 10 per cent of the sons of laborers were themselves laborers.[18]

By applying these rates to the occupational composition of each group of older foreign born males in a city, the 'expected' occupational distribution of each second generation group of younger males was obtained. Assuming that second generation males between the ages of twenty-five and forty-four in 1950 were the sons of immigrant males of the same nationality who were at least forty-five years old in 1950 in a given city and, further, barring questions of differential fertility, mortality, and migration, it is possible to compare the actual occupational composition of second generation males with the composition expected on the basis of the society's intergenerational occupational mobility rates.

Despite the admittedly arbitrary nature of the assumptions, the results in Table 8.5 indicate that for a number of groups a fairly good prediction of the occupational composition of second generation males could have been made simply on the basis of the general social pattern of intergenerational mobility. That is, knowledge of the occupations of the fathers of second generation males combined with the general intergenerational occupational mobility patterns yields predictions of the occupational composition of second generation members that is fairly close to their actual occupational distributions. But, further, the magnitudes of the deviations in Table 8.5 are related to the degree of residential segregation of the foreign born groups from native whites in 1950. The correlations shown in col 3 of Table 8.4 indicate a persistent pattern in which the more segregated an immigrant group, the greater its deviation from the general intergenerational occupational mobility patterns that exist in our society.

Summary and conclusion

The magnitude of an immigrant group's residential isolation from the native white population in a city influences other dimensions of the group's

Table 8.5   Indexes of dissimilarity between the actual occupational distribution
of selected groups of second generation males (25 to 44 years of age)
and the occupational distribution expected on the basis of intergenerational mobility patterns in several large United States cities,
1950

Groups	Boston	Chicago*	Cleveland	Phila-delphia*	Pittsburgh
England and Wales	5·04	5·78	11·76	11·68	12·68
Ireland	13·64	12·26	8·28	8·98	11·63
Norway	—	10·01	—	—	—
Sweden	15·42	13·72	—	—	—
Germany	9·70	8·66	10·34	12·54	14·45
Poland	8·82	13·71	15·54	16·14	20·35
Czechoslovakia	—	9·30	13·42	—	20·51
Austria	—	8·51	11·98	7·28	19·69
Russia	25·22	23·79	19·04	22·61	14·66
Italy	7·68	8·99	5·75	9·07	10·43

* Indexes of dissimilarity adjusted for the group's estimated proportion of the total male population in the
four cities for which generational mobility patterns were obtained. These adjustments led to minor changes
and did not affect the groups' rank order in either Chicago or Philadelphia.

assimilation. Highly segregated groups are less apt to become citizens or speak English; and these associations hold after differences between groups in their length of residence are taken into account. In addition, the degree of intermarriage is influenced by an immigrant group's residential segregation. That is, keeping in mind that an admittedly crude indicator was used, groups highly segregated residentially tend to have low rates of intermarriage. Finally, applying intergenerational mobility tables to the occupational patterns of second generation groups in five metropolises for which such data were available, it was found that highly segregated first generation groups were more apt to have second generation members deviate from the general pattern of intergenerational occupational choice.

These results may be viewed in two closely related contexts. First, the differential residential segregation of ethnic groups in American cities is an important factor in the assimilation of ethnic groups. Segregation is not only a significant dimension to assimilation but, further, the magnitude of a group's segregation appears to influence other aspects of the group's assimilation. In this respect, support is offered for Hawley's hypothesis that residential dispersion is a basic prerequisite for ethnic assimilation.

Secondly, the results of this inquiry may be used in calling to the reader's attention the fact that examination of the spatial distributions of human populations or social institutions is not merely a convenient tool or indicator for research purposes – as important as this may be – but is, additionally, a potentially significant factor in interpreting and predicting differences in social behavior.

S. *Lieberson*

Notes and References

This study was supported by a grant from the Ford Foundation to the Population Research and Training Center, University of Chicago. This is paper number 8 in the series 'Comparative Urban Research'.

1. Otis Dudley Duncan and Stanley Lieberson, 'Ethnic segregation and assimilation', *Am. J. Sociol.*, **64**, (Jan. 1959), 364–74 [7].
2. Leo Kuper, Hilstan Watts, and Ronald Davies, *Durban: A Study in Racial Ecology*, London: Cape, 1958).
3. Eva R. Younge, 'Population movements and the assimilation of alien groups in Canada', *Canadian Journal of Economics and Political Science*, **10**, (Aug. 1944), 372–80.
4. Robert Gessain and Madeleine Doré, 'Facteurs comparés d'assimilation chez des Russes et des Arméniens', *Population*, **1**, (Jan.–Mar. 1946), 99–116.
5. Jerzy Zubrzycki, 'Ethnic segregation in Australian cities', paper read at International Population Conference, Vienna, 1959.
6. Amos H. Hawley, 'Dispersion versus segregation: apropos of a solution of race problems', *Papers of the Michigan Academy of Science, Arts, and Letters*, **30**, (1944), 674. See, also, Royal Institute of International Affairs, *Nationalism*, Oxford University Press, 1939, 281–3.
7. William M. Kephart, 'Negro visibility', *Am. Sociol. Rev.*, **19**, (Aug. 1954), 462–7.
8. Stanley Lieberson, 'Ethnic groups and the practice of medicine', *Am. Sociol. Rev.*, **23**, (Oct. 1958), 542–9.
9. For a list of cities for which such data were gathered in 1930, see Howard Whipple Green and Leon E. Truesdell, *Census Tracts in American Cities (Census Tract Manual)*, rev. edn, Washington: United States Department of Commerce, Bureau of the Census, 1937.
10. Otis Dudley Duncan and Beverly Duncan, 'Residential distribution and occupational stratification', *Am. J. Sociol.*, **60**, (March 1955), 493–503 [4]; Duncan and Lieberson, *loc. cit.*; Kuper, Watts, and Davies, *loc. cit.*
11. W. Burton Hurd, 'Racial origins and nativity of the Canadian people', in Dominion Bureau of Statistics, *Seventh Census of Canada, 1931*, **13**, *Monographs*, Ottawa: Edmond Cloutier, 1942, 662.
12. Bureau of the Census, *Fifteenth Census of the United States: 1930, Population*, vol. *II*, Washington: Government Printing Office, 1933, 401.
13. Franco Savorgnan, 'Matrimonial selection and the amalgamation of heterogeneous groups', *Population Studies*, supplement (Mar. 1950), 59–67.
14. Duncan and Lieberson, *loc. cit.*, 370.
15. See, for example, Marvin R. Koller, 'Residential and occupational propinquity', in Robert F. Winch and Robert McGinnis, eds, *Marriage and the Family*, New York: Henry Holt, 1953, pp. 429–34.
16. Hawley, *loc. cit.*, 672.

120

17. For a description of the study, see Gladys L. Palmer, *Labor Mobility in Six Cities*, New York: Social Science Research Council, 1954.
18. For the complete table, see Stanley Lieberson, 'Comparative ethnic segregation and assimilation', PhD dissertation, University of Chicago, 1960, 255.

Karl E. Taeuber and A. Taeuber

9 The Negro as an immigrant group*

During the last half of the nineteenth century and the early decades of the twentieth, millions of immigrants from Europe entered the United States. Many of these immigrants settled initially in ethnic colonies in large northern cities and found jobs as unskilled laborers in burgeoning mass-production industries. With the onset of World War I in Europe, and with the passage of restrictive legislation in the United States in the early 1920s, the period of massive overseas migration came to an end. At the same time, however, there developed a large-scale migration of Negroes from the South to the same large northern industrial cities. Like the immigrants from abroad, the Negro migrants to northern cities filled the lowest occupational niches and rapidly developed highly segregated patterns of residence within the central cities.

In view of many obvious similarities between the Negro migrants and the various immigrant groups preceding them, it has been suggested that northern urban Negroes are but the latest of the immigrant groups, undergoing much the same processes of adaptation to city life and of assimilation into the general social structure as the European groups preceding them.[1] The persistence of Negroes as a residentially segregated and underprivileged group at the lowest levels of socioeconomic status, however, is frequently interpreted in terms of distinctive aspects of the Negro experience, particularly their historical position in American society.[2]

The question of whether or not a northern urban Negro population can fruitfully be viewed as an immigrant population, comparable to European immigrant populations of earlier decades with respect to the nature and speed of assimilation, will be explored on the basis of data permitting analysis of recent trends in racial and ethnic segregation in Chicago.

The process by which various immigrant groups have been absorbed into

* Reprinted from *American Journal of Sociology*, **69**, no. 4 (January 1964) 374–82.

American society are complex and have been studied from a variety of viewpoints. Unfortunately there is no sociological consensus on a definition of assimilation and there is nothing approaching a definitive study of the processes of assimilation for any one immigrant group. It is beyond the scope of our task here to attempt to provide such a definition. We feel that a distinctively sociological approach to the topic must view assimilation as a process of dispersion of members of the group throughout the social structure. Cultural and psychological processes, we feel, should not be incorporated into a sociological definition, although their relationship to institutional dispersion should, of course, be retained as one focus of research on assimilation.

For our purposes, it will suffice to have a working definition of the process of assimilation considerably less sophisticated than that required for a general sociological theory. Accepting the view that both immigrant groups and Negro migrants originally settled in segregated patterns in central areas of cities and ranked very low in terms of socioeconomic measures, assimilation then consisted in large part of a process of social and economic advancement on the part of the original members of the group and their descendants, along with a decreasing residential concentration in ethnic colonies. Our concern with diminishing residential segregation as a necessary concomitant of the assimilation process derives from Myrdal's discussion of the 'mechanical' importance of residential segregation in facilitating other forms of segregation and discrimination, and Hawley's discussion of the impact of spatial patterns on race relations. Our concern with socioeconomic advance reflects the initially low status of the groups with which we are concerned, whereas a more general treatment would need to reckon with the unusually high status of some immigrant stocks, as well as with other aspects of social status and institutional dispersion than those for which we have data.

The data in Table 9.1 illustrate for selected immigrant groups the patterns of socioeconomic advance and residential dispersion from highly segregated ethnic colonies. For each of the larger ethnic groups, data for 1950 show the average standing on three measures of socioeconomic status, standardized for age, of the first generation (the foreign-born white, FBW) and the second generation (native white of foreign or mixed parentage, NWFMP). The nationality groups are split into 'old', 'new', and 'newer' groups in an extension of the traditional system. On the average, comparing with the first or within the second generation, the 'old' immigrant groups are the best off on these measures, the 'new' groups are intermediate, and the 'newer' groups are the worst off. It cannot be determined from these data to what extent the old immigrants are better off by virtue of their longer average length of residence in the United States, or to what extent they may have been better off at their time of immigration than the newer immigrants were at the time of their move.

123

Comparisons between the first and second generations might appear to be a more direct means for assessing the extent of socioeconomic advance, particularly since the emphasis in the literature on assimilation is on intergenerational processes rather than simply on processes of upward mobility through time in the status of the original immigrants. Comparisons of corresponding status measures for the first and second generations in Table 9.1 reveal, in general, the expected pattern of intergenerational advance. Data such as these, however, do not refer directly to a specific set of immigrant parents and their native-born children and must be interpreted with great caution.[4] For instance, it would be unwarranted on the basis of these data to assume that descendants of German immigrants are not as well off as their parents in terms of education. It is more credible

Table 9.1 Selected characteristics (age-standardized) of foreign-born and native ethnic populations in 1950, and indexes of residential segregation of selected groups of foreign stock from native whites of native parentage, 1930 and 1960, Chicago*

Country of origin	Per cent high-school graduates (males age 25 and over)		Per cent with income above $3,000 (persons with income)		Per cent with white-collar jobs (employed males)		Index of residential segregation (compared with NWNP)		
	FBW	NWFMP	FWB	NWFMP	FBW	NWFMP	1930	1960	Change
'Old' immigrant groups:									
England and Wales	45	50	53	58	49	51	11	18	+7
Ireland	24	47	47	56	22	47	23	31	+8
Norway	31	47	54	57	24	51	44	37	−7
Sweden	25	48	59	60	23	51	26	30	+4
Germany	37	34	53	55	34	42	22	19	−3
'New' immigrant groups:									
Austria	29	40	54	57	33	44	30	16	−14
Czechoslovakia	25	33	44	54	22	36	59	37	−22
Italy	15	27	47	53	24	37	52	32	−20
Poland	18	25	42	49	25	30	63	38	−25
USSR	35	60	60	69	59	74	51	44	−7
'Newer' immigrant groups:									
Mexico	14	16	38	29	8	13	71	54	−17
Puerto Rico†	13	29	16	37	22	36	†	67	†

* Data for 1930 and 1950 refer to foreign white stock (foreign-born plus native of foreign or mixed parentage); data for 1960 refer to total foreign stock. Abbreviations used are FBW for foreign-born white, NWFMP for native white of foreign or mixed parentage, and NWNP for native white of native parentage. The three socioeconomic characteristics refer to the Standard Metropolitan Area population, while the segregation indexes are based on community areas within the city. Age-standardization was by the direct method, using age groups 25–44 and 45 and over, with the Standard Metropolitan Area age composition as a standard.

† Socioeconomic characteristics for Puerto Rican population refer to total United States; Puerto Rican population by community areas for Chicago available for 1960 only.

Source: Characteristics from U.S. Bureau of the Census, *US Census of Population: 1950, Vol. IV, Special Reports*, Pt 3, chap. A, 'Nativity and parentage,' and chap. D, 'Puerto Ricans in continental United States.' Distributions of population by community areas for 1930 and 1960 from data on file at Chicago Community Inventory, University of Chicago.

that recent immigrants from Germany, under our immigration laws, include a large proportion of persons of high socioeconomic status.

Measures of the changing residential patterns of the immigrant groups are given in columns 7–9 of Table 9.1. The measure, an index of residential segregation between the total foreign stock (FBW + NWFMP) of each nationality and the total native whites of native parentage (NWNP), assumes a value of 100 for maximum residential segregation and a value of 0 if the residential distributions are identical.[5] The indexes were computed from the distribution of each group among the seventy-five community areas of the city of Chicago for 1930 (the last previous census year that included information on the total foreign stock) and 1960. The degree of residential segregation from the native population is highest for the 'newer' immigrants and lowest for the 'old' immigrants. Between 1930 and 1960, most of the ethnic groups became less segregated from the native population. Only for England, Ireland, and Sweden did the indexes fail to decline, and these were already at relatively low levels.[6]

This general approach to the measurement or assimilation of immigrant groups has been pursued for a number of cities and longer time periods by Lieberson. He found a remarkably persistent and consistent association through time between residential desegregation of an ethnic group and increasing socioeconomic similarity to native whites, and cross-sectionally between the position of each group as compared to others on measures of residential segregation and its relative levels on status measures.[7]

The index of residential segregation between Negroes and NWNP for 1930 was 84, and for 1960, 82. These values are higher than any of those for specific immigrant stocks. Furthermore, each of the immigrant stocks was highly segregated from Negroes in 1930 and 1960. There is relatively little intermixture of Negro residences with those of any group of whites. Even the 'newer' immigrant groups, the Puerto Ricans and Mexicans, are not joining or replacing Negroes in established Negro areas but are moving into separate ethnic colonies of their own at the periphery of Negro areas. Negroes clearly occupy a distinctive position as the most residentially segregated of the principal migrant groups. The separation of Negroes from all groups of whites is sharper than any of the patterns of residential segregation between ethnic groups or between socioeconomic groups within the white population.[8] Apparently this pattern has developed during the last few decades. Lieberson has demonstrated that, although prior to the great Negro migrations of World War I there were instances of immigrant stocks being more segregated from native whites than were Negroes, since 1920 there has been a general tendency for Negro residential segregation to be highest.[9]

Data pertaining specifically to the comparison between whites and non-whites (97 per cent of Chicago's non-whites are Negroes) on measures of socioeconomic status and of residential segregation are presented in

125

Table 9.2. For each of four measures reflecting socioeconomic status,

**Table 9.2 Selected socioeconomic characteristics (unstandard-
ized) of whites and non-whites, Chicago, 1940, 1950,
and 1960**

Characteristic	Non-white	White
*Residential segregation index, whites v. Negroes:**		
1930	85	
1940	85	
1950	79	
1960	83	
Per cent high school graduates, ages 25 + :		
1940	16	25
1950	25	37
1960	29	37
Per cent white collar, male:		
1940	17	40
1950	17	41
1960	21	40
Per cent home-owners:		
1940	7	26
1950	12	33
1960	16	39
Per cent multiple-person households with 1·01 or more persons per room:		
1940	41	17
1950	46	14
1960	34	10

* These values differ slightly from those cited in the text for Negroes as compared to native whites of native parentage.

Source: Data for 1940 from the 1940 Census Tract Bulletin for Chicago; for 1950 from Philip M. Hauser and Evelyn M. Kitagawa (eds), *Local Community Fact Book for Chicago, 1950*, Chicago Community Inventory, 1953; and for 1960 from the 1960 Census Tract Bulletin for Chicago.

there was improvement in the status of the non-white population between 1940 and 1960. (For whites, improving status would be more clearly evident if the data referred to the entire metropolitan area rather than just the city of Chicago.) The indexes of residential segregation between whites and Negroes, in the top panel of the table, show minor fluctuations around an extremely high level and give no indication of the decline anticipated on the basis of the socioeconomic advancement of the Negro population. That this is not an atypical finding is indicated by reference to other data showing a long term historical trend toward increasing residential segregation between whites and non-whites. Increasing racial residential segregation was evident in most large cities of the United States between 1940 and 1950, while during the 1950s, southern cities continued to increase in segregation and northern cities generally registered modest declines.[10]

In broad perspective, the historical trend toward improving socio-economic status of immigrant groups has gone hand in hand with decreasing residential segregation. In contrast, Negro residential segregation from whites has increased steadily over past decades until it has reached universally high levels in cities throughout the United States, despite advances in the socioeconomic status of Negroes.

We have been unable to locate any data permitting a comparison between Negroes long resident in Chicago, or born and raised in the North, and Negroes with lesser periods of residence in the city. Thus we are not able to make even the crude intergenerational comparisons for Negroes that are possible for the immigrant groups. The only analysis of this type possible with census data is a comparison between recent migrants and the rest of the population, and the only published data are residential distributions, with no socioeconomic characteristics. For 1960, with the seventy-five community areas of Chicago as units, the index of residential segregation between non-whites resident in the metropolitan area five years or more and native whites of native parents is 80·5. Comparing non-whites with less than five years' residence in the metropolitan area and NWNP, the index was 81·0. Comparing the recent in-migrants with the non-whites who were resident in the metropolitan area five years or more, the index was 13. Thus the recent non-white in-migrants are distributed differently from the rest of the non-white population, but each group is highly segregated from the native whites. Unfortunately, these results cannot be readily interpreted in terms of the general assimilation and dispersion processes under consideration. Possibly there are trends toward socioeconomic advancement and residential dispersion on the part of 'second generation' Negroes in Chicago that are confounded in the data for the total Negro population.

Decreasing residential concentration of immigrant groups occurred despite the efforts of many nationality organizations to maintain the ethnic colonies.[11] Few Negro organizations have been as explicitly segregationist. In some immigrant groups, many members were dispersing from the ethnic colonies even while large-scale immigration of that group was still under way. For every immigrant group, diminishing residential segregation has been evident since the cessation of large-scale immigration. For Negroes, however, residential segregation has increased since the first period of large-scale immigration to northern cities, and this increase in residential segregation continued during the late 1920s and 1930s when the volume of migration was at a low level. These observations tend to discredit the argument that a major barrier to residential dispersion of the Negro population of Chicago is its continuing rapid increase. However, the size of the Negro population and the magnitude of its annual increase are larger than for any single ethnic group in the past, and comparisons with smaller groups are not completely convincing. That rapid increase of Negro popu-

127

lation does not necessarily lead to increasing residential segregation was demonstrated directly in the intercity comparative study previously cited. There was no definite relationship between increase in Negro population and increase in the value of the segregation index. Indeed, during the 1950–1960 decade, there appeared to be a slight relationship in the opposite direction.[12]

More significant in accounting for the divergent trends in residential segregation may be the different urban contexts in which the immigrant and Negro populations found themselves. Comparing the residential locations of Italian-born and Polish-born in Chicago in 1899 and in 1920, Wallace observed:

> It can be seen that the areas of greatest dispersion, low proportion, and presumably of 'second' settlement for many immigrants were those which were not settled at all in 1899.
>
> The implication of this fact is that the so-called 'assimilation' process was not reflected by the geographic dispersion of the immigrant populations into 'cosmopolitan American areas'. The dispersal was more directly related to an increase in housing alternatives as the city grew at the periphery.[13]

By the time the Negro concentrations were forming near the central areas of Chicago, the city was built up and the urbanized area extended well beyond the present boundaries. Residential alternatives at a price Negroes could afford and located sufficiently close in to permit inexpensive commuting were no longer available.

It has been suggested that considerable time is required for Negroes to make the transition from a 'primitive folk culture' to 'urbanism as a way of life'.[14] Several types of data indicate that large and increasing proportions of the Negro urban population are city-born and raised. For instance, there is a rapidly decreasing color differential in the percentage of the Chicago population born in the state of Illinois. In 1960, 44 per cent of the native-born, non-white residents of Chicago were born in Illinois, as contrasted to 66 per cent of the white population.[15] National estimates for 1958 showed that of all males aged 45–64 living in metropolitan places of 500,000 or more population, 65 per cent of the non-whites, as compared to 77 per cent of the whites, had lived in this size city for twenty years or longer.[16] Estimates of the components of growth of the non-white population of Chicago indicate that between 1950 and 1960 natural increase was as important as net in-migration, and that natural increase will in the future account for rapidly increasing proportions of the growth of the non-white population.[17]

Unfortunately there is inadequate knowledge of the specific length of time under specified conditions for the required cultural transformation to occur. Wallace's observations indicate a significant degree of dispersal over time among first-generation immigrants. Such processes are more often conceived as primarily intergenerational. That many of the 'first generation' Negro migrants to northern cities have lived there for twenty years or more and that in the younger adult ages there are sizable numbers of 'second generation' urban Negroes suggests that there has been ample time for any necessary adjustment to urban living, at least for large proportions of the Negro population. It is also clear that if northern Negroes remain inadequately educated for urban living and fail to participate fully in the urban economy, the 'primitive folk culture' of the South can less and less be assigned responsibility, and northern cities will be suffering from the neglect of their own human resources.

The 'visibility' of Negroes due to skin color and other features which make the large majority of second-, third-, and later-generation descendants readily identifiable as Negroes is often cited as a basic factor in accounting for the distinctive position of Negroes in our society. It is exceedingly difficult to assess the significance of visibility. There is no other group that is strictly comparable to Negroes regarding every factor except visibility. It is not completely irrelevant, however, to note that non-white skin color, by itself, is not an insurmountable handicap in our society. The socioeconomic status of the Japanese population of Chicago in 1950 substantially exceeded that of the Negro population; and their residential segregation from whites, although high, was considerably lower than that between Negroes and whites.[18] Unfortunately there are no trend data available on the characteristics of the Japanese in Chicago. A more appropriate Japanese population for comparison, however, is the much larger one in the San Francisco area. A recent study there affirmed that 'ethnic colonies of Japanese are gone or rapidly going' and documented their rapid socioeconomic advance.[19]

In the traditional immigrant pattern, the more recent immigrants displaced the older groups at the bottom socioeconomic levels. How do the Negroes compare with the other 'newer' immigrant groups, the Mexicans and the Puerto Ricans? The limited data now available suggest that the Negroes may soon be left alone at the bottom of the social and economic scale. We have already noted (from data in Table 9.1) that the 'newer' groups were, in 1950, of very low status compared to the other immigrant groups, and that their residential segregation from the native whites of native parentage was the highest of all the immigrant groups. For 1960, data on distribution within Chicago of persons born in Puerto Rico are available separately from data on those persons born in the United States of Puerto Rican parentage. Thus it is possible to compute indexes of residential segregation for first- and second-generation Puerto Ricans. For Chicago in 1960, these index values were 68·4 for the first generation and 64·9 for the second generation, indicating that residential dispersion has already begun for the Puerto Ricans. This difference actually understates the amount of dispersion, since the second generation consists in large proportion of children still living with their first-generation parents.

Selected socioeconomic measures for the Puerto Rican and the non-white populations of Chicago in 1960 are shown in Table 9.3. On every measure, the Puerto Rican population is less well off – it is less educated, has lower income, is more crowded, is less likely to own homes, is less well housed, and lives in older buildings. Yet the index of residential segregation (computed with respect to NWNP) for Puerto Ricans is 67 as compared with 82 for Negroes.

Up to now we have been making comparisons between Negroes and immigrant groups, demonstrating that residential dispersion has not accompanied socioeconomic advance by Negroes in the way that it did for immigrant groups. Economic status and expenditure for housing, however, are clearly correlated, and there is also a correlation between economic status and residential segregation. By virtue of variations in the type, age, and quality of housing, and in the patterns of residential choice by persons of varying socioeconomic status, the subareas of a city are differentiated in terms of the average status of their residents. Since Negroes are of much lower average status than whites, they would be expected to be disproportionately represented in low-status residential areas. In fact, an extreme position regarding the relationships between patterns of socioeconomic residential segregation and racial residential segregation would attribute all of the latter to the former. Such a position is sometimes offered as a counterargument to charges of racial discrimination against the real estate business. To the extent that this position is correct, it might be expected that future economic advances on the part of the Negro population should be translated into decreased residential segregation.

The task of partialing out a component of racial segregation due to economic factors involves some difficult methodological problems, and no method is entirely satisfactory.[20] Our approach utilizes indirect standardization of available census data. Let us delineate the status of a residential area in terms of, say, the income distribution of its residents. Specifically, consider for each community area of Chicago the number of families with incomes below $1,000, from $1,000–1,999, from $2,000–2,999, and so forth. For the city as a whole in 1960, 44 per cent of all families with an income below $1,000 were non-white, as were 44 per cent of families with incomes from $1,000–1,999, and 40 per cent of families with incomes from $2,000–2,999. For each community area, we can apply these city-wide percentages to the observed income distribution to obtain the number of non-white families expected if income alone determined the residential locations of whites and non-whites.

By the method of indirect standardization just outlined, we obtain an expected number of non-white and white families for each of the seventy-five community areas. We can then compute an index of residential segregation between expected numbers of non-white and white families. This index can be regarded as the amount of racial residential segregation attributable to patterns of residential differentiation of income groups. For

**Table 9.3   Selected socioeconomic characteristics (unstandard-
ized) of Puerto Ricans and non-whites, Chicago, 1960**

Characteristic	Non-white	Puerto Rican
Residential segregation *v.* whites	83	67
Per cent high school graduates, total	29	11
Median family income	$4,742	$4,161
Per cent families earning < $3,000	28	27
Per cent families earning > $10,000	9	4
Per cent home-owners	16	6
Per cent substandard dwellings	26	33
Per cent 1·01 or more persons per room	34	52
Per cent housing units built since 1940	12	6
Median gross rent	$88	$79
Median number of rooms	3·9	3·7
Median number of persons	3·0	4·0

Source: Data are from the 1960 Census Tract Bulletin for Chicago.

1950, the index of residential segregation between the numbers of whites and non-whites expected on the basis of income was 11, as compared with the actual segregation index of 79. As a rough measure, then, we can attribute 11/79, or 14 per cent, of the observed racial residential segregation in Chicago in 1950 to income differentials between whites and non-whites. For 1960, the corresponding values are 10 for the expected index, 83 for the observed index, and 12 per cent for the racial segregation attributable to income differentials.

In a recent study of the relationships between housing consumption and income, Reid has demonstrated many pitfalls in the uncritical use of income distributions in the analysis of housing patterns.[21] We have therefore repeated the above analyses, using distributions by major occupational groups and distributions by educational attainment. For 1960, the index of residential segregation computed from the numbers of whites and non-whites expected on the basis of patterns of occupational differentiation is 9, and that expected on the basis of patterns of educational differentiation is 3. The results using income distributions are thus supported by the results from other measures of socioeconomic status, and the conclusion seems clear that patterns of socioeconomic differentiation of residential areas can account for only a small proportion of observed racial residential segregation.

Reid demonstrated that differences between whites and non-whites in observed patterns of housing consumption are largely attributable to income differentials between whites and non-whites. Our analysis suggests

131

that residential segregation cannot be attributed to these differentials. Apparently the economic structure of the housing market for whites is similar to that for non-whites, even though non-whites are excluded from a large share of the housing supply for which their economic circumstances would allow them to compete.

The judicious conclusion from our review of a variety of pieces of data is that we simply do not yet know enough about immigrant assimilation processes and any corresponding processes among Negro migrants to northern cities to be able to compare the two. We believe that this very lack of knowledge makes questionable any attempt to reason from presumed patterns of assimilation among immigrants in the past to current racial problems in northern cities. Furthermore, such evidence as we could compile indicates that it is more likely to be misleading than instructive to make such comparisons.

Our definition of assimilation as involving socioeconomic advancement and residential dispersion is simple, and greater differences between groups would appear were a more complex definition adopted. Restriction of portions of the analysis to the city of Chicago had little effect on the measures for non-whites, but probably led to an understatement of the degree of assimilation of the immigrant stocks insofar as higher-status members of these groups have moved to the suburbs. The segregation indexes probably overstate somewhat the residential isolation of small groups, such as particular immigrant stocks, as compared with larger groups such as total native whites of native parents. Taking account of any of these limitations in our data would tend to increase the differences between Negroes and immigrant groups. Even so, our data showed that second-generation persons from several countries are of higher socioeconomic status than the total native whites of native parentage. Relatively few Negroes in Chicago have white-collar jobs or incomes above the median level for whites, and yet there are large numbers of adult Negroes who were born in the city. Basic differences between the Negroes and the immigrant groups seems to us implicit in the failure of residential desegregation to occur for Negroes while it has continued for the immigrant groups.

In view of the fundamental impact of residential segregation on extralegal segregation of schools, hospitals, parks, stores and numerous other facilities, the failure of residential dispersion to occur strikes us as an especially serious social problem. Socioeconomic advance and residential dispersion occurred simultaneously for the various immigrant groups. It is apparent that the continued residential segregation of the Negro population is an impediment to the continued 'assimilation' of Negroes into full and equal participation in the economy and the society at large.

Notes and References

Paper no. 15 in the series, 'Comparative Urban Research', was issued from the Population Research and Training Center, University of Chicago, under a grant from the Ford Foundation. A preliminary version of this paper was read at the 1962 annual meetings of the American Statistical Association. We appreciate the reactions of Stanley Lieberson, Judah Matras, and Margaret G. Reid to that version.

1. Philip M. Hauser, 'On the impact of urbanism on social organization, human nature and the political order', *Confluence*, **7**, (Spring, 1958), 65. Elsewhere Hauser has expressed a more cautious view, emphasizing the lack of definitive knowledge; see his *Population Perspectives*, Rutgers University Press, 1960, 129.
2. D. J. Bogue, 'Chicago's growing population problem', *Commerce*, **59**, (July 1962), 31.
3. Gunnar Myrdal, *An American Dilemma*, New York: Harper, 1944, I, 618; Amos H. Hawley, 'Dispersion versus Segregation: apropos of a solution of race problems', *Papers of the Michigan Academy of Science, Arts, and Letters*, **30**, (1944), 667–74.
4. For an enumeration of some of the difficulties see C. A. Price and J. Zubrzycki, 'The use of inter-marriage statistics as an index of assimilation', *Population Studies*, **16**, (July 1962), 58–69.
5. The index of residential segregation is an index of dissimilarity between the residential distributions of each group. For further discussion, see Otis Dudley Duncan and Beverly Duncan, 'A methodological analysis of segregation indexes', *Am. Sociol. Rev.*, **20**, (April 1955), 210–17 [2].
6. For a more detailed discussion of these patterns, using data for 1930 and 1950, see Otis Dudley Duncan and Stanley Lieberson, 'Ethnic segregation and assimilation', *Am. J. Sociol.*, **64**, (Jan. 1959), 364–74 [7].
8. S. Lieberson, *Ethnic Patterns in American Cities,* Free Press of Glencoe, 1963.
9. For a discussion of class residential segregation in Chicago see Otis Dudley Duncan and Beverly Duncan, 'Residential distribution and occupational stratification', *Am. J. Sociol.*, **60**, (Mar. 1955), 493–503 [3].
9. Lieberson, *op. cit.*, 120–32.
10. Karl E. Taeuber, 'Negro residential segregation, 1940–1960: changing trends in the large cities of the United States', paper read at the Annual Meetings of the American Sociological Association, 1962.
11. David A. Wallace, 'Residential concentration of Negroes in Chicago', unpublished PhD dissertation, Harvard University, 1953.
12. Taeuber, *op. cit.*
13. Wallace, *op. cit.*, 205.
14. Philip M. Hauser, 'The challenge of Metropolitan growth', *Urban Land*, **17**, (Dec. 1958), 5.

15. Data from US Bureau of the Census, *US Census of Population, 1960: General Social and Economic Characteristics, Illinois. Final Report* PC(1)-15C, Tables 72 and 77.

16. Karl E. Taeuber, 'Duration-of-residence analysis of internal migration in the United States', *Milbank Memorial Fund Quarterly*, **39**, (Jan. 1961), Table 3.

17. D. J. Bogue and D. P. Dandekar, *Population Trends and Prospects for the Chicago–Northwestern Indiana Consolidated Metropolitan Area: 1960 to 1990*, University of Chicago, Population Research and Training Center, 1962.

18. Although the maximum value of the residential segregation index is less than 100 for ethnic groups of small size, this is not sufficient to vitiate the Negro-Japanese comparison.

19. Harry H. L. Kitano, 'Housing of Japanese-Americans in the San Francisco Bay area', in Nathan Glazer and Davis McEntire, eds, *Studies in Housing and Minority Groups*, University of California Press, 1960, 184.

20. A general discussion of this problem can be found in the section on explanation of areal variation in Otis Dudley Duncan, Ray P. Cuzzort, and Beverly Duncan, *Statistical Geography*, Glencoe: Free Press, 1961.

21. Margaret G. Reid, *Housing and Income*, University of Chicago Press, 1962.

N. Kantrowitz

10 Ethnic and racial segregation in the New York Metropolis*

It appears to be both a fact of city life and a common indicator of cultural differences that people with similar traits tend to live together, apart from other groups, whether in a 'Chinatown' or 'on the better side of the tracks'. In the modern American metropolis, ethnic and racial neighborhoods can be analytically abstracted from those with other bases of separation, such as rich-poor or Protestant-Catholic. In this mélange, such ethnic segregation as the separation of Catholic Irish from Catholic Italians is usually seen as succumbing to a process of assimilation, as the enclaves of immigrant nationalities are replaced by religious and racial neighborhoods distributed along an economic axis from central-city slums to affluent suburbs.[1] Moreover, it would seem to be a reasonable extension of this idea to conclude that, since the multiplicity of ethnic neighborhoods is disappearing, opposition to Negro integration is almost entirely racial. We do not agree. We think voluntary ethnic segregation is still a viable force.

Our own study of New York in 1960, and our examination of research done for other cities has led us to believe that, although ethnic segregation has indeed weakened, the reports of its demise are exaggerated. Indeed, even among those white ethnicities that are similar to one another – such as the Protestant Swedes and Norwegians – we judge that ethnic separatism remains fairly high into the second generation. This conclusion has pessimistic implications for the problem of Negro desegregation. Especially in the central city, where Negroes are most concentrated and ethnicities are most distinct, we suspect that the major opposition to Negro dispersion tends to come, not from whites in general, but from specific white ethnic populations. As a consequence, the cause of racial desegregation must bear the burden, not only of an often noted racial prejudice, but also of a usually

* Reprinted from *American Journal of Sociology*, **74** (May 1969), 685–95.

overlooked ethnic separatism.

In support of the contention that the segregation of European ethnic populations remains strong, we can present only limited new evidence. Even though this is the first intensive study of ethnic and racial segregation in the nation's largest metropolis, and one of the few such studies of any metropolis to include the suburbs as well as the central city, it is still but a single case study. Moreover, the data and methods are limited to ethnic (foreign stock and Puerto Rican) and racial (Negro) segregation index numbers, calculated from the census tract statistics of the 1960 New York–Northeastern New Jersey Consolidated Statistical Area.[2] So that we may reach a conclusion with this limited amount of original evidence, our argument will splice together several parts of our own and others' findings. In order to connect the Consolidated Area of 1960 with the recent past for other American cities, we shall first evaluate in detail the evidence for a decline in ethnic segregation in these other cities, and then, in order to create a parallel, we shall show how New York's segregation patterns resemble those of Chicago.

Having indicated why we consider that New York is similar to other cities, where the decline of ethnic segregation has been minimal, we can focus on this metropolis, presenting new data from the most recent census, which includes both suburb and city. But before analyzing segregation in New York, we must dispose of the argument that our results are trivial because they are based on only immigrant populations which constitute a small proportion of the total population of the metropolis. We shall show, on the contrary, that, because the census classification 'foreign stock' is so heavily weighted by the second generation, our 1960 indexes measure more than just immigrant enclaves; in fact, the data include the great majority of the area's population. Finally, we will discuss the metropolis and its component cities and suburbs, to assess their levels of interethnic segregation and the extent to which Negro segregation is but a racial reinforcement of existing ethnic separatism.

As a prefatory methodological note to our argument, it should be mentioned that the segregation index number we have used, the Index of Dissimilarity (or delta), has been closely studied and extensively applied by earlier researchers.[3] However, a major problem in its evaluation is the matter of determining what values of delta between 0 (no segregation) and 100 (total segregation) constitute 'high' and 'low' segregation, and what magnitude of numerical change can be taken as indication of an important change in segregation level. In theory, there is no answer to this problem, but in practice we can resolve it by considering deltas upward of 70 (which usually separates Negroes from whites) as 'high', deltas of 30 or less as 'low', and variations in level of less than five points as unimportant, unless they are otherwise correlated.[4]

Returning to out argument, our first step is to reassess the evidence for a decline in ethnic segregation. Our central concern is a comparison which emphasizes the segregation of specific ethnicities from one another, such as Irish from Italian. The major relevant study is Lieberson's *Ethnic Patterns in American Cities*, an analysis of segregation from 1910 to 1950 in ten northeastern and midwestern central cities. Lieberson found convincing evidence of assimilation among the foreign-born; the segregation of immigrant groups from one another as well as from all native whites consistently declined as their socioeconomic status rose. From his larger study, we should like to discuss one small part, the segregation of foreign-born whites by country of birth in city wards between 1910 and 1920 and in census tracts between 1930 and 1950.

For each of his ten cities, Lieberson calculated the segregation index of each ethnic group from each of the others, so that he derived perhaps fifty deltas per city for such comparisons as Irish with Italian, German with Irish, and Italian with Russian. There was a small decline in the (equally weighted or, as we shall call them, unweighted) average of the deltas, city by city. For example, Cleveland's average decreased, by wards, from 50·6 in 1910 to 43·5 in 1920; by census tracts, from 60·8 in 1930 to 54·3 in 1950.[5] In the remaining nine cities, the declines were similarly consistent and small. This decline of approximately five points between 1930 and 1950 in the average of segregation indexes is not very impressive when one realizes that it was wrought by depression, war, the maturation of a new generation, and a postwar expansion of settled areas within and beyond the cities' legal boundaries.

The decline in average delta continued to be consistent but small when Lieberson made the common distinction between those of the foreign-born who came from northern Europe – the 'old' immigrants, whose greatest immigration wave preceded the final quarter of the nineteenth century – and those from southern and central Europe – the 'new' immigrants, whose greatest immigration wave was more recent. If we again take Cleveland as an example, the average segregation index among northern European ethnicities fell from 35·5 to 30·3 between 1930 and 1950; between northern and southern Europeans it fell from 59·8 to 53·9; and among southern Europeans, from 65·4 to 58·1. If the segregation indexes themselves reflect real differences between, for example, Irish and Italians, then these consistent but small declines indicate the existence of relatively stable immigrant enclaves.[6]

The data shown in Table 10.1 permit us to draw a parallel between foreign-born segregation in the ten central cities in 1950, and foreign-stock segregation in the New York metropolis in 1960. Although the data are based on different years, geographical units, and definitions of ethnicity, so that it is impossible to draw fine conclusions, we can see one broad similarity: New York's averages resemble those of other places. Turning again to Cleveland as an example, we see that its over-all mean of 54·3 is higher than New York's 46·4. But once we examine northern and southern European ethnicities, the advantage vanishes: Cleveland's 'old versus old' average of 30·3 is lower than New York's 40·5, its 'new versus new'

Table 10.1   Unweighted averages of interethnic segregation indexes among the foreign-born whites of ten central cities in 1950* and among persons of foreign stock in the New York–Northeastern New Jersey Standard Consolidated Area in 1960†

Place	Total	Old v. Old	Old v. New	New v. New
Central cities, 1950:*				
Boston	50·6	28·5	55·0	61·5
Buffalo	52·0	33·2	55·4	62·3
Chicago	50·1	34·0	52·1	53·3
Cincinnati	48·4	35·8	51·3	51·0
Cleveland	54·3	30·3	53·9	58·1
Columbus	49·3	36·3	49·7	52·4
Philadelphia	53·0	32·9	56·9	53·4
Pittsburgh	51·6	32·0	53·4	54·8
St Louis	49·9	35·6	48·5	56·0
Syracuse	53·8	39·6	56·5	57·0
Foreign stock				
New York Consolidated Area, 1960†	46·4	40·5	51·2	40·8

* Stanley Lieberson, *Ethnic Patterns in American Cities* (New York: Free Press, 1963), Tables 9 and 22.
† From Tables 10.5 (of this paper), second column, last three rows.

average of 58·1 is higher than New York's 40·8, and the 53·9 index for 'old versus new' approximates New York's 51·2. All in all, then, it is apparent that, when we consider Lieberson's ten northeastern and midwestern central cities, the decline in foreign-born segregation, although real, is too small to be interpreted as a destruction of ethnic enclaves. Moreover, the 1950 foreign-born levels bear at least a broad resemblance to the 1960 foreign-stock levels of the New York metropolis.

Lieberson's comparative study was made before 1960 census statistics were available. The only more recent report is a case study of changes from 1930 to 1960 in Chicago city segregation between individual ethnic foreign stocks (immigrants and their children combined)[7] and the totality of all native whites of native parents. This, of course, differs from the interethnic segregation we have just considered in our discussion of Lieberson's work, for the Taeubers compare an ethnicity with an average base line. Thus, if we compare, say, Irish foreign stock against a base line of native whites of native parents, we are comparing a single ethnicity against an average base line composed of those whose immigrant forebears were no more recent than their grandparents, an average base line which is itself weighted to an unknown extent by a changing mix of grandchildren of immigrants from different countries – including, of course, the grandchildren of Irish immigrants. Obviously, such a comparison does not measure changes in

138

interethnic segregation, as between, for example, Irish and Italians.[8]

The Taeubers' purpose was to demonstrate the decline in ethnic segregation in contrast to the high, and stable, Negro-white segregation figure. As we did with Lieberson's work, we wish to focus on a small part of these data in a different context. If we consider the 'old versus new' dichotomy, the data document the 1930–60 changes: among ethnicities from northern Europe, levels of segregation remained stable and low, while among southern Europeans, segregation levels, originally higher, declined precipitously.[9]

Comparison of our 1960 data for the New York metropolis and data for the city of Chicago (Table 10.2) indicates an overall congruence. For

Table 10.2   Indexes of residential segregation by race and by selected ethnicities (foreign stock) from a base population of native whites or native parents,* New York–Northeastern New Jersey Standard Consolidated Area (CA) for 1960, City of Chicago for 1930–60†

	Consolidated area (CA), 1960							City of Chicago, 1930–60		
		New York part (New York SMSA)		New Jersey part						
				Newark SMSA						
Ethnicity and race	Total CA	Total	City only	Total	City only	P-C-P‡ SMSA	JC# SMSA	1930	1960	Change
'Old':										
United Kingdom	21·2	22·1	25·0	16·2	20·9	15·3	32·9	11 □	18	+7
Ireland (Eire)	37·4	38·0	37·1	27·9	28·1	20·4	21·4	23	31	+8
Norway	48·2	50·2	62·5	42·6	72·5	33·8	39·1	44	37	−7
Sweden	34·1	35·0	41·6	31·3	53·2	27·4	38·2	26	30	+4
Germany	26·7	28·3	31·9	20·6	26·0	16·5	30·4	22	19	−3
'New':										
Poland	42·5	44·3	42·5	38·3	39·6	40·0	34·9	63	38	−25
Czechoslovakia	41·6	42·8	43·5	39·4	41·0	40·5	40·3	59	37	−22
Austria	40·4	41·2	38·2	34·0	42·8	30·9	25·2	30	16	−14
Hungary	42·7	42·8	40·8	32·0	36·3	38·0	29·2	△	△	
USSR	51·9	50·7	47·5	45·4	54·0	39·0	34·2	51	44	−7
Italy	37·7	33·7	39·2	37·2	33·4	31·6	23·9	52	32	−20
Negro†	80·2	81·8	84·4	75·5	64·5	79·1	72·1	84	82	−2
Puerto Rican	82·2	81·6	78·5	75·6	59·6	69·2	68·1	△	67	—
White†:										
Total	12·9	14·2	13·2	7·9	8·7	7·4	5·4	△	△	—
Native of foreign or mixed parentage	19·8	20·5	17·1	16·7	13·4	14·0	8·5	△	△	—
Foreign-born	35·8	36·0	29·5	25·8	23·0	24·6	18·2	△	△	—

* Non-Puerto Rican. Data are from Table 10.5, below, second column, last three rows.

† From Taeuber and Taeuber, 'The Negro as an Immigrant Group,' *op. cit.*, Table 1.

‡ Paterson-Clifton-Passaic.

Jersey City.

□ England and Wales.

△ Not available.

example, in 1960, Chicago's delta between Negroes and native whites born of native parents is 82, in the Consolidated Area, between Negroes and non-Puerto Rican whites born of native parents, it is 80·2. Moreover, we find a correlation of 0·87 between Chicago and New York when we rank each of twelve ethnicities and races in their segregation from the base population.[10] We think it reasonable to conclude that neither Chicago nor any other city differs substantially from New York in the pattern of ethnic segregation.

Now that we have demonstrated that ethnic segregation in general has declined very little, and that ethnic segregation in New York resembles that of other cities, we can focus on just the Consolidated Area of 1960. We wish to show that we are not considering just some quaint immigrant fragments of a bygone past, now scattered through a much larger population. First, we should emphasize that the 1960 census data on the foreign stock are weighted not so much by the immigrants themselves as by the second generation. Table 10.3 shows that the percentage of foreign-born ranges from 27·3 for the Irish to 43·4 for the Norwegians. On the average, only about a third of any ethnic population are themselves immigrants. Moreover, both generations are old enough to consist of adults living in their own homes. We do not know the age distributions for the Consolidated Area as a whole, but we do know it for each state. In New York, for example, the median age for the foreign-born was 57·3 years; for the native-born of foreign parentage, it was 43·7; and for the native-born of mixed native and foreign parentage, it was 31·0.[11] In effect, we can consider our ethnic population to be primarily the children of immigrants who left their parental homes and began their own families.

Table 10.3 **Percentage of foreign-born among selected foreign stock, New York–Northeastern New Jersey Standard Consolidated Area, 1960***

Ethnicities	Total foreign stock (in thousands)	Foreign-born as a percentage of total
Norway	68	43·4%
Germany	654	40·2
Hungary	183	40·0
Czechoslovakia	128	36·9
United Kingdom	413	36·3
Poland	668	35·9
Sweden	64	34·1
Austria	342	33·1
USSR	787	32·5
Italy	1,531	29·6
Eire	504	27·3

* US Bureau of the Census, *U.S. Census of Population, Vol. I: Characteristics of the Population*, Part 34 (New York, US Government Printing Office, Washington, DC, 1963), Table 99.

Moreover, the ethnicities usually number large enough populations to fill neighborhoods, although individual foreign stocks range considerably in size. As Table 10.3 indicates, except for the Swedes, who constitute only 0·4 per cent of the Consolidated Area's total population, and the Norwegians, who constitute 0·5 per cent, all others exceed 100,000: they range from the Czechs, who constitute 0·9 per cent, to the Italians, who constitute 10·4 per cent.

Table 10.4   Percentage distribution of population by race and nativity, New York–Northeastern New Jersey Standard Consolidated Area and Component SMSA's, 1960*

	Consoli-dated Area	New York SMSA		Newark SMSA		Paterson-Clifton-Passaic SMSA	Jersey City SMSA
		Total	*City*	*Total*	*City*		
Total population (in thousands)	14,759	10,695	7,782	1,689	405	1,187	611
Race and nativity:							
Negro†	10·6%	11·5%	14·0%	13·3%	34·1%	3·6%	6·8%
Other non-white†	0·5	0·6	0·7	0·2	0·3	0·1	0·2
Puerto Rican	4·6	5·9	7·9	0·8	2·4	0·8	2·4
Non-Puerto Rican whites:							
Native-born of native parents	40·4	36·2	28·8	49·5	29·3	52·5	45·5
Foreign stock	43·9	45·8	48·6	36·2	33·9	43·0	45·1
Total	84·3	82·0	77·4	85·7	63·2	95·5	90·6
Total	100·0%	100·0%	100·0%	100·0%	100·0%	100·0%	100·0%

* 1960 census of population (Nathan Kantrowitz and Donnell M. Pappenfort, '1960 Fact Book for the New York–Northeastern New Jersey Standard Consolidated Area: The Non-White, Puerto Rican, and White Non-Puerto Rican Populations,' *Social Statistics for Metropolitan New York*, No. 2 [March, 1966]; US Bureau of the Census, *U.S. Census of Population: 1960*, Vol. I, Parts 32, 34, Tables 72, 79).
† Includes non-white Puerto Ricans.

A final clarification emerges from Table 10.4, where we see that the census data for just interethnic segregation include a significant part of the population of the metropolis. The excluded population – non-Puerto Rican, native-born whites with two native-born parents – ranges from a high of 52·5 per cent in the Paterson-Clifton-Passaic SMSA to a low of 36·2 per cent in New York. As we go from the SMSA to the inner city, the excluded population drops still more; for example, it is 28·8 per cent in New York City, and even lower in such residential areas as the Bronx (26·7 per cent). Moreover, this omitted population tends to contain a large proportion of children and very young adults. For example, we esti-mate that in New York City 40 per cent of our excluded population is under fifteen years of age. If we assume that all these youngsters live with their parents, so that their residential distribution would not affect the housing pattern, and that many of the parents themselves are second generation, then our ethnic and racial segregation indexes should include at least 75 per cent of New York City's population. In summary, we can reasonably

141

conclude that the Consolidated Area's 1960 segregation patterns are not unique to a minor part of a fragmented and miniscule immigrant population. Rather, New York's segregation pattern is similar to that of other cities which have had relatively stable ethnic segregation; moreover, an analysis of New York includes the great majority of the residents of that metropolis.

Turning to the segregation index numbers of the Consolidated Area, we want to show, first, that the deltas for the individual SMSA's resemble one another closely enough so that the total for the Consolidated Area summarizes characteristics of the metropolis as a whole. Table 10.5 indicates that differences among the four SMSA's are relatively minor. The largest

Table 10.5 Unweighted mean indexes of segregation for Negroes, Puerto Ricans, and foreign stock, New York–Northeastern Consolidated Area and Component SMSA's, 1960

Populations compared	Number of comparisons	Total CA	New York		Newark		Paterson-Clifton-Passaic SMSA	Jersey City SMSA
			SMSA Total	City only	SMSA Total	City only		
Negro × Puerto Rican	1	66·0	63·8	62·2	55·8	48·7	54·9	69·4
Negro × foreign stock:								
Negro v. all foreign stock	11	81·0	81·7	83·7	76·9	71·6	79·8	75·2
Negro v. old stock	5	82·0	82·7	84·8	78·8	72·2	81·2	79·2
Negro v. new stock	6	80·1	80·9	82·8	75·4	71·2	78·7	71·8
Puerto Rican × foreign stock:								
PR v. all foreign stock	11	80·2	79·2	77·9	77·5	70·3	68·9	72·8
PR v. old stock	5	82·4	81·6	80·0	80·5	71·3	73·1	74·8
PR v. new stock	6	78·3	77·2	76·1	75·1	69·5	65·3	71·1
Interethnic foreign stock:								
Total	55	46·4	46·2	49·3	42·6	53·3	38·4	42·7
Old v. old	10	40·5	41·1	46·2	37·6	51·9	27·5	43·4
New v. new	15	40·8	38·9	40·3	38·4	46·0	34·1	38·0
Old v. new	30	51·2	51·6	54·9	46·4	57·4	44·2	44·9

range of differences – 15·9 points, between the Jersey City and the Paterson-Clifton-Passaic SMSA's for the 'old versus old' interethnic foreign-stock average – is not even approached by any of the other ranges. More typical is the 9·1 difference between the total New York and Jersey City SMSA's for the 'Negro versus new' stock comparison. Generally, the SMSA's vary by only seven or eight points, in no particular order, except that New York's tend to be higher than New Jersey's.[12] Consequently, we shall refer to the average for the total Consolidated Area, shown in the second column of Table 10.5, to make the point that interethnic segregation can be regarded as relatively high.

We see here that the European ethnic populations are almost equally segregated from Negroes, whether we consider 'old' stock (82·0) or 'new' (80·1). Moreover, an equivalent ethnic segregation appears to apply to the Puerto Ricans, again whether we consider their segregation from the 'old' (82·4) or 'new' (78·3) European stock. It is only speculation, but we think that the appreciably lower (66·0) segregation between Negroes and Puerto Ricans stems in large measure from the recent date of both their migrations: the greatest number of European migrants came prior to World War I; most Negro migrants came since World War I; and most Puerto Ricans, since World War II.

But whatever reasons we posit for the very large segregations between European ethnicities and Negroes or Puerto Ricans, we assume that a guide to the lower bounds of these segregations will be found in the segregation between European ethnicities. We can see in Table 10.5 that the level of average segregation among northern Europeans in the Consolidated Area (40·5) is virtually identical with that among southern Europeans (40·8). But the average segregation between northern and southern Europeans is markedly higher (51·2). We think it reasonable to consider this average delta of 51·2 as the lower bound for 1960 segregation of foreign stock from Negroes or Puerto Ricans.[13] In effect, nearly forty years after the end of large-scale European migration, a segregation index number encompassing both the migrants and their children (but primarily the children) in a highly suburbanized metropolis indicates that, on the average, 51·2 per cent of the population of southern European origin would have to be redistributed in order to achieve full integration with the northern European population. Consequently, we expect that any given Negro-white segregation index number will exceed this base. How much of a differential it is reasonable to 'expect', is, of course, a subjective matter. But whatever judgment one makes, we think it likely that any reduction of racial segregation will involve the reduction, not of just Negro-white segregation, but rather of Negro-white European ethnic segregation – a task made difficult by the high level of interethnic segregation.

To enable us to focus more closely on just this interethnic segregation, Table 10.6 presents the indexes for eleven selected ethnicities, plus Negroes and Puerto Ricans. It is instructive to consider two ethnicities which together comprise but 0·9 per cent of the population. The segregation index between the Norwegians and Swedes, 45·4, indicates a separation between two Protestant Scandinavian populations which have partially intermarried and even have at least one community in common (the 'Bay Ridge' neighborhood in Brooklyn). But the high delta does represent ethnic separation, for each national group still maintains its own newspaper, and each lives in neighborhoods separate from those inhabited by the other. If Swedes and Norwegians are not highly integrated with each other, it is likely that they are even less integrated with other ethnic populations. And this is the case, for the Swedish-Norwegian delta is the lowest for the Norwegians and the fourth lowest for the Swedes.

We can carry out a more general analysis of the Consolidated Area's interethnic segregation if we focus on those ethnicities which are relatively

Table 10.6 Indexes of residential segregation in 1960, between selected ethnicities (foreign stock), total New York–Northeastern New Jersey Standard Consolidated Area (above the diagonal), New York Standard Metropolitan Statistical Area (below the diagonal)*

Ethnic population	1	2	3	4	5	6	7	8	9	10	11	12	13
1. United Kingdom	—	30·9	49·7	31·6	25·9	44·9	42·3	40·6	42·5	51·6	43·3	79·8	81·4
2. Eire	28·1	—	56·1	41·8	33·8	50·2	47·5	45·5	47·4	55·4	45·5	79·0	76·9
3. Norway	51·4	58·7	—	45·4	52·4	65·9	64·1	64·5	66·4	70·7	58·9	87·7	88·2
4. Sweden	31·8	41·3	45·8	—	37·4	56·9	52·2	52·6	53·8	61·3	51·5	83·4	84·9
5. Germany	25·6	33·3	56·4	38·2	—	45·8	41·2	39·0	40·8	51·4	42·9	80·2	80·6
6. Poland	45·0	51·7	67·9	57·9	47·1	—	40·1	23·3	34·4	27·7	50·6	78·6	76·6
7. Czechoslovakia	39·5	44·5	65·6	51·1	39·5	41·7	—	41·3	34·4	53·2	51·3	81·6	80·8
8. Austria	40·2	47·1	68·0	54·2	40·4	20·3	39·9	—	30·2	21·4	50·4	80·2	77·2
9. Hungary	39·1	44·2	68·3	52·9	38·7	31·3	33·9	24·7	—	39·9	54·0	80·4	78·8
10. USSR	50·2	57·1	72·9	62·2	52·1	20·0	49·0	19·0	32·7	—	59·4	81·1	78·1
11. Italy	44·9	48·0	60·2	51·9	45·6	52·7	51·6	53·0	53·9	60·5	—	78·9	78·2
12. Negro	80·3	80·3	88·4	83·7	80·6	79·7	81·9	81·1	80·4	81·8	80·5	—	66·0
13. Puerto Rican	79·8	76·5	88·2	83·9	79·7	75·5	78·6	76·6	76·3	78·1	77·8	63·8	—

* New York SMSA indexes are included to present a more complete record for reference.

Source: US Bureau of the Census, *1950 Census of Population* (see text).

144

integrated – say, with deltas of less than 35·0. Such a comparison highlights the usual 'old versus new' European dichotomy, which is most likely attributable to the differential mixture of Jews, and to common periods of migration. Although we admit that we are being outlandishly speculative, we are intrigued by the observation that the segregation among the 'new' ethnicities reflects the map of central Europe in the nineteenth century. For example, if we consider these ethnic populations in order of size of delta, we would entirely exclude the Italians and encompass the ethnicities of the old Austro-Hungarian Empire and their cousins, the Slavs.[14] Most closely connected are the Austrians and the Russians (21·4), followed by the Austrians and the Poles (23·3), the Poles and the Russians (27·7), the Hungarians and the Austrians (30·2), the Hungarians and the Poles (34·4), and the Czechs and the Hungarians (34·4). We do not entirely discount the influence of the Old World; despite the fact that many of these groups were in conflict, there are forces which bring people together – perhaps shopping districts, perhaps nationality-group realtors.[15] Similarly, a second cluster combines the Anglo-Saxons – the United Kingdom and Germany (25·9) each of these with the Irish, and the Swedes with the United Kingdom.

Two ethnicities remain, highly segregated from all others: the Italians and Scandinavians. We might expect that the Italians, a southern European or 'new' stock, would remain highly segregated but we would have no reason to anticipate that they are more integrated with the 'old' northwestern Europeans than with the 'new' southern and central Europeans.[16] Even less expected is that the Norwegians are highly segregated from other ethnic groups. We have already noted that their lowest segregation is from the Swedes (45·4). Perhaps, then, it should not surprise us that their highest segregation, from the USSR (70·7) (primarily Slavic Jews), approaches their segregation from Negroes (87·7). If we assume that residential segregation numbers reflect degrees of cultural acceptance, we think it a fair speculation that Norwegian segregation from Negroes differs in degree, but not in kind, from their separatism from Slavic Jews.[17]

Some of these New York patterns are, of course, unique to the 1960 Consolidated Area. But we judge, from this first study of the New York metropolis, that its 1960 ethnic segregation patterns are similar to those of Chicago and most other northeastern and midwestern cities and that its ethnic segregation index numbers reflect a social reality which will remain viable at least for the foreseeable future. Certainly for the present, the strong prejudice against Negroes on the part of whites only compounds an existing separatism, for if Protestant Norwegians hesitate to integrate with Protestant Swedes, and Catholic Italians with Catholic Irish, then these groups are even less likely to accept Negro neighbors.

Notes and References

Revision of a paper prepared for discussion at the Columbia University Seminar on Population and Social Change, December 1967. This research was supported by the Columbia University School of Social Work–Mobilization for Youth Research Project (Richard A. Cloward, director), under a grant from the National Institute of Mental Health. I wish to thank many people for their assistance, particularly John Beresford, Patricia Golden, and members of the staff of the US Bureau of the Census, who programmed and calculated the segregation index numbers; and Nathan Glazer, Stanley Lieberson, Donnell M. Pappenfort, and members of the Population Seminar.

1. Noel P. Gist and Silvia F. Fava, *Urban Society* (New York: Crowell, 1964); Scott Greer, *The Emerging City* (Free Press of Glencoe, 1962). Nathan Glazer and Daniel P. Moynihan, 'Introduction', *Beyond the Melting Pot*, Cambridge, Mass.: MIT Press, 1963. Much of the literature on ethnicity and assimilation focuses on such factors as voting or intermarriage. In large measure, our conclusions are an extension of these ideas to residential segregation.

2. Census tract statistics for 1960, published in the US Bureau of the Census, *US Censuses of Population and Housing: 1960 Census Tracts* (PHC [1] series), were obtained for this study from the census bureau's computer tract tally tapes 29I and 29B. The seventeen counties of the Consolidated Area are defined and outlined in US Bureau of the Census, *1960 Census of Population: 1960, vol. I: Characteristics of the Population*. Parts 32 (New Jersey) and 34 (New York), Tables 11, 11a. The census bureau's definition of 'foreign stock' and 'Puerto Rican' is based on the respondent's place of birth (or his parents' birthplaces). Consequently, it does not differentiate ethnicity among those whose parents are native-born. The European ethnicities presented here include all those tabulated by the census bureau for the Consolidated Area. For definitions of race and of European or Puerto Rican ethnicity, see U.S. Bureau of the Census, *US Census of Population, 1960, vol. I: Characteristics of the Population*, Part 1, US Summary, 'Introduction'.

3. A major study comparing delta with other segregation indexes is Otis Dudley Duncan and Beverly Duncan, 'A Methodological Analysis of Segregation Indexes', *Am. Sociol. Rev.*, **20**, (April 1955), 210–27[2]; for more recent applications of delta which contain theoretical discussions and guides to the literature, see Stanley Lieberson, *Ethnic Patterns in American Cities* (Free Press of Glencoe, 1963), chap. 2; and Karl E. Taeuber and Alma F. Taeuber, *Negroes in Cities*, Chicago: Aldine Publishing Co., 1965, Appendix A. Some scholars have other methodological preferences. See, for example, James M. Beshers, Edward O. Laumann, and Benjamin S. Bradshaw, 'Ethnic congregation-segregation, assimilation, and stratification', *Social Forces*, **42**, (May 1964), 482–9. Any segregation index number is, of course, a limited statistical summary device, which is useful for analysis. It reflects 'real segregation' no more

than the IQ reflects 'real intelligence' or the US Bureau of Labor Statistics' Consumer Price Index reflects the 'real cost of living'.

4. These cutting points reflect my judgment as to how delta has been interpreted in the literature. Moreover, the data lend plausibility to this decision. For example, consider the segregation index numbers for the Consolidated Area in Table 10.6. The deltas range from 21·4 to 70·7, with a median of 45·8 (as compared with our interpretation of 30 as 'low' and 70 as 'high'); the median has a semi-interquartile range of 6·6 (as compared with our five-point 'un-important' variability).

5. Lieberson, *op. cit.*, Table 9, p. 57. Lieberson points out (pp. 58–9) that the various deltas for a given city in any one year are not independent of one another. The larger size of Cleveland's average delta calculated by census tracts in 1930 (60·8) over that calculated by ward boundaries in 1920 (43·5) is an artifact of the statistical characteristics of delta. In general, the use of a smaller geographic unit results in a larger delta. Since census tracts are smaller than wards, deltas calculated from census tract statistics are usually larger than deltas calculated from ward statistics.

6. *Ibid.*, Table 22, pp. 84–5. A similar conclusion can be drawn from the segrega-tion of the foreign-born from native whites (see Lieberson, Table 4, p. 46, and Table 13, pp. 66–7). We are emphasizing a point already recognized by Lieberson; see his comment on 'dynamic equilibrium' (p. 46).

7. Karl E. Taeuber and Alma F. Taeuber, 'The Negro as an immigrant group: recent trends in Racial and Ethnic Segregation in Chicago', *Am. J. Sociol.*, **69**, (Jan. 1964), 374–82[9].

8. We cannot give precise reasons for the differences between segregation index numbers calculated between individual ethnicities (such as Irish and Italian) or between an ethnicity and a base line (such as Irish immigrants and all native whites). The latter is more sensitive to changes in the city as a whole. For example, a case study of Chicago has concluded, from map inspection, that the dispersion of its Polish and Italian communities to approximate more closely the average base line during 1898–1920 in large part resulted from the construc-tion of new housing within the city after 1899 (see David Wallace, 'Residential concentration of Negroes in Chicago', [unpublished PhD dissertation, Harvard University], 1953, pp. 197–210).

9. Taeuber and Taeuber, 'The Negro as an immigrant group,' *op. cit.*, Table 1, pp. 376–7. We concur with the Taeubers' observation that ethnicities have become less segregated over time. Our purpose is to highlight the fact that segregation between specific ethnicities differs from segregation of a specific ethnicity from a base-line population. The latter is a weighted average, so that, for example, all native whites are weighted differently in 1960 than in 1930.

10. Coefficient of Spearman rank correlation. Within this broad pattern of similarity, some differences can be noted. For example, the slight but con-sistently higher level of segregation in the Consolidated Area as compared with Chicago city probably stems from the use of different spatial units: the

Consolidated Area is divided into more than 4,000 census tracts, the city of Chicago into but seventy-five 'community areas'. Other variations which probably derive from the changing mix of the base line populations are the slightly lower indexes for entire Standard Metropolitan Statistical Areas (SMSA) than for just their central cities and the slightly higher indexes for the New York SMSA's than for the New Jersey ones. The higher segregation of Negroes from every other population in New York (as well as in nearly every other study of American cities) is so constant throughout every part of the metropolis that we need not point it out repeatedly. We shall not discuss the segregation of Puerto Ricans here because we have described their adjustment in the following: 'Socio-economic segregation among the nonwhite, Puerto Rican, and non-Puerto Rican white populations, New York, 1960', a paper presented at the annual meeting of the Population Association of American, 1968; and 'Social mobility of Puerto Ricans: education, occupation, and income changes among children of migrants, New York, 1950–1960', *International Migration Review*, **2**, (Spring 1968), 52–72.

11. US Bureau of the Census, *US Census of Population: 1960*, subject reports: *Nativity and Parentage, Final Report* (PC [2]-1A), Table 15, p. 103.

12. There are only small differences between the average deltas of the total Newark or New York SMSA's and their central cities; we guess that some of this stems from continued ethnic separatism in the suburbs. We suspect also that work-residence patterns may affect segregation levels. We have seen that the New York SMSA has higher levels; the relatively minor variations among New Jersey SMSA's have been ignored because commuter-stream analysis indicates that these SMSA's are segments of a large but unfocused urban tangle which is interwoven with a highly centralized New York SMSA. (See Nathan Kantrowitz, 'The organization of commuter flows, New York, 1960' the Research Center, Columbia University School of Social Work, 1968.)

13. Alternative approaches to studying the effects of non-racial factors are outlined in Taeuber and Taeuber, *Negroes in Cities*, chap. 4.

14. C. Grant Robertson and J. G. Bartholomew, *An Historical Atlas of Modern Europe from 1789 to 1922*, London: Oxford University Press, 1924; Carlton J. H. Hayes, *A Political and Social History of Modern Europe*, New York: Macmillan Co., 1929, II, 427.

15. Attempts to partition ethnicities into Jew and gentile (or Catholic and Protestant) result only in guesses. For example, Herbert Seidman, Lawrence Garfinkel, and Leonard Craig conclude: 'In New York City the Russian-born are heavily Jewish. The Polish-born, the Austrian-born, and the Hungarian-born are largely Jewish. The Italian-born and Irish-born are heavily Catholic. The Scandinavian-born and British-born are predominantly Protestant. The German-born and the natives are distributed with large proportions in each of the three major religious groups' ('Death rates in New York City by socio-economic class and religious groups and by country of birth, 1949–1951', *Jewish Journal of Sociology*, **4**, no. 2 [Dec. 1962], 264). See also Ira Rosenwaike,

'The utilization of census tract data in the study of the American Jewish population', *Jewish Social Studies*, **25**, (Jan. 1963), 42–56. This pattern appears to be unique to New York. In contrast to the Consolidated Area in 1960, Chicago's pattern of foreign-born white segregation in 1930 and 1950 shows separate England-Eire and Germany-Austria connections becoming linked with each other through the English (and the Swedes through the Irish) in 1950 (Otis Dudley Duncan and Stanley Lieberson, 'Ethnic segregation and assimilation', *Am. J. Sociol.*, **64**, [Jan. 1959], 364–74 [7]). We do have some fragmentary evidence of ethnic clustering and persistence. Robert Park and Herbert Miller, in *Old World Traits Transplanted*, University of Chicago, Society for Social Research, 1925, particularly in the discussion of the map facing p. 146, point out how the Italian colony in New York City's Bowery recreated the provinces and villages of southern Italy on contiguous blocks of the city. David Wallace, in *Residential Concentration of Negroes in Chicago*, p. 209, judges that in Chicago, nationality-group real-estate operators have manipulated home buildings and loans in order to control and preserve their market.

16. This appears to be unique to the Consolidated Area: in our Table 10.5, the average delta for the fifteen 'new *v.* new' interethnic deltas is 40·8; if we abstract from these fifteen the five interethnic deltas which include the Italians, we find that the average among just these five (53·1) is much higher than among the remaining ten (34·5). However, when we consider the city of Chicago (from Duncan and Lieberson, 'Ethnic Segregation and assimilation', [7] *op. cit.*, Tables 2, 3, 4), we find that the Italians are similar to other ethnic groups: the overall 'new *v.* new' segregation for foreign-born whites in 1930 (55·8) and in 1950 (53·5) compares with the analogous 'Italian *v.* new' average segregation in 1930 (59·5) and 1950 (54·6).

17. Duncan and Lieberson present evidence that ethnic residential segregation is correlated with some attitude scales used by Bogardus to study the acceptance or rejection of ethnic minority groups, at least by the general population ('Ethnic segregation and assimilation', *op. cit.*, pp. 272–3). We do not know whether the Consolidated Area's Norwegian segregation is peculiar to this area, since data for other cities are lacking.

R.L.Morrill

11 The Negro ghetto: problems and alternatives*

'Ghettos', as we must realistically term the segregated areas occupied by Negroes and other minority groups, are common features of American urban life. The vast majority of Negroes, Japanese, Puerto Ricans, and Mexican-Americans are forced by a variety of pressures to reside in restricted areas, in which they themselves are dominant. So general is this phenomenon that not one of the hundred largest urban areas can be said to be without ghettos.[1]

Inferiority in almost every conceivable material respect is the mark of the ghetto. But also, to the minority person, the ghetto implies a rejection, a stamp of inferiority, which stifles ambition and initiative. The very fact of residential segregation reinforces other forms of discrimination by preventing the normal contacts through which prejudice may be gradually overcome. Yet because the home and the neighborhood are so personal and intimate, housing will be the last and most difficult step in the struggle for equal rights.

The purpose here is to trace the origin of the ghetto and the forces that perpetuate it and to evaluate proposals for controlling it. The Negro community of Seattle, Washington, is used in illustration of a simple model of ghetto expansion as a diffusion process into the surrounding white area.

From the beginning of the nineteenth century the newest immigrants were accustomed to spend some time in slum ghettos of New York, Philadelphia, or Boston.[2] But as their incomes grew and their English improved they moved out into the American mainstream, making way for the next group. During the nineteenth century the American Negro population, in this country from the beginning but accustomed to servitude, remained predominantly southern and rural. Relatively few moved to the North, and those who did move lived in small clusters about the cities. The Negro

* Reprinted from *The Geographical Review*, **55**, no. 3 (July 1965).

ghetto did not exist.[3] Even in southern cities the Negroes, largely in the service of whites, lived side by side with the white majority. Rather suddenly, with the social upheaval and employment opportunities of World War I, Negro discontent grew, and large-scale migration began from the

Table 11.1 Major destinations of net 3,000,000 Negroes moving north, 1940–60 *(Estimates only)*

New York	635,000	Washington, DC	201,000
Chicago	445,000	San Francisco	130,000
Los Angeles	260,000	Cleveland	120,000
Detroit	260,000	St Louis	118,000
Philadelphia	255,000	Baltimore	115,000

Table 11.2 Minority populations of major urbanized areas, United States, 1960

City	Minority population	Total population	Minority %
1. New York City	2,271,000	14,115,000	16
Negro	1,545,000		
Puerto Rican	671,000		
2. Los Angeles	1,233,000	6,489,000	19
Negro	465,000		
Mexican	629,000		
Asian	120,000		
3. Chicago	1,032,000	5,959,000	17
4. Philadelphia	655,000	3,635,000	18
5. Detroit	560,000	3,538,000	16
6. San Francisco	519,000	2,430,000	21
7. Washington, DC	468,000	1,808,000	26
8. Baltimore	346,000	1,419,000	24
9. Houston	314,000	1,140,000	28
10. San Antonio	303,000	642,000	47
11. St Louis	287,000	1,668,000	17
12. Cleveland-Lorain	279,000	1,928,000	15
13. New Orleans	265,000	845,000	31
14. Dallas–Fort Worth	252,000	1,435,000	18
15. Atlanta	207,000	768,000	27
16. Birmingham	201,000	521,000	38
17. Memphis	200,000	545,000	37

Source: Census of Population 1960: vol. 1, Chap. C, General Social and Economic Characteristics; vol. 2, Subject Reports: Nonwhite Population by Race.

rural south to the urban north, to Philadelphia, New York, Chicago, and St Louis, and beyond.

The influx was far larger than the cities could absorb without prejudice. The vision of a flood of Negroes, uneducated and unskilled, was frightening both to the whites and to the old-time Negro residents. As the poorest and newest migrants, the Negroes were forced to double up in the slums that had already been created on the periphery of business and industrial districts.

The pattern has never been broken. Just as one group was becoming settled, another would follow, placing ever greater pressure on the limited area of settlement, and forcing expansion into neighboring areas, being emptied from fear of inundation. Only in a few cities, such as Minneapolis–St Paul and Providence and other New England cities, has the migration been so small *and* so gradual that the Negro could be accepted into most sections as an individual.

America has experienced four gigantic streams of migration: the European immigration, which up to 1920 must have brought thirty million or more; the westward movement, in which from 1900 to the present close to ten million persons have participated; the movement from the farms to the cities, which since 1900 has attracted some 30 million; and the migration of Negroes to the North and West, which has amounted since World War I to about five million, including some three million between 1940 and 1960 (Table 11.1). The pace has not abated. Contributing also to the ghetto population have been 900,000 Puerto Ricans, who came between 1940 and 1960, largely to New York City; about 1,500,000 Mexicans, descendants of migrants to the farms and cities of the Southwest; and smaller numbers of Chinese, Japanese, and others.[4] Economic opportunity has been the prime motivation for all these migrant groups, but for the Negro there was the additional hope of less discrimination.

The rapidity and magnitude of the Negro stream not only have increased the intensity and size of ghettos in the North but no doubt have also accelerated the white 'flight to the suburbs' and have strongly affected the economic, political, and social life of the central cities.[5] In the South, too, Negroes have participated in the new and rapid urbanization, which has been accompanied by increased ghettoization and more rigid segregation.

As a result of these migrations, the present urban minority population consists, in the North and West, of 7·5 million Negroes and 4 million others, together 12·5 per cent of the total regional urban population; in the South, of 6·5 million Negroes, 20 per cent; in total, of 18 million, 14 per cent.[6] The proportion is increasing in the North, decreasing in the South. Minority populations in large American cities are presented in Table 11.2.

The nature of the ghetto

If we study the minority population in various cities, we can discern real differences, in income, education, occupational structure, and quality of homes.[7] For example, median family income of Negroes ranges from $2,600 in Jackson, Mississippi, to $5,500 in Seattle; and as a proportion of median white family income, from 46 per cent to 80 per cent respectively. The United States median family income for Negroes in urban areas is only $3,700, as compared with $6,400 for whites, but it is more than double the figure for Negroes still living in rural areas, $1,750. It is not hard, therefore, to understand the motivation for Negro migration to the northern cities, where striking progress has really been made.

But the stronger impression is of those general characteristics which are repeated over and over. The ghetto system is dual: not only are Negroes excluded from white areas, but whites are largely absent from Negro areas. Areas entirely or almost exclusively white or non-white are the rule, areas of mixture the exception. The ghettos, irrespective of regional differences, are always sharply inferior to white areas; home ownership is less and the houses are older, less valuable, more crowded, and more likely to be substandard.[8] More than 30 per cent of Negro urban housing is dilapidated or without indoor plumbing, as compared with less than 15 per cent for whites. The ghetto is almost always in a zone peripheral to the central business district, often containing formerly elegant houses intermingled with commercial and light industrial uses. As poor, unskilled labor, Negroes settled near the warehouses and the railroads, sometimes in shacktowns, and gradually took over the older central houses being abandoned by the most recently segregated groups – for example, the Italians and the Jews – as their rise in economic status enabled them to move farther out. More than one ghetto may appear on different sides of the business district, perhaps separated by ridges of wealthy, exclusive houses or apartments.

The Negro differs fundamentally from these earlier groups, and from the Mexicans and Puerto Ricans as well. As soon as economic and educational improvements permit, the lighter-skinned members of the other groups may escape the ghetto, but black skin constitutes a qualitative difference in the minds of whites, and even the wealthy Negro rarely finds it possible to leave the ghetto. Color takes precedence over the normal determinants of our associations.[9]

In the southern city Negroes have always constituted a large proportion of the population and have traditionally occupied sections or wedges, extending from the center of the city out into the open country. Indeed, around some cities, such as Charleston, South Carolina, the outer suburban zone is largely Negro. Figure 11.1 depicts the ghetto pattern for selected cities.

The impact of the ghetto on the life of its residents is partly well known, partly hidden. The white person driving through is struck by the poverty, the substandard housing, the mixture of uses, and the dirt; he is likely to feel that these conditions are due to the innate character of the Negro. The underlying fact is, of course, that Negroes on the average are much poorer, owing partly to far inferior educational opportunities in most areas, but more to systematic discrimination in employment, which is only now beginning to be broken. Besides pure poverty, pressure of the influx into most northern cities itself induces deterioration: formerly elegant houses, abandoned by whites, have had to be divided and redivided to accommodate the newcomers, maintenance is almost impossible, much ownership is by

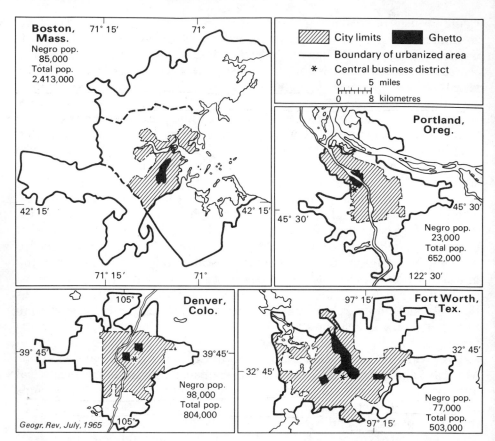

Fig. 11.1 A group of representative ghettos. The dashed-line boundary on the Boston map indicates the inner urbanized area. *Source.* 1960 census data.

absentee whites. Public services, such as street maintenance and garbage collection, and amenities, such as parks and playgrounds, are often neglected. Residential segregation means *de facto* school segregation. Unemployment is high, at least double the white average, and delinquency and crime are the almost inevitable result. A feeling of inferiority and hopelessness comes to pervade the ghetto. Most important is the enormous waste of human resources in the failure to utilize Negroes to reasonable capacity. The real cost of maintaining the ghetto system is fantastic. In direct costs the city spends much more in crime prevention, welfare payments, and so forth than it can collect.[10] The ghetto is the key to the Negro problem.

What are the forces that operate to maintain the ghetto system? Four kinds of barriers hinder change: prejudice of whites against Negroes; characteristics of the Negroes; discrimination by the real-estate industry and associated financial institutions; and legal and governmental barriers.

Naked prejudice is disclaimed by a majority of Americans today. Today's prejudice is not an outright dislike; it is, rather, a subtle fear, consisting of many elements. The typical white American may now welcome the chance to meet a Negro, but he is afraid that if a Negro moves into his neighborhood it will break up and soon be all Negro. Of course, on a national average there are not as many Negroes as that – only one or two families to a block – but the fear exists because that is the way the ghetto has grown. A greater fear is of loss in social status if Negroes move in. This reflects the culture-bred notion that Negroes are inherently of lower standing. Some persons are terrified at the unlikely prospect of intermarriage. Finally, people are basically afraid of, or uncertain about, people who are different, especially in any obvious physical way. These fears combine into powerful controls to maintain segregation: refusal to sell to Negroes, so as not to offend the neighbors; and the tendency to move out as soon as a Negro enters, in order not to lose status by association.

The Negro himself contributes, however unwillingly, to ghettoization. It is difficult to be a minority as a group, but more difficult still to be a minority alone. Consequently the desire to escape the ghetto and move freely in the larger society is tempered by a realization of the problems in store for the 'pioneer' and hesitancy to cut neighborhood ties with his own kind. Few people have such courage. In most cities, even if there were no housing discrimination, the ghetto would still persist, simply because a large proportion of Negroes could not afford, or would be afraid, to leave. Most Negroes achieve status and acceptance only within the Negro community. Usually Negroes who leave the ghetto prefer Negro neighbors; the risk is that this number, however small, is enough to initiate the conversion to full-scale ghetto.[11]

The Negro today suffers from his past. The lack of initiative and the family instability resulting from generations of enforced or inculcated subservience and denial of normal family formation are still present and are a barrier to white acceptance. The far lower levels of Negro income and education, no matter how much they are due to direct neglect and discrimination by the white majority, are nevertheless a strong force to maintain the ghetto. Studies show that whites will accept Negroes of equivalent income, education, and occupation.[12]

The strongest force, however, in maintaining the ghetto may well be real-estate institutions: the real-estate broker and sources of financing. It has always been, and continues to be, the clear-cut, official, and absolute policy of the associations of real-estate brokers that 'a realtor should never be instrumental in introducing into a neighborhood a character of property or occupancy, members of any race or nationality, or any individuals whose presence will clearly be detrimental to property values in that neighborhood'.[13] Many studies have attempted to resolve this problem. In the long run, property values and rents exhibit little if any change in the transition from white to Negro occupancy.[14] Sale prices may fall temporarily under panic selling, a phenomenon called the 'self-fulfilling prophecy' – believing that values will fall, the owner panics and sells, and thus depresses market values.[15]

The real-estate industry opposes with all its resources not only all laws but any device, such as cooperative apartments or open-occupancy advertising, to further integration. Real-estate and home-building industries base this policy on the desirability of neighborhood homogeneity and compatibility. Perhaps underlying the collective action is the fear of the individual real-estate broker that if he introduces a Negro into a white area he will be penalized by withdrawal of business. There is, then, a real business risk to the individual broker in a policy of integration, if none to the industry as a whole. Segregation is maintained by refusal of real-estate brokers even to show, let alone sell, houses to Negroes in white areas. Countless devices are used: quoting excessive prices, saying the house is already sold, demanding unfair down payments, removing 'For sale' signs, not keeping appointments, and so on. Even if the Negro finds someone willing to sell him a house in a white area, financing may remain a barrier. Although his income may be sufficient, the bank or savings institution often refuses to provide financing from a fear of Negro income instability, and of retaliatory withdrawal of deposits by whites. If financing is offered, the terms may be prohibitive. Similar circumstances may also result when a white attempts to buy a house – for *his* residence – in a heavily minority area.

Through the years many legal procedures have been used to maintain segregation. Early in the century races were zoned to certain areas, but these laws were abolished by the courts in 1917. The restrictive covenant, in which the transfer of property contained a promise not to sell to minorities, became the vehicle and stood as legal until 1948, since when more subtle and extralegal restrictions have been used.

Until 1949 the federal government was a strong supporter of residential segregation, since the Federal Housing Administration required racial homogeneity in housing it financed or insured. As late as 1963, when the President by Executive order forbade discrimination in FHA-financed housing, the old philosophy still prevailed in most areas. Finally, many states, and not just those in the South, still encourage separation. Even in the few states with laws against discrimination in housing, the combined forces for maintaining segregation have proved by far the stronger.

The process of ghetto expansion

The Negro community in the North has grown so rapidly in the last forty years, almost doubling in every decade, that even the subdivision of houses cannot accommodate the newcomers. How does the ghetto expand? Along its edge the white area is also fairly old and perhaps deteriorating.

Many whites would be considering a move to the suburbs even if the ghetto were not there, and fears of deterioration of schools and services, and the feeling that all the other whites will move out, reinforce their inclination to move. Individual owners, especially in blocks adjoining the ghetto, may become anxious to sell. Pressure of Negro buyers and fleeing white residents, who see the solid ghetto a block or two away, combine to scare off potential white purchasers; the owner's resistance gradually weakens; and the transfer is made.

The role of proximity is crucial. On adjacent blocks the only buyers will be Negroes, but five or six blocks away white buyers will still be the rule. In a typical ghetto fringe in Philadelphia the proportion of white buyers climbed from less than 4 per cent adjacent to the ghetto itself to 100 per cent five to seven blocks away.[16] Figure 11.2 illustrates the great concentration of initial entry of new street fronts in a band of two or three blocks around a ghetto. The 'break' zone contains 5 per cent or fewer Negroes, but 60 per cent of the purchases are by Negroes. Typically, a white on the edge does

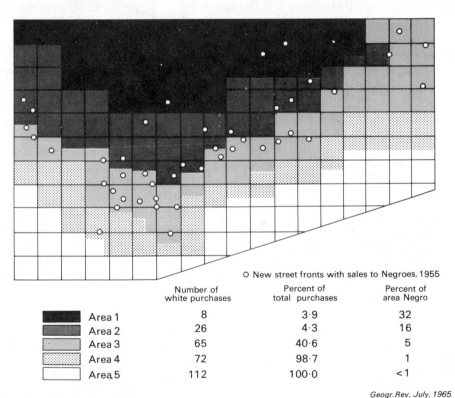

O New street fronts with sales to Negroes, 1955

		Number of white purchases	Percent of total purchases	Percent of area Negro
▄	Area 1	8	3·9	32
▦	Area 2	26	4·3	16
▨	Area 3	65	40·6	5
▦	Area 4	72	98·7	1
□	Area 5	112	100·0	< 1

Geogr. Rev, July, 1965

Fig. 11.2 Distribution of Negro purchases on the edge of the ghetto, showing initial entry of street fronts, in one year (1955). Adapted from diagram in Rapkin and Grigsby (see text note 11 for reference), p. 76.

not mind one or two Negroes on the block or across the street, but if a Negro moves next door the white is likely to move out. He is replaced by a Negro, and the evacuation-replacement process continues until the block has been solidly transferred from white to Negro residence. Expansion of the ghetto is thus a block-by-block total transition.

In this process the real-estate agent is also operative. If the demand for Negro housing can be met in the area adjacent to the ghetto, pressure to move elsewhere in the city will diminish. The real-estate industry thus strongly supports the gradual transition along the periphery. After the initial break the real-estate broker encourages whites to sell. The transition is often orderly, but the unscrupulous dealer sometimes encourages panic selling at deflated prices, purchasing the properties himself and reselling them to Negroes for windfall profits. The probability of finding a white seller is high in the blocks adjacent to the ghetto but falls off rapidly at greater distances, as whites try to maintain familiar neighborhood patterns and conceive this to be possible if the Negro proportion can be kept small. The process of transition is destructive to both groups, separately and together. Whites are in a sense 'forced' to sell, move, and see their neighborhoods disband, and Negroes are forced to remain isolated; and total transition reinforces prejudice and hinders healthy contact.

Spread of the Negro ghetto can be described as a *spatial diffusion* process, in which Negro migrants gradually penetrate the surrounding white area. From some origin, a block-by-block substitution or diffusion of a new condition – that is, Negro for white occupancy – takes place. The Negro is the active agent; he can move easily within the ghetto and can, though with difficulty, 'pioneer' outside it. The white is passive, an agent of resistance or inertia. Resistance against escape of Negroes from the ghetto takes two forms: rebuff of attempts to buy; and diminishing willingness to sell with increasing distance from areas or blocks that already have Negroes. On the average the Negro will have to try more than once to consummate a sale, or, conversely, the owner will have to be approached by more than one buyer. Once the block is broken, however, resistance falls markedly, and transition begins. Although a complete model would take into account that a few whites continue to purchase in transition areas, the rate is insufficient, the net flow clear-cut, and the transition inevitable.

The proposed diffusion model is of the probabilistic simulation type.[17] It is probabilistic rather than deterministic for several reasons. We do not have sufficient definite information concerning the motivations for specific house-to-house moves of particular persons, but only general ideas concerning the likelihood of movement and how far. We are not dealing with a large aggregate of migrants, but with only a few individuals in a short period of time in a small area. If we had a thousand migrants, we could safely predict how many would move how far, but at the micro-level a probabilistic approach is required to evaluate individual decisions in the face of a complex of possible choices. Rather than determine that a specific migrant moves from one particular house to another, we find the probability of a typical migrant's move from a block to any and all other blocks, and we use random numbers to decide which destination, among the many possible, he chooses. We thus obtain a spatial pattern of moves, which spreads settlement into new blocks and intensifies it in old blocks.

The model is simulated rather than 'real' because it does not purport to predict individual behavior of actual people, but to simulate or pretend moves for typical households. Simulation is a valuable technique in science and technology, in which a model is constructed to depict artificially certain *major* features of some real process.

The simulation of diffusion model is important in biology, in rural and general sociology, and in communications, and has been used in geography.[18] It is an ideal vehicle for the characteristics of ghetto expansion – a process of growth in time, concerning behavior of small groups in small areas in small units of time, in which a powerful element of uncertainty remains, even though the general parameters of the model tend to channel the results. This randomness is evident in the real situation, since we observe that the ghetto, like a rumor or an innovation, does not progress evenly and smoothly in all directions but exhibits an uneven edge and moves at different rates in different directions, here advancing from block to block, there jumping over an obstacle.

We do not expect the simulated patterns to match precisely the actual patterns. We do want the model to generate a pattern of expansion that corresponds in its characteristics to the real pattern, and we can satisfy ourselves of the correspondence by visual and statistical tests. The purpose and hope are to discover and illustrate the nature of the ghetto expansion process, in full knowledge that the detail of the ultimate step is omitted – how the actual individual decides between his specific alternatives. The omission is justified, because we know that the combined effect of many individual decisions can often be described by a random process. The real test here is whether the spread, over a period of time, has the right extent, intensity, solidity or lack of it, and so on.

The model

A model of ghetto expansion must incorporate several elements: natural increase of the Negro population; Negro immigration into the ghetto; the nature of the resistance to Negro out-migration and its relation to distance; land values and housing characteristics; and the population size limits of destination blocks.

Beginning with the residential pattern at a particular time (in the Seattle example, 1940), migration and the spread of Negro settlement are simulated for ten two-year periods through 1960. The steps are as follows.

A. Taking into account natural increase for each period of the Negro population resident in the Seattle ghetto, at the observed rate of 5 per cent every two years.

B. Assigning immigrants who enter the study area from outside at the observed mean rate of 10 per cent every two years of the Negro population at the beginning of a period. These are assigned by random numbers, the probability that an area will be chosen being proportional to its present Negro population. Presumably, immigrants entering the area will find it easier to live, at least temporarily, and will find opportunities in houses or apartments or with friends, in approximate reflection of the number of Negro units available. After initial residence in the ghetto, the model allows these immigrants to participate in further migration.

C. Assigning internal migrants, at the rate of 20 per cent of the Negro households (including natural increase and immigration) of each block every two years, in the following manner:

1. Each would-be migrant behaves according to a migration probability field (Fig. 11.3) superimposed over his block. This migration probability field can be shifted about so that each would-be migrant can in turn be regarded as located at the position indicated by X. The numbers in the blocks show where the migrant is to move, depending on which number is selected for him in the manner described below. Blocks adjoining position X have three numbers (for example, 48–50); more distant blocks have two numbers (for example, 54–55); and the most distant have one number (for example, 98). Since 100 numbers are used, the total number of these numbers used in any one block may be regarded as the probability, expressed as a percentage, that any one migrant will move there. Thus a movable probability field, or information field, such as this states the probabilities of a migrant for moving any distance in any direction from his original block. Probability fields are often derived, as this one was, from empirical observations of migration distances. That is, if we look at a large number of moves, their lengths follow a simple frequency distribution, in which the probability of moving declines as distance from the home block increases. Such probabilities reflect the obvious fact of decreasing likelihood of knowing about opportunities at greater and greater distances from home. Thus the probability is higher that a prospective migrant will move to adjacent blocks than to more distant ones. The probability field provides a mechanism for incorporating this empirical knowledge in a model.

2. Randomly selected numbers, as many as there are migrants, are used to choose specific destinations, according to these prob-

1	2	3	4	5	6	7	8	9
10	11	12	13	14–15	16	17	18	19
20	21	22	23	24–25	26	27	28	29
30	31	32	33–34	35–37	38–39	40	41	42
43	44–45	46–47	48–50	x	51–53	54–55	56–57	58
59	60	61	62–63	64–66	67–68	69	70	71
72	73	74	75	76–77	78	79	80	81
82	83	84	85	86–87	88	89	90	91
92	93	94	95	96	97	98	99	00

			2	2	
1	5	10	10	5	1
5	10	15	15	15	4

		$\frac{1}{2}$	$\frac{3}{4}$		
5	6–10	11–20	21–30	31–35	36
37–41	42–51	52–66	67–81	82–96	97–00

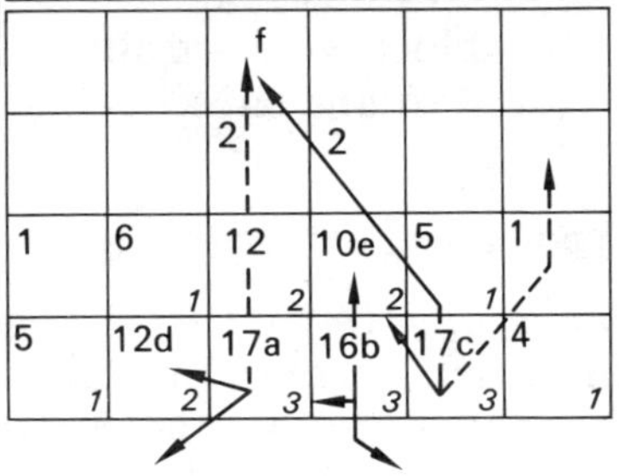

Fig. 11.3 The migration probability field.
Fig. 11.4 Negro residents at start of period.
Fig. 11.5 Distribution of immigrants. Tally marks indicate entry into appropriate blocks.
Fig. 11.6 Movement of migrants from three sample blocks. Large figures, resident Negroes; italic figures, number of migrants; broken lines, contact only; solid lines, actual moves.

		f			
		2	2		
1	6	12	10e	5	1
5	12d	17a	16b	17c	4

abilities, as will be illustrated below. The probability field as such makes it as likely for a Negro family to move into a white area as to move within the ghetto. A method is needed to take into account the differential resistance of Negro areas, and of different kinds or qualities of white areas, to Negro migration. Modification of the probability field is accomplished by the following procedures.

(a) If a random number indicates a block that already contains Negroes, the move is made immediately (no resistance).

(b) If a random number indicates a block with no Negroes, the fact of contact is registered, but no move is made.

(c) If, however, additional numbers indicate the same block contacted in b, in the same or the next two-year period, and from whatever location, then the move is made. This provides a means for the gradual penetration of new areas, after some persistence by Negroes and resistance by whites. Under such a rule, the majority of Negro contacts into white areas will not be followed by other contacts soon enough, and no migration takes place. In the actual study area chosen, it was found that resistance to Negro entry was great to the west, requiring that a move be allowed there only after three contacts, if the simulated rate of expansion was to match the observed rate. This is an area of apartments and high-value houses. To the north and east, during this period, resistance varied. At times initial contacts ended in successful moves and transition was rapid; at other times a second contact was required. These facts were incorporated into the operation of this phase of the model.

D. There is a limit (based on zoning and lot size) to the number of families that may live on a block. Thus when the population, after natural increase and immigration, temporarily exceeds this limit, the surplus must be moved according to the procedures above. Obviously, in the internal-migration phase no moves are allowed to blocks that are already filled. The entire process is repeated for the next and subsequent time periods.

Hypothetical example of the model

Immigration (A and B). Let us assume at the start that the total Negro population – that is, the number of families – including natural increase is 100, distributed spatially as in Fig. 11.4. Here the numbers indicate the number of families in each block. Ten immigrant families (10 per cent) enter from outside. The probability of their moving to any of the blocks is proportional to the block's population and here, then, is the same in percentage as the population is in number. In order that we may use random numbers to obtain a location for each immigrant family, the probabilities are first accumulated as whole integers, from 1 to 100, as illustrated in Fig. 11.5. That is, each original family is assigned a number. Thus the third block from the left in the second row has two of the one hundred families, identified by the numbers 1 and 2, and therefore has a 2 per cent chance of being chosen as a destination by an immigrant family. The range of integral numbers 1–2 corresponds to these chances. The bottom left-hand block has a 5 per cent probability, as the five numbers 37–41 for the families now living there indicate. If, then, the random number 1 or 2, representing an immigrant family, comes up, that family will move to the third block in the second row. For the ten immigrant families we need ten random numbers. Assume that from a table of random numbers we obtain, for example, the numbers 91, 62, 17, 08, 82, 51, 47, 77, 11, and 56. The first number, 91, falls in the range of probabilities for the next to the last block in the bottom row. We place an immigrant family in that block. The second number, 62, places an immigrant family in the third block from the left in the bottom row. This process is continued until all ten random numbers are used. The final distribution of immigrant families is shown by the small tally marks in various blocks in Fig. 11.5. The population of blocks after this immigration is shown in Fig. 11.6. Here the large numerals indicate the number of families now in the blocks. It should be made clear that the migrants could not have been assigned exactly proportional to population, because there are not enough whole migrants to go around. The first two blocks, for example, would each have required two-tenths of a migrant. In the probabilistic model, however, this difficulty does not exist.

Local migration (C). Twenty per cent of the Negro families of each block, rounded off to the nearer whole number, are now taken as potential migrants. The rounding off yields a total of nineteen families who will try to migrate from the blocks, as indicated by the italic numerals in Fig. 11.6. To illustrate, let us consider migration from the three blocks identified by *a*, *b*, and *c* in the bottom row. Random numbers are now needed to match against the migration probability field, Fig. 11.3. Let the random numbers now obtained from the table of random numbers be 49, 75, 14, 50, 36, 68, 26, 12, and 33. The first migrant from *a* is represented by the random number 49. This provides a location one block to the left of the migrant's origin, *X*, to *d*. The second migrant's random number, 75, provides a location two blocks down and one to the left, which is beyond the study area. We interpret this as moot, as though he were replaced by another migrant from the blocks, as indicated by the italic numerals in Fig. 11.6. To location three blocks up, location *f*. Since this block has no Negroes, this is only a contact, and no move is made at the time. This is indicated by a dashed line. Now let us proceed to migration from block *b*. The first migrant's number, 50, provides a location one block to the left, in block *a*, and the move is made. The second migrant's number, 36, provides a location one block up, in block *e*, and the move is made. The third migrant's number, 68, provides a location beyond the area. From block *c* the first migrant's number is 26, a location two blocks up and one to the right. This is an area with no Negroes, and only a contact path is shown. The second migrant's number, 12, provides a location three blocks up and two to the left. This location coincides with the contact made earlier by the third migrant from block *a*, and the move is made. The third migrant's number, 33, provides a location one block up and one to the left, or block *e* again, and the move is made. The net result of all this migration is the opening of one new block to settlement, the reinforcement of three blocks, and two lost contacts.

Northward expansion of the ghetto in Seattle

The ghetto in Seattle, with only 25,000 residents, is of course smaller than those in the large metropolises, and it may seem less of a threat to the

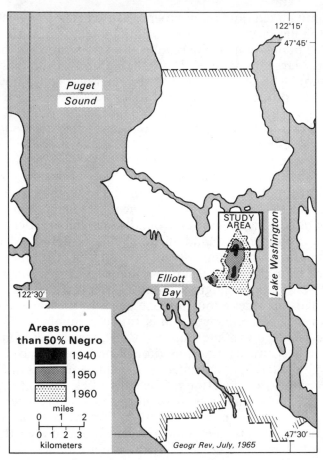

Fig. 11.7 The ghetto area of Seattle: non-white concentrations, 1940, 1950 and 1960. *Source.* Census data for the relevant years.

surrounding area.[19] Nevertheless, the nature of expansion does not differ from one ghetto to another, though the size of the ghetto and the rate of expansion may vary.

The expansion of the Seattle ghetto is shown on Fig. 11.7, on which the study area is indicated. From 1940 to 1960 the Negro population in the study area more than quadrupled, from 347 families to 1,520. Except for a few blocks just north and east of the 1940 Negro area, expansion was into middle-class single-family houses. To the west, where expansion was least, apartments offer increasing resistance, and to the northwest and along the lake to the east houses reach rather expensive levels. Expansion was easiest along the major south–north and southwest–northwest arterial streets, and northward along a topographic trough where houses and land were the

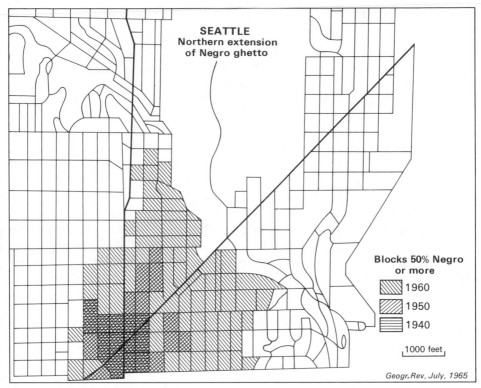

Fig. 11.8 Blocks predominantly Negro in the northern part of Seattle's ghetto. *Source.* Census of Housing, 1960. (Block statistics for Seattle.)

least valuable. The solidity of the ghetto core, the relatively shallow zone of initial penetration, and the consequent extension of the ghetto proper are shown on Figs. 11.8 to 10. As the ghetto became larger and thus more threatening, transition became more nearly solid.

The model was applied to the study area for ten two-year periods, beginning with the actual conditions of 1940 and simulating migration for twenty years. For each two-year period the natural increase of the Negro population was added to the resident population at the beginning of the period. Immigrants were assigned as in the model. Migrants were assigned according to the probability field (Fig. 11.3) and the rules of resistance. One example of the simulation of migration is shown on Fig. 11.11, for 1948–1950. Typically, out of 147 potential migrants, 131 were successful and 16 made contacts, but only 8 of the movers pioneered successfully into new blocks. The results of the simulation are illustrated by Figs. 11.12 and 13, which summarize the changes within two larger periods, 1940–50 and 1950–60.

165

Evaluation of the results

A comparison of Figs. 11.9 and 12, and 11.10 and 13, showing actual and simulated expansion of the Seattle ghetto for 1940–50 and 1950–60 respectively, indicates a generally close correspondence in the patterns. The actual pattern extended more to the north and the simulated pattern more to the northwest. A field check revealed that neither the quality nor the value of homes was sufficiently taken into account in the model. Topography, too, was apparently crucial. By 1960 the Negroes were rapidly filling in the lower-lying, nonview land. The ridge and view properties remained more highly resistant. The model did not recognize the rapid movement northward along the topographic trough.

According to the most stringent test of absolute block-by-block conformity the model was not too successful. Less than two-thirds of the simulated new blocks coincided with actual new blocks. However, the model was not intended to account for the exact pattern. Sufficient information does not exist. The proper test was whether the simulated pattern of spread had the right extent (area), intensity (number of Negro families in

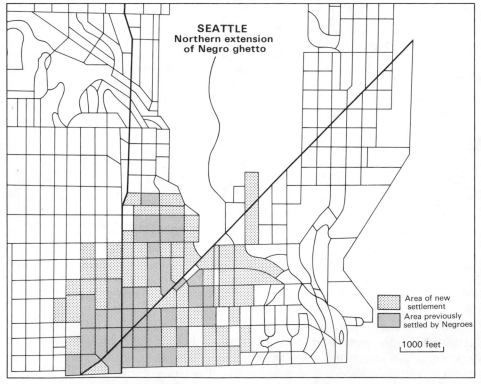

Fig. 11.9 Expansion of Negro population 1940–50. *Source.* Census of Housing, 1950. (Block statistics for Seattle.)

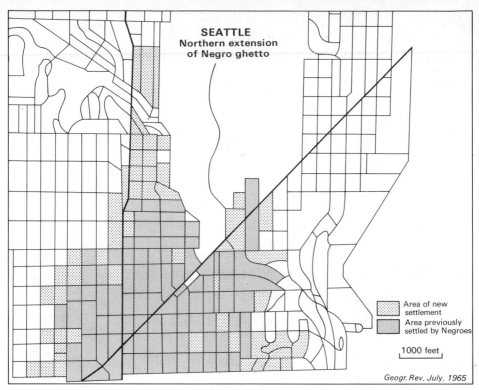

Area of new
settlement

Area previously
settled by Negroes

1000 feet

Geogr. Rev, July, 1965

Fig. 11.10 Expansion of Negro population 1950–60. *Source.* Census of Housing, 1950. (Block statistics for Seattle.)

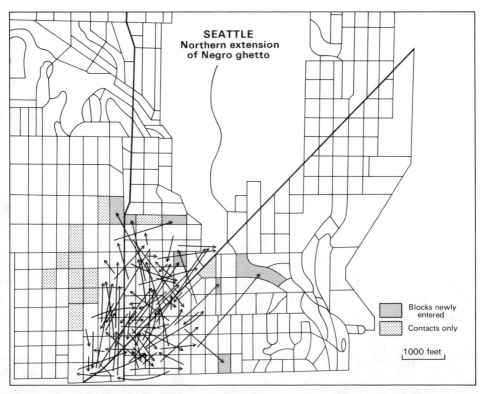

Blocks newly
entered

Contacts only

1000 feet

Fig. 11.11 Simulation of migration 1948–50.

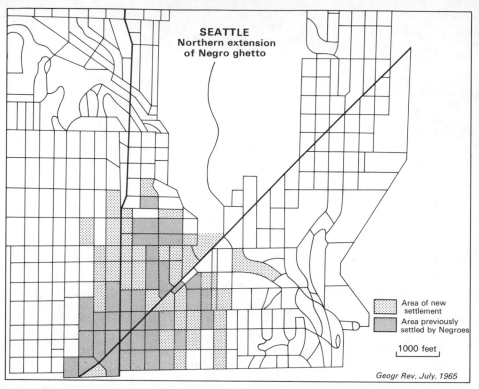

Fig. 11.12 Simulated expansion of ghetto 1940–50.

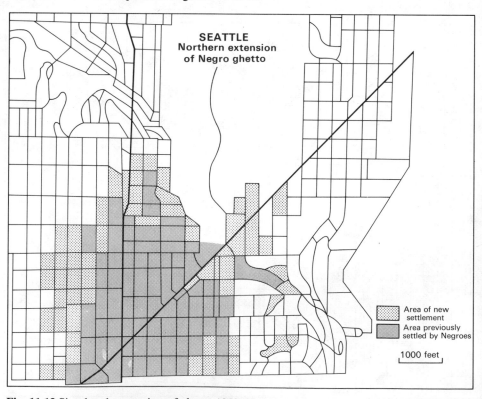

Fig. 11.13 Simulated expansion of ghetto 1950–60.

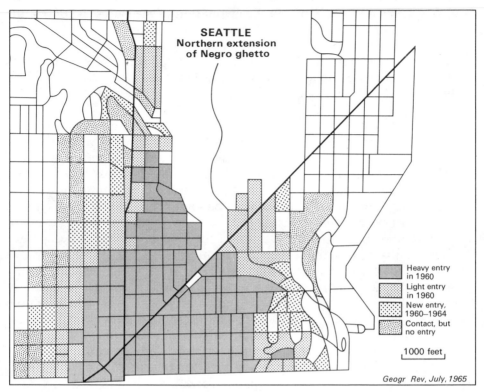

Fif. 11.14 Simulated expansion of ghetto 1960–64.

blocks), and solidity (allowing for white and Negro enclaves), and in these respects the performance was better. The number of blocks entered was close, 140 for the simulation to 151 for the actual; the size distribution of Negro population was close; and similar numbers of whites remained within the ghetto (with the model tending toward too great exclusion of whites). This similarity, rather than conformance, indicated that both the actual and the simulated patterns *could have occurred* according to the operation of the model. This is the crucial test of theory.

A predictive simulation, as a pattern that could occur, using as the base the actual 1960 situation, was done for the periods 1960–62 and 1962–64 (Fig. 11.14). A limited field check showed that this pattern is approximately correct, except, again, with too much movement to the northwest and not enough to the north. No prediction from 1964 has been attempted, because of risk of misinterpretation by the residents of the area.

Alternatives to the ghetto

The model attempted merely to identify the process of ghetto expansion

169

and thus helps only indirectly in the evaluation of measures to control the ghetto. We know that such a diffusion process is common in nature – the growth from an origin or origins of something new or different within a parent body. Reduction of this phenomenon would seem to require a great weakening of the distinction between groups, here Negroes and whites, either naturally through new conceptions of each other or artificially by legal means.

In ghetto expansion the process is reduced to replacement of passive white 'deserters' by active Negro migrants. Is there an alternative that would permit the integration of minorities in the overall housing market and prevent the further spread and consolidation of ghettos? Is it possible to achieve stable interracial areas, in which white purchasers, even after Negro entry, are sufficiently numerous to maintain a balance acceptable to both? Three factors have been found crucial: proximity to a ghetto; proportions of white and nonwhite; and preparation of the neighborhood for acceptance of Negro entry.[20] Proximity to a ghetto almost forbids a stable interracial situation. Fear of inundation either panics or steels white residents. Only wealthy areas can maintain any interracial character in such a location, since few, if any, Negroes can afford to enter. Negroes entering areas remote from the ghetto are more easily accepted (after initial difficulties), because the great body of Negroes does not 'threaten' neighborhood structures.

The proportion of Negroes in an area is critical for continued white purchasing. Whites are willing to accept 5 per cent to 25 per cent (with a mean of 10 per cent) Negro occupancy for a long time before beginning abandonment – depending on such factors as the characteristics of the Negroes moving in, the proximity of the ghetto, and the open-mindedness of the resident white population. On the other hand, although the Negro is accustomed to minority status, he usually prefers a larger proportion of his own group nearby than the critical 10 per cent. Thus a fundamental dilemma arises, and there are in fact few interracial neighborhoods. For cities with low Negro ratios, say less than 10 per cent, the long-run possibilities are encouraging, especially with the rise of Negro education and income, increased enforcement of nondiscrimination laws, and the more liberal views of youth today. For urban areas with high Negro ratios, such as Philadelphia, with 20 per cent (40 per cent in the city proper), it is difficult to imagine an alternative to the ghetto. The same conclusion holds for southern cities. No spatial arrangement, given present levels of prejudice, will permit so large a proportion of Negroes to be spread throughout the city without serious white reaction.

Private interracial projects have begun integration and have been successful and stable, if few in number.[21] From these experiments it has been learned that white buyers in such developments are not unusually liberal but are a normal cross section. Also, the spatial arrangement that permits the largest stable proportion of nonwhites has been found to be a cluster pattern – small, compact colonies of a few houses – rather than dispersed isolates.[22] This makes possible easy contact within the minority group, but also good opportunity for interaction with the white group, while minimizing the frequency of direct neighbors, which few whites are as yet able to accept.

Integrated residential living will become more acceptable as Negroes achieve equality in education and employment, but housing integration will probably lag years or decades behind. At most we may expect an arrest of the extension of existing ghettos, their internal upgrading, and prevention of new ones. Experience certainly indicates a long wait for goodwill to achieve even internal improvement; hence a real reduction in ghettoization implies a governmental, not a voluntary, regulation of the urban land and housing market – that is, enforced open-housing ordinances. Everything short of that has already been tried.

The suggested model of diffusion-expansion still describes the dominant ghettoization pattern. In the future we may be able to recognize an alternative 'colonization' model, in which small clusters of Negroes or other minorities break out of the ghetto and spread throughout the urban area under the fostering or protection of government.

Notes and References

1. Census Tract Reports, 1960, *Ser. PHC(1)*, selected cities. Subject Reports (Census of Population, 1960, vol. 2), 1960, *Ser. PC(2): Nonwhite Population by Race; State of Birth*, US Bureau of the Census, various dates.
2. Oscar Handlin, *The Newcomers* (New York Metropolitan Region Study [vol. 3]; Cambridge, Mass., 1959).
3. Charles Abrams; *Forbidden Neighbors* (New York, 1955), p. 19.
4. *Ibid.*, pp. 29–43.
5. Davis McEntire, *Residence and Race: Final and Comprehensive Report to the Commission on Race and Housing*, Berkeley, 1960, pp. 88–104.
6. *Nonwhite Population by Race* [see note 1 above].
7. Census Tract Reports [see note 1 above].
8. McEntire, *op. cit.*, pp. 148–56.
9. Abrams, *op. cit.*, p. 73.
10. John C. Alston, *Cost of a Slum Area*, Wilberforce State College, Ohio, 1948.
11. Chester Rapkin and William G. Grigsby, *The Demand for Housing in Racially Mixed Areas*, Special Research Report to the Commission on Race and Housing, Berkeley, 1960, pp. 27–30.
12. Nathan Glazer and Davis McEntire, eds. *Studies in Housing and Minority Groups: Special Research Report to the Commission on Race and Housing*, Berkeley, 1960, pp. 5–11.
13. McEntire, *op. cit.*, p. 245.

14. Luigi Mario Laurenti, *Property Values and Race: Studies in 7 Cities: Special Research Report to the Commission on Race and Housing*, Berkeley, 1960; [Homer Hoyt:] *The Structure and Growth of Residential Neighborhoods in American Cities*, Federal Housing Administration, Washington, DC, 1939; Lloyd Rodwin, 'The theory of residential growth and structure', *Appraisal Journ.*, **18**, (1950), 295–317.

15. Eleanor P. Wolf, 'The invasion-succession sequence as a self-fulfilling prophecy', *Journ. of Social Issues*, **13**, (1957), 7–20.

16. Rapkin and Grigsby, *op. cit.*, pp. 56–8.

17. Herbert A. Meyer, ed. *Symposium on Monte Carlo Methods, Held at the University of Florida . . . , March 16–17, 1954*, New York and London, 1956; Everett M. Rogers, *Diffusion of Innovations*, New York, 1962; Warren C. Scoville, 'Minority migrations and the diffusion of technology', *J. Econ. Hist.*, **11**, (1951), 347–60.

18. Torsten Hägerstrand, 'On Monte Carlo simulation of diffusion', in W. L. Garrison, ed., *Quantitative Geography*, Forrest R. Pitts, 'Problems in computer simulation of diffusion', *Papers and Proc. Regional Science Assn.*, **11**, (1963), 111–19.

19. Calvin F. Schmid and Wayne W. McVey, Jr, *Growth and Distribution of Minority Races in Seattle, Washington* [Seattle] 1964; Walter B. Watson and E. A. T. Barth, *Summary of Recent Research Concerning Minority Housing in Seattle*, Institute for Social Research, Department of Sociology, University of Washington, 1962; John C. Fei, 'Rent differentiation related to segregated housing markets for racial groups with special reference to Seattle', unpublished Master's thesis, University of Washington, 1949.

20. Eunice Grier and George Grier, *Privately Developed Interracial Housing: an analysis of experience: special research report to the Commission on Race and Housing*, Berkeley, 1960, pp. 29–30.

21. *Ibid*, p. 8.

22. Reuel S. Amdur, 'An exploratory study of 19 Negro families in the Seattle area who were first Negro residents in white neighborhoods, of their white neighbors and of the integration process, together with a proposed program to promote integration in Seattle', unpublished Master's thesis in social work, University of Washington, 1962; Arnold M. Rose and others, 'Neighborhood reactions to isolated Negro residents: an alternative to invasion and succession', *Am. Sociol. Rev.*, **18**, (1953), 497–507; L. K. Northwood and E. A. T. Barth, *Neighborhoods in Transition: the new American pioneers and their neighbors*, University of Washington, School of Social Work, Seattle, pp. 27–8.

H.M.Rose

12 The development of an urban subsystem: the case of the Negro ghetto*

The internal development of individual urban places has not traditionally been one of central focus in geography. This probably stems in part from the overriding emphasis on regions in general and the urban geographer's concern with the interrelationships among individual urban nodes. American geographers have only recently turned their attention to the internal structure of urban areas, no doubt an outgrowth of general interest in central place theory. Increasing interest in urban subsystems has resulted in a concomitant interest in the spatial structure of these systems. This paper attempts to provide insights on the spatial dynamics of a single subsystem within the metropolitan system, the Negro ghetto.

The Negro ghetto, as a universal and viable urban subsystem within the American urban system, has evolved with the rise of the Negro population in northern urban centers beginning with the decade prior to World War I.[1] The almost continuous flow of Negroes from both the rural and urban South to the North and West has permitted and promoted the development of Negro ghettos in all of the nation's major population centers. By 1960 more than 30 per cent of the nation's Negro population resided in twenty metropolitan areas. Whereas the Negro ghetto is found in nearly all 200 metropolitan areas in the United States, the basic concern of this study is with the processes responsible for its change in scale in northern urban centers. The previous legality of a system of racial separation in the American South served as an exogenous factor, overriding all others, in the promotion and maintenance of residential clusters based on race. For a brief period there existed laws which were specifically designed to maintain residential segregation based on race. The Supreme Court outlawed attempts to maintain a legal system of residential separation in 1917, in the case of Buchanan *versus* Warley.[2] Such a legalized role-prescription tends

* Reprinted from *Annals of the Association of American Geographers*, **60**, no. 1 (March 1970) 1–17.

173

to reduce the fruitfulness of a behaviorally oriented study, and thereby accounts for the limiting of this investigation to northern cities.

To date, only Morrill's pioneer work might be described as a spatial behavioral approach to the study of the changing state of the ghetto.[3] The model he assembled was employed to replicate the process of ghetto development in Seattle. Other researchers are beginning to show increasing concern for the general problem, with emphasis on the spatial dimension. Beauchamp recently suggested the use of Markov Chain Analysis as a means of specifying or identifying territorial units as ghetto or non-ghetto by investigating the dynamic changes taking place in the racial composition of areas.[4]

The process of the changing ghetto state has been described elsewhere as a diffusion process.[5] Diffusion models have attracted the interest of a small number of geographers who have employed them as a means of describing the spatial spread of an innovation. The more notable of these are associated with the work of Hägerstrand. The suitability of diffusion models as a means of describing the spread of the ghetto, however, is questionable. It appears that the spread of the ghetto is a phenomenon of a different type. More specifically, it appears that the spread of the Negro ghetto is a function of white adjustment to a perceived threat. The distinction between adjustment and diffusion was recently reviewed by Carlsson.[6] He averred that motivation and values transcend knowledge, in importance, in explaining certain types of behavioral change.[7] If the diffusion thesis is accepted as a means of explaining rather than describing the expansion of the Negro ghetto, then it must be assumed that each metropolitan system operates as a closed system. Since this is not the case, the adjustment hypothesis which Carlsson supports is undeniably more appealing than the diffusion hypothesis as a means of explaining the spread of the ghetto. Admittedly, whites must first be aware of the presence of Negroes if a change in their normative mobility pattern is to occur, but awareness here promoted the kind of behavior which has also become accepted as normative. Thus, the necessary adjustment is made as a means of maintaining the steady state condition. The kind of behavior inferred here was described by Zelinsky as social avoidance.[8] Morrill, who previously described the ghetto development process in terms of diffusion, now describes processes of this general type, which are interactional in nature, as quasi-diffusionary.[9]

Intra-urban population mobility

The spatial mobility of the American population, both in terms of long distance moves and intraurban shifts, was intensified during the decade of the 1950's. As major metropolitan systems were the target of most long distance moves, these moves resulted in the rapid dispersion of population into what was previously part of the rural countryside. The latter phenomenon has attracted the attention of researchers from a vast array of disciplines, geographers included. Geographers have also focused particular interest on the centrifugal flow of population, as this flow has had the most obvious impact on the form and areal magnitude of urban systems. But to consider the latter and ignore the role of the centripetal movement weakens the analysis of population shifts within the system and of the ensuing patterns which evolve.

Movements toward the periphery of the urban system, both from within the system and from without, have been principally responsible for the increase in the size of individual metropolitan aggregates. At the same time many central cities within metropolitan systems have suffered absolute losses in their populations. Thus, the centripetal flow into the central cities of metropolitan systems has seldom been sufficiently large to offset the counter flow. The most rapid and easily observed flow into the nation's larger central cities is that of Negro in-migration, a phenomenon which has far-reaching effects on the color composition of metropolitan areas.[10] By the mid-sixties there was official evidence that this process was continuing. The city of Cleveland, Ohio, undertook a special census on April 1, 1965. The results showed that the city had lost 91,436 white residents during the five years that had elapsed since the last census, while gaining an additional 26,244 Negro residents.[11] The Negro proportion of Cleveland's population rose by five percentage points during that period, from twenty-nine to thirty-four per cent. Since the census was confined to the political city of Cleveland, it is impossible to determine the extent to which Negroes entered the stream of movers destined for suburbia.

In response to the changing magnitude and composition of metropolitan populations, a network of transport links has evolved to facilitate the spatial redistribution of the population. Where an individual chooses to locate himself within the urban system is a function of occupational status, income, place of employment, and social taste. The operation or interaction of these factors has produced a strongly segmented pattern of urban occupance. A change in an individual's socioeconomic status frequently results in relocation within the metropolitan system. As the nation's occupational structure is being rapidly altered in the direction of a larger proportion of white collar workers, especially technical and professional workers, with a concomitant alteration in the income structure, spatial mobility is further accelerated. Changes of this nature tend to produce shifts in territorial status assignment in urban space. Davis, in a recent study, described the magnitude of territorial shifts in the location of middle-class housing areas in a selected group of American cities.[12] With the redistribution of the population towards the periphery, there has subsequently been an outward shift of the inner boundary of the zone of middle-class housing. As a consequence, these shifts frequently create gray areas which act as zones of transition or buffers between middle and lower-class occupance.

It is within these gray areas, with their high vacancy rates, that most of the centrifugal Negro flow is destined. The growing intensity of mobility within the metropolitan system has affected all segments of the population, although somewhat differentially. The pattern of movement of whites and nonwhites in urban space is akin to the pattern of inter-regional movement within the nation as a whole. In both instances nonwhite moves are characterized by short distance, whereas whites are more frequently engaged in long distance moves.

The nature of population movement within the urban system is highly related to the magnitude and form of the set of urban subsystems which evolve. The Negro ghetto which comprises one such subsystem or social area is directly related to this process. Since spatial mobility is related both to age and income, one would expect to observe the evolution of a series of patterns which reflect the economic health of a specific metropolitan system, the nature of its economic base, and its subsequent ability to attract population through the process of internal migration; the latter phenomenon has the effect of altering the age distribution of the population. If ability to purchase was the single most significant variable influencing the distribution of population in metropolitan space, it should be easy to predict the kind of sorting-out which eventually occurs. Although this can be done in a rather general manner, purchasing ability alone is far from adequate in explaining the development of the ghetto.[13] The relative stability of the Negro's economic position vis-à-vis the white's during the last several years may have reduced or severely limited the ability of individual Negroes to cross critical rent isolines. On the other hand, the brisk hiring of Negroes to salaried positions by an increasing number of firms pledged to the goal of equality of opportunity, could have the effect of increasing the length of the individual move. It is impossible at this time to specify with any degree of precision the effect of either factor upon the pattern of Negro movement, even though they both may be significant.

Territoriality

The existence and persistence of the Negro ghetto as a spatially based social community may best be explained within the framework of the social assignment of territory. Once a slice of physical space is identified as the territorial realm of a specific social group, any attempt to alter this assignment results in group conflict, both overt and covert. Stea recently described this behavior in the following way: 'We have reason to believe that "territorial behavior", the desire both to possess and occupy positions of space, is as pervasive among men as among their animal forbears.'[14] Webber attributed this kind of behavior simply to working class groups for whom physical space is an extension of one's ego.[15]

Human ecologists have employed terms such as invasion and succession to describe the process of residential change in which members of competing

176

groups struggle for territory. Henderson recently questioned the employment of the term invasion to describe the process of Negro entry into areas bordering on the ghetto.[16] Admittedly the term invasion appears to be appropriate only within the context of territorial conflict. Viewed outside this context, the term does not appear to be meaningful. A further point, no doubt the one which concerned Henderson, is that the term invasion not only reflects the white resident's perception of events, but the perception of the researcher as well. It has been said, 'When our own tribe engages in this behavior we call it nationalism or aggression.'[17] From another vantage point, it would appear that the term retreat describes the process more accurately. Since both terms, invasion and retreat, refer to territorial conflict, no major point is settled by substituting one for the other. Nevertheless, it should be kept in mind that the nature of the behavior which occurs within this context does so within the context of a fear-safety syndrome.

The territorial acquisition by advancing Negro populations cannot always be viewed as a gain in this game of psychological warfare, for once the territory is transferred from one group to the other, it is perceived by the white population as having been contaminated and, therefore, undesirable. The formalization or codification of this attitude is associated with the Federal Housing Administration's policy of promoting racial homogeneity in neighborhoods during the period 1935–50.[18] Hoyt's classic study on the growth of residential neighborhoods strongly supported this position, and possibly served to support and justify the government's position.[19] Thus, the whole notion of stable property values revolves around the transfer of the status designation from a group to the territory occupied by the group. More recently Bailey observed in one case that unstable property values were associated with those zones located in the shadow of the ghetto rather than in the ghetto itself.[20] However, it is the slack demand for housing in a racially changing neighborhood that is likely to drive down housing values. The unwillingness of whites to compete with non-whites for housing in a common housing market, coupled with vacancy rates which frequently exceed Negro demand, could eventually lead to a lessening of values. Thus, land abandoned by whites on the margins of the Negro ghetto at some single point in time is almost never known to be retrieved by such residents.

The behavior described above is rapidly leading to the development in the United States of central cities within which territorial dominance is being relinquished to the Negro population. This fact has undoubtedly had much to do with the increasing demand by Negroes for black power, and logically so. If one inherits a piece of turf it is only natural for him to seek control of the area of occupance. Thus, both the critics and supporters of black power have traditional white behavior and the public decisions stemming therefrom for its overt crystallization. Grier recently noted that it was not until President Kennedy signed his executive order of 1962, which treated the problem of discrimination in housing, had the federal government ever gone on record as opposing discrimination in housing.[21] Yet even today, as the nation's ghettos continue to expand, public policy abets their existence and expansion.

The model

The previous description of a set of general processes goes far in explaining the continuous expansion of the Negro ghetto. The processes described reflect the values of society and, as Pahl recently pointed out, residential patterns are a reflection of the functioning of a social system.[22] It is possible within the framework of systems analysis to devise a model which replicates the total process of metropolitan systems development, but such an understanding exceeds the skills of a single researcher or the knowledge and focus of a single academic discipline. However, a single researcher might attempt to develop a simple model which replicates some aspect of the development of the metropolitan system. A model of this nature, although promoting keener insights into an understanding of processes operative at the micro-level, is characterized by serious shortcomings as it basically reflects the operation of endogenous processes. Nevertheless, the advantages emanating from the development of such models outweigh the previously specified shortcomings.

Components of the model

A model of ghetto development is of the type described by Chorley and Haggett as normative.[23] An effective model describing ghetto development should include at least three basic components: 1. a demographic component, 2. a producer component, and 3. a consumer component. The data employed to describe these components serve as input for the model. The demographic component is employed to determine housing demand, the producer component to determine availability, and the consumer component to determine allocation. The operation of and subsequent interaction associated with these components permits the model to be placed in the category of behavioral models. The demographic and producer components are generated deterministically, whereas the consumer component is generated probabilistically. Thus, the spread of the ghetto is described in an indeterminate manner. The weakness of the simulation lies primarily in the gross assumption employed in the producer component and secondarily in the projections derived from the operation of the demographic components, both of which acutely affect the emerging pattern of ghetto development.

The demographic component Gross changes in the magnitude of the ghetto are associated basically with the changing demographic character of the Negro population. The demographic characteristics of the white population residing in ghetto space will likewise influence the pattern or form of

the ghetto at any point in time. The competition for housing and its subsequent allocation is largely influenced by the demographic characteristics
of both the white and Negro populations. In order to better understand the
role of population dynamics on ghetto development, interest is focused on
the population occupying what is here identified as 'ghetto space'.[24]
Ghetto space in the city selected for testing the model, Milwaukee, Wisconsin, spreads out over a twelve square mile area extending north and west
from the central business district. The area in 1960 contained approximately
217,000 persons of which only 20 per cent was nonwhite. Nested within
ghetto space was a much smaller area, approximately four square miles in
extent, which had already become identified as the ghetto. This smaller
area included 92,000 persons of whom approximately 68 per cent were
nonwhite. Thus, the area identified as the Negro ghetto was slightly more
than two-thirds Negro and included many blocks which did not contain a
single Negro household. In identifying the twelve square mile area as
ghetto space, an assumption is posited that the spread of the Negro population will be largely confined to this area in the city of Milwaukee during the
current decade and no doubt the decade which follows. By adopting this
assumption it is clear that the model being developed here is a strict
segregation model.

The principal reason for incorporating a demographic component in the
model is to arrive at a reasonable estimate of housing demand. Demand is
generated through the employment of an appropriate set of age-specific
rates. Age-specific birth and death rates, by color, were applied to the
population at one year intervals for a ten year period. This prodecure permitted the recording of year by year changes in the population resulting
from an excess of births over deaths. Since in-migration is also an important
aspect of population change in the Negro population, a migration factor
was included. Migration was not thought to contribute significantly to net
changes within the white population residing in ghetto space and was
omitted as a growth producing factor.

A major weakness of the above described procedure is that it allows a
piling up of population in census tracts. This condition is an outgrowth of
the absence of a mechanism which would generate data on white out-
movement at the tract level. The application of age-specific intracounty
mobility rates could be applied to the white population as a means of
generating a more accurate measure of the population actually in residence
in a census tract at any given point in time. The employment of a correction
factor of this type possesses the added advantage of enabling one to
compare the actual rate of white movement from tracts with the expected
rate; the expected rate would represent the number of movers generated
through the use of intracounty mobility rates.

The producer component The producer component is employed to create
housing vacancies which might allow a Negro household to establish

residence in a given block located in ghetto space. As few new housing units are constructed in older neighborhoods, residential space is essentially made available by white abandonment. It is generally agreed that there exists some level of tolerance beyond which whites will no longer continue to share a common residential space with Negroes. On the other hand, there is no general agreement on what whites perceive to be an acceptable residential mix. Nevertheless, a curve in which the leaving rate of whites is a function of the increase in the proportion of Negro households in a block may be described intuitively. Although it would be more logical to describe the leaving process as indeterminate rather than determinate, there is an absence of sufficient data upon which a stochastic process might be based. As the general leaving process becomes better understood, it may be described stochastically.

A shortcoming of the producer component based on assumed white leaving-rates is that it produces an excessive number of vacancies in those parts of the ghetto space which are somewhat remote from the main body of the ghetto. The social distance effect is not as pervasive over space as the vacancy-creating mechanism suggests. Some constraints should be placed upon the territorial limits of ghetto space that would be open to Negro occupancy during any given time interval, under conditions of strict segregation (in order to effect a more realistic description of the actual process). The problem by nature suggests that ghetto space should be made available incrementally. These increments, which are unlikely to fall within the sphere of Negro residential search behavior during the initial time period, should not be influenced by the vacancy creating mechanism. The creation of vacancies on the periphery of ghetto space results in a series of random residential assignments which leads to a more dispersed settlement pattern than that which actually occurs. This suggests that interaction along what is perceived as the ghetto edge during any single time period is far more pervasive in its impact upon the actual ghetto form than interaction about individual clusters, which might evolve under conditions of random residential assignment if the total ghetto is available for entry throughout a ten-year time interval.

Consumer component The consumer component of the model is a residential assignment mechanism. The housing demand of the Negro population during any one-year period is derived by means of determining the number of households formed during the interval. Household formation is deduced by applying an appropriate set of age-specific marriage rates to that segment of the population classified as single. In a situation where in-migration is responsible for a significant proportion of the increase in the local population, it is difficult to choose the most appropriate marriage rates to be employed. In this case the rates characterizing the North Central region were employed. It is suspected that the employment of such rates under conditions of heavy in-migration is likely to produce a larger than actual number of marriages. The existence of a sizeable number of single persons in a new environment is thought to have a depressing effect on the formation of new households.

Negro household assignments were made annually on the basis of the group's known propensity to purchase (or rent) housing in specific price categories. In order to generate household assignments, every block in ghetto space was assigned a probability of receiving a Negro home seeker. The highest probabilities were assigned to those blocks in which the median rent was in the $60–69 range, as blocks characterized by such rents housed the largest percentage of the Negro population in 1960. An assignment could not be made in a block wherein an appropriate number of vacancies did not exist.

The model oversimplifies the process of housing competition in ghetto space in not permitting whites and Negroes to compete for housing in a common market. Obviously, whites continue to seek housing in ghetto space until some critical threshold level is attained. Data on white entry into census tracts in ghetto space which had a minimum of forty per cent Negro occupancy by 1960, confirms that whites continue to seek housing in close physical proximity to Negroes until Negro occupancy attains a

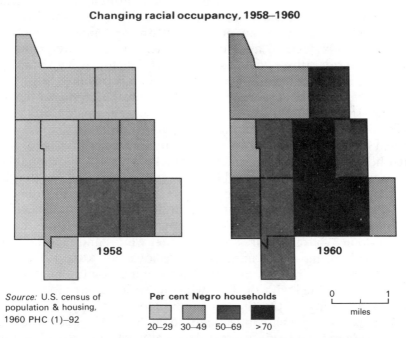

Changing racial occupancy, 1958–1960

1958   1960

Source: U.S. census of population & housing, 1960 PHC (1)–92

Per cent Negro households

20–29   30–49   50–69   >70

0 ⊢——⊣ 1
miles

Fig. 12.1 The changing intensity of Negro occupance within a segment of ghetto space over a two-year interval is graphically demonstrated. It is evident that the rate of change is essentially linked to the intensity of Negro occupance in contiguous units in the previous time period.

181

level of approximately 30 per cent. And even then about one-fifth of the housing seekers continue to be white, but falling off sharply thereafter. In the one census tract in ghetto space which exceeded 70 per cent Negro occupance in 1958, there was only a negligible number of white entrants; less than 2 per cent. Thus, the exodus of whites at the tract level takes place within a very short period of time, seemingly as a function of the Negro build up in contiguous space. This fact implies an initial saturation at the block level, proceeding outward from blocks with an already heavy Negro concentration (Fig. 12.1). Changes in Negro-white relations during the past few years may have altered the expected behavior in contiguous physical space.

The continual expansion of the ghetto is essentially dependent upon the collective behavior of individual residents of ghetto space, white and black. A strict segregation model, such as that developed here, is an attempt to add to an understanding of the operation of the residential market existing within ghetto space. Although knowledge of the behavior of individuals based on race aids in this understanding, it is by no means the only force operating to promote the expected pattern of residential behavior. The operation of exogenous forces are more unpredictable, but critically affect the ensuing pattern of racial residential development. In order to better understand the operation of the internal variables it is necessary to gain insights into the residential search behavior of prospective Negro home seekers as well as white propensity for residential desegregation. Morrill's ghetto residential assignment model was basically governed by the former consideration, whereas the model developed here emphasizes the latter as a means of shedding light on the dual problem.

Whereas Negroes move more often than whites, the lengths of the moves are usually shorter. A sample of Negro movers occupying units on the edge of the ghetto in 1950 exemplifies the pattern of intraurban movement attributed to Negro home seekers. Only four per cent of the Negro movers selected housing located more than ten blocks beyond the original ghetto neighborhood, 39 per cent selected housing within five blocks of the ghetto, while 41 per cent acquired housing within the same neighborhood (Fig. 12.2).[25] A similar pattern apparently continued to persist as is evidenced by the number of Negro households occupying units located on the fringe of the ghetto in 1960. It seems safe to say that whites and Negroes seldom compete for housing in a common market over an extended period of time. Wolf, in analyzing the concept of the tipping point in neighborhood change, was concerned with the following question as one of those critical to an understanding of the tipping point: Does the tipping mechanism refer to the point at which whites begin to enter?[26] The answer is yet unclear, but it is apparent that both factors are at work. The model developed here is based on the former question, and some of its weaknesses undoubtedly stem from an initial ignorance of the latter question. An

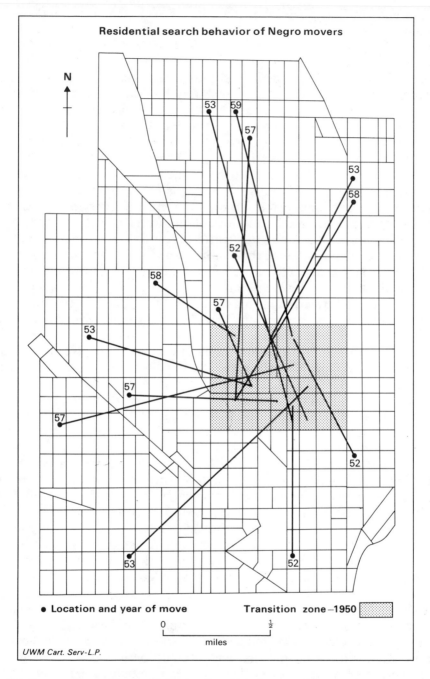

Fig. 12.2 Vectors are employed to show the direction, distance, and time of move of a sample of Negro movers who were residents of the ghetto edge in 1950. None of the sample movers chose to settle beyond the confines of ghetto space.

examination of the success of the model will demonstrate this more effectively.

Evaluation of the model

Once a model of the type described above has been assembled, it can be treated in one of two ways. It may simply be judged on the basis of the logic employed in its construction or it might be made operational as a means of actually testing its validity. The latter course of action has been chosen in this instance. The construct described here is recursive, and is designed to generate changes in the spatial pattern of Negro occupance over a ten-year period. An evaluation of the results of such a model is no mean task. The first problem is selecting the most appropriate method of evaluation. Opinion relative to this matter is mixed. Some researchers have employed various statistical techniques as a means of evaluating the goodness of fit between the simulated pattern and the actual pattern. Others have been content to evaluate the results empirically. Because of the nature of the data and the lack of precise information which can be employed to describe the actual pattern, an empirical analysis will be conducted. The lack of precise information in this case stems from the fact that the model which utilizes census data as input has been calibrated by employing the results of the 1960 census. The yearly changes in the spatial pattern of residential occupance occurring after the base year can only be crudely evaluated at this time. Only after the results of the 1970 census are available can the model output be subjected to a more rigorous analysis.

A second question concerns the appropriate spatial unit to be employed in the evaluation. Data have been assembled at the block level, for it is generally assumed that race as a factor in the promotion of residential mobility has its most pervasive impact at this level. Yet the prevalence of other forces located within what Wolpert identified as the action space of the individual must not be overlooked.[27] Any meaningful analysis on a block-by-block basis would strongly suggest the use of statistical rather than empirical treatment. Even then, the results of statistical tests applied to the aggregation of blocks constituting ghetto space could prove misleading. In order to eliminate a modicum of the chaos which might arise in this type of analysis, a subaggregation of blocks has been chosen for investigation. These subaggregations may be considered housing market areas.

Only two of the housing market areas in ghetto space have been chosen for intensive observation. One of these is situated on the western edge of the ghetto, and the other is situated several blocks to the north of the original Negro core. Considering the characteristics of these areas at the beginning of the period, they may be described as a declining blue collar housing area and a stable housing area of skilled and semi-skilled workers, respectively. These two prospective appendages of the ghetto are identified, respectively, as the West Central housing market area and the Keefe-Capitol-Congress housing market area. These two housing market areas contained approximately 7,500 housing units in 1960, a number sufficient to satisfy approximately one-half of the anticipated Negro housing demand during the following ten years. The quality of housing in the two market areas differs significantly, with the quality in the West Central market being generally lower than that which Negroes had previously inherited on the northern margins of the ghetto. Thus, given a choice of housing available in close proximity to the existing ghetto boundaries, the Keefe-Capitol-Congress market area, with its more attractive housing, should prove to be the major target area for Negro occupance during the ensuing ten-year period.

The Keefe-Capitol-Congress area is in many ways similar in housing quality and population characteristics to the Baxter area of Detroit, an area whose pattern of racial change was recently described by Wolf.[28] The Keefe-Capitol-Congress area includes the only sizable volume of single family detached structures in close proximity to the ghetto.

In 1960 the total number of Negro households situated in these two housing market areas numbered less than 150, with the great majority of these located in blocks contiguous to the ghetto. The northern and western margins of the market areas were beyond the distance which most Negro movers travel to seek housing accommodations. This being the case, one would normally expect a block by block filling in, proceeding from areas heavily built up with Negro households to those without Negro households in the initial time period. As a means of comparing the actual process of racial change with the results generated by the simulation model, it was necessary to devise a sampling frame. The question of the type of sample to be employed had to be confronted. Because of the nature of the question to which answers are being sought, it was finally decided that two different sampling techniques would be employed. As a means of gaining insights into the general pattern of household mobility in the two market areas, a stratified random sample stratified by block was employed. In order to reveal more clearly the changes in the pattern of racial occupance, a quadrat or cluster sample was also introduced. The latter technique allowed observation of all changes taking place within a micro-housing environment through time.

The results of the stratified random sample demonstrate that the West-Central housing market area is far less stable than its northern counterpart. Samples drawn from the two census tracts which largely comprise the West-Central market showed that 60 per cent of the 1960 residents in the tract nearest the ghetto, and 52 per cent of the residents of the tract more distant from the ghetto, were no longer residents of this housing market area by 1965. Likewise, Negro householders served as the basic replacement population in the eastern half of the housing market area, which in 1965 possessed a vacancy rate of 20 per cent. The western segment of this market, although exhibiting signs of instability, was not yet receiving large numbers of Negro householders. Negroes at this date constituted fewer than 10 per cent of the housing market entrants. The fact that five years had elapsed and Negro entrance into the western segment of the market was minimal, strongly supports the contention that Negroes do not search for housing far beyond the margins of already heavily built up Negro areas. The vacancy rate in the western segment of this housing market area was considerably less than that which characterized the east.

In the Keefe-Capitol-Congress housing market, residential mobility was less than half that which characterized the West-Central market. In the northern segment of this market only 20 per cent of the original residents had abandoned the area by 1965. The higher level of stability in this housing market was no doubt influenced by its greater physical attractiveness, its higher incidence of owner occupancy and the prevalence of older families. The latter factor is only a temporary contributing factor which will have the opposite impact on stability at a later time. As was true in the eastern half of the West-Central housing area, Negro families represented the chief replacement households in the southern half of the Keefe-Capitol-Congress area. Only about one-third of the replacement households in the northern segment of the market were Negro. The peripheral segment of each of these housing market areas received a smaller number of Negro households during the five-year interval than did those segments of the market contiguous to the ghetto.

A number of blocks were selected at random within the two housing areas in which to observe the pattern of residential mobility of the universe of occupants located within those blocks. The city directory was employed as the basic source of information on the moves of individual occupants of the sample blocks on a year by year basis. It is often possible to determine the rate of entering households on the basis of name, place of previous residence, and occupation data, all of which can be derived from the city directory. Although this technique is not without its shortcomings, it does enable one to arrive at crude index of racial change within a local housing environment.

Twenty-one sample blocks, or in this case quadrats, as the block configuration employed here is the census block rather than the linear block, were selected for intensive investigation (Fig. 12.3). Eleven of these quadrats are located in the Keefe-Capitol-Congress housing market area, and the remaining ten are in the West-Central housing market area. The sample blocks in the West-Central area are characterized by rental levels which were prevalent in areas already heavily Negro in 1960. The median rental levels of the sample blocks in the northern market were generally higher than those occupied by the Negro population in the initial year. Thus, the probability of a Negro household receiving an assignment in the latter market area is less than that of receiving such an assignment in the former area.

A sequential running of the model over a five-year period allowed comparison of the simulated pattern of Negro entry in the sample blocks with the observed actual pattern. In all but one of the sample blocks in the Keefe-Capitol-Congress area, the model underpredicted the number of entrants. The basic flaw leading to underprediction in these blocks is the lack of an owner-occupancy mechanism in the model. These are blocks in which most homes are owner occupied structures. This results in high median rental values being assigned them, thereby reducing the probability of a Negro occupant receiving an assignment. In actuality, this area is one in which Negro home purchases have been rather substantial, as Negroes constituted the principal entrants by 1965. A combination of distance and high rents led to a nearly congruent relationship between the actual and simulated pattern in the northernmost blocks in the housing market area.

In the West-Central housing market area the model tended to underpredict in those blocks nearest the ghetto edge and to overpredict in those blocks farther removed. In only three of the sample blocks was there any real similarity between the actual and simulated pattern of Negro entries. Overprediction near the margins of the ghetto suggests that the vacancy creating mechanism in the model requires modification as a means of improving its sensitivity to the presence of small numbers of Negro households within blocks. This lack of sensitivity results in too little concentration along the ghetto edge and too much dispersion in the outer areas of ghetto space, especially when blocks in the outer areas possess similar rental characteristics to those in the ghetto. This weakness was apparent in the overall simulation pattern characterizing ghetto space, as well as in individual housing market areas (Figs 12.4 and 5).

A total view of the ghetto configuration is described in Fig. 12.4. Figure 12.5 reveals the simulated state of the ghetto in 1968. The overall weakness of the model can best be detected by viewing the excessive dispersion of the Negro population along the western edge of ghetto space and the current under concentration along the northern margin of the ghetto (Fig. 12.5). Several nonresidential blocks within the interior of the ghetto are shown on these maps, without shading. Maps of the type represented by Figs 12.4 and 5 can be produced for each year, over the ten-year period, from computer output generated by the model.

In evaluating the model it is apparent that the model's performance in the Keefe-Capitol-Congress housing market surpassed its performance in the West-Central market. This fact partially reflects the lack of constraints other than housing costs, to access to all housing in ghetto space. The sequential opening of segments of ghetto space within a time frame should result in a general improvement in the level of model performance. This further indicates that the ghetto resident is engaged in a series of short distance moves, seldom exceeding a ten-block distance and most fre-

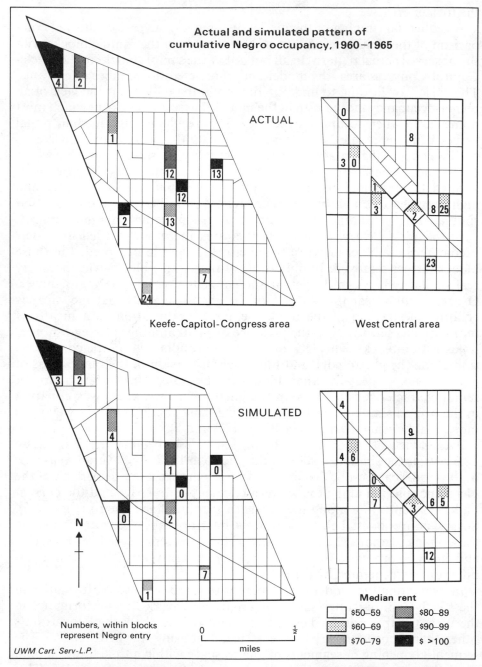

Fig. 12.3 The actual and simulated number of Negro movers entering two ghetto fringe housing market areas. Visual variations in the goodness of fit can be observed within the set of sample blocks.

188

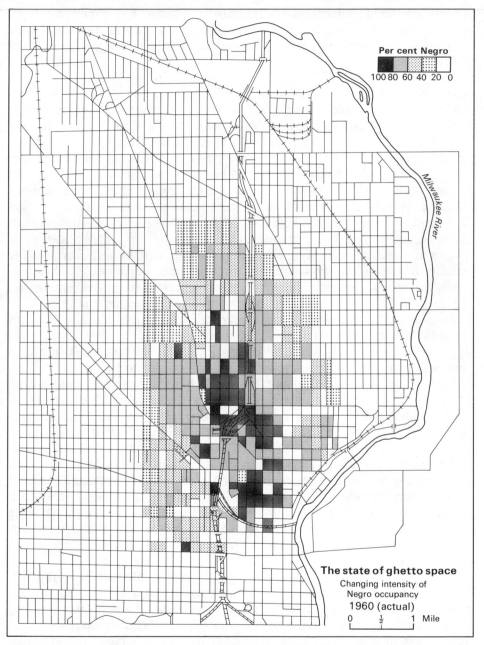

Per cent Negro

100 80 60 40 20 0

Milwaukee River

The state of ghetto space

Changing intensity of
Negro occupancy

1960 (actual)

0   ½   1 Mile

Fig. 12.4 The actual intensity of Negro occupancy within the context of ghetto space, as of 1960. The non-shaded blocks within the interior of the ghetto represent non-residential blocks, or blocks with a minimal number of housing units.

quently confined to distances of less than six blocks. This practice permits whites to continue to compete for housing only a short distance from the margin of the ghetto, as the slow process of filling-in occurs along the ghetto edge.

The validity of the conceptual model

The previous discussion which dealt with the behavior of whites and non-whites in a common housing market was an attempt to demonstrate the soundness of the use of the previously specified components as input in a ghetto developer model. As the behavior of the individual decision maker operating within a common market is based on a host of factors, it is an inconceivable task to disaggregate all factors impinging on one's decision to move. Nevertheless, the role of the racial composition of the population in housing sub-markets has been employed as the principal factor generating a reduction of white demand and a corresponding intensification of Negro demand in such areas. The question which arises here concerns the validity of the assumptions employed as the basis for model calibration. Since the model described here is a strict segregation model, employing the terminology of Thompson, it may be considered by many to be a distortion of the real-world process of residential household allocation.[29] Admittedly, it is an oversimplification of the process, but it generally appears to provide a closer approximation of racial residential patterns than an open system operating without social constraints.

Unless there is a radical departure in the behavior of individual householders, both white and black, as well as the innumerable exogenous forces whose impact is heavily felt in influencing the racial makeup of residential space, the strict segregation model will be effective in simulating the pattern of ghetto developments for some time to come. Ghetto maintenance is strongly rooted in the nation's institutional mores. Whereas some question the wisdom of maintaining the ghetto intact, especially after a series of very hot summers, it appears that many professionals and a much larger segment of the lay population feel either that the task of breaking it up is an impossible one or that its maintenance is desirable. The recent flurry of open occupancy laws, at both the state and national level, do not alter this fact.

It appears that many social scientists, regardless of their basic motivations, currently support what Downs describes as a ghetto enrichment strategy.[30] Piven and Cloward, writing recently, strongly suggest that efforts at integration have worked against the Negro's acquisition of adequate housing.[31] This same type of reasoning was recently but somewhat more subtly stated by Spengler, who tends to emphasize the role of a satisfactory social environment.[32] Keller, a planner and strong advocate of the promotion of homogeneous communities, denied that one must favor complete segregation, but admitted that one should use caution in

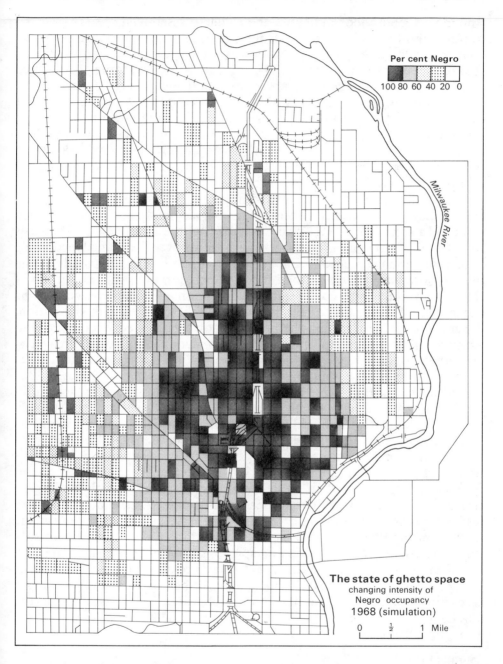

Fig. 12.5 The simulated pattern of Negro residential expansion through an eight-year period can be observed above. The simulation is subject to maximum error along the eastern and western edges of the simulated zones of intensive Negro occupance.

mixing neighborhoods in light of the evidence assembled.[33]

Thus, those in the ghetto who strongly advocate the development of black power and likewise opt for an enrichment strategy, and who consequently tend to be generally opposed to dispersion, seem to have strong professional backing. Downs, unlike Piven and Cloward, in evaluating the enrichment strategy, expressed uncertainty about its potential for success. Yet Grier has openly stated that public policy in the United States should be aimed at allowing the Negro to enter the mainstream of American life and not to solidify the structure of the ghetto.[34] After reviewing the evidence there appears to be strong support for the conceptual validity of something approaching a strict segregation model.

Depending upon the direction and impact of public policy on individual residential location choices, an alternative model might be developed. Such a model might generate specific levels of ghetto escapement on the basis of changing patterns of behavior, growing out of modified economic policies and social relations. But even if all future housing demands on the part of a rapidly growing urban black population are satisfied outside of the ghetto, the ghetto configuration will continue to generate conditions which may be thought to be inimical to the best interests of the nation. There is little question that the phenomenon treated here is complex and transcends the more simplistic problem of understanding housing markets. The ghetto is not simply a spatial configuration, but a social and ideological configuration that has spatial expression.

Models of the type described here might be employed with some modifications to aid in the planning process, if the ghetto enrichment strategy is chosen. Similarly, with additional modifications, such models might be employed as an aid in predicting the location and intensity of certain types of economic and social problems. If one opts for a strategy of dispersal, the strict segregation model will no longer represent a conceptually valid construct. An open system model might be developed which could generally be described as a 'ghetto destroyer' model. At the moment there exists no body of information which might serve as a foundation for the development of a model of this type. Furthermore, such a model could only be employed to generate residential spatial patterns which do not currently exist on any meaningful scale. Yet, these currently non-existent patterns could become a reality by altering human behavior as a result of major decisions emanating from both the public and private sectors of the economy.

Summary and conclusions

An attempt has been made here to describe the basic behavior of individuals which gives rise to residential ghettos in northern metropolitan systems. After gaining limited insights into the behavioral dimension, a model was developed using these basic insights as input. The model, described as a ghetto-developer model, was employed to predict the future state of the ghetto. The state of the ghetto reflects the intensity of the spatial concentration of the Negro population within a contiguous area. Although models of this type can never be expected to duplicate the existing pattern, they can replicate in a general way the real-world process, which leads to the development of spatial patterns that bear varying degrees of similarity to the actual pattern. Whereas models of this type have some predictive value, the real merit derived from them is the gaining of additional understanding of the processes one is attempting to simulate.

The ghetto-developer model was run using data from Milwaukee, Wisconsin. The results provided evidence of deficiency in some of the basic assumptions incorporated in the model, both in terms of the aggregate simulated ghetto spatial pattern, as well as the resulting pattern occurring within individual housing market areas. The employment of the model to generate ghetto expansion in a series of urban systems should permit one to ascertain if a general set of assumptions might be employed to describe fairly accurately the process of ghetto formation.

Models of the type described above are attempts to replicate an actual ongoing process. The initiation of strategies designed to alter the existing process would tend to invalidate the model. At the same time, models may be developed based on the behavior necessary to modify the existing residential spatial pattern. Models of this type could very well serve as planning models, providing that in this case there is a national opting for an alternative strategy. The strict segregation model currently generates a spatial pattern that approaches the actual pattern, even though, in reality, ghetto escapements occur. But the extent of such occurrences are not sufficiently significant to alter the spatial configuration of the ghetto.

Notes and References

1. A. Meier and E. M. Rudwick, *From Plantation to Ghetto*, New York: Hill and Wang, 1966, pp. 191–2.
2. R. L. Rice, 'Residential segregation by law', *The Journal of Southern History*, **34**, (1968), 194–9.
3. R. L. Morrill, 'The Negro ghetto: problems and alternatives', *Geogrl. Rev.*, **55**, (1965), 339–61.
4. A. Beauchamp, 'Processual indices of segregation: some preliminary comments', *Behavioral Science*, **11**, (1966), 190–2.
5. Morrill, *op. cit.*, 348, fn. 3; R. L. Morrill, *Migration and the Spread and Growth of Urban Settlement*, Lund (Sweden): Gleerup, 1965, p. 186.
6. G. Carlsson, 'Decline of Fertility: innovation or adjustment process', *Population Studies*, **20**, (Nov, 1966), 149–50.

7. Carlsson, *op. cit.*, 150, fn. 6.
8. W. Zelinsky, *A Prologue to Population Geography*, New York: Prentice-Hall, 1965, 45–6.
9. R. L. Morrill, 'Waves of spatial diffusion', *Journal of Regional Science*, **8**, (Summer 1968), 2.
10. See H. Sharp and L. F. Schnore, 'The changing color composition of metropolitan areas', *Land Economics*, **38**, (1962), 169–85.
11. Special Census of Cleveland, Ohio, April, 1965, *Current Population Reports*, Series p-28, no. 1390 (1965).
12. J. T. Davis, 'Middle class housing in the central city', *Economic Geography*, **41**, (1965), 238–51.
13. For a methodological discussion of this point see K. E. Taeuber and A. F. Taeuber, *Negroes in Cities*, Chicago: Aldine Publishing Co., 1965, pp. 78–95.
14. D. Stea, 'Space, territory and human movements', *Landscape*, **15**, (1965), 13.
15. M. M. Webber, 'Culture, territoriality and the elastic mile', *Regional Science Association Papers*, **13**, (1964), 61–3.
16. G. C. Henderson, 'Negroes into Americans: a dialectical development', *Journal of Human Relations*, **14**, (1966), 537.
17. Stea, *op. cit.*, 13, fn. 14.
18. E. Grier and G. C. Grier, 'Equality and beyond: housing segregation in the great society', *Daedalus*, **95** (1966), 82.
19. H. Hoyt, *The Structure and Growth of Residential Neighborhoods in American Cities*, Washington, DC: Government Printing Office, 1939, pp. 62 and 71.
20. M. J. Bailey, 'Effects of race and other demographic factors on the values of single-family homes', *Land Economics*, **42**, (1966), 214–18.
21. G. C. Grier, 'The Negro ghettos and Federal housing policy', *Law and Contemporary Problems* (Summer 1967), 555.
22. R. E. Pahl, 'Sociological models in Geography', in R. J. Chorley and P. Haggett, eds., *Models in Geography*, London: Methuen, 1967, p. 239.
23. Chorley and Haggett, *op. cit.*, p. 25, fn. 22.
24. Ghetto space represents the area presently identified as the ghetto as well as that expanse of contiguous territory thought to be sufficiently adequate to house the net increase of Negro households over a ten year period.
25. The zone of transition shown on Fig. 12.2 is areally coincidental with what has been described above as the same neighborhood.
26. E. P. Wolf, 'The tipping point in racially changing neighborhoods', *Journal of American Institute of Planners*, **29**, (1963), 219.
27. J. Wolpert, 'Behavioral aspects of the decision to migrate', *Regional Science Association Papers*, **15**, (1965), 163.
28. E. P. Wolf, 'The Baxter area: a new trend in neighborhood changes?' *Phylon*, **26**, (1965), 347–8.
29. W. R. Thompson, *A Preface to Urban Economics*, Baltimore: Johns Hopkins Press, 1965, 309–13.
30. A. Downs, 'The future of American ghettos', *Daedalus*, **97**, (1968), 1346–7.

31. F. F. Piven and R. Cloward, 'The case against urban desegregation', *Social Work*, **12**, (1967), 12.

32. J. J. Spengler, 'Population pressure, housing habitat', *Law and Contemporary Problems*, **32**, (1967), 172.

33. S. Keller, 'Social class in physical planning', *International Social Science Journal*, **18**, (1966), 506–7. .

34. Grier, *op. cit.*, 560, fn. 21.

B. J. L. Berry

13 Monitoring trends, forecasting change and evaluating goal achievements: The ghetto v. desegregation issue in Chicago as a case study*

Introduction

I am inclined to agree with Yehezkel Dror (1968) who introduced his reevaluation of public policy-making by saying:

> much of the practical sterility . . . of the contemporary 'modern sciences of society' . . . results from mistaken notions about whether 'factual inquiry' should be, or even can be, divorced from social reality and social problems, from the construction of abstract theories, and from introspective contemplation. Such notions lead to an unsophisticated disregard of the interdependence of 'facts', 'values', and 'action'.

It has, I think, been quite comfortable for scientists to perpetuate the myth of science – that before the emergence of science there were only two domains of decision in organized society, individual choice and authority, but that science introduced into human affairs the third and more general domain of objective reality.

Individual choice was exercised in such matters as food, clothing, habitation, recreation, etc., within the limits of social choice and the availability of supplies. Authority applied to most other facets of life, with the nature and source of sanctions depending on the level of authority in a hierarchy determined by custom, law and religion. But, the myth continues, with the emergence of science, the human mind became aware of 'nature' as an objective reality amenable to human understanding by observation and experiment, and verification of observations and inferences by others. Science, therefore, the myth concludes, introduced into human affairs a

* Colston Papers No. 22, Regional Forecasting Ed. M. Chisholm, A. E. Frey and P. Haggett London, Butterworths 1971.

third domain of objective reality which cannot be changed by authority, however high its status, or by personal choice or preference.

Many geographers, like their peers in other fields, have used this myth as a means of retreating to the indolence of their cozy armchairs in warm offices hidden away in unobtrusive ivory towers. Others, certain of the objectivity of their scientific knowledge and asserting the universality of their concepts, have attempted to move beyond the university into the public arena, if for no other reason than because it is the greatest source of research funds. The questions asked of them have always been the same: What will happen if policy A is instituted, and what if policy B (or what *did* happen because C *was* done)? What are (were) the costs and benefits? How far will (did) they achieve the goals? Will there be (were there) undesirable consequences requiring additional remedial actions?

The cognitive dissonance involved in responding to these questions and still perpetuating the scientific myth was immense. Such dissonance can only be tolerated up to some threshold, however, a threshold that was exceeded some time ago for anyone with intellectual honesty and social sensitivity.

We face, along with our sister disciplines, a real crisis of social science as a result. Enough has been learned to know how complex social systems are and to be scared of simplistic concepts and intervention, because of the multiplex ways in which actions can breed negative reactions. Regrettably, however, we know very few ways to intervene subtly when thinking in systemic terms.

Ideally in our urban analysis we should be able to identify and measure the impact of urban programmes and policies, to develop indicators that will permit us to learn how well the instruments of planned intervention are achieving goals, and to monitor programmes during their operation by providing an intelligence system both sensitive to ongoing change and potentially useful in providing 'alerting' signals that warn of new problems. Of course, this kind of policy-oriented research can only be effective when policies are articulated theoretically and thereby become researchable. This is perhaps the key factor in bringing social research to bear on the formulation and assessment of action programmes. For geography, it resolves to being able to answer such questions as: What is the most probable future map? What is the map likely to be as a result of A, B or C? And, to introduce the normative element: What is the most desirable future map?

The prime question that emerges in this process is the identification, assessment and articulation of the assumptions made when it is asserted that programmes will realize policy objectives. Some of the assumptions used today may be consistent with existing bodies of well-tried social theory. More frequently, the sets of assumptions underlying suggested solutions to problems are simply untested premises, and they invite clarification, investigation and analysis. But such a process requires in turn:

1. Continuing reexamination and specification of goals, and their translation into a hierarchy of objectives and achievable criteria.
2. Analysis and clarification of the array of instruments that are intended to realize the stated objectives, and the search for new instruments.

Identification and specification of the causal links between instruments and goals, either by further theoretical work or by controlled experiment, is the basis for the generation of:

1. Measures of the impact of instruments on the urban environment.
2. Measures of the performance of the instruments in terms of goal achievement.
3. Translation of the measures into sensitive social indicators and urban programme monitors.

But these in themselves represent goals for 'relevant' social science, and so in what follows the first halting steps in developing such a scheme in the arena of anti-discrimination policy in housing in Chicago are illustrated, using such limited bases as it is now possible to assemble in a policy-oriented framework. No pretence is made that what is described is very satisfactory, but it is a first step – in the spirit of that perceptive soul who said about women 'They aren't much, but they're the best other sex we have'.

Racial segregation in Chicago

The context is one of racial segregation in Chicago's housing market, forced on the Negro and maintained by institutional means. Chicago's Negro population did not always live in segregated residential neighbourhoods. In 1898, only a quarter of the city's 30,000 Negroes resided in areas that were more than 50 per cent Negro, and over 30 per cent lived in areas that were at least 95 per cent white (Cressy, 1930). As late as 1910, Negroes were less highly segregated from native whites than were Italian immigrants (Lieberson, 1960).

It was not until the early twentieth century that segregation was forced on the Negro in Chicago. This increased residential separation of the city's black and white populations accompanied mass movement of Negroes from the southern states to the north during World War I. At this time, blacks became more visibly evident in the city and began to offer competition in the job market to blue-collar whites. In 1910, Chicago's black population had been 44,000, whereas by 1920 it had risen to 110,000. Most of the increase in black residents occurred in eighteen months in 1917–18, when an estimated 50,000 Negroes arrived in Chicago (Chicago Commission on Race Relations, 1968).

Just as these Negroes had left the south in search of increased opportunity and in the face of worsening race relations in that region – recall that the Ku Klux Klan had been re-established in 1915 – so, arriving in Chicago, they were forced to live in increasingly segregated neighbourhoods as racial fears in the white population increased. Many methods were used to achieve this result: violence, activities of such organizations as the Hyde Park Improvement Protective Club (which 'induced' real-estate agents to develop dual listings to confine Negroes to designated Negro 'Districts', and even proposed that the city enact a residential segregation ordinance), and by the general acquiescence or active support of the majority of the white community (Spear, 1967). And to cement the racial fears of Chicago's white community, in 1919 and 1920 the city's *Property Owners' Journal* impressed on them the idea that Negroes destroy property values (Commission on Race Relations, 21–2).

As a result, after World War I Chicago's growing Negro population became progressively more highly segregated, and the housing market lapsed into duality. White hostility, boycotts and violence, and the institutionalization of white attitudes in the practices of the real-estate industry effectively limited the housing choice of Negroes and forced the growing black population to live in a limited 'Black Belt'. In response, the Negro community turned inward and created a 'Black Metropolis' (Drake and Cayton, 1962). In 1920, 11·3 per cent of Chicago's Negro population lived in tracts with less than 10 per cent of their population black. By 1950 only 2·8 per cent and 1960 1·5 per cent of the city's Negroes were in this position. Conversely, in 1920 none of Chicago's Negroes lived in tracts that were more than 90 per cent Negro; in 1950 66·9 per cent did so (De Visé, 1967). Of the eleven metropolitan areas in the United States with Negro communities over 200,000, Chicago in 1960 consequently manifested the greatest degree of racial segregation (Clark, 1965; Taeuber and Taeuber, 1965).

In the intervening years, the city's Negro population grew, and along with it the physical limits of the ghetto, but the dual housing markets created by the institutional barriers introduced in the early twentieth century within the real-estate industry only permitted the Negro housing supply to expand by outright transfer of property from the white to the Negro market. This took place geographically on a block-by-block basis through a process of 'invasion' and 'succession' on the margins of the ghetto.

Figure 13.1 shows the sequence of expansion. Table 13.1 portrays the result in 1960, but understates the segregation of the Negro in using the Census 'nonwhite' category, because other nonwhites tend to have greater flexibility than Negroes in their housing choice.

Even with that, only 3 per cent of the city's white population, but 93 per cent of the nonwhite population, lived in areas 50 per cent or more black in 1960. If the scale were relaxed to areas only 25 per cent or more black,

199

Table 13.1 Racial intermixture in Chicago, 1960

Per cent of census tract population non-white	Per cent of the white population	Per cent of the nonwhite population
Under 1·0	85·8	0·6
1 – 9·9	6·8	0·9
10 – 29·9	3·9	3·2
30 – 49·9	1·0	2·3
50 – 74·9	1·5	8·6
75 – 89·9	1·0	19·1
90 – 97·4	0·4	27·7
97·5–100·0	0·1	37·9
	100·0	100·0

the figures would be 5 per cent of the white population and 97 per cent of the nonwhite population, thus emphasizing the sharpness of separation of black from white in the city.

The integration goal

In its momentous 1948 decision (*Shelley v. Kramer*), the United States Supreme Court ruled that restrictive covenants used in the real-estate industry to discriminate on the basis of race were unconstitutional. Later Federal legislation has declared that integration is a principal national goal, to be achieved with all speed in all aspects of life, thus reversing previous Federal housing policy, as revealed for example in the 1947 Federal Housing Administration *Underwriting Manual* (Par. 1354(1)), which said in its guidelines

> Protective covenants are essential to the sound development of proposed residential areas since they regulate the use of the land and provide a basis for the development of harmonious, attractive neighbourhoods suitable and desirable to the user groups forming the potential market.

In such guidelines, the institutionalized basis of segregation in expanding suburban communities supported by FHA financing is clear.

But in spite of the reversal of policy, the pace of change has been infinitesimal. As a consequence, during the summer of 1966, Chicago's racial problems exploded in headlines across the country. The Rev. Dr Martin Luther King, Jr of the Southern Christian Leadership Conference, along with the Chicago Freedom Movement, initiated a series of marches and demonstrations in and around Chicago, to try to alter the rate of change. At a rally held in Soldier Field, Dr King said, 'For our primary target we have chosen housing. As of 10 July we shall cease to be accomplices to a housing system of discrimination, segregation and degradation. We shall begin to act as if Chicago were an open city.' Rioting broke out on the west side in July and 3,000 National Guardsmen were called out to restore order. Violence and hostility characterized the marches in various areas throughout the summer, and the demonstrations culminated in a series of historic meetings between the leadership of business, labour, government, civil rights, housing, industry and religious groups.

Each of the groups present at these meetings made specific commitments to aid in creating a single, nondiscriminatory housing market throughout the Chicago metropolitan area. A *Leadership Council for Metropolitan Open Communities* was designated, formally, on 6 December 1966, in a Chicago 'Summit Agreement', as the organization to carry this mandate. Financing was obtained from the Department of Housing and Urban Development (HUD) to support the work of the Leadership Council, and the Centre for Urban Studies of the University of Chicago was asked by HUD to monitor and evaluate this work from its inception in 1968 to see if they were achieving their stated aim of eliminating the dual housing market, and therefore segregation. What follows is a synopsis of this evaluation work, which we are in process of reporting in more detail elsewhere (Berry, Smith *et al.*, 1969).

Operationalizing the goal

The first problem was to operationalize the general goal of 'integration' as it applies to housing. Clearly, it cannot simply mean mixture of black and white in all areas proportional to the national or citywide population ratios insofar as a housing policy is concerned, because abilities to pay, family structures, and therefore housing demands differ, as does the mixture of housing available in each local area.   To be sure, the different income distributions of black and white are also in large measure the product of segregation, but to the extent that this results from segregated education or discriminatory practices in the job market that can only be overcome by longer term strategies, they cannot be tackled directly, in the short run, by a housing policy. Thus it does not seem unreasonable to think of finding an operational expression for the goal of integrating housing that takes as given whatever the income distributions of black and white happen to be at any point in time, as well as the spatial distribution of the available housing supply, recognizing that over a span of years both of these may change – the former through educational and job market policies, and the latter through new home building and urban renewal. An added advantage of using this as a point of departure is that it enables a determination to be made of the extent to which the present residential separation of black and white is a product of differences in the ability to pay for housing, and the extent to which it reflects differences in access to housing supplies holding income differences constant, given that there are clear unmet pressures for home ownership among black Americans.

201

A simple procedure was proposed by Zelder (1968). In this procedure, called one of *income-standardization*, the distribution of households by income class (e.g. $5,000–$5,999, $6,000–$6,999, etc.) within each census tract regardless of race is taken as given. Likewise, for the metropolitan area as a whole, the proportion of blacks and whites in each of these income classes is taken as given. The intermixture potential of a tract is computed by assuming that in a colour-blind housing market the proportional black–white split of families in any income category in any census tract is the same as the proportional split of all families in that category in the entire metropolitan area.

Symbolically, if there are m census tracts and n income categories, and h_{ij} represents the number of families of tract i in income category j, the tractwise distribution of families by income can be arrayed in a matrix as follows:

$$
\begin{array}{cccccc}
h_{11} & h_{12} & h_{13} & . \quad . \quad . & h_{1n} & \Sigma_n h_{1n} = H_{1.} \\
h_{21} & h_{22} & h_{23} & . \quad . \quad . & h^2{}_n & \\
. & & & & . & \\
. & & & & . & \\
. & & & & . & \\
h_{m1} & h_{m2} & h_{m3} & . \quad . \quad . & h_{mn} & \\
\Sigma_m h_{m1} = H_{.1} & & & & &
\end{array}
$$

A row sum indicates the number of families in a tract (e.g. $\Sigma_n h_{1n} = H_{1.}$ in tract 1) whereas a column sum indicates the total number of families in an income category (e.g. $\Sigma_m h_{m1} = H_{.1}$ in category 1). The latter, for the metropolitan area, is composed of white and black parts ($H_{.1} = W_{.1} + B_{.1}$) and therefore the mix coefficient $\mu_1 = B_{.1}/H_{.1}$ is the metropolitan-wide proportion of families in income category 1 who are black. Thence $\mu_1 h_{11}$ is the expected number of black families of income category 1 in tract 1, $\mu_2 h_{12}$ of category 2 in tract 1, etc. Therefore $\Sigma_n \mu_n h_{1n} = \hat{B}_{1.}$ is the expected number of black families in tract 1, and $100\hat{B}_{1.}/H_{1.}$ is the expected black percentage, $\hat{P}_{1.}$. The difference between the actual black percentage $P_{1.}$ and the expected $\hat{P}_{1.}$ is a measure of the effects of segregation in the housing market.

Figure 13.2 shows the distribution of the black population in metropolitan Chicago as it might be expected on the basis of income standardization, using 1960 census data. The greatest black concentrations are only 27 per cent of any tract population, and the least are around 10 per cent. Figure 13.3 portrays the changes required in the 1960 distribution of the black population to achieve income-standardized equality. Ghetto concentrations would have to be reduced by 60 to 80 per cent, and the black population of the suburban areas would have to be increased to 10 per cent of the total population. This fact should serve to refute the argument that income differences were responsible for the present pattern of ghettoization. The reasons, instead, reside in some interacting mixture of prejudicial discrimination against blacks by home sellers and their agents, and the preference in most ethnic groups for residential exclusivity.

Other formulations of the goal

Of course, a variety of changes in the detailed criteria for measuring intermixture potentials will result in various expressions of the goal. For example, one similar procedure involves *expenditure-standardization*. Households are arrayed in a matrix with the m tracts as rows and with k columns representing owner-occupied housing units by price-range and renter-occupied units by rental-range. Thus $H_{.1}$ is the number of families in the metropolitan area in a particular tenure and valuation category, $B_{.1}$ the number of such families who are black, and $\alpha_1 = B_{.1}/H_{.1}$ the proportion black. $H_{1.}$ is, as before, the number of families in tract 1. Similarly, the expected numbers of black residents may be calculated $[\Sigma_n \alpha_n h_{1n} = \hat{B}_{1.}]$, the intermixture potentials obtained $[100\hat{B}_{1.}/H_{1.} = \hat{P}_{1.}]$, the results mapped, and the required equalizing redistributions revealed.

Figure 13.4 shows the resulting expenditure-standardized distribution of the black population, and is again the map of the *desirable* spatial pattern achieving the goal. The degree of tractwise concentration is approximately the same as with the income-standardized results, but the spatial pattern is somewhat different because of the greater proportion of the region's rental property in the central city and the greater current concentration of blacks in rented rather than owner-occupied units. Again (Fig. 13.5), the redistribution of the black population to achieve expenditure-standardization is of the same order of magnitude as that for income-standardization.

An alternative future: present trends continue

To determine whether the activities of the Leadership Council were making a difference – such is the essence of evaluation – we had to develop a sensitive reading of the ongoing processes of ghetto expansion before 1968, so that we could simulate what would have been likely to happen in 1968, 1969 and thereafter in the absence of the Council's work. Formal evaluation of success in changing the system could then be made in terms of movement away from the 'present trend' future towards the integration goal, as operationalized earlier.

We were initially confounded by scarcity of data, however. The last complete census which included racial data was in 1960. This is hopelessly outdated, since we are now on the eve of the 1970 census. Moreover, the last census before 1960 was conducted in 1950, providing us with data on only two points in time a decade apart, with the first 20 years in the past. The inadequacy of these data needs little discussion. The need for more recent reliable data on racial mix was inescapable.

Use of racial headcounts in the schools

One annual source worthy of exploitation was found to be the Fall-semester racial headcount in the public elementary schools of the City of Chicago (Berry and Sööt, 1969). Although these data were available on an individual school basis only for the central city, this did not represent a serious handicap in that approximately 90 per cent of the blacks in the Chicago Consolidated Area live in Chicago, and the data do provide an annually available statistical series.

In 1968, the map showing percentage of public elementary school enrolment black (Fig. 13.6) picked out the outlines of the ghetto. Declining black percentages with increasing distance from the core of the ghetto mirror the extent of 'penetration', and racial 'succession' in that year. Equally, a map showing percentage changes in racial headcounts in the period 1963–68 (Fig. 13.7) picks out the wavelike character of ghetto spread. The Chicago Urban League and the courts have used such data, together with spot checks in sample city blocks, to estimate the spread of the ghetto each year since 1960 (Fig. 13.8). The question we asked was whether the relationship presumed by such uses could be quantified, and then built into a forecasting process that embodied the four stages said by the Duncans (1957) together to comprise a complete wavelike cycle of succession:

1. *'Penetration'* – the stage of initial entry of Negroes.
2. *'Invasion'* – takes place when substantial numbers of Negroes move in.
3. *'Consolidation'* – continued increase in numbers and the proportion of Negroes.
4. *'Piling up'* – increasing numbers after virtually complete Negro occupancy has been achieved.

We were not sure that the relationship between the percentage of a community's population that was black and the percentage of black children in the public elementary schools was at all simple, however, because of differences in the population pyramids in white and black areas and the high percentage of whites attending private schools, particularly on the leading edge of the black ghetto.

Therefore we turned to data available in the 1960 census and performed a series of regression analyses, ultimately to calibrate in the proper functional form the relationship between the percentage of the population that was black and the percentage of public elementary school enrolment that was black.

In the census, the elementary enrolment is only classified as public or private, and is not differentiated by race. Racial distinction is, however, made by age categories, and thus persons of elementary school age are utilized as a surrogate for elementary enrolment. The census age category which most closely aligns with elementary enrolment (grades 1–8) is 5–14.

The linear regression equation for census tracts between (A) elementary enrolment and (B) population 5–14 is:

$$(A) = 2 \cdot 85 + 0 \cdot 85 \ (B).$$

This relation had an R^2 of 0·991 for 329 census tracts (229 tracts with more than 400 blacks, as well as 100 tracts selectively chosen throughout the city to capture other types of sectoral and zonal variation in white areas). The regression line runs remarkably close to the origin, since the numbers fitted range from 120 to 4,030.

But it was observed in the residuals from this regression that black areas had high percentages of the population 5–14 attending elementary schools, while the white areas near the fringe of the central city, in contrast, had low percentages (low 80's). Quite expectedly, the majority of suburban areas, even the partially black suburbs, had lower percentages than these in the central city. The cause for the differences may be varied, although they generally relate to the configurations of the parochial schools of the Catholic Archdiocese – and suffice it here to observe the phenomenon.

With the relation between elementary enrolment and population 5–14 established, and operating on the assumption that most private enrolment is white in areas of ghetto expansion, the 329 census tracts were then analyzed to obtain the needed relationship between black population and black public elementary school enrolment.

However, once again the neatness of analysis was confounded by the census, for instead of Negro population we had to work with the census category 'Nonwhite'. In most areas of the city these are synonymous, but differences will exist in those areas with substantial numbers of Oriental residents.

Because the annual racial headcounts refer to public elementary school enrolment also, private enrolments had to be extracted, and the regression equation therefore took the form

$$B = f(E)$$

where B is the proportion of the census tract's population nonwhite in 1960, and

> E is the imputed nonwhite proportion in the public elementary schools, computed as $E = (N - R)/N$

and N is the nonwhite population 5–14, with
  R the enrolment in private elementary schools.

Several equation forms were fitted to the data, but the large variation in the middle zone (25–75 per cent nonwhite) contributed to the highest R^2 ($= 0.935$) for the linear form

$$B = -0.04 + 0.90E$$

A plot of the residuals indicates that a parabolic or exponential curve would also fit the data well, nevertheless, none yielded a higher R^2 than the linear equation. An exponential form:

$$B = -0.16E^{1.05}$$

($R^2 = 0.917$; log–log equation) substantiated the accuracy of the linear form.

The linear equation suggests that due to the variations in age composition and propensity among blacks to attend public schools, the public schools attain a 100 per cent black level when the area has become 86 per cent black. Similarly the black public enrolment is 60 per cent when the community is half black. The other relations may be determined directly from the equation.

The forecasts

Markov probability matrices based on the recent annual shifts in racial headcounts in the schools were then used to develop the 'present trends' forecasts of ghetto expansion, together with the regression equations translating school enrolments into neighbourhood population mixes. Markov models, of course, are designed for studying succession as a continuous dynamic process. In this case, 'succession' involves the transition of schools from one 'state' to another, where the states are defined as the decile classes of percentage of enrolment black (1–10, 11–20 . . .). Basically a Markov process consists of establishing a matrix of transition probabilities between all combinations of these states.

A Markovian process makes it possible to assign to a school X_t, which occupies a particular condition or state i at time t, a probability that it will occupy state j at time $t+1$.

The matrix P_{ij} is the Markovian transition probability matrix. When the constituent probability elements in these matrices p_{ij} are independent of the time dimension t, they are referred to as stationary transition probabilities. The matrices are of the form

$$p_{ij} = \begin{matrix} p_{11} & p_{12} & p_{13} & p_{14} & \cdot & \cdot & \cdot \\ p_{21} & p_{22} & p_{23} & p_{24} & \cdot & \cdot & \cdot \\ p_{31} & p_{32} & p_{33} & p_{34} & \cdot & \cdot & \cdot \\ p_{41} & p_{42} & p_{43} & p_{44} & \cdot & \cdot & \cdot \\ & \cdot & \cdot & \cdot & \cdot \end{matrix}$$

In this study, the first row of the probability distribution is the probability of a school X shifting from black percentage category $i = 1$ to category j during one time interval as a result of ghetto expansion. Clearly, as transition states, the probabilities satisfy the conditions

$$p_{ij} = 0 \qquad i, j = 1, 2 \ldots m$$

$$\sum_{j=1}^{m} p_{ij} = 1{\cdot}0 \qquad i = 1, 2 \ldots m$$

Derivation of subsequent distributions depends on the particular mode of matrix analysis employed. Given an initial vector of school states X_t, and an initial transition matrix P_{ij} the operation

$$X_{t+1} = X_t * P_{ij}$$
$$X_{t+2} = X_t * [P_{ij} * P_{ij}]$$
$$X_{t+3} = X_t * [P_{ij} * P_{ij}{}^2]$$

$$\cdot \qquad \cdot$$
$$\cdot \qquad \cdot$$
$$\cdot \qquad \cdot$$

provides estimates of a new state vector at the end of each time period. An elementary school can make sequential moves in either direction of degree of integration as dictated by the matrix P_{ij}

Tests of the stationarity of the transition matrices were undertaken. Thus the annual 1967–1968 matrix of transition probabilities (Table 13.2) was taken to the fourth power to simulate the four-year transition period 1963–1967 (Table 13.3) and compared with the actual 1963–1967 four year matrix of changes in school states (Table 13.4). By comparing the effects of the two non-overlapping time periods, it was determined that the rates of racial change remained essentially stable for the two time periods. However, since a contiguity test could not effectively test for the similarity between these two matrices and since the principal objective is the distribution of schools, the relevant test of similarity was on the vectors of schools (calculated by multiplying the respective matrices by the 1963 school vector).

A cursory examination of the changes in these vectors over time (Table 13.5) indicates quite clearly how rapidly schools move through degrees of integration from complete segregation (all white) to integration to segregation again (all black). The fact that the number of schools between 10 per cent and 90 per cent black is experiencing little change is further evidence that the presence of schools in this range merely represents a temporary stage in the move toward 90 per cent-plus black. The transition matrix indicates that some schools move rather slowly, and may even be stable, yet in a four-year period, many schools have undergone a complete turnover

Table 13.2   Actual 1967–68 transition probabilities*

State from	State to									
	0–10	11–20	21–30	31–40	41–50	51–60	61–70	71–80	81–90	91–100
0–10	953	35	12	0	0	0	0	0	0	0
11–20	125	250	250	375	0	0	0	0	0	0
21–30	0	0	400	400	0	0	0	0	200	0
31–40	0	0	0	250	250	0	0	250	0	250
41–50	0	0	0	200	600	200	0	0	0	0
51–60	0	0	0	0	0	375	125	500	0	0
61–70	0	0	0	0	0	250	125	250	375	0
71–80	0	0	0	0	0	0	0	375	625	0
81–90	0	0	0	0	0	0	0	0	166	834
91–100	0	0	0	0	0	0	0	0	5	995

* Schools receiving black students by bus are excluded.

Table 13.3   Expected four-year transition probabilities (1967–68 matrix to fourth power)

State from	State to									
	0–10	11–20	21–30	31–40	41–50	51–60	61–70	71–80	81–90	91–100
0–11	860	33	30	30	8	0	0	7	8	14
11–20	149	9	40	111	121	32	2	93	100	321
21–30	0	0	25	87	112	32	2	85	97	553
31–40	0	0	0	48	110	55	8	91	94	587
41–50	0	0	0	88	203	124	23	194	153	208
51–60	0	0	0	0	0	36	13	141	226	577
61–70	0	0	0	0	0	27	9	96	151	710
71–80	0	0	0	0	0	0	0	19	60	917
81–90	0	0	0	0	0	0	0	0	6	991
91–100	0	0	0	0	0	0	0	0	5	992

Table 13.4   Actual four-year (1963–67) transition matrix

State from	State to									
	0–10	11–20	21–30	31–40	41–50	51–60	61–70	71–80	81–90	91–100
0–10	902	16	12	15	4	7	8	11	0	23
11–20	125	375	125	0	0	125	0	125	125	0
21–30	0	0	333	0	334	333	0	0	0	0
31–40	0	0	0	0	0	0	250	0	0	750
41–50	0	0	0	0	286	143	285	0	0	286
51–60	0	0	0	0	0	500	250	250	0	0
61–70	0	0	0	0	0	250	250	250	0	250
71–80	0	0	0	0	0	0	250	0	500	250
81–90	0	0	0	0	0	0	0	77	0	923
91–100	0	0	0	0	0	0	0	0	7	993

Table 13.5   Actual and predicted vectors of schools*

State percentage (black)	Actual 1963	Predicted 1964	1965	1966	Actual 1967	Predicted 1967	Actual 1968	Predicted 1968
0–10	255	246	237	229	231	221	222	213
11–20	8	9	9	9	8	9	9	8
21–30	3	6	8	8	5	8	9	8
31–40	4	7	8	10	4	10	3	10
41–50	7	5	5	5	4	6	4	6
51–60	4	4	3	2	8	2	6	2
61–70	4	1	1	1	7	1	2	0
71–80	4	6	6	6	7	6	9	6
81–90	13	7	7	7	4	7	10	7
91–100	147	158	165	172	171	179	175	187

* Schools receiving black students by bus are excluded.

of racial composition. These changes are found, quite expectedly, on the expanding fringe of the ghetto.

The actual rate at which the racial mix is changing has remained relatively uniform in the period 1963–68, and can be verified by Kolmogorov–Smirnov test for goodness of fit. The test, based on the cumulative frequency distribution of data points, indicates that at the 30 per cent rejection level, the 1967–68 changes run over a four-year period resemble quite closely the cumulative annual pace of the 1963–67 changes. This conclusion facilitates the use of either the actual five-year 1963–68 matrix or the annual matrix for forecasting future racial mix, in accordance with the assumption of continuing stability.

Further examination of Table 13.5 reveals that the calculated distribution for 1966 lies between the actual vectors for 1966 and 1967, however, suggesting that there may be some time differences in the rate of change. Apparently, transitions in the 1967–68 period were slightly more rapid than in the years 1963–67. As a result, when the 1967–68 transition probabilities are applied iteratively to the 1963 school vector, the 1966 predictions fall a little short of the 1967 actual, and the 1967 predictions a little beyond it, on the way to 1968. However, because of the similarity of the two modes of the distributions (0–10 per cent and 91–100 per cent black), the application of the K–S test reveals that the fit of the 1966 calculated vector is just as close as the 1967 calculated vector with the 1967 'actual'. Therefore based on the results of the Kolmogorov–Smirnov test, we felt justified in accepting the hypothesis of stability in the transition matrix, although realizing that either the forecasts may be somewhat anticipatory, or may on the other hand reflect an acceleration of the pace of ghetto spread in 1967–68.

The forecasts were then made in two ways: (*a*) by successive multiplication by the annual transition matrix (1967–68), and (*b*) using the five-year transitions (1963–68). Results are shown in Table 13.6, and from this we

209

developed our 'future ghetto' maps – not presented here because of the political and legal implications that could follow in Chicago from their publication.

Table 13.6 Actual and predicted vectors of schools

Percentage (black)	Actual		Predicted						
			Annual	Annual	5 yr	Annual	5 yr	Annual	5 yr
	1963	1968	1970	1975	1975	1980	1980	2000	2000
0–10	255	240	224	187	195	156	170	76	97
11–20	8	9	9	8	9	6	8	3	4
21–30	3	9	9	7	10	6	11	3	7
31–40	4	5	10	10	3	8	2	4	2
41–50	7	6	5	6	6	5	6	3	4
51–60	4	6	3	2	5	2	6	1	5
61–70	4	2	1	0	2	0	4	0	7
71–80	4	10	8	6	11	5	13	3	12
81–90	13	11	10	8	10	7	8	5	7
91–100	147	199	220	262	247	295	268	376	343

The evaluation

Regardless of evaluating the Leadership Council's efforts, we had found a source of data that enabled us to monitor ongoing racial changes in Chicago on an annual basis, and this itself had a variety of useful by-products, just as we had been able to develop a reasonable evaluation methodology, centering on the effort to measure degree of goal-achievement. Alas, the Council achieved less, as it noted in its own annual report, however:

> [The] experimental programme was designed to stimulate and supplement the existing real-estate market, so as to make it equally accessible to everyone . . . We envisioned the focus of our efforts to be a drive to enlist the active *cooperation* of real estate interests in our work. This approach, based upon what we perceived to be a new spirit of good will among professional real estate dealers, proved essentially fruitless.
>
> It became increasingly clear that despite the commitments made during the 1966 Summit Agreement, the real estate industry had no real commitment or intention to accommodate its practices to the needs of minority home seekers.

As might be expected, our Markov chain models therefore forecast the actual extent of the ghetto quite accurately. With Spear (1967) we could again conclude that at the end of 1969

> . . . in many significant ways, remarkably little had changed since 1920. Increased numbers had vastly expanded the ghetto, but had not changed its basic structure. Negroes were still unable to obtain hous-

ing beyond the confines of the ghetto, and within the back belt the complex of separate institutions and organizations that had first developed between 1890 and 1920 continued to serve an isolated Negro populace. The same restrictions that had limited Negro opportunities in the early twentieth century still operated in 1966. In fact, four civil rights bills, dozens of court decisions, and thousands of brave words about Negro rights had barely touched the life of Chicago's Negroes. It remained as constricted as it had been two generations earlier. And the bitter hostility of the residents of Gage Park, Belmont-Cragin, and Cicero towards Dr. King's marches demonstrated that thousands of white Chicagoans were still determined to preserve the status quo.

Housing in Chicago essentially remained locked into a racist real estate system that continued to constrain and pattern residential choice.

The only positive sign of progress was that the Leadership Council had persuaded some fifty suburbs in the Chicago Metropolitan Area to adopt open housing ordinances. Before 1962 only 10 black families had lived in otherwise white suburbs in Metropolitan Chicago. Thereafter, the number of annual move-ins was as follows: 1963, 26; 1964, 45; 1965, 75; 1966, 165; 1967, 191; 1968, 353. Of the 353 finding homes in white neighborhoods, all but nineteen moved into suburbs with open housing ordinances, and sixty-six suburbs in all had at least one black family (Fig. 13.9). But a small percentage of the suburbs is involved, and less than one-third of one per cent of all black families in Metropolitan Chicago. The rest remain ghettoized, and for them the integration goal remains confounded by Zeno's paradox – in perpetually moving half way between the present position and the ultimate goal, one is condemned never to reach that goal.

Concluding remarks

Ideally, any programme of evaluation should have a model that can be manipulated to illustrate the effects of alternative assumptions about goals, plans and projections, but the work reported here has hardly reached that stage yet. A more complete model would permit simulation of the consequences of alternative forecasts on a given plan of action, and the consequences of various plans embodying different instruments and objectives on future projections, while capturing important feedback relationships (Milliman, 1967). I doubt whether such a model can, however, yield single-valued optima, for these can only be derived if the model is oversimplified and the goals one-dimensional. Rather, the model should enable us to visualize the sets of consequences likely to arise under varying sets of goals and assumptions about the nature of society and social change, to outline the costs, effectiveness and risks associated with a variety of alternative policies, and thereby to aid the decision-maker choose a reasonable course of action leading to a desirable future. This is far from the ivory tower, but it is how the geography we will describe to our students tomorrow will have emerged from the geography of today.

Notes and References

Berry, B. J. L., Smith, K. B., Vorwaller, D. and Wertymer, J. (1969) *Down from the Summit*, Center for Urban Studies, University of Chicago.

Berry, B. J. L. and Sööt, S. (1969) 'Future expansion of Chicago's black population. A Markov Process approach', *Chicago Regional Hospital Study*.

Berry, B. J. L. and Horton, F. (1970) *Geographic Perspectives on Urban Systems*, Prentice-Hall.

Berry, B. J. L., Peery, P., Thomas, E. N., Vorwaller, D. and Whitley, Y. (1970) *Social Goals in Urban Policy*, Center for Urban Studies, University of Chicago.

Chicago Commission on Race Relations (1968) *The Negro in Chicago*, Arno Press.

Clark, K. B. (1965) *Dark Ghetto*, Harper & Row.

Cressy, P. (1930) 'Succession of cultural groups in Chicago', PhD dissertation, University of Chicago.

De Visé, P. (1967) *Chicago's Widening Color Gap*, Interuniversity Social Research Committee, University of Chicago.

Drake, St Clair and Cayton, H. (1962) *Black Metropolis*, Harper & Row.

Dror, Y. (1968) *Public Policymaking Reexamined*, Chandler Publishing Co.

Duncan, O. D. and Duncan, B. (1957) *The Negro Population of Chicago*, University of Chicago Press.

Kemeny, J. G. and Snell, J. L. (1960) *Finite Markov Chains*, Van Nostrand.

Lieberson, S. (1960) 'Comparative segregation and assimilation of ethnic groups', PhD dissertation, University of Chicago.

Lowry, I. S. (1967) 'Seven models of urban development: a structural comparison', paper presented to Highway Research Board, Conference on Urban Development Models.

Milliman, J. W. (1967) 'Large-scale models for forecasting regional economic activity: a survey', unpublished paper, Indiana University.

Morrill, R. L. (1965) 'The Negro ghetto. Problems and alternatives', *Geographical Review*, **55**, 346–50.

Spear, A. H. (1967) *Black Chicago*, University of Chicago Press.

Taeuber, K. E. and Taeuber, A. (1965) *Negroes in Cities*, Aldine Publishing Co.

Zelder, R. E. (1968) 'Racial segregation in urban housing markets', paper prepared at Western Michigan University.

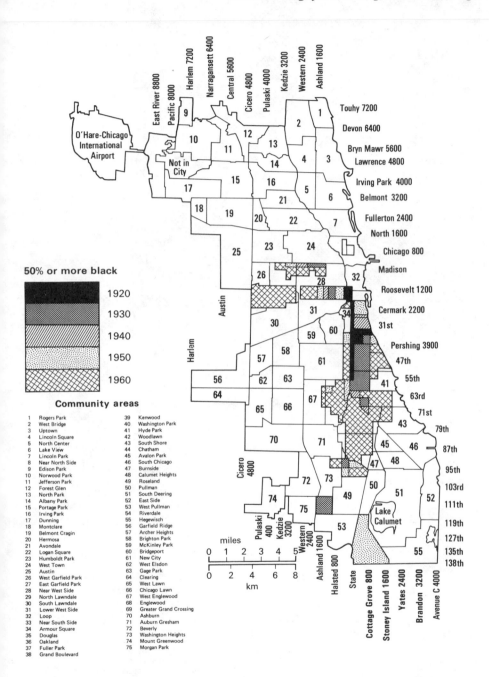

Fig. 13.1 Growth of black residential areas, 1920–60.

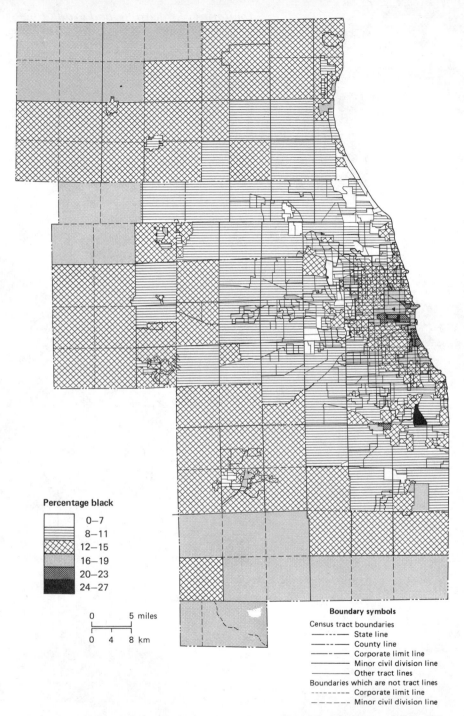

Fig. 13.2 Distribution of the black population in a colour-blind housing market. I. Income standardization.

214

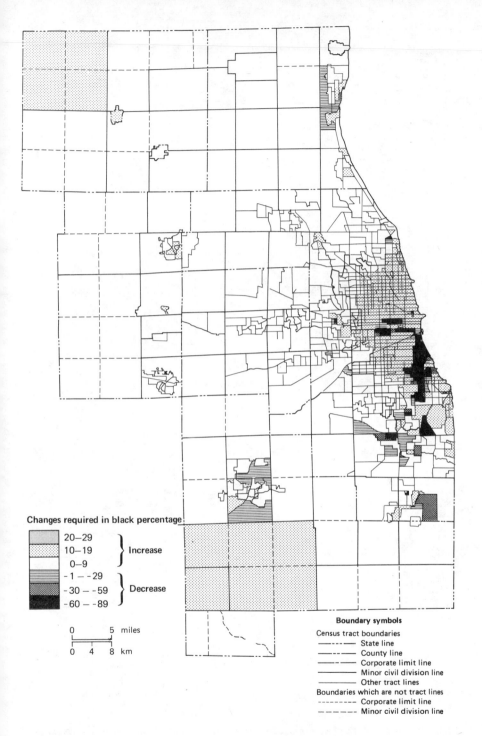

Fig. 13.3 Redistribution of the black population to achieve income-standardized equality.

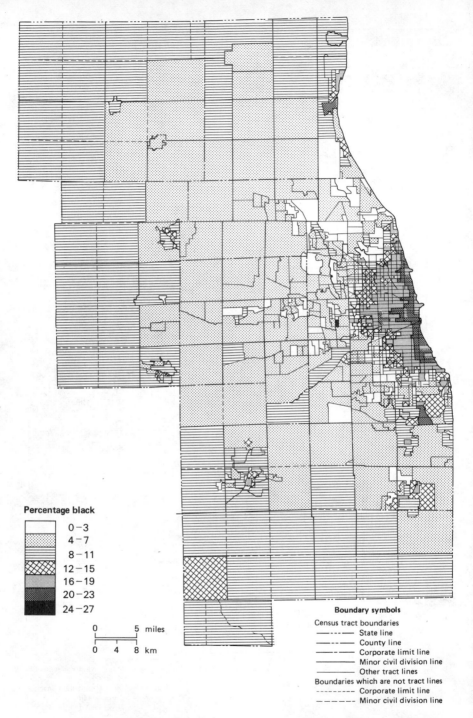

Percentage black

	0 – 3
	4 – 7
	8 – 11
	12 – 15
	16 – 19
	20 – 23
	24 – 27

0   5 miles

0   4   8   km

Boundary symbols

Census tract boundaries
- - - - - State line
- - - County line
—— Corporate limit line
—— Minor civil division line
—— Other tract lines

Boundaries which are not tract lines
- - - - - - Corporate limit line
— — — — Minor civil division line

Fig. 13.4 Distribution of the black population in a colour-blind housing market. II. Expenditure standardization.

216

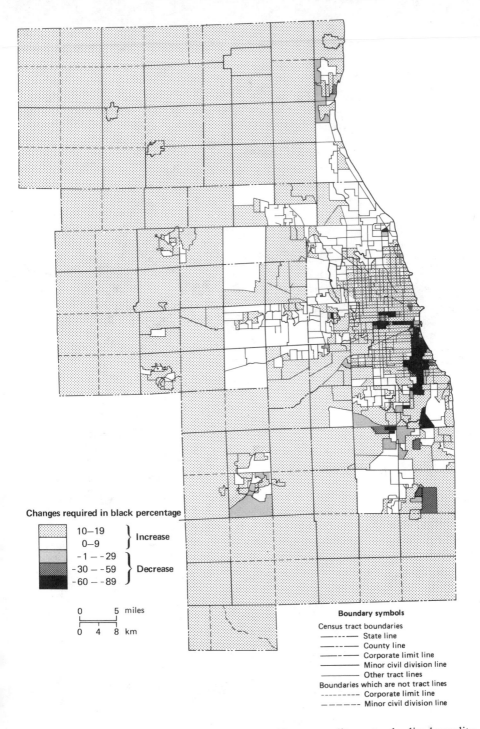

Changes required in black percentage

10—19 ⎫ Increase
0—9 ⎭

-1 — -29 ⎫
-30 — -59 ⎬ Decrease
-60 — -89 ⎭

0   5   miles
0   4   8   km

Boundary symbols

Census tract boundaries
————————— State line
————·———— County line
———— —— Corporate limit line
————————— Minor civil division line
————————— Other tract lines
Boundaries which are not tract lines
- - - - - - - - Corporate limit line
— — — — — Minor civil division line

Fig. 13.5 Redistribution of the black population to achieve expenditure-standardized equality.

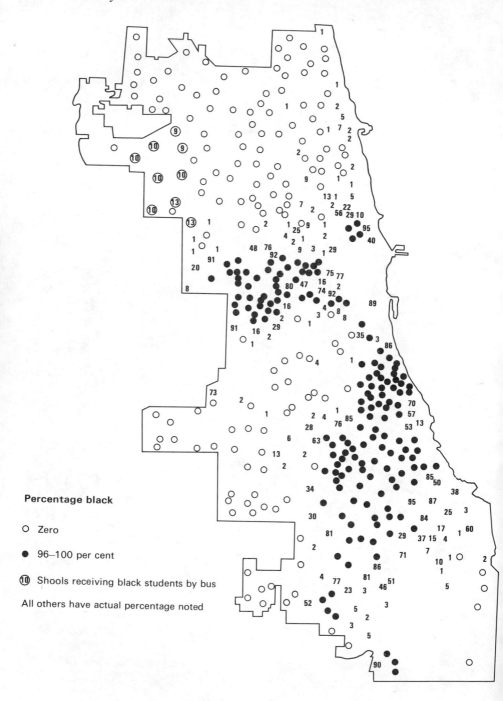

Fig. 13.6 Percentage of public elementary school enrolment black in 1968.

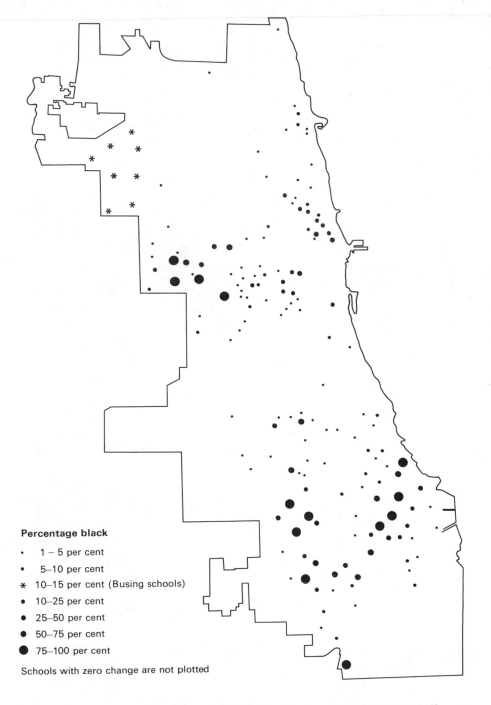

Percentage black

- ·   1 – 5 per cent
- ·   5–10 per cent
- ∗   10–15 per cent (Busing schools)
- •   10–25 per cent
- •   25–50 per cent
- ●   50–75 per cent
- ●   75–100 per cent

Schools with zero change are not plotted

Fig. 13.7 Increase in percentage of elementary public school enrolment black 1963–68.

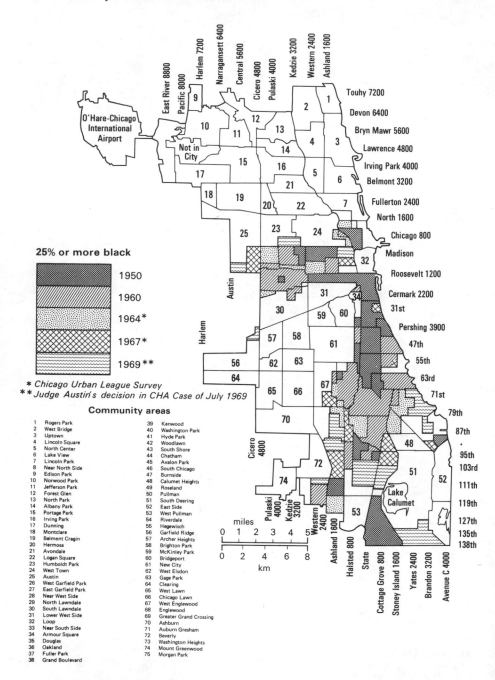

Fig. 13.8 Growth of black residential areas, 1950–69.

220

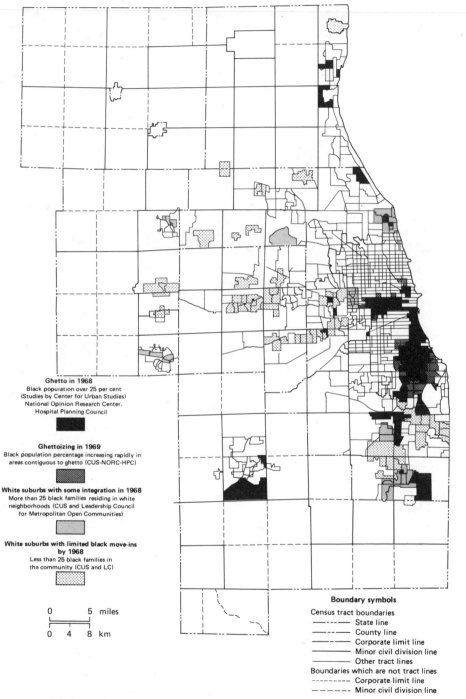

Ghetto in 1968
Black population over 25 per cent
(Studies by Center for Urban Studies)
National Opinion Research Center.
Hospital Planning Council

Ghettoizing in 1969
Black population percentage increasing rapidly in
areas contiguous to ghetto (CUS-NORC-HPC)

White suburbs with some integration in 1968
More than 25 black families residing in white
neighborhoods (CUS and Leadership Council
for Metropolitan Open Communities)

**White suburbs with limited black move-ins
by 1968**
Less than 25 black families in
tha community (CUS and LC)

0   5 miles

0   4   8 km

Boundary symbols
Census tract boundaries
––––––– State line
––·––·– County line
–––––– Corporate limit line
–––––––– Minor civil division line
–––––––– Other tract lines
Boundaries which are not tract lines
–––––––– Corporate limit line
–––––––– Minor civil division line

Fig. 13.9 Racial status and trends in metropolitan Chicago.

221

Part IV

The United Kingdom

Emrys Jones

14 The segregation of Roman Catholics and Protestants in Belfast *

The charter of the borough of Belfast, issued by James II in 1613, nowhere implies that there should be any differentiating in the new town between the English and Scots on the one hand and the Irish on the other. Discrimination was written into some charters, and this is not really surprising. Towns were the gift of invading peoples, and the whole institution was an alien introduction in Ireland; to the incoming forces they represented vantage points and pockets of 'civilization' which must be protected and usually walled; to the native population they were a new challenge. There are many parallels to the exclusion of native peoples from bastide towns when indigenous and intrusive cultures clash. In Ulster this clash was also that of protestant and catholic, a fundamental and deep-rooted division which was to dominate social intercourse from that time onwards.

But even if discrimination was not explicit in this particular charter – and in many cases even the explicit was ignored – it is tempting to read into the first map of Belfast a parallel to those bastide towns where the quarters of the native population were in fact a mere appendage to the invaders' walled town;[1] for before the settlement of Scots and English under Sir Arthur Chichester there was no town on this site.

Phillips' map of 1685 shows the town's defences clearly enough.[2] Inside the walls, the main thoroughfare, High Street, runs from west to east on either side of the Farset river (a tributary of the Lagan). But this line of houses is continued outside the walls, and Phillips seems to indicate that these houses were on the whole much smaller and meaner; symbols of single storied cottages predominate. These extra-mural houses were probably little more than thatched cabins, and they are reminiscent of contemporary scenes of Carrickfergus, another garrison town, in which clusters of mud and wattle cabins are shown outside the walls.[3] The

* Reprinted from *Sociological Review*, **4**.

Belfast 'suburb' is also associated with the earliest grist mill, and the site is still called Mill Street. Mill Street is now the apex of the main sector of catholic population in Belfast. Has Phillips' map in fact preserved whatever segregation there was in the seventeenth century? Parallels suggest it, and so does the subsequent growth of the Irish population from that one point on the periphery of the walled town.

But direct evidence of the number and social position of the Irish is as scarce as that of their distribution. Petty in 1659 gives the number of English in the town as 366, and the number of Irish as 223.[4] It has been presumed that the total population of Belfast at the end of that century was about 2,000, yet a letter written by a sovereign of the town in 1708 says that there were only seven catholics in Belfast.[5] The figure is extremely doubtful, but such a small number might indicate that no account was taken of those who lived outside the town, who – if the supposition concerning the 'suburb' is correct – would be Irish. There must have been many more Irish than Macartney claims, and it is not difficult to imagine that they were associated with that sector which continuity of tradition has preserved as Irish.

In 1757 the catholics in Belfast numbered 556 out of a total population of 8,549 (6·5 per cent).[6] A Record Office return for the parish for 1776 enumerates 256 catholic families out of a total of 3,033.[7] The parish extended beyond the limits of the town (an average of five per family would give a population of over 15,000, but the town population was not yet 13,000), giving a percentage of 8·4. This might indicate that the proportion of catholics was higher in the rural areas of the parish. They did have strong links with the south-west, for they were served by a priest from Derriaghy,[8] and later there was considerable movement inwards along the Falls Road. Where this sector had its apex the first catholic chapel was built in 1783, near a house in Mill Street where mass had been celebrated for some time.

There is no evidence of segregation during the latter part of the eighteenth century. Relations between the two sects were apparently cordial, if the fact is taken into account that much of the money which went to the building of the new chapel was subscribed by Presbyterians;[9] though one should also remember Arthur Young's warning that subscription in this case can be no safe guide to the true relations between the sects;[10] the rift, supported by penal laws, was very deep. It is true that this decade saw the Volunteer Movement at its height in championing the cause of the catholics, and the great endeavours made to repeal the Penal Code were mainly protestant inspired. The civic condition of the minority was deplorable,[11] and it was common sense as much as a new spirit of liberalism which convinced protestants that if catholics were to play their part it could be as full citizens only. Many would not subscribe to full emancipation, but realized that it was too much to expect loyalty from an unhappy minority.

It is hard to imagine deliberate segregation in such mounting liberal thought; there is no evidence either way, but it is also certain that liberalism in thought did not relieve the catholics of their long-established poverty. Retail trading was the best they could attain in employment, and there is no reason to believe that their well-established sector in the west was broken down in any great degree. Theoretically, those catholics who could afford to do so could move into the more select residential streets of Belfast; but in practice they were probably too few to upset the well-established pattern.

The number and proportion of catholics rose remarkably in the first half of the nineteenth century. The first definite count is given in the report of the Royal Commission of Public Institutions, in 1834. The total population of the town is given as 60,813, of which 19,712 were catholics, or 32·4 per cent. Barrow stated in 1835 that he thought 18,000 was an exaggerated estimate; he was nearer the true figure than he thought.[12] Belfast was beginning its vast industrial expansion, and labour was beginning to come in from all parts of Ireland. Within a few years 'some four or five thousand raw, uneducated catholic labourers from the south . . . had poured into the city' and they were 'rapidly increasing in proportion to the rest'.[13]

The 1841 census shows that 15,334 people had been born outside the town, but in Ireland; and although the majority came from Ulster, where the proportion of the two religious sects was approximately 50/50, very many came from the other three provinces, where the catholic population accounted for about nine in ten of the total.

The next count of religion was taken in 1861, when the catholics numbered 41,237 in a total population of 119,444, or 34·1 per cent. Although the town was growing at a phenomenal rate the numbers of catholics were increasing even more rapidly. The industrial growth of Belfast coincided with the rural depopulation of Ireland, which reached its peak in the famine years of the late 1840s. They were not town folk who struggled into Belfast from the west and south, on foot, by road and later by rail, to find relief from hunger; they were country folk, and the majority came from catholic areas.

It is difficult to gauge accurately attitudes towards these incomers in this period. The support which was given to the extreme anti-papist attitude of Henry Cooke[14] was probably an expression of protestant dismay at the great increase in the numbers of the other sect. Tension certainly rose as their numbers increased. The Party Procession Act of 1850 was enforced to end the 'practice of assembling and marching . . . in a manner calculated to perpetuate animosity between different classes of Her Majesty's subjects'.[15] This was modified ten years later by the Party Emblems Act,[16] but it was not repealed until 1875. Friction between protestants and catholics had led to severe rioting in 1857,[17] and later the discontent caused by the Party Procession Act led eventually to the riots of 1864,[18] and to repeated demonstrations on the twelfth of July. A bye-law prohibiting sectarian language seems merely to have provided ready funds for the judicial purse. The split was a wide one; even the shipyard, which had kept a balance of protestants by importing specialist labour from the Clyde and the Tyne, was spoken of as having two hostile camps.[19]

Reports on the rioting in the mid-century make it clear that in the western section of the town there was a considerable degree of segregation which became accentuated whenever disturbances arose. By 1857 the industrial region west of Durham Street, between Divis Street and Sandy Row, was divided into two segments by Albert Street. The Pound, between Divis Street and Albert Street, had been predominantly catholic 'for many years', and Sandy Row had been mainly protestant; though

> there was some intermixture, and a few Roman catholics resided in the Sandy Row districts, and a few protestants in the Pound district. Since the commencement of the late riots (1857) however the districts have become exclusive, and by regular systematised movement on both sides, the few catholic inhabitants of the Sandy Row district have been obliged to leave it, and the few protestant inhabitants of the Pound district have been also obliged to leave that district.[20]

This was the mechanism of segregation, although the report stresses that except in July (when the protestants celebrated the victories of William III) the two groups 'met in peace: in business there were ordinarily no distinctions made, and protestant, catholic and Orangeman lived together in friendship'.[21]

The situation was aggravated by the poverty of the incoming Irish population, which led to their congregating in crowded working-class areas, together with the tradition of the catholic sector in the west, which grew along the axis of the Falls Road. A similar sector of working-class protestants was establishing itself a little to the north, along the Shankill and Crumlin Roads: this, and the older Sandy Row area, successfully contained the catholic axis.

It is not until the last few decades of the nineteenth century that we can measure statistically the irregular distribution of the catholic population in the general population. Figures of religious sects are given in the census from 1871 to 1891 inclusive, for the five wards. Generalized though these figures are they give some indication of irregular distribution. In Table 14.1 the number of catholics in each ward is expressed as an index, derived by dividing the percentage of catholics in each ward by the percentage of catholics in Belfast. If there are no catholics in a ward, the index will be 0; if all are catholics the index will be 100 divided by the percentage in Belfast – this maximum index for various years is given in Table 14.1. Unity means the same percentage as that for the town as a whole.

In the north (Dock) the proportion is only a little above unity, and varies insignificantly in thirty years. Cromac, representing the entire east and south-east,[22] is considerably below unity in 1871, and decreases even by

Table 14.1

Ward	Index 1871	1881	1891
Cromac	0·76	0·72	0·70
Dock	1·08	1·08	1·10
St Anne's	0·84	0·74	0·65
St George's	1·15	1·34	1·50
Smithfield	1·31	1·20	1·30
% RCs in Belfast	31·8	28·8	26·3
Maximum Index	3·15	3·47	3·76

Note: The index should be read in relation to the maximum index which is stated for each year and which varies with the decrease in the percentage of catholics in the city from 1871 to 1891. The maximum index affects the comparison of any one ward, year by year. For example, if the maximum index is higher in 1891 than 1881, then a similar index in fact shows a slightly lower segregation.

1891 as the population on the Down side of the river is drawn from its own strongly protestant country. St Anne's ward is considerably below unity, representing the more northerly part of the western industrial sector, and again there is a decrease as people are drawn in along the north-western route from the strongly protestant Antrim. Smithfield, immediately west of the city centre, where the nucleus of the catholic population had long been, and in which the first chapel was built, remains with fairly high but static index. Catholic predominance is on the increase in St George's ward, which includes the Falls Road, the major axis of the Irish population.

The proportions of catholics remained high in these last two wards in spite of the fact that, as the table shows, the percentage in the total population was decreasing. The distribution corresponds with the comparatively lower socio-economic status of this group compared with the protestants, which was referred to above. In 1881, for example, when the catholics were 28·8 per cent of the total population, their proportion in certain selected groups of occupations was as follows:

Legal profession: 17·2 per cent   Medical: 9·7 per cent   Engineering: 7·1 per cent   Merchants: 14·7 per cent   Brokers, etc.: 8·9 per cent.

(The fact that there was none in the officer ranks of the army contrasted strangely with the proportion in the ranks, which was 31·9 per cent.)[23]

Their relative social position is emphasized in the illiteracy rates in the town. In 1881 the illiteracy of all persons over five years of age in Belfast was 11·9 per cent: among catholics it was 17·9 per cent for males and 22·9 per cent for females. Even in 1901, when the town rate was only 7·7 per cent, the catholic rate was still 12·2 per cent. The effects of the disabilities of the Penal Code were very slow in being erased.

The ward tables reveal that there was, then, a concentration of catholics in the immediate west of the town and in the south-west. It is known too that there was a small concentration in Cromac which was hidden by the size of the ward, and that even in the north, which is near unity in the table, this sect was found mainly immediately north of the city centre, an area which from the very beginnings of industrialization had been a zone of decay, spreading outwards as the century progressed.

In 1896 the expansion of the city demanded an extension of the boundaries and a change in the wards: their number was increased from five to fifteen. The new wards reveal that the distribution of religious groups contained a much more radical degree of segregation than was ever suggested by the figures for the five wards.

Table 14.2

Ward	Index 1901	1911	1926	1937	1951
Clifton	0·86	0·93	1·10	1·28	1·31
Court	0·76	0·96	0·99	1·04	1·08
Cromac	0·90	0·90	0·85	0·93	0·92
Dock	1·49	1·61	1·77	1·92	1·94
Duncairn	0·71	0·72	0·43	0·44	0·51
Falls	3·17	3·40	3·58	3·88	3·59
Ormeau	0·57	0·60	0·30	0·35	0·38
Pottinger	0·73	0·70	0·63	0·59	0·56
St Anne's	1·43	1·39	1·68	1·59	1·57
St George's	0·40	0·39	0·20	0·18	0·17
Shankill	0·31	0·29	0·19	0·21	0·25
Smithfield	3·58	3·68	3·95	3·86	3·52
Victoria	0·39	0·35	0·24	0·20	0·25
Windsor	0·62	0·61	0·72	0·64	0·60
Woodvale	0·44	0·41	0·21	0·19	0·31
% Belfast	24·3	24·1	23·0	23·8	25·9
Maximum index	4·11	4·15	4·35	4·20	3·86

Table 14.2 shows that in 1901, for example, four wards have an index of less than 0·5, one as low as 0·31; seven are between 0·55 and 0·9; and four are well over unity, two a little under 1·5, one is 3·17 and one is 3·58. The last two indices are high compared with the maximum index of 4·11 (i.e. the index if the ward were 100 per cent catholic). The ward with an index of 3·17 is Falls; this was carved out of the former St George's, the remainder of which, representing south Belfast, is in 1901 only 0·40. This indicates that the new ward boundaries were taking into account the marked difference in religious composition of the several regions of the city. Smithfield ward becomes smaller: it no longer represents the industrial west, but only a small part of it immediately near the city centre. Here the index is extremely high. Part of the old Smithfield ward has now become part of the new Shankill ward (0·31), revealing how sharp was the religious split in this

western industrial population; for this ward, with the lowest index of all, is as protestant as the old is now catholic. In the same way the new St Anne's and Dock wards are much more restricted than the old and contain a much higher proportion of catholics as a result.

No radical change had occurred in the late nineteenth century in the distribution of these groups, but certainly the more detailed indices of the new wards bring out much more clearly the restriction in the distribution of the catholic population. Tradition and economic position determined this. Still greater segregation was to result from the religious and political disorders of this century.

Table 14.2 enables us to trace the changes of indices in these wards over the last fifty years. During this period, as in the four decades preceding it, the increase in catholics was not keeping pace with the increase in the whole population. Consequently there was a decrease in the proportion from the peak of 34·1 per cent in 1861 to 23·0 per cent in 1926, though since that time there has been a gradual and an increasing rise. Again it should be remembered that the maximum index varies according to the proportion of catholics in the city, and the columns must be read in conjunction with the maxima. But they vary less than in the nineteenth century, so that comparisons are easier. In the majority of wards there is very little change in the first decade apart from a rise in those wards which are already predominantly catholic. The significant changes occur in the next fifteen years, for the next census was taken in 1926. Four wards (Woodvale, Shankill, Victoria and St George's) which already had low indices (below 0·4 in 1911) drop markedly. Two others (Duncairn and Ormeau) drop equally sharply from, respectively 0·72 to 0·43 and from 0·60 to 0·30. Those wards with big catholic populations increase: Clifton from 0·93 to 1·10, St Anne's from 1·39 to 1·68, Dock from 1·61 to 1·77, Falls from 3·40 to 3·58 and Smithfield from 3·68 to 3·95. This increase in segregation in certain parts of the city is of course a reflection of the bitter rioting which occurred in the city between 1920 and 1923,[24] reflected in the Special Powers Act of 1922 which empowered setting of curfews, banning of processions, emblems and so on.[25] There had been considerable displacement of population, especially in those localities where the trouble had been worst – i.e. near the city centre, among the industrial workers of the north, north-west, west, south-east and east.

Relaxation of this segregation since 1926 has been slight, and in some wards, where the catholic proportion is high, segregation has increased between 1926 and 1937 (Falls, Dock and Clifton). Since 1937 the position has been fairly static with the exception of Falls and Smithfield, both of which show a sharp decrease. Much of this can be accounted for by the absolute decrease of population in areas near the city centre. Depopulation has been especially marked in Smithfield, many families having been resettled in new housing estates on the periphery of the city since 1945.

Although the ward figures for the proportions of the two religious elements in the population reveal interesting data on general distribution, it is obvious that the unit is too large to disclose any accurate information; and within such a large unit a considerable degree of segregation could be hidden entirely if a concentration of catholics were split and included in two wards in which the overwhelming majority was protestant. The map of the distribution of catholics in 1951, however, is based on the enumeration districts of Belfast (Fig. 14.1). These are units in which the population is usually about 2,000, in an area which can be covered conveniently by a single census enumerator. As they are later built up into ward figures these data are not published.[26] There are 231 enumeration districts in Belfast,

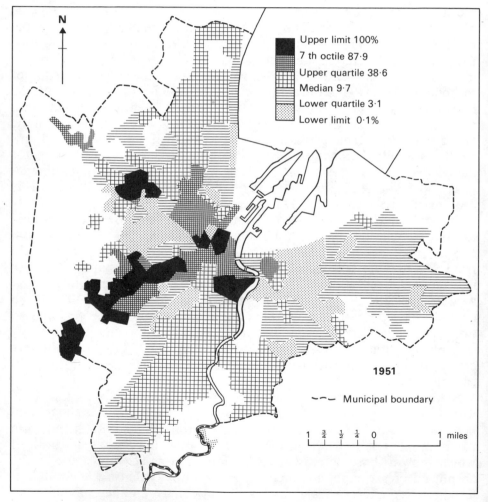

Fig. 14.1 Belfast: density of Roman Catholics.

and consequently any information which is mapped on this basis will reveal a very close and accurate pattern which would be hidden in the ward figures. It will be appreciated that when population is sparse in any district then the enumeration district will be large; this is true especially on the periphery, and in order to offset any great distortion the built up area only has been shaded to show the appropriate distribution.[27]

In one other respect should it be stressed that these are statistical units and not social regions. Although they are small enough to be built up into social regions it is inevitable that at times they will overlap two such regions. This means that an enumeration district showing 25·9 per cent catholics can suggest that it has an even distribution: whereas in fact one part of such a district might be exclusively catholic and the other exclusively protestant – that is, far from it being an even scatter, segregation may be complete. We will be more concerned with this when discussing segregation; in the general distribution this fact may blur the edges of the larger social regions, but it will not seriously affect the pattern.

The detail revealed in this map differs considerably from that which would be shown in a ward distribution map. In east Belfast, for example, what could previously be interpreted as a slight scatter of catholics through-out Victoria and Pottinger wards is now seen to be nothing of the kind; there is, rather, one small concentration of very high density (over 70 per cent) in the centre of Ballymacarrett, and outside this the distribution is almost negligible.

The outstanding concentrations, those in the eighth octile – i.e. over 87·9 per cent catholic, are the following:

(*a*) The greatest concentration, and the most important, is that which follows the Falls Road, running from a point near the centre of the city, southwestwards right up to the boundary. Within this block there are several enumeration districts in which the percentage is 100. The apex is that point – already referred to above – where the indigenous population probably first settled, and where the first chapel was built. The grist mill which used the waters of the Farset at this same point was the first hint of the use which was to be made of the tributary streams which flowed from the western plateau. By the time steam power had replaced water power – and partly because water itself was essential in the linen industry – west Belfast had been established as a purely industrial sector. It grew in the nineteenth century as countless numbers of the peasantry poured into the town. It is a sector with two axes, for its northern part, along the Shankill Road, al-though similarly industrial, is almost purely protestant. The concentration of the catholics along the Falls Road is made more complete by the fact that (i) a line of factories along the Farset is often the line of demarcation between it and the protestant area to the north; and (ii) it is effectively cut off from the Malone ridge of south Belfast by the low-lying floodable meadows of the Blackstaff river, an area which is only partly, and recently, built-up. One other feature of the Falls Road sector is its continuation beyond the purely industrial zone into continually more substantial suburban residential land use. This axis represents the entire socio-economic scale, from unskilled labouring and manual work near the centre (and today, near the periphery, in new housing estates) to professional classes in the detached area of Andersonstown, near the city boundary.

(*b*) Immediately south-east of the city centre, but to the west of the Lagan (the main river, and shown on the map), is a second compact concentration of catholic population. This is the Cromac region; that part of Cromac lying nearest the river was reclaimed early in the nineteenth century, and on it were built the expanding markets of the town. Part of it also became the site of the gas works in the 1820s, and there was a mill and several brick-fields in the vicinity at the same period.[28] From its inception, therefore, this area was industrial, but it was restricted. The river prevented spread eastward, and to the west the residential sector of south Belfast, moving steadily further south towards the Malone ridge, checked its expansion in that direction.

(*c*) There is a third concentration of catholics north of the city centre. This is mainly in the grid sections on either side of York Street, laid out in the early nineteenth century. The main streets are exceptionally wide, but they were never graced with the substantial dwellings which characterized similar late Georgian planning in the south. When the planned units of the north were built up it was with a mixture of factories and warehouses – closely connected with shipping – as well as with mean housing. Most of its inhabitants today live in tiny crowded streets, overwhelmed and over-shadowed by industry and trade. Density of dwellings here, and consequently of population, is among the highest in Belfast.

(*d*) The fourth compact area of catholics is a seemingly detached area in the north-west of the industrial sector. This is Ardoyne, a comparatively recently built locality to which there was a wholesale movement of catholics from the other industrial sectors in the late 1930s. This again has a mill population, and apart from the more pleasant and more open building of this century, compared with the squalid bye-law streets of the last century, there is not much difference between this population and that of the other industrial sectors of the city.

We now come to those areas where the concentration of catholics lies between the upper quartile and the seventh octile, i.e. between 38·6 per cent and 87·9 per cent. There are many enumeration districts in this category lying on either side of the Falls Road axis which need no further discussion. In the north-west extremity of the map is another concentration in the former mill village of Legoniel. For the remainder the following areas are worth mentioning.

(*a*) To the east of the Lagan there is a marked concentration in Bally-macarrett. This former small industrial suburb grew enormously during the latter part of the nineteenth century, partly due to the development of ship-building and its associated industries on the Down side of the river. Drawing its population mainly from the east, Ballymacarrett has a comparatively small number of catholics. Two things are significant; they again occupy the industrial hub of purely working-men's houses, and secondly they form quite a compact unit in an industrial population in which, for the most part, protestants account for 96·9 per cent of the total population.

(*b*) The city centre has a very small resident population indeed, and the extent of certain densities here is misleading: the densities really indicate the situation immediately around the periphery of the city centre, just where it impinges on the densely populated industrial belt.

(*c*) The third is a much more extensive area in north Belfast which is far from being homogeneous and which cannot be explained entirely by one simple set of facts. In the first place there is an extension north of the mixed warehousing-factory-dwelling region of York Street in which the catholics are often the predominant element. Secondly there is a region around the lower Crumlin Road in which there is a fairly high proportion of professional men. This region, closely associated with the Mater Hospital, was formerly a select residential district, together with part of the Antrim Road. It was the nucleus from which the main residential sector of north Belfast spread in the later nineteenth century. Some professional men, especially doctors, still occupy some of the larger houses. But when the upper middle class moved still further north from the growing city centre they left many streets of substantial terrace houses into which crowded the growing industrial population. These streets became regions of decay and transition, for their upkeep was far beyond the newcomers, and often houses are shared by many families, giving rise to deplorable conditions. Such decay is found elsewhere in the city where the rich have moved into suburbia and the poor have taken over the older dwellings;[29] but they are more extensive in this north-western sector. This physical decay of property from the centre outwards is one which was emphasized by the Chicago urban sociologists. The older centre having been rebuilt, this zone was once peripheral to the centre and between it and the zone of workingmen's houses which lay beyond. In Chicago, Burgess associated certain social groups with this zone, and he evolved a generalization which might be true of many North American industrial cities; that this is the immigrant zone, where incoming groups, low on the socio-economic scale and least integrated into the society of their choice, occupy whatever dwellings are easily available.[30] Most of this zone of transition in Belfast is occupied by catholics, and although the main reason is their socio-economic grouping it is interesting to see a situation parallel with that of immigrant groups in an American city.[31] Belfast began as a foreign town: it was an English-Scot protestant establishment to which the native population only slowly and gradually moved. Consequent growth maintained the protestant ascendancy, and Irish people were looked upon almost as immigrants. They had an alien tongue, a different religion, a lower socio-economic position, and they were by no means integrated with the new culture. They occupied, in addition to their traditional sector in the south-west, the zone of transition and decay.

The remainder of the map may be discussed very briefly, as some further details can be dealt with more appropriately when discussing present-day segregation. The almost exclusively protestant sector in the industrial west, corresponding to that of the catholic sector has already been mentioned; also the overwhelmingly protestant population of the industrial area in the east outside the immediate hub of Ballymacarrett. This leaves the mainly residential north and south Belfast (the Antrim Road, and the Malone ridge with Ormeau, respectively) and the residential rim of the east. In the last the number of catholics is very small for two reasons. The geographical orientation of the two main sects is such that the greater number of catholics remains on the Antrim side of the Lagan; naturally the majority of those who move into the better residential areas, as they move up the social scale, remain on that side and are to be found north and south. These latter are the old residential sectors which have by now expanded into prosperous suburbs: their links with the old town are firmly established, whereas the newer eastern residential sector has no long-standing traditional links with the more prosperous parts of the old town. The older sectors have a higher proportion of the professional classes, which form the upper middle class in Belfast society.

The map of the distribution of catholics in 1951 has revealed a social phenomenon which was only hinted at in the figures of distribution by wards for the half century before (though, as the tables showed, segregation alters in relation to different social and political circumstances). If figures were available it would be illuminating to compare such detailed maps over the last half century. All that can be said, however, is that the 1951 pattern of distribution does illustrate ecological segregation. By 'ecological segregation' is implied this: that if the factor being studied – in this case religion – has an effect on the residence of people, then its distribution will not be a random distribution, but irregularities will occur which will exhibit segregation. Many American sociologists have produced indices of segregation,[32] but they usually apply to entire cities. The problem here is to find a simple index for each enumeration district.

If the catholic population was randomly distributed in the city one would expect the percentage in any enumeration district to be the same as that for the city as a whole – in this case it would be 25·9 per cent. Any departure from this shows some degree of segregation, although the small departures admittedly will not be significant. If there are no catholics in an enumeration district then segregation is complete. Similarly it is complete when the population of a district is 100 per cent catholic. So at 0 per cent and at 100 per cent there is complete segregation; at 25·9 per cent there is total absence of segregation. Between 25·9 per cent and 0 per cent in one direction and between 25·9 per cent and 100 per cent in the other direction, segregation increases. Segregation at 0 per cent and 100 per cent is therefore given the index 1. At 25·9 per cent, where there is no segregation, the index is 0. If the percentage of catholics falls between 25·9 per cent and 0 per cent or between 25·9 per cent and 100 per cent, then the index is calculated as a ratio: e.g. half way between 0 per cent and 25·9 per cent and half way

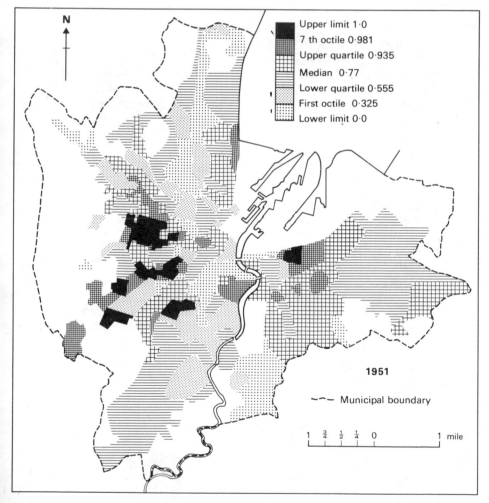

Fig. 14.2 Belfast: segregation index.

between 25·9 and 100 per cent both give an index of 0·5. Segregation calculated on this basis was mapped by enumeration districts (Fig. 14.2).

It was stated above that, although the enumeration districts are small enough to give a fine-grained and accurate pattern of social data, there are cases where they break down in registering segregation: 25·9 per cent catholics in a district does not always indicate the random spread which it suggests. One could only remove this error by reducing still further the size of the unit,[33] though an over-reduction would lead to an absurdiy complete segregation throughout. But there are several districts which show a comparative absence of segregation in which in fact there is more or less complete segregation. They are districts which overlap two distinct social regions, and the segregation on all sides of them is likely to be very high. This has been checked in some cases against a map of the distribution of school children of both sects, which gave a street distribution,[34] and it was found that these districts are on the periphery of the densely populated catholic majority areas near the centre of the city.

In Fig. 14.2 the focus has shifted from the distribution of one group (although that explained in a negative way the distribution of the other) to an examination of the expression in both groups of one particular social fact. Any correlations which can be made will be against the total social situation in the city.

It is obvious from the map that there is an ecological relationship between areas of very high segregation and the industrial regions in the town; the lower indices in north, south and east are striking. To test the hypothesis that the degree of segregation varies in relation to socioeconomic class – which is suggested by the map – the degree of segregation was correlated with occupational rank, and the result is shown in the scatter-diagram (Fig. 14.3).

The Northern Ireland Census does not use a method of ranking occupations into socio-economic groups as the Census for England and Wales does; so the first step was to group together occupations in classes which were roughly similar to those of England.[35] To produce a simple index, the five groups which were in this way obtained were further reduced to three categories, roughly corresponding with non-manual, skilled manual and unskilled occupations. Of the total male and female workers in Belfast the vast majority fell into the third category – 147,314 out of 212,349; there were 34,150 in the first category and 30,885 in the third.

The relative numbers and percentages of each category were made available for each enumeration district, and in order to produce an occupational rank index for each district, category I was weighted four times, category II was weighted twice. The three categories were now added for each district and the total represented the index. These were ranked (142–365) and split into four groups by finding the median and the two quartiles. This gave an approximate rank grouping based on occupation.

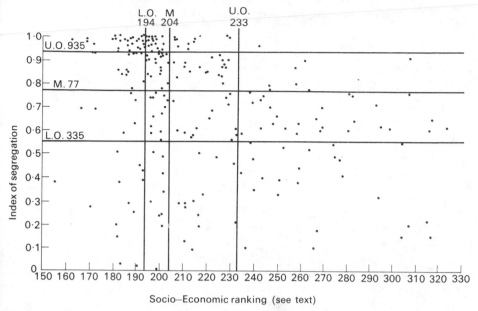

Fig. 14.3 Belfast: correlation of degree of segregation with occupational rank.

The scatter-diagram shows the relationship between this socio-economic ranking and segregation. The diagram has been divided into sixteen compartments by the inclusion of medians and quartiles for both indices. The number of enumeration districts falling within each compartment is an indication of whether or not there is any correlation between these two factors.

With the exception of the bottom left square the figures seem to suggest that there is a broad correlation, that generally speaking segregation is more marked in the lower socio-economic classes than it is in the higher. The category referred to is considerably swollen in number, 11, because it contains several of those enumeration districts mentioned above in which segregation is hidden by the overlapping of two mutually exclusive distributions. This applies to seven districts in the bottom left square which should be in the upper left-hand square as showing extreme segregation. The figure 9 in the next square on the lowest left-hand side is similarly swollen by two enumeration districts in which segregation is almost complete and by two districts which cover the city centre and in which evaluation of the true position is very difficult.

Generally speaking segregation seems to decrease with a rise in socio-economic ranking. It is most marked in those enumeration districts which rate very low on the socio-economic scale. There is more variation in those districts which rate higher on the socio-economic ranking. A comparison of the segregation map with that showing socio-economic ranking (Fig.

Number of enumeration districts

				Seg. index
29	18	10	1	
13	19	18	8	UQ 0·94
5	12	15	26	M 0·77
11	9	14	23	LQ 0·55

Segregation ↑

LQ   M   UQ

→ Rank

4th   3rd   2nd   1st

Percentages

12·55	7·99	4·33	0·43
5·63	8·23	7·79	3·46
2·17	5·20	6·50	11·25
4·76	3·90	6·06	10·0

Segregation ↑

→ Rank

14.4) will help to show that the correlation appears closer when geographical factors are taken into account.

The map suggests that both segregation and social rank are closely linked with spatial factors, and that their distribution does reflect the several urban regions into which the city could be divided. To consider such regions in detail is beyond the scope of this paper, but the broad outline of the urban pattern is as follows: the whole of the western sector is industrial, and, with the exception of the upper Falls Road area, residential use is limited to the merest fragmentary rim: northern and southern sectors are residential, both with an older core which approaches very near the city centre and which expanded outwards to the present streets and avenues; east again there is a wide peripheral zone of residential land use beyond industrial Ballymacarrett – but this has no older core, and it is in all respects newer than similar districts to the west of the Lagan. Social rank reflects these different urban environments very well, but without revealing those differences in age which still further distinguish the eastern residential area from the northern and southern.

Segregation shows a wider variation from the urban pattern than does social rank. For example, segregation is much less marked in parts of the northern and southern residential areas (especially the northern axis and the Ormeau district) than in the corresponding eastern residential area; in

240

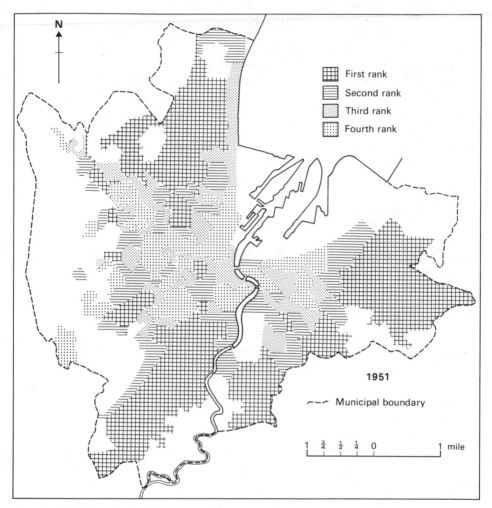

First rank
Second rank
Third rank
Fourth rank

1951

--- Municipal boundary

1 ¾ ½ ¼ 0   1 mile

Fig. 14.4 Belfast: social rank.

the latter there are districts in which segregation is higher than the median. The index is also high in a wide area around Ballymacarrett. The density map may provide a part answer for these phenomena, for the absolute number of catholics east of the river is very much smaller than that to the west. Traditionally the main inflow of Irish population has been from the west, settling in the already well-defined sectors of the old town. Development east of the Lagan is much newer. The spread of the catholic population into the newer suburbs is one which distinguished between those residential areas which grew from older cores – north and south – and that in the east which did not do so; there is no comparable movement from Ballymacarrett to Knock.

241

Differences in segregation, therefore, are not linked simply with social rank; but rather do they reflect the type and evolution of certain sectors of the city and the spatial relations of these sectors with one another.

The mapping of distribution and segregation in no way explains these two phenomena. It does suggest correlations with the distribution of socio-economic data; but its main function is to illustrate differences in various sectors of the city, and these sectors themselves have historical and environmental characteristics of their own in which lie some of the complex factors governing religious distribution. This paper does nothing more than state the problem and suggest that spatial relations are one essential in explaining social phenomena. But it should be a starting point only of a sociological study of the total social situation in which the human relationships which have been dealt with above exist and develop.

Notes and References

1. As, for example, in Caernarfon and Cardigan in Wales.
2. British Museum. Copy in Linen Hall Library, Belfast.
3. See illustration of Carrickfergus in 1680, reproduced in G. Camblin, *The Town in Ulster*, 1951, plate 16.
4. W. Petty, (ed. S. Pender), *A Census in Ireland, c. 1659*, 1939, p. 8.
5. George Macartney to Mr Secretary Dawson, March 24th, 1708: quoted in G. Benn, *History of Belfast*, 1877, pp. 416–17.
6. Benn, *op. cit.*, p. 622.
7. P. C. J. Rogers, 'The Belfast Volunteers and the Catholic Question (1778–1793)', D Litt. thesis, Queen's University, Belfast, 1932, p. 5.
8. J. O'Laverty, *Historical Account of Down and Connor*, II, 408.
9. *Belfast News Letter*, June 8th–11th, 1784.
10. Arthur Young, *A Town in Ireland* (1776–9), II, part ii, p. 48: 'I must be free to own that when I have heard gentlemen who have favoured the laws as they now stand, urge the dangerous tenets of the church of Rome, quote the cruelties which have disgraced that religion in Ireland, and led them into the common routine of declamation on that side of the question . . . when I have been a witness to such conversations I could not but smile to see subscriptions handed about for building a mass house, at the very time when the heaviest vengeance of the law fully executed fell upon those who possessed a landed property, or ventured a mortgage upon it'.
11. Rogers, *op. cit.*, p. 5. Real property was forbidden, and the positions from which a Roman catholic was excluded included: magistracy, the corporation, university, bench, bar, voting, holding office of constable, sheriff, jury, teaching; they could neither inherit nor receive land, were restricted to two apprentices except in the linen trade, and were not allowed to inter-marry with protestants.

12. J. Barrow, *A Tour round Ireland*, 1835, p. 37.
13. *Ibid.*, p. 33.
14. J. Jamieson, 'The influence of the Rev. Henry Cooke on the political life of Ulster', unpublished MA thesis, Queen's University, Belfast, 1950, chap. 2.
15. 13 & 14 Vic. Cap. II, 1850. An Act to restrain party processions in Ireland. Firearms, weapons and emblems were also banned under this Act.
16. 23 and 24 Vic. Cap. CXLI, 1860.
17. *Report of the Commission of Inquiry into the Riots in Belfast in July and September, 1857*, HMSO, 1858.
18. T. Henry, *History of the Belfast Riots*, 1864.
19. Thomas McKnight, *Ulster As It is*, 1896, I, 33, 36.
20. *Report of the Commission of Inquiry into the Riots in Belfast in July and September, 1857.* p. 2.
21. *Ibid.*
22. The catholic group near Cromac Square was in a compact area west of the river. The ward covered a vastly greater district to the south, extending east of the Lagan.
23. *Census of Ireland*, 1881.
24. *Belfast News Letter*, July 1920–June 1922.
25. 12 & 13 George V Cap. 5, 1922, Civil Authorities (Special Powers) Act. This included powers to impose curfews, ban processions, emblems, arms, etc. The powers could be delegated by the Minister to the police.
26. Thanks are due to the Registrar General of Northern Ireland for making these figures available.
27. To produce this map, the densities in all the enumeration districts were arrayed, and then subdivided on the basis of median, quartiles and octiles: these provided the classes.
28. O.S. map, first edition, 6 in. to 1 mile, 1832.
29. E. Jones., 'Social geography of Belfast', *Journal of the Statistical and Social Inquiry Society of Ireland*, **20**, (1953–54).
30. E. W. Burgess, *Proc. Am. Sociol. Soc.*, **18**, (1929), 88–9.
31. W. L. Warner and L. Strole, *The Social Systems of American Ethnic Groups*, 1945.
32. J. Jahn, C. F. Schmidt and C. Schrag: 'The measurement of ecological segregation', *Am. Sociol. Rev.*, **12**, no. 3, (1947), 293–303. Discussed further in: R. A. Hornseth, *Am. Sociol Rev.,* **12**, no. 3 (1947), 603–4; J. J. Williams, *Am. Sociol. Rev.*, **13**, no. 3 (1948), 298–303; O. D. Duncan and B. Duncan, *Am. Sociol. Rev.*, **20**, no. 2 (1955), 210–17.
33. D. O. and M. S. Cowgill: 'An index of segregation based on block statistics', *Am. Sociol. Rev.*, **16**, no. 6 (1951), 825–31.
34. E. Jones: 'Belfast, a survey of the City', *Belfast in its Regional Setting,* British Association Handbook, 1951.
35. Group 1—Occupational Order XIX, Code Nos. 760–819.
    Group 2—   ,,   Orders XVI, XVIII, C. Nos. 610–629, 710–759.

Group 3—	,,	Orders II, IV–XV (inc.), XVII, XX, XXI, XXII, XXIII, XXVII, C. Nos. 010–030, 060–609, 630–709, 820–895, 961–976.
Group 4—	,,	Orders I, III, XXIV, XXV, C. Nos. 000, 040–059, 900–921.
Group 5—	,,	Order XXVI, C. Nos. 930–950.

This is approximately the classification introduced by the Census of England and Wales in 1911, in which the first group included professional, higher administrative and managerial-executive: the second, inspectorial and supervisory (all non-manual): the third, skilled manual and routine non-manual: the fourth, semi-skilled manual, and the fifth, unskilled manual.

For further discussion see J. Hall and C. Jones, 'Social gradings of occupations', *British Journal of Sociology*, **1**, (1950), 31–55; D. V. Glass, *Social Classes and Mobility in England*, 1954.

F. Boal

15 Social space in the Belfast urban area*

The classic work of Emrys Jones[1] has provided a more comprehensive urban geography of Belfast than is perhaps available for any other city of comparable size. This is an excellent foundation on which further study is being based. Much of his work used data obtained from the 1951 census of population, and most of the analysis was restricted to the County Borough of Belfast. However, since 1951 the population of the County Borough has declined by over 44,000, while the built-up area outside the city had, at the 1966 census, a population of 161,000, or about 29 per cent of the total population of the whole urban area. On these grounds alone a further analysis seems justified. In addition, there is now a greater range of data available for the whole of the urban area, derived from the 1966 Census of Population, from the Belfast Area Travel Survey, and from various planning surveys. Finally, the availability of computers makes it possible to use new techniques for analysis of the data.

Urban social geography in general has been heavily orientated towards the description of the areal distribution of a range of socio-economic characteristics. This is in line with the social area analyses of sociologists such as Shevky and Bell.[2] However, the spatial aspects of interaction between areas has received little attention except in transportation studies and investigations of shopping patterns. Because of the system nature of urban complexes it would appear that social area analysis can be improved by a study of interaction both within and between such areas. The present study then, will consist of two principal parts: first an analysis of the whole urban area leading to its subdivision into a series of broad socio-economic regions, and second, an analysis of some aspects of interaction within the broader context established in the first part of the study.

* Reprinted from *Irish Geographical Studies*, published by the Department of Geography, The Queen's University of Belfast, in honour of E. Estyn Evans, Belfast, 1970.

Urban area analysis

Urban areas have been characterized in terms of a number of gradients. E. W. Burgess suggests a positive gradient outwards from the city centre in terms of class – working class in the inner areas grading through to the highest income groups on the periphery.[3] Colin Clark, and subsequent workers, have demonstrated the existence of a general negative gradient of population density with distance from the city centre.[4] Both sets of

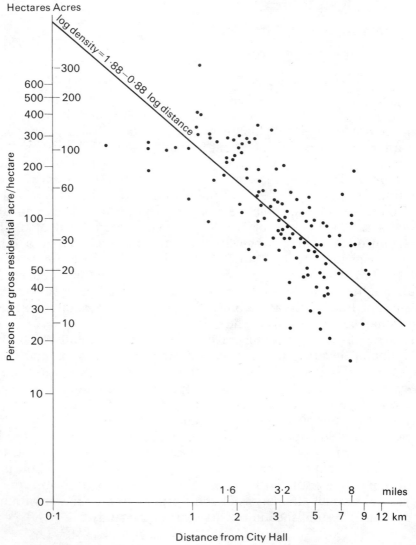

Fig. 15.1 The relationship between the population density of 119 census zones and their distance from the City Hall (1966).

246

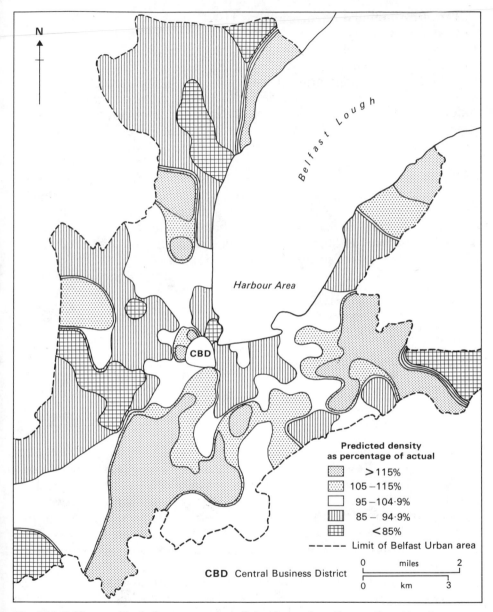

Fig. 15.2 Belfast: residuals from regression of density against distance from the city centre. The regression equation used to obtain residuals was log gross residential density (persons per acre) = 1·88–0·88 log distance (miles). For locations named in text see Fig. 15.5.

gradients indicate a concentric arrangement of various socio-economic characteristics focused on the central business district. These concentric models will be taken as a point of departure in this study.

247

The gross population density for 119 Census data zones within the Belfast area, ranging from 0·6 km (0·35 mile) to 10·5 km (6·54 miles) from the city centre (City Hall) is shown in Fig. 23.1. The data has been plotted on double log axes and a least squares regression line fitted which is based on the equation, log population density = 1·88 − 0·88 log distance (where density is persons per gross residential acre and distance is in tenths of a mile). The negative form of the density gradient is obvious. At the same time it is clear that individual data zones differ considerably from the general trend. These deviations from the regular 'model' density surface can be computed and mapped in terms of residuals from the regression (Fig. 15.2). The spatial distribution of the residuals displays a well defined pattern and can be described in terms of thirteen sectors forming an alternating series in which density is either over- or under-predicted. Where density is over-predicted, actual densities are less than expected from the model, and conversely where under-predicted actual densities are higher than expected. The two sets of sectors are indicated in Table 15.1.

Table 15.1   Positive and negative residual sectors

Over predicted (positive residual areas)	*Under predicted (negative residual areas)*
Outer North Lough Shore	Inner North Lough Shore–Rathcoole
Antrim Road	Crumlin Road–Ligoniel
Ballygomartin Road (weak)	Springfield Road–Falls Road
Malone Road	Ormeau Road (weak)
Ravenhill–Saintfield Roads	Castlereagh Road
Upper Newtownards–Belmont Roads	Inner South Lough Shore
Outer South Lough Shore	

This suggests an overall sector distribution of density rather than a concentric one. However, while sectors can be distinguished, within any one sector the negatively sloped density gradient can still be distinguished, and is illustrated in Fig. 15.3A where density is shown along two high density and two low density sectors. The same gradient feature, though now positive, can be demonstrated for socio-economic status (Fig. 15.3B). The differences between sectors and the overall density gradient are both apparent.

Density (x) in Belfast is negatively correlated with distance (y) from the city centre ($r \log x. \log y = -0.72$) but as noted above, with distinctive differences in density levels between sectors. In European and North American cities there is also a high correlation between density and other socioeconomic characteristics. Belfast is no exception, where, for instance, a general index of socioeconomic status (*a*) based on occupation has a high negative correlation with density ($r_{a.x} = -0.70$), while there is a similar negative correlation between density and car ownership (*b*) ($r_{b.x} = -0.67$). If we take four general indicators of socioeconomic status (density,

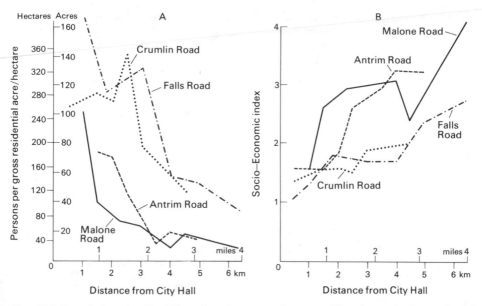

Fig. 15.3 Population density (A) and socio-economic status (B) measured along selected sectors in Belfast.

occupational index[5], car ownership and male unemployment) and correlate them against a general array of variables for the 119 Belfast data zones, the correlation matrix shown in Table 15.2 is obtained.

The four general indicators are all highly intercorrelated. At the same time they are highly correlated with a number of other variables. It would seem possible, therefore, to substitute one of the indicators as a general socioeconomic index. However, instead of using just one variable it was considered desirable to employ a technique that would involve the use of the full array of the twenty-six available variables. This number was finally reduced to twenty-five by the omission of the distance variable in case this had too strong a patterning effect on its own. The technique used was principal components analysis whereby linear combinations of variables are obtained which are uncorrelated, and whereby the first linear combination (component) is a normalized combination with maximum variance; the second component is uncorrelated with the first and has as large a variance as possible and so on. The initial data was standardized.

The first five principal components obtained absorbed 79 per cent of the total variance of the twenty-five variables as follows:

	Component					
	1	2	3	4	5	1–5
Percentage of variance	41·4	18·0	8·8	6·4	4·5	79·1

The component scores were computed. The data zones were then ranked

249

Table 15.2 Correlations between selected variables for the Belfast urban area. In addition the correlations between twenty-five variables and the first two components are also given (data are untransformed)

	Density	Occupational index[5]	Car Ownership	Male unemployment	Correlation between variables and component Component 1	Component 2
Per cent population $\leqslant$ 14 years						0·88
Per cent population $\geqslant$ 65 years						−0·92
Persons per household						0·73
Persons per room			−0·51	0·50	0·61	0·63
Distance from City Hall	−0·59	0·62	0·59		NA	NA
Gross residential density		−0·70	−0·67	0·72	0·78	
Gross dwelling density	0·92	−0·78	−0·72	0·57	0·81	
Occupational index	−0·70		0·86		−0·62	−0·88
Cars per household	−0·67	0·86			−0·57	−0·89
Per cent of population 15–19 years in full-time education	−0·64	0·70	0·75		−0·79	
Per cent of population with driving licences	−0·75	0·88	0·89	−0·65	−0·91	
Per cent of heads of household socio-economic group A_i	−0·75	0·70	0·77		−0·72	
Per cent of heads of household Socio-economic group A_{ii}	−0·50	0·66	0·53		−0·63	
Per cent of heads of household Socio-economic group B						0·62
Per cent of heads of household Socio-economic group C	0·62	−0·74	−0·74	0·54	0·83	
Per cent population over 15 years occupied						0·71
Per cent occupied males out of work	0·72	−0·62	−0·57		0·68	
Per cent workers employed in CBD						
Per cent journey to work by bus			−0·55		0·52	
Per cent journey to work by car	−0·75	0·88	0·91	−0·63	−0·92	
Per cent journey to work on foot	0·70	−0·72	−0·66	0·67	0·76	
Age of housing		−0·62			0·55	−0·73
Migrants as per cent of total population	−0·53	0·58	0·51		−0·61	
Internal area migrants						
In migrants from rest of Northern Ireland		0·58	0·50		−0·58	
Per cent of population Roman Catholic					0·57	

Only correlation coefficients > 0·5 shown. All coefficients significant at 0·01 level. NA – not available.

according to the value of their scores on each component, and then grouped by deciles. A map of the zonal groups derived from the first principal component is shown in Fig. 15.4. The component is most highly correlated positively with the following initial variables (see Table 15.2): persons per room, gross residential density, gross dwelling density, percentage of heads of household in socioeconomic group C (semi-skilled and unskilled manual workers), percentage of normally occupied males out of work and percentage of people who journey to work on foot. The component is negatively associated with occupational index, car owner-ship, percentage of population with driving licences, percentage of popu-lation between fifteen and nineteen years in full-time education, percentage of heads of household in socioeconomic group A_i (managerial and pro-fessional), and percentage who make the journey to work by car. These variables are generally indicative of socioeconomic status, and on this basis the first principal component has been named the socioeconomic component.

The pattern displayed shows a close association with the pattern of residuals from the density analysis (Fig. 15.2) and the sectoral form is striking. Those zones that score highly on this component are areas of low socioeconomic status, whereas at the other end of the scale are the high status areas. Particularly striking are the low status sectors along the inner parts of the north and south lough shores and the massive low status sector extending west and south-west from the city centre, along the Crumlin–Ligoniel and Falls–Springfield axes, with the Shankill Road in the middle. The most clearly defined high status sectors are on the lines of the Antrim, Malone, Ravenhill-Saintfield, and Upper Newtownards-Belmont Roads, together with the two outer lough shore areas.

One vital aspect of the low status sector extending west and south-west from the city centre is not included in the pattern derived from the first component – this is the high degree of religious segregation that exists.[6] Unfortunately, religious data was not obtained in the 1966 population census, necessitating the use of estimates derived from a series of surveys. This provides a sample cover for about 50 per cent of the urban area, but when considered with the pattern discussed by Jones[7] a fairly complete picture can be obtained. The main elements of the highly segregated religious area in the centre and western low status sector of the city is shown in Fig. 15.5, where a highly segregated area is defined as having more than 90 per cent Protestants or more than 90 per cent Roman Catholics. The main Roman Catholic concentration extends from the city centre south-westwards along the spine of the Falls Road for a distance of about 6 km (3·7 miles). There are separate and much smaller concentra-tions north of the middle Crumlin Road (Ardoyne), immediately west of the city centre, south-east of the centre (Cromac), and east of the centre (part of Ballymacarrett). Between Ardoyne and the Falls Road sector, there is the very well developed and almost entirely Protestant Shankill Road area, while lying south-east of the Falls sector is the equally pre-dominantly Protestant Sandy Row area.

The result is that within the western low status area there is a Roman Catholic–Protestant alternation of sub-sectors. The actual divides between these sub-sectors are, almost without exception, very sharp. In some cases

251

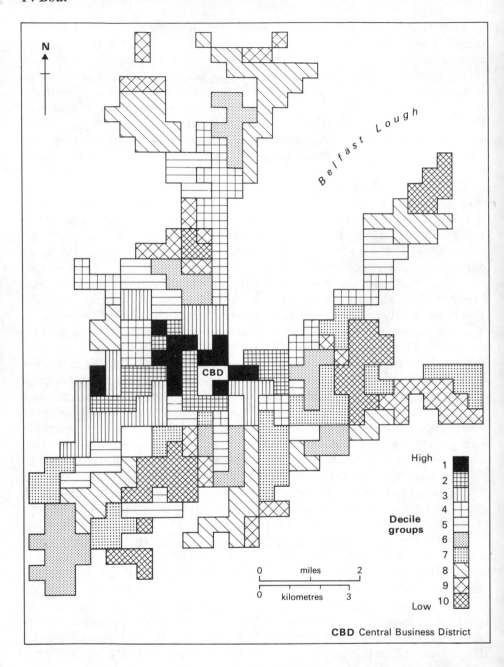

Fig. 15.4 Belfast urban area: census data zones ranked according to their component scores on the socio-economic component. The boundaries of the census zones have been adjusted to a grid format.

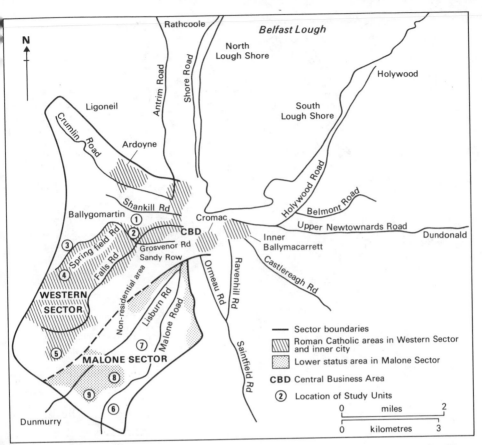

Fig. 15.5 Roman Catholic areas in central and west Belfast, and general key to locations mentioned in the text. Study units: (1) Shankill; (2) Clonard; (3) New Barnsley; (4) Turf Lodge; (5) Ladybrook; (6) Upper Malone; (7) Inner Malone; (8) Taughmonagh; (9) Erinvale. *Note.* Dock area excluded.

the division is composed of non-residential areas, such as factory sites and railway tracks, while in others, the residential areas come into direct contact with each other, and the transition from Protestant to Catholic occurs within the width of a street of houses. An example of this is shown in Fig. 15.6, on the divide between the Falls and Shankill sub-sectors.[8]

Thus far the basic socioeconomic picture of the Belfast urban area we have obtained is one of a city centre focussed gradient, positively sloped in terms of social status, and negatively sloped in terms of density. Superimposed on this general surface are the alternating high and low status sectors, while the western low status sector displays a further set of internal sub-sectors distinguished on the basis of religion.

When the data zones are ranked on their scores for component 2 the

253

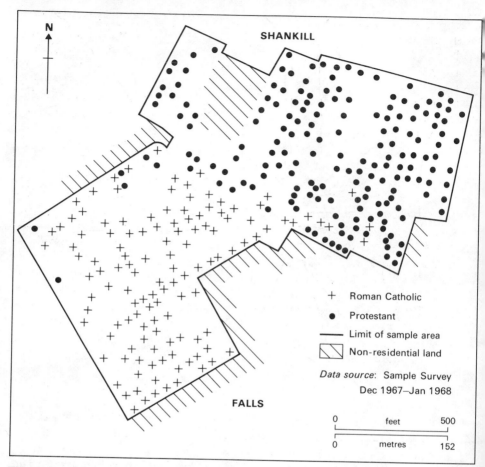

N

SHANKILL

+ Roman Catholic

● Protestant

— Limit of sample area

▨ Non-residential land

Data source: Sample Survey
Dec 1967–Jan 1968

FALLS

| 0 | feet | 500 |
| 0 | metres | 152 |

Fig. 15.6 Religious distribution in a small area of west Belfast at the contact of the Shankill and Falls sub-sectors. The map is based on a ten per cent sample of persons over the age of twenty-one.

pattern produced is much less sectoral in character. In fact, the highest scoring zones are the peripheral ones and the lowest scoring the central zones, with inner high status areas scoring lowest of all. The initial variables most heavily weighted in this component are those associated with demographic characteristics. Zones with high scores have large proportions of the population under fourteen, a low proportion over sixty-five, and large households. A large proportion of the population has also been involved recently in a house move, and the houses occupied are relatively new. The component picks out the growing periphery of the urban area. This growth is of very mixed socioeconomic character, in that there is Local Authority and Northern Ireland Housing Trust rental housing, low to medium cost private estates, and a limited development of high cost housing. Government developed housing (Local Authority and Housing Trust) is quite widespread on the periphery and has been constructed at the outer ends of a wide range of socioeconomic sectors. However, there is a predominance of rental housing on the outer fringes of low status sectors. Where Government housing lies on the lines of higher status sectors, the population generally has a higher socioeconomic status than for similar housing on the lines of the low status sectors. Thus, while the demographic characteristics of the urban area have a general concentric pattern, a strong sectoral influence can still be seen.

The presence of both sectoral and concentric residential patterns corresponds with the findings reported by Berry for American cities.[9] He notes that there are three dimensions of socioeconomic variation: the sectoral variation of neighbourhoods by socioeconomic rank, the concentric variation of neighbourhoods according to family structure and the localized segregation of particular ethnic groups. However, if we consider the religious groups as 'ethnic' the segregation pattern in the Belfast context is predominantly sectoral, as noted above. Thus, while Jones found a 'sector residential pattern' in the west,[10] the present analysis suggests the co-existence of 'sectors' and 'rings' over much of the urban area.

Before proceeding to the activity analysis it should be stressed that there is some loss of 'information' in the analysis of the Belfast data zones. This applies particularly to parts of the periphery, where the data zones are quite large and include a wide range of housing types. The general picture is not distorted greatly but locally considerable statistical homogenization has been imposed.

Activity analysis

Up to this point, the analysis has dealt with the whole urban area, and has concentrated on standard socioeconomic data. An attempt will now be made to examine a series of sample areas in much greater detail, and in particular to carry out an analysis of some activity patterns to see how activity linkages are distributed and how activity is related to the basic socioeconomic structure of the urban area outlined above.

Nine study units were selected and a random sample of persons over the age of twenty-one was interviewed in each area. The study units were selected from the western low status sector and the Malone high status sector. Pairs of units were also selected to allow comparison, while holding religion, socioeconomic status and age of housing constant. The study units and certain of their characteristics are listed in Table 3 while their locations are shown in Fig. 15.5. The sharp differences of religion within the western sector and between the two semi-detached private housing

Table 15.3 Study unit characteristics

Sector	Study unit name	Type of housing	Persons per net residential hectare (acre)	Households per net residential hectare (acre)	Religion (per cent RC)	Size of household	Occupational index[5]	Persons sampled
	Shankill I	Victorian terrace	438 (177)	138 (54)	1	3·3	1·68	158
	Clonard	Victorian terrace	353 (143)	90 (36)	98	3·9	2·27	113
Western	New Barnsley	Corporation estate*	195 (79)	34 (14)	12	5·7	2·47	101
	Turf Lodge	Corporation estate*	259 (105)	37 (15)	99	7·0	2·13	116
	Ladybrook	Semi-detached private	96 (39)	23 (9)	90	4·2	3·26	61
	Inner Malone	Large detached	34 (14)	8 (3)	14	4·1	4·11	65
Malone	Upper Malone	Large detached bungalows	30 (12)	8 (3)	8	3·7	4·20	66
	Erinvale	Mainly semi-detached private	125 (51)	33 (13)	10	3·8	3·32	77
	Taughmonagh	Corporation 'pre-fab' estate	107 (44)	19 (8)	13	5·7	2·58	92

* Maisonette areas excluded.

areas, one in the western sector, the other on the outer edge of Malone, are evident.

Clearly, Shankill, Clonard, New Barnsley and Turf Lodge are low status areas, while Inner and Upper Malone are high status areas. On the other hand Ladybrook, Erinvale and Taughmonagh, do not conform to the particular low or high status characteristics of their respective sectors. In fact, these three areas lie on the flanks of the two sectors, Ladybrook being lower middle income and predominantly Roman Catholic, Erinvale being lower middle income and Protestant. Taughmonagh is a highly non-conforming insertion of Corporation housing on the central axis of the Malone sector. The non-conforming nature of these three study units is also evident in the activity analysis.

The activity analysis applied depends on the examination of a set of linkages within the Belfast urban area. The present residence of the inter-viewee forms one point and the links between that point and three other sets of points are established. The three other sets of points are the pre-vious address of interviewee (if there is one), the origin points of social visits to interviewee or points interviewee visited during a one week period, and the pre-marriage addresses of interviewee and spouse (if applicable). The first step in the analysis required the establishment of the extent to which points associated with the three social attributes (previous address, visits and pre-marriage address) corresponded with each other for any one study unit. The extent to which the three point distributions were congruent for each of the study units is shown in Fig. 15.7, cells for which three or two attributes were congruent being indicated, together with the cells for which only one attribute was present.

If we confine our attention to those cells where two or three attributes are congruent a number of features emerge. Firstly, all the study units display 'core areas' where all three attributes are congruent. The simplest and most sharply developed are those for the inner low status areas of Shankill and Clonard. Secondly, we can note the more elongated well-developed cores for the outer housing estates of New Barnsley and Turf Lodge and the somewhat more fragmented core pattern for the private estate of Ladybrook. In the Malone sector two distinct patterns emerge, rather weakly developed elongated cores for the high status Upper and Inner Malone units, and more strongly developed but discontinuous cores for the Erinvale private estate and the Taughmonagh Corporation Hous-ing area. Viewed differently we can say that all the low and middle status areas display well-developed cores while the high status units are weaker in this respect.

Well-developed cores indicate a closely knit spatial system wherein, for each study unit, there are a series of congruent linkages – the area or areas concerned are connected to the study unit in terms of visiting, an im-mediately previous address and the pre-marriage location of at least one

257

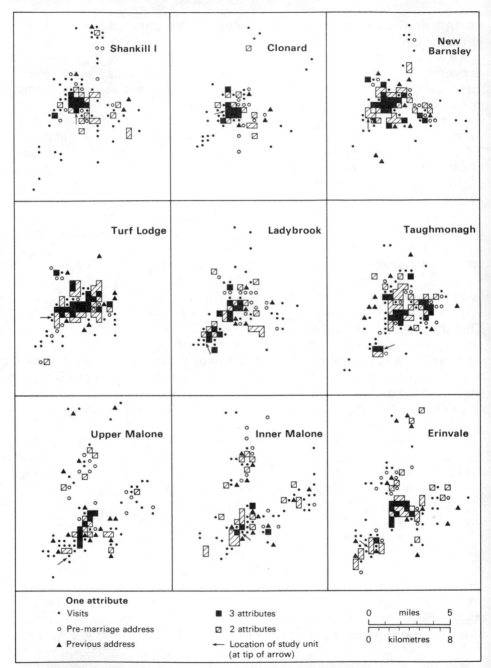

Fig. 15.7 Congruence of social activity attributes for sample residents in each of nine study units. The congruence is measured within a 0·5 km² grid superimposed on the Belfast urban area.

Note. The degree of concentration of attributes in the three and two attribute cells is not shown.

partner. In the instances in which all these linkages occur within the same area, this is taken to indicate the existence of a tightly knit 'spatial community', which Fried claims is an indication of a standard working class community pattern, 'an overlapping series of close knit networks'.[11] The core areas occur either where there are old established fairly static groups (Shankill and Clonard) or where there has been movement from a small part of the inner city to new housing areas on the urban periphery (New Barnsley, Turf Lodge, Taughmonagh, which are Local Authority housing areas, and Ladybrook and Erinvale, which are higher status private housing areas deriving a significant proportion of their population from a restricted section of the inner city).

The two high status Malone areas do not show the close knit networks to the same degree, though even here reasonably well defined cores are evident. However, in these two cases, not only are the various social attributes less congruent within the Belfast urban area but they also show much stronger linkages outside the urban area altogether. This is shown in Table 15.4 where the percentage concentration of the various attributes is given for the Malone sector and also outside the urban area.

The five study units within the western sector show high levels of concentration for all three social attributes (Table 15.5). A very high proportion of total interaction is restricted to the western low status sector. A further degree of concentration can also be distinguished, in that the two predominantly Protestant study units (Shankill and New Barnsley) have very high levels of linkage within the Protestant sub-sectors, while the

Table 15.4 Percentage allocation of previous addresses, pre-marriage addresses and visit connections for the Malone sector sample units

		Malone sector (percentage of urban area connections)		Low status sub-sector + Sandy Row (percentage) of urban area connections	Outside urban area (percentage of all connections)	
	Sample units	*Total*	*High status sub-sector*		*Northern Ireland*	*Abroad*
Previous address	Upper Malone	65	48	20	11	20
	Inner Malone	60	52	10	11	11
	Erinvale	25	4	35	20	12
	Taughmonagh	15	4	24	7	4
Pre-marriage address	Upper Malone	33	27	3	24	42
	Inner Malone	25	25	0	28	30
	Erinvale	24	7	30	33	9
	Taughmonagh	9	2	32	11	6
Visit connections	Upper Malone	71	66	9	17	4
	Inner Malone	63	58	6	22	5
	Erinvale	44	4	52	26	0
	Taughmonagh	27	1	36	6	3

Table 15.5 Percentage allocation of previous addresses, pre-marriage addresses and visit connections for the western sector sample units

	Sample units	Western sector (percentage of urban area connections)			Outside urban area (percentage of all connections)	
		Total	Within Protestant sub-sectors	Within Catholic sub-sectors	Northern Ireland	Abroad
Previous address	Shankill	87	82	5	4	4
	Clonard	81	5	76	4	5
	New Barnsley	75	67	8	2	9
	Turf Lodge	85	5	80	0	2
	Ladybrook	87	11	76	9	14
Pre-marriage address	Shankill	91	89	2	5	1
	Clonard	85	7	78	7	8
	New Barnsley	79	71	8	7	4
	Turf Lodge	83	7	76	2	3
	Ladybrook	86	13	73	19	6
Visit connections	Shankill	83	79	4	3	1
	Clonard	93	5	88	3	2
	New Barnsley	84	76	6	5	1
	Turf Lodge	85	5	80	1	0
	Ladybrook	79	8	71	10	2

three Roman Catholic units have strong links within the Catholic sub-sectors. The different 'orientation' of the Protestant and Roman Catholic sub-sectors can also be indicated in terms of newspaper readership and support for certain football teams. In this case Catholic loyalties lie with Glasgow Celtic and the *Irish News*, while Protestant loyalties lie with Linfield football club and there is an 'inverted' loyalty to the *Irish News*. Probably television and the *Belfast Telegraph* evening paper are the two news and cultural media that both sectors have in common but there is little else (Table 15.6).

Table 15.6 Newspaper readership, football team support and presence of television sets, Western sector study units

	Percentage Roman Catholic	Percentage reading Irish News	Percentage supporting Glasgow Celtic	Percentage supporting Linfield	Percentage reading Belfast Telegraph	Percentage with TV sets
Clonard	98	83	73	0	58	77
Turf Lodge	99	74	63	0	70	97
Ladybrook	90	39	11	0	62	100
Shankill	1	3	0	74	68	86
New Barnsley	12	3	1	63	72	97

The three outer units within the western sector (New Barnsley, Turf Lodge and Ladybrook) show clearly the centre-periphery nature of much interaction, for previous addresses are located in the inner parts of the subsectors as are pre-marriage addresses. The tendency towards out-migration along sectors has been noted previously by Jones,[12] and is a generally observed feature of residential moves within the Belfast urban area. If a move to a new house is contemplated, people express a strong preference for a location in the outer reaches of the sector within which they already reside. This is clearly related to familiarity and ease of movement from the new housing area back to the 'home' district.

The study units in the Malone sector display a less concentrated set of linkages in terms of the sector itself. Even so the two high status (Upper and Inner Malone) do show considerable degrees of sector concentration in terms of previous addresses and visit connections, even though there are significant linkages outside the urban area altogether. For these two areas the pre-marriage address is more dispersed, both within and outside the urban area, though the urban area distribution is almost entirely restricted to high status sectors.

The two lower status units in the Malone sector are the most weakly linked in terms of the sector within which they are present. This is because both units are non-conforming as far as the socioeconomic characteristics of most of the sector are concerned. On social status grounds they have low probabilities of connection with the high status predominant portion of the sector. However, both study units show strong links with an inner low status area (Sandy Row), which until now we have considered part of the Western sector. In terms of potential interaction this interpretation needs to be relaxed because the innermost parts of all sectors west of the river are close to each other and it is questionable to which sector they should be allocated. From the restricted evidence available it would appear that Sandy Row is more strongly linked to the lower status outer parts of the Malone sector than to the outer parts of the Western sector, particularly since the outer parts of the western Protestant sub-sector are 'cut-off' from Sandy Row by the overwhelmingly Catholic sub-sector of Falls.

The non-conforming nature of Erinvale and Taughmonagh is further emphasized when the distances of the linked points from the study units are considered. For instance, the mean distance of visit links for Taughmonagh is not significantly different from that for Upper Malone, while it is significantly greater than that for Inner Malone ($p = 0.05$) despite the considerable socioeconomic differences between the units.

The pattern of connectivity which has been analysed would seem to be influenced by a number of factors. Firstly, linkages will occur predominantly with areas which are similar in socioeconomic and religious characteristics. Secondly, the linkages are further constrained by distance, and by the general accessibility pattern of the various potential linkage areas

F. Boal

to any particular study unit. Where there is a high dependence on walking and use of buses, distances are small unless movement is channelled in and out along a radial road where there is a good bus service. With the present radial arrangement of bus routes between city centre and periphery, lateral (inter-sector) movement is difficult, particularly where the spine roads of the sectors are far apart. As noted earlier, however, since the spine roads are much closer together in the inner parts of the city, inter-sector movement is easier here. The availability of a car and to some extent of a telephone also tends to free movement from the radial network. But all the low status study units have two-thirds to three-quarters of households without cars, and in the western sector there is no significant difference between the inner and outer low status areas (Table 15.7). Thus,

Table 15.7 Mobility potential of households in the sample units

	Cars per household	Percentage of households with no car	Percentage of households with telephone
Shankill	0·14	85	2
Clonard	0·29	71	7
New Barnsley	0·19	82	5
Turf Lodge	0·24	77	2
Ladybrook	0·77	23	16
Upper Malone	1·55	2	96
Inner Malone	1·68	6	99
Erinvale	0·77	30	35
Taughmonagh	0·35	67	0

in this case peripheral location is not compensated for by higher personal mobility using a car and consequently, movement by bus on the spine roads is a major constraint on linkage patterns.

At the other end of the spectrum lie the two high status Malone units where practically every household has at least one car, and about half the households have two or more cars available. About three quarters of the households in the middle status units (Erinvale and Ladybrook) have cars. The existence of a telephone is even more marked in the inequality of its distribution, ranging from just about saturation in the Malone units to almost insignificance in the low status areas. The telephone distribution pattern suggests a whole sub-system of interaction as far as the high status areas are concerned.

The lack of cars and to some extent of telephones in the low status units, together with the enforced radial nature of bus travel, suggests why so much social interaction is sectoral in nature, and the constraints of religion and social status further affect the pattern. In this context it is still striking to observe the degree to which the interaction for the Malone high status units is also restricted to a considerable extent to the Malone sector, despite much greater potential physical mobility. There are elements of Fried's 'close knit networks'[13] present here too.

Conclusion

This analysis has disclosed the existence of clearly developed sectors in the Belfast urban area. The 'static' socioeconomic sector pattern disclosed in the earlier part of the study is further emphasized by the sectoral congruence of selected activity systems. The sector pattern, when viewed both from a social pattern and activity analyses viewpoint, indicates very high levels of segregation, that is segregation by socioeconomic group and by religious affiliation.

It remains to comment briefly on the significance of these sector-segregated patterns from a planning standpoint. Currently segregation based on religion is viewed with disfavour by external observers, while in the past, in many cities, segregation by class has been looked upon with equal disfavour, although these attitudes are not generally held in the segregated areas concerned. In fact, one could argue that highly segregated sectors are the most efficient form for the existing system of interaction. Where areas that are non-conforming in terms of the general character of the particular sector occur, this only seems to generate more extended linkages to other areas that do conform. On the other hand, it could be argued that the existing segregated activity patterns are a consequence of the homogeneous sectors or sub-sectors. In the Belfast area, in so far as people have any residential choice, they exercise it by moving from less segregated to more segregated housing groups or else they move within an existing highly segregated sector. In the case of one Corporation housing estate which initially was integrated in terms of religion, subsequent moves have produced an almost entirely Roman Catholic estate. The Ladybrook and Erinvale private estates are both highly segregated, with only ten per cent of the particular minority religious group present in each case. Catholics have opted for Ladybrook, Protestants for Erinvale. This highlights a further factor in segregation, namely the availability of schools. As might be expected the voluntary (Roman Catholic) schools, and the Roman Catholic churches, are restricted to a large extent to the Catholic sectors. A Catholic family buying a house, or obtaining a rented housing allocation outside the Catholic sectors is faced subsequently with long and difficult school journeys, a particularly important factor in the case of primary schools.

Planning proposals for the Belfast urban area have been produced recently,[14] and these suggest that 'the strengthening of the identity and sense of community of townships and city sectors is important socially'. To achieve this a structuring of the urban area into a series of 'Districts' is proposed. While the 'Districts' may have meaning where they focus on

pre-existing outlying settlements such as Dunmurry, Dundonald and Holy-
wood (Fig. 15.5), the 'Districts' proposed for much of the rest of the area
run quite counter to existing community identities. The findings of the
current study indicate that well defined areas with marked identity already
exist whereas the proposed new 'Districts' break right across these. This is
particularly true for the proposed West Belfast District which would not
allow the strengthening of existing communities. The only intention can
be to completely restructure the western sector by attempting to link into
one 'District' at least four sharply defined sub-sectors. This aim should
have been stated unequivocally and the advantages and disadvantages of
such a policy carefully assessed.

In the Belfast urban area physical segregation and social segregation are
highly correlated. Whether physical desegregation, in terms of religion and
social class, would lead to social desegregation (that is, social interaction)
is open to question. The possible consequences of physical desegregation
need to be examined in depth. In fact, actual experiment may be the most
effective, though not necessarily the least painful way of providing the
necessary data. Analyses such as the present study, or experiments as
suggested above, cannot provide substitutes for judgement as to the desirability of desegregation, but they can provide a firmer basis on which the
judgement can be made.

Notes and References

The survey work on which part of the study is based was made possible by generous
grants from the Frederick Soddy Trust, the James Munce Partnership and The
Queen's University of Belfast. I would also like to thank Miss J. Orr, Mr W.
McGaughey and Mr G. Bullock of the Department of Geography in the university
for their assistance, and Building Design Partnership for providing data for the
Belfast urban area.

This chapter was completed in September 1968. The communal disturbances during 1969 and 1970, many of which occurred in the vicinity of the edges of the
religious subsectors in the western part of the city, are, in consequence, not
discussed here.

1. E. Jones, *A Social Geography of Belfast*, London, 1960.
2. E. Shevky and W. Bell, *Social Area Analysis*, Stanford University Press, 1955.
3. E. W. Burgess, 'The growth of the city', in R. E. Park and E. W. Mackenzie,
   eds., *The City*, Chicago, 1927.
4. C. Clark, 'Urban population densities', *Journal of the Royal Statistical Society*,
   114, (1951), 490–6.
5. The Occupational Index is derived from the formula:

$(0.05 \times P_1) + (0.04 \times P_2) + (0.03 \times P_3) + (0.02 \times P_4) + (0.01 \times P_5)$ where P_1, P_2, $\ldots P_n$ are percentages of heads of households in the given area whose socio-economic groups are 1, 2 ... n respectively. See R. Travers Morgan & Partners, *Travel in Belfast*, (Belfast, 1968), 188.

6. See E. E. Evans, 'Belfast: the site and the city', *Ulster Journal of Archaeology*, 3rd ser., **7**, (1944), 25–9; and Jones, *op. cit.*, 172–206.

7. Jones, *op. cit.*, p. 196.

8. F. W. Boal, 'Territoriality on the Shankill-Falls divide', Belfast, *Irish Geography*, **6**, no. 1 (1969), 30–50.

9. B. J. L. Berry, 'Internal structure of the city', *Law and Contemporary Problems* (Winter 1965), 115.

10. Jones, *op. cit.*, p. 273.

11. M. Fried, 'Functions of the working class community in modern urban society – implications for forced relocations', *J. Amer. Inst. Planners*, **33**, no. 2 (March 1967), 92.

12. Jones, *op. cit.*, p. 145–6.

13. Fried, *op. cit.*, p. 92.

14. Building Design Partnership, *Belfast Urban Area—Interim Planning Policy*, Belfast, 1967, pp. 72–106.

P. Collison

16 Immigrants and residence*

This paper presents measures of the segregation and certain other features of the residential distribution of various groups in the City of Oxford together with some data for the English conurbations. The data is taken from the census 1961. Although we are interested in substantive rather than methodological issues the following four points of methodological interest must be borne in mind:

Firstly, we are limited to categories or groups of categories recognized by the census.[1] The census does not recognize racial or ethnic divisions although it records information on birthplace. We are obliged to assume, therefore, that birthplace relates to the groupings we have made. Thus we assume that those born in various areas of Africa are 'non-white' although there must obviously be cases where this assumption is false. It may be noted that some groupings are sub-categories of others (Asians and West Indians, for example, are both included in non-white). The categories are as follows:

Natives, birthplace England or Wales
Foreign, birthplace other than England or Wales
Scots, birthplace Scotland, Isle of Man or Channel Islands
Irish, birthplace Ireland, North or South
Non-white, birthplace India, Pakistan, Ceylon, British West Africa, British
    East or Central Africa, or British Caribbean Territories
Asians, birthplace India, Pakistan or Ceylon
West Indians, birthplace British Caribbean Territories

Secondly, the analysis is confined to 'residents' of England and Wales. The definition of residence in the census is somewhat subjective. An overseas student, for example, or an immigrant employed here could state that

* Reprinted from *Sociology*, **1**, no. 3, (September 1967) 277–92.

his residence was in his home country.[2] Such people would be classified as 'non-resident' and of necessity excluded from our analysis.

Thirdly, any analysis of residential distribution has to be based on some type of geographical area. We use 'census tracts'. There are thirty-six of these areas for Oxford each having a population of about 3,000. The tracts were defined for the census of 1951.[3] Tracts are aggregations of 'enumeration districts' and for certain purposes we use these smaller areas.[4]

Fourthly, following previous work on the ecology of Oxford[5] and similar studies in the United States[6] we employ the Index of Dissimilarity to measure the residential separation between one group and another and the

Table 16.1

	Oxford		England and Wales	
1	*2*	*3*	*4*	*5*
	Group as %	*Sex ratio*	*Group as %*	*Sex ratio*
Group	*of population*	*male : female*	*of population*	*male : female*
Natives	89·9	1·0	93·6	0·9
Scots	1·9	1·1	1·5	1·0
Irish	2·9	1·2	1·8	1·0
Foreign	10·1	1·1	6·4	1·0
Non-whites	1·5	1·6	0·9	1·4
Asians	0·7	1·7	0·4	1·4
West Indians	0·6	1·5	0·3	1·3
Total Population	106,291 (= 100%)	1·0	46,104,548 (= 100%)	0·9

Index of Segregation to measure the residential separation between any particular group and the remainder of the population.[7] These Indexes range from 0 indicating no residential separation to 100 indicating complete separation. In order to measure the extent to which groups are concentrated in particular types of area we use the Index of Concentration[8] which ranges from +100 to −100, positive values indicating a greater or less tendency for the group under consideration to live in areas of a certain type and negative values the reverse.

Table 16.1 presents information about Oxford with comparable material for England and Wales.[9] Comparing the figures in Table 16.1, col 2 with those in col 4 it is apparent that for Oxford Natives constitute a smaller proportion of the population than for England and Wales as a whole. Even so the figure of almost 90 per cent for Oxford indicates that by far the larger part of the residents are native born.[10] The remaining groups are all over-represented in Oxford, although in various degrees, compared with the country as a whole.

The ratios in Table 16.1, col 5 show that all the groups except Natives and Irish contain a higher proportion of males. The Irish group contains as many males as females while the Native group contains more females than males. These differences are, no doubt, due to differences in age composition and to differences in the stage and character of immigration for particular groups. Oxford (Table 16.1, col 3) diverges from the national pattern in having in each case a higher male to female ratio.

Table 16.2 shows for each group the census tracts where the group in question is most heavily represented. Thus in census tract 1, 94 per cent of the population is Native and this is the highest figure for all thirty-six tracts. 94 per cent[11] of the population in tract 31 is also Native. Table 16.2, col 4 shows the percentage of the group in the tract. Thus 2 per cent of all Oxford's Natives are in tract 1 and 3 per cent are in tract 31.

It is clearly possible for concentrations to occur in areas smaller than tracts so the figures in cols 5 and 6 have been provided to take the analysis down to enumeration district level.[12] Table 16.2 col 5 shows the percentage distribution of groups over the enumeration districts within the tracts.[13] Tract 1, for example, has three enumeration districts containing, respectively, 32, 37 and 31 per cent of the Natives in the tract. Table 16.2, col 6 gives the percentage of the enumeration district population in the group in question. Thus it is evident that for the three enumeration districts in tract 1 the percentage of the population in the Native group are 95, 91 and 97 per cent respectively.

Looking at the figures in Table 16.2, col 3, it is apparent that most of our groups constitute only a small proportion of tract populations. Scots, for instance, form only 3 per cent of the population even where they are most heavily concentrated (tract 5). The highest figure for Irish is 6 per cent in tract 13 and for Non-whites, 4 per cent in tract 11. Foreign provides the one possible exception and it is evident that this group constitutes 21 per cent of tract 5 and 17 per cent of tract 8.

From Table 16.2, col 6 it can be seen that in tract 5 Scots constitute no more than 5 per cent of the population even in the enumeration district where Scots are most heavily represented in this tract. Similarly for Irish in tract 13 the highest figure is no more than 7 per cent and for coloureds in tract 11 it is no more than 9 per cent. For Foreign in tract 5, however, the figure in the case of one enumeration district is 29 per cent. So far as the Native is concerned these figures suggest that in every part of the City the great majority of his fellow residents in tract and enumeration district are also Natives. Even in the case of the enumeration district where Foreign are most heavily represented more than two out of three of the residents are Native. Moreover it is, of course, unlikely that Foreign is a unitary group either in the way that it is perceived or treated, or in the way it acts.

To see the position from the side of the immigrant groups rather than the Natives we may look at the figures in Table 16.2, col. 4. It is apparent that

Table 16.2   Distribution by tract and enumeration district

1	*2*	*3* Group as % of tract population	*4* % of Group in tract	*5* % Tract group in ED	*6* % of ED population
Group	*Tract*				
Natives	1	94	2	32	95
				37	91
				31	97
	31	94	3	22	91
				19	96
				26	97
				33	92
Scots	5	3	7	15	3
				13	3
				12	2
				28	5
				32	4
	2	3	5	13	2
				31	4
				18	2
				27	4
				11	2
Irish	13	6	5	49	7
				23	4
				28	6
	15	4	5	26	4
				23	5
				30	5
				21	5
Foreign	5	21	9	13	15
				14	19
				18	23
				23	29
				32	23
	8	17	3	32	18
				40	17
				28	17
Non-whites	11	4	5	49	9
				8	1
				43	5
	8	3	3	33	4
				46	4
				21	2

Table 16.2 *(continued)*   **Distribution by tract and enumeration district**

1 Group	*2* Tract	*3* Group as % of tract population	*4* % of Group in tract	*5* % Tract group in ED	*6* % of ED population
Asians	5	2	12	15	2
				12	1
				23	3
				21	2
				29	2
	10	2	5	80	4
				3	0
				0	0
				18	1
West Indians	11	3	9	58	7
				9	1
				33	2
	19	2	10	7	1
				17	1
				76	5

12 per cent of Oxford's Asian residents live in tract 5, 10 per cent of West Indians live in tract 19 and 9 per cent in tract 11, while 7 per cent of Scots live in tract 5. These figures suggest some degree of concentration. The enumeration district figures (Table 16.2, col 5) for Asians tract 10 and for West Indians tract 19 suggest that there is in these cases at any rate further concentration within the tracts. Taken as a whole, however, the figures in cols 4 and 5 indicate a fairly wide dispersal.[14]

Table 3, col 7 gives the Indexes of Segregation calculated on tracts for the groups. The limits of the index are 0 and 100. It is apparent that West Indians with an Index of 42 are residentially the most segregated group. Asians and Non-whites follow with indexes of 32 and 31 respectively. At the other extreme are Scots with an Index of 12 and Irish with one of 15.

The Indexes of Dissimilarity (Table 16.3, cols 1 to 6) show the degree of residential segregation between one group and another. For Natives it is evident that the degree of separation in area of residence is lowest with Scots where there is an index of 13 and is only marginally higher with Irish, index 15, and Foreign, index 17. There is then a sharp rise to 32 in the index with Non-whites and a further rise to 43 in the index with West Indians. The greatest degrees of residential separation occur between Asians and West Indians (index 52) and between Asians and the remainder of the Non-whites (index 51). Other studies suggest that social distance is reflected in residential separation[15] and if this is the case here it would seem that social distance is least between Natives and Scots and is only slightly greater

Table 16.3

	Dissimilarity						Segregation
	1	*2*	*3*	*4* *Non-*	*5*	*6* *West*	*7*
	Scots	*Irish*	*Foreign*	*whites*	*Asians*	*Indians*	
Natives	13	15	17	32	33	43	17
Scots		20	15	28	30	44	12
Irish			25	29	37	36	15
Foreign				21	24	42	17
Non-whites					38	51	31
Asians						52	32
West Indians							42

between Natives and Irish and Natives and Foreign. Social distance is comparatively great between Natives and West Indians and is greatest between Asians and West Indians.

The Indexes of Concentration in Table 16.4 have been prepared to determine if there is any tendency for groups to be concentrated in areas of particular type. The limits of the Index are -100 and $+100$. The figures in Table 16.4, cols 2 to 6 relate to the occupational composition of the tracts.[16] The figure $+26$ for Asians in col 2 indicates a tendency of this order for Asians to be concentrated in tracts having a relatively high proportion of the occupational force in the 'Professionals . . .' group. At the other extreme -20 for West Indians in col. 2 indicates a tendency of this order for West Indians to live away from tracts having a high proportion of 'Professionals . . . .'

Apart from under-representation in areas of 'Professionals . . .' the figures for Natives (cols 2 to 6) indicate some concentration in areas of 'Skilled . . .' and 'Personal service' workers and a slighter degree of concentration in areas of 'Unskilled' and 'Non-manual'. The figures for Scots and Irish are all fairly low although the Irish have some tendency to be concentrated in 'Unskilled manual' areas and away from 'Professionals . . .' areas. Foreign and Non-whites both show some tendency to concentration in 'Professionals . . .' areas and the opposite tendency in respect of the remaining types of area. The figures for Asians and West Indians indicate relatively marked patterns although of different kinds. The Asians are comparatively heavily represented in 'Professionals . . .' areas and under-represented in 'Skilled . . .', 'Personal service' and 'Unskilled manual' areas. The West Indians on the other hand are distinctly under-represented in 'Profes-

271

Table 16.4 Concentration by character of residential area

1 Group	2 Pro- fessionals employers managers	3 Non- manual	4 Personal service	5 Skilled Own- account workers	6 Unskilled manual	7 Average rateable value	8 Persons per room	9 Centrality
Natives	−10	+3	+12	+16	+6	−9	+5	−14
Scots	+8	+1	−6	−6	−5	+6	−1	+2
Irish	−10	−1	+7	+5	+11	−12	+4	+4
Foreign	+10	−3	−12	−16	−6	+9	−5	+14
Non-whites	+9	−11	−15	−26	−4	+6	−12	+27
Asians	+26	−12	−31	−36	−20	+23	−13	+31
West Indians	−20	−11	+10	−9	+21	−22	−14	+20

sionals . . .' areas and over-represented in 'Unskilled manual' areas.

The figures in Table 16.4, col 7 have been calculated on the average rateable value of dwelling houses in each tract.[17] Positive values indicate a tendency to concentration in areas of high average rateable value and negative values the reverse. Asians, it is apparent, show the sharpest tendency to live in areas of high average rateable value while West Indians show an almost equally sharp but opposite tendency. For Foreign, Non-whites and Scots there is some tendency to residence in areas of high average rateable value and for Natives and, to a somewhat greater extent for Irish, there is the opposite tendency.

Table 16.4, col 8 shows the indexes calculated on the basis of persons per room for each tract.[18] For this calculation the ranking has been made with the tract having the highest figure for persons per room given rank 1 and so on. This means that positive values in Table 16.4, col 8 indicate a tendency for concentration in areas with relatively high room occupancy rates and negative values the reverse. It is evident that Natives and Irish tend to be concentrated in areas with high room occupancy rates although the values for the Indexes are not very high. West Indians, Asians and Non-whites on the other hand tend to be concentrated in areas where occupancy rates are comparatively low, as do Foreign and Irish although the Indexes for Foreign is only −5 and for Irish only −1.

The figures in Table 16.4, col 9 give an indication of the extent to which groups tend to concentrate toward the centre of the City,[19] a matter of traditional interest to the urban sociologist. For this calculation, Carfax, the centre of the City, was taken as the centre of two concentric circles, the first having a radius of one mile and the second a radius of two miles. This provided three areas, the first within one mile of Carfax, the second more than one mile but less than two miles from Carfax and the third consisting of the parts of the City more than two miles from Carfax. In Table 16.4, col 9 positive values indicate a greater or less tendency to concentration towards the centre and negative values the reverse.

Asians it can be seen show the greatest tendency to be concentrated towards the City centre and they are followed fairly closely in this by Non-whites and then by West Indians and Foreign. Irish and Scots also show some degree of concentration towards the centre although the indexes are small. Natives by contrast show a tendency to residence away from the City centre.

Turning now to a discussion of this material we may first draw attention to council housing as a factor underlying a number of our findings. In Oxford council housing for historical reasons tends to be located towards the City peripheries. It also has low average rateable value and high occupancy rates in terms of persons per room.[20] As regards occupation council house residents tend to be manual workers with the unskilled and semi-skilled heavily represented.[21]

It is also probably the case that groups of recent immigrants have not yet obtained full access to council housing and certainly had not done so by 1961 when the census was taken. No doubt this is due to residence requirements for council housing and perhaps also to the demographic features of some, at least, of the immigrant groups.[22]

The position is illustrated by Table 16.5 which presents in column 1 the percentage of the population falling in the various groups for tract 28 which consists very largely of council housing built shortly after the last war. It is evident that Natives compared with their representation in the population of Oxford (Table 16.5, col 3) are over-represented in this tract, as are the Irish. All remaining groups are under-represented. Table 16.5, col 2 shows comparable figures for another tract also consisting largely of

Table 16.5   Council housing and immigrants

	1 Tract 28 %	2 Tract 46 %	3 Oxford %
Natives	93·2	91·1	89·9
Scots	1·8	1·8	1·9
Irish	3·6	4·4	2·9
Foreign	6·8	8·9	10·1
Non-whites	0·2	0·7	1·5
Asians	0·1	0·1	0·7
West Indians	0·1	0·5	0·6

council housing but built more recently and after the commencement of recent immigrations. Comparing the figures in column 2 with those in column 3 it is clear that Natives are again over-represented as are the Irish while all the remaining groups are under-represented. But if the figures in columns 1 and 2 can be taken as representing a trend it seems that the proportion of Natives on council estates is falling, the proportion of Scots and Asians remains constant while for all the remaining groups the proportions are increasing.

Given the character of council housing the over-representation of Natives and Irish, and the under-representation of other groups, must go some part of the way in explaining, for example, the indexes in table 16.4. Thus the concentration of Natives in council housing together with the under-representation of 'Professionals . . .' would tend to produce the negative index for Natives in Table 16.4, col 1.

The degree to which the different groups are represented in council housing will also affect the indexes in Table 16.3. Obviously if certain groups are excluded in some degree and for whatever reason from council estates the degree of residential separation between the excluded group and others will increase. In view of this the indexes in Table 16.3 may seem surprisingly small. Certainly the figures in Tables 16.2 and 3 offer no support for the view that 'ghettoes' have been established either of Non-whites or of any of the other groups considered. Moreover, if we are right in our interpretation of the figures in Table 16.5 and there is a tendency for some, at least, of the new immigrant groups to find their way into council housing we can expect the degree of separation between such groups and, for example, the Natives to fall.[23]

It is notable that the greatest degree of residential dissimilarity occurs between the Asians and the West Indians and that the Indexes of Concentration for these groups (Table 16.4, cols 2 to 8) show strikingly contrasting patterns. This suggests that the Non-whites are not a socially homogeneous group. If there is discrimination in this society it would seem to be against negroes and not against Non-whites as a whole. Or, alternatively, if there is discrimination against Non-whites it would seem that Asians are better able to overcome it than are West Indians, or it may be less intense for the former than for the latter. On the whole, however, our data suggests that the society is very open and it is notable that the Foreign group as a whole (Table 16.4) is distinctly better placed in the matter of housing than are Natives.

The position of Asians is particularly striking and the data in Tables 16.2 and 16.4 suggests strongly that this group taken as a whole had already by 1961 merged into the socially privileged elite. There is a widespread tendency to assume that immigrants and particularly Non-white immigrants are necessarily underprivileged members of the society. Davison, for example, in a recent book expresses disbelief in and surprise at data showing that Indians and Pakistanis in certain London boroughs, although in somewhat different ways and degrees, are overall in 'superior' occupations compared with other groups and particularly the 'English'.[24] He is similarly surprised at other data in relation to housing.[25] We think it now time to question the assumption that immigrants are necessarily and everywhere underprivileged and to consider seriously the hypothesis that

British society is more open so far as immigrants are concerned than is generally supposed and that the energy and enterprise often shown by immigrant groups can carry them rapidly up the social hierarchy. In the case of Asians our data suggest that this process is already well under way.

Certain qualifications have, of course, to be made. It is possible, although we think improbable, that some Asians are Asian in terms of birthplace only. The children born to English military or civil service families resident in earlier times in India might form such a group. It is also possible that some of our results could be explained by differential enumeration of immigrants at the census, those in poor areas being under-enumerated and those elsewhere fully enumerated. But in the light of local circumstances this too we think improbable. In addition we know that the majority of Oxford Asians are Indian[26] and it may be that our findings do not apply to Pakistanis for example. Finally it may be the case that Oxford is quite unlike other parts of the country in these matters.

It is helpful to look at our findings against the data in Tables 16.6 and 7. Table 16.6[27] shows for the English conurbations the socio-economic groups of males according to certain birthplace categories. Comparing the figures in column 3 with those in column 1 it is evident that only 47 per cent of Indians are in manual work (Table 16.6, lines 8–11) compared with 59 per cent for the male work force as a whole. On the other hand 9·5 per cent of Indians are in professional occupations (lines 3 and 4) compared with only 4 per cent for the community as a whole. In respect of employers and managers (lines 1 and 2) the proportion for Indians is somewhat lower but for clerical workers (lines 5 and 6) rather higher.

The West Indians present a sharp contrast both with the Indians and the community as a whole having a particularly large proportion (86 per cent) engaged in manual work and only small proportions engaged in managerial, professional and clerical work. The Pakistanis also have a high proportion engaged in manual work (74 per cent) and particularly in unskilled manual work (32 per cent). The proportion engaged as professionals is about the same as for the work force as a whole while in the employer/managerial and clerical groups the Pakistanis are under-represented.

The Africans have the lowest proportion (43 per cent) in manual work and the highest (12 per cent) in the professions. They are also heavily represented in the clerical groups but rather under-represented among employers and managers. Finally the Maltese and Cypriots show a fairly small proportion in manual work (50 per cent), although the proportion is larger than for Indians or Africans, and large proportions for employers and managers of small establishments and for personal service workers.

Although the pattern of occupation for different groups may vary from area to area the data in Table 16.6 fits well with the Oxford data.

West Indians, for example, are concentrated in the lower reaches of the socio-economic hierarchy, and this no doubt is reflected in their residential

Table 16.6   Conurbations: males, selected socioeconomic groups

	1 All eco- nomically active males %	2 West Indians %	3 Indians %	4 Pakistanis %	5 Africans %	6 Maltese and Cypriots %
1. Employers and man- agers in central and local government, industry and commerce etc. – large establishments	4·0	0·3	3·9	1·5	2·4	0·3
2. Employers and man- agers in industry, com- merce etc. – small establishments	6·3	0·5	4·3	3·3	2·2	11·2
3. Professional workers – self employed	0·7	0·3	2·0	0·2	1·4	0·3
4. Professional workers – employees	3·3	0·6	7·5	3·5	10·9	1·4
5. Intermediate non- manual workers	4·1	1·7	5·2	1·5	8·5	2·0
6. Junior non-manual workers	15·3	4·5	23·0	7·3	23·3	6·7
7. Personal service workers	1·1	1·1	1·4	2·6	2·4	17·3
8. Foremen and supervisors – manual	3·4	0·2	0·9	0·5	0·3	0·9
9. Skilled manual workers	32·1	36·4	21·4	14·5	18·1	27·7
10. Semi-skilled manual workers	14·6	23·5	17·1	26·2	16·7	10·5
11. Unskilled manual workers	8·9	25·9	7·4	32·4	8·0	11·3
12. Own account workers (other than professional)	3·4	1·0	2·3	3·6	1·4	7·2

location in Oxford. There is some evidence that Indians are favourably placed in the socio-economic hierarchy and particularly in respect of the professions. It is not surprising therefore to find Oxford Asians, who are largely Indians, advantageously placed in respect of residential location and providing a sharp contrast with West Indians.

It may be noted that the fact that a high proportion of, for instance, Indians are engaged in the professions does not establish that there is no prejudice or discrimination against immigrants or Non-whites in general or Indians in particular. It could be that even more Indians are qualified for professional or other high status work than have found such employment and that the figures for Indians in Table 6, lines 1–4, are from some points of view lower than they should be.

We may also draw attention to the figures for Foremen (Table 16.6, line 8) which indicate that only a small proportion of each of the groups has reached this status compared with the work force as a whole, even though the West Indians and Pakistanis have particularly large proportions in manual work. Further the West Indians have more than a third in skilled manual work, from which one might expect foremen and supervisors to be drawn. It could be that the society is less open in some ways or on some levels than others and that immigrants, or immigrants of certain type, find some opportunities closed to them even though others are open.[28]

Table 16.7,[29] lines 1–4, presents data on household tenure. From line 1 it is evident that almost 48 per cent of Indian households are owner occupied compared with only 38 per cent of all households. The Indians are followed

Table 16.7   Conurbations: households by selected tenures

	1	2	3	4	5	6
	All households %	West Indian %	Indian %	Pakistani %	African %	Maltese and Cypriot %
1. Owner occupiers	38·0	27·6	47·8	45·2	23·7	37·6
2. Rented from local authority or new town corporation	23·0	2·2	8·4	8·4	3·5	8·3
3. Rented unfurnished from private person or company	30·0	56·8	21·2	28·4	57·3	21·9
4. Rented furnished from private person or company	5·9	12·5	19·7	15·5	13·9	28·4
5. Percentage of households at 1 or > 1 person(s) per room	30·3	84·4	47·6	68·2	72·9	68·9

closely by the Pakistanis with 45 per cent. The Maltese and Cypriots have a proportion almost identical with that for all households while the proportions for West Indians and particularly African households are noticeably smaller than that of any other group. Owner occupation is usually regarded as the most desirable form of tenure and in so far as this is true, it would seem that Indians are again favourably placed, as are the Pakistanis although to a slightly smaller extent. The Africans and once again the West Indians seem here to be placed disadvantageously.

Renting from a local authority is also widely regarded as a desirable form of tenure and it is evident (Table 16.7, line 2) that the figures for immigrants are in every case much smaller than the figure for all households. It is striking that the figure for West Indians is only just over 2 per cent while the figure for Indians, Pakistanis and Maltese and Cypriots is in each case over 8 per cent.

Renting unfurnished from a private landlord (Table 16.7, line 3) can be more or less attractive according to circumstances although it is usually regarded as less desirable than owner occupation or renting from a local authority. It is apparent that Africans and West Indians are heavily represented in this type of tenure compared with all households while Pakistanis and particularly Indians and Maltese and Cypriots are under-represented.

The remaining type of tenure, renting furnished from a private landlord (Table 16.7, line 4) is probably the least desirable and it is evident that all the groups show higher proportions in this category than all households. There is some variation between the groups and it is apparent that the Maltese and Cypriots have the highest proportion in this category and the West Indians the lowest.

Table 16.7, line 5, shows the percentage of households living at one or more than one person(s) per room and gives some idea, therefore, of relative crowding. All the groups show higher proportions than for all households. There are, however, large variations between groups, the West Indians having the particularly high figure of 84 per cent and the Indians the relatively low figure of 48 per cent. Between these are the Africans with 75 per cent and the Pakistanis and the Maltese and Cypriots each with rather more than 68 per cent.

Looking back now at the Oxford data it is clearly not surprising to find Asians providing a sharp contrast with West Indians in the matter of residential location. On all counts the former are markedly more privileged than the latter and unless some general mechanism of colour discrimination is operating it would be surprising if residential patterns were similar. It could be that non-white is not a significant social category but that negro is. There is some evidence in Tables 16.6 and 7 that Africans are also disadvantageously placed but it is not consistent and so far as this study is concerned the relative position of negroes and other non-whites remains indeterminate.

It is clear from Tables 16.6 and 7 that in some ways Indians are advantageously placed relative to the community as a whole and to the extent that this is true we would also expect it to be reflected in their pattern of residence. On the other hand the position of Indians in relation to the rest of the community is not entirely consistent and in some matters Indians appear to be at something of a disadvantage. There are likely, of course, to be variations from place to place in the position of particular groups and it is possible that Indians in Oxford are better placed socially and economically than are Indians in general.

Notes and References

This paper was read at the British Association meeting, Nottingham, September 1966. We are grateful to Mrs J. Lay of the Atlas Laboratory, Harwell, for her generous assistance in computing.

1. See *Census Statistics for Wards, Parishes and Enumeration Districts Presented on Punched Cards* (100 *per cent data*) *and* (10 *per cent data*), GRO, duplicated, n.d.
2. GRO, personal communication.
3. See, *Census* 1951, *Oxford Area: Selected Population and Housing Characteristics by Census Tracts*, Oxford, Oxford Census Tract Committee, 1957. One tract was added for the 1961 census because of a City boundary extension.
4. An enumeration district is the area covered by one census enumerator. For Oxford the Registrar General defined the enumeration districts for 1961 in such a way that they aggregated into the pre-existing tracts. It is important to remember that enumeration districts are defined in terms of administrative convenience for census purposes. Their populations vary considerably in size and in some cases institutions such as colleges or schools are treated as enumeration districts. Unless this is borne in mind enumeration districts may sometimes appear to have some odd demographic characteristics.
5. Peter Collison and John Mogey, 'Residence and social class in Oxford', *Am. J. Sociol.*, **54**, no. 6 (1959), 599–605; Peter Collison 'Occupation, education, and housing in an English city', *Am. J. Sociol.*, **55**, no. 6 (1960), 588–97.
6. Otis Dudley Duncan and Beverly Duncan, 'Occupational stratification and residential distribution', *Am. J. Sociol.*, **50**, no. 5 (1955), 493–503 [3]; Stanley Lieberson, *Ethnic Patterns in American Cities*, Free Press of Glencoe, 1963; Karl E. Taeuber and Alma B. Taeuber, *Negros in Cities, Chicago*, Aldine, 1965.
7. The Index of Dissimilarity is $\frac{1}{2}\sum(X_i - Y_i)$ where X is the percentage distribution of a particular group over tracts and Y is the percentage distribution of another group over tracts. The absolute values of the differences are taken, i.e. negative signs are ignored. The Index of Segregation is the same except that Y relates to the total population less X. For discussions of these Indexes see Otis Dudley Duncan and Beverly Duncan, 'A methodological analysis of segregation indexes', *Am. Sociol. Rev.*, **20**, no. 2 (1955), 210–17 [2], and Taeuber and Taeuber *op cit.*, 195–245.
8. The Index of Concentration is $\sum X_{i-1}Y_i - \sum Y_{i-1}X_i$ where X is the cumulated

percentage distribution of a particular group over tracts and Y is the cumulated percentage distribution of the remainder of the population over tracts, tracts being first ranked on the criterion under consideration. Thus to produce the indexes in Table 4 column 2 tracts were ranked high to low on the percentage of the male work force falling into the combined 'Professional, employer and manager' group. For the indexes in Table 16.4, col. 7 tracts were ranked high to low on average rateable value of dwelling houses. The theoretical limits of the Index are, in fact, $+ 10,000$, $- 10,000$. For convenience of presentation we treat the limits as $+ 100$, $- 100$.

9. Calculated from GRO, *Census* 1961, *England and Wales, Birthplace and Nationality Tables*, London HMSO, 1964. A number of authors report under-enumeration of immigrants in the 1961 census. After examining statistics from a number of sources G. C. K. Peach suggests that West Indians were under-enumerated by at least 20 per cent. See his 'Under-enumeration of West Indians in the 1961 Census', *Sociological Review*, **14**, NS, (1966), 78.

10. Although we ought perhaps to note that 3,316 people born in Wales are included among Natives.

11. The figure in fact is slightly lower but has been 'rounded up'.

12. It is also possible for groupings of tracts to occur. The indexes we employ (Table 16.3) are insensitive to possible patterns occurring between tracts.

13. Enumeration districts with populations of 300 or less are excluded from this table.

14. London also shows a much wider geographical dispersion of immigrants than is usually supposed. Among the several thousand enumeration districts for London A.C. in 1961 there were only two in which West Indians formed more than 30 per cent of the total population and none in which all 'new minorities' together formed a majority of the population. See, Ruth Glass and John Westergaard, *London's Housing Needs*, London: Centre for Urban Studies, 1965, 41.

15. For example, Duncan and Duncan, 'Occupational stratification and residential distribution' [3]: Collison and Mogey, *op. cit.*; Collison, *op cit.*

16. The information is from the 10 per cent sample data of the 1961 census. People not included in the groupings of occupations shown in Table 16.4, cols 2–6 have been excluded from the calculations. Thus to obtain the rank order of tracts, which is the first step in the calculation of the Index, we have calculated, in the case of the figures in col. 2, the number of 'Professionals, employers and managers' in eact tract as a percentage of the sum of all five occupational groupings in the particular tract. The percentage for each occupational group overall for the range over tracts are 'Professionals etc.' 15 per cent, range 2 per cent to 46 per cent: Non-manual 19 per cent, range 10 per cent to 44 per cent: Personal service 19 per cent, range 4 per cent to 23 per cent: Skilled and own account workers 35 per cent, range 4 per cent to 40 per cent: Unskilled manual 12 per cent, range 2 per cent to 33 per cent.

18. See Oxford Census Tract Committee (note 4 above), *op. cit.*, Table 11. The

figures for rateable value relate to 1953 while the census figures relate to 1961. One tract added for the census 1961 has not been included in these calculations. The range for average rateable value is from £13 to £55.

18. Where possible enumeration districts relating to institutions as opposed to ordinary dwelling houses have been excluded from the calculation. Overall the figure for persons per room is 0·676 and the range for tracts is from 0·546 to 1·076.

19. Oxford has an unusual ecological pattern in that overall groups high in the socio-economic scale tend to live towards the City centre. See Collison, *op. cit.*, 596.

20. Collison, *op. cit.*, 593. For England and Wales in 1961 the figures for persons per room were: owner occupiers, 0·59; rented from a local authority or New Town Corporation, 0·83; rented unfurnished from a private person or company, 0·64; rented furnished from a private person or company, 0·82. See, GRO, *Census 1961. Housing Tables, Part 2, Tenure and Household Arrangements*, London, HMSO, 1965, Table 20.

21. Collison, *loc. cit.*

22. The high male to female ratios in the case of Pakistanis in particular suggest that many immigrants were single men or married men whose families remain in the country of origin. As such they would be unlikely to qualify for council housing.

23. In 10 cities in the United States Stanley Lieberson notes a tendency for the residential separation of Negroes to increase although for other groups it is decreasing. See Lieberson, *op. cit.*, 16.

24. R. B. Davison, *Black British*, Oxford University Press, 1966, 69–70. He suggests that Indians and Pakistanis may have upgraded themselves although there seems no reason for assuming that they would do this more than others.

25. *Op. cit.*, 48–9. To explain the relatively high proportion of Indian and Pakistani households having a hot water supply, Davison suggests that Indians and Pakistanis are more concerned with personal cleanliness than others. In a Foreword to Davison's book Philip Mason comments on this finding by remarking that 'to anyone who has visited the Indian sub-continent it will suggest that Indians and Pakistanis have brought with them their intense regard for personal cleanliness . . .' Irish households show the smallest proportion having access to a hot water tap.

26. GRO, *Census 1961, England and Wales. County Report. Oxfordshire*, London, HMSO, 1964, Table 10.

27. The figures in Table 6.6, col. 1 are taken from GRO, *Census 1961. England and Wales. Socio-Economic Group Tables*, London, HMSO, 1966, Table 1. These figures relate to 'economically active males'. The figures in cols 2–6 are taken from GRO, *Census 1961, England and Wales. Commonwealth Immigrants in the Conurbations*, London, HMSO, 1965, Table A.5. These figures relate to males 'in employment'. All data are from the census 10 per cent sample. People born in the Union of South Africa are not included in col. 5.

Socio-economic groups 13–17 are small and are not shown. Because these groups are not shown the percentages do not sum to 100.

28. In a position similar to that in which the Jews have often found themselves. One recalls Max Weber's advice to Jews aspiring to enter academic life. See H. H. Gerth and C. Wright Mills, eds, *From Max Weber*, London, Routledge, 1948, 134.

29. The figures in Table 16.7, col. 1 are taken from GRO, *Census* 1961. *England and Wales. Housing Tables. Part* 2, *Tenure and Household Arrangements*, Table 21. The figures in cols 2–6 are based on the 10 per cent sample and are taken from GRO, *Census* 1961. *England and Wales. Commonwealth Immigrants in the Conurbations*, Table B.3. Households are classified as 'West Indian', 'Indian' etc. if either the head of the household or the spouse was born in the territory in question.

Not all tenure categories are shown and in consequence the percentages do not sum to 100.

Part V

Australia, New Zealand and the West Indies

F. Lancaster Jones

---

17 Ethnic concentration and assimilation: an Australian case study*

Urban sociologists have long used census tract data to throw light upon the relationship between urban social structure and the social characteristics of residential areas.[1] As many studies have shown, in urban societies composed of persons of diverse origins, backgrounds, and interests, individuals with similar social positions and cultural origins become residentially differentiated. Residential proximity increases the probability of social interaction, and persons with similar social positions, values, and expectations tend to locate in relatively close proximity so that group interaction can be maximized and group norms maintained. Over time the different residential areas of a city acquire a social evaluation reflecting the social characteristics of their resident populations, and spatial distance becomes an indicator of social distance.[2] The emergence of ethnic concentrations in cities can be viewed both as an instance of this general process of residential differentiation among urban populations, and as an aggregate effect of socioeconomic and cultural differences.

A number of studies have shown that ethnic groups vary considerably in the degree of their residential concentration.[3] As residential proximity to persons of the same ethnic origin provides one important means of preserving, at least for a time, familiar cultural patterns and preferred modes of behavior, variations in ethnic residential concentration have often been used as an indicator of differential assimilation. This paper sets out to examine changes in residential concentration among the eight most numerous ethnic groups in Melbourne, Australia's second largest metropolis, in 1954 and 1961, and to relate these findings to three other commonly used indicators of group assimilation – occupational composition, intermarriage, and naturalization – in order to assess how closely these indicators are associated with residential concentration and how far, if at all,

* Reprinted from *Social Forces*, **45**, no. 3 (March 1967).

they effect systematic differences in the rates of assimilation among these groups. It is expected that groups showing a high degree of residential concentration will also show a high degree of occupational concentration, a high proportion of ethnic inmarriages, and a high proportion of unnaturalized aliens. It is argued that insofar as systematic differences among these groups exist according to these indicators, they reflect differences in cultural and social distance from the receiving society and consequently in the rate of group assimilation to that society.

Data and methods

The statistics on which the analysis of residential concentration is based are drawn from the results of the 1954 and 1961 censuses of Australia and deal mainly but not exclusively with the summary statistics for the population of census collectors' districts in Melbourne in 1961 (CDs are the basic areal unit of enumeration in Australian censuses). These summary statistics provide univariate distributions of such characteristics as ages of the population in each CD, conjugal condition, workforce characteristics, religion, birthplace, nationality, period of residence of the foreign born, and some information on dwellings. No questions on income or education were included in the 1961 census, and although industry and occupation are available for some geographic units, only industry categories are available for CDs. In this paper, however, only the birthplace data will be systematically examined, using the eight main ethnic groups distinguished in the CD statistics. Since in 1954 detailed CD statistics were not available, the analysis of changes between 1954 and 1961 uses broader areal units.

In 1961 Melbourne's population of 1,911,895 persons was distributed over 2,107 CDs, giving an average CD population of 907 persons. As the following figures indicate CDs varied considerably in population size: 10 per cent contained fewer than 500 persons, 22 per cent 500 to 749 persons, 31 per cent 750 to 999 persons, 23 per cent 1,000 to 1,249 persons, 10 per cent 1,250 to 1,499 persons, and 4 per cent 1,500 persons or more. More importantly, this variation in size was not random. Closer examination indicated that over time CDs in areas of population decline had become systematically smaller than those in areas of population stability or recent population growth. Thus, in the central City of Melbourne the average CD size had declined to only 680 persons, compared with 1,200 persons in the rapidly growing outer area of Box Hill. As one of the methods used in this study involved ecological correlations, in which each areal unit receives equal weighting, it seemed unreasonable to tolerate nonrandom variation in CD size.[4] As a first step, therefore, an aggregation of adjacent CDs up to a population of about 3,000 persons was made in an attempt to limit the range of areal variation, to eliminate any systematic variation, and to improve the reliability of some measures. Prior to aggregation the central business district and CDs with predominantly 'institutional' accommodations (as indicated by an overall ratio of six or more persons per dwelling) were excluded for separate analysis. Profiles of the remaining 2,042 CDs were constructed, showing the percentage of private houses, the percentage of owner-occupied private houses, and the percentage of private houses built since the previous census (1954). An initial aggregation of CDs to an optimum size of approximately 3,000 persons was made, the only controls being that CDs so aggregated must be contiguous and in the same Local Government Area. The profiles of aggregated CDs were then compared and where possible dissimilar CDs were regrouped. As a crude index of dissimilarity the semi-interquartile ranges of the three measures in the profile were adopted (12·5, 20·0, and 10·0 per cent respectively). This regrouping yielded a new series of 611 areal units, with an average population of 3,080 persons. Since the component CDs themselves averaged 907 persons, a range in the size of the new areal units was inevitable. Fifty-nine per cent contained between 2,500 and 3,499 persons, two per cent fewer than 2,000 persons, and three per cent 4,000 or more. This variation had, however, now been effectively randomized and was not related to differential population change in the various parts of the city.[5] Although it is obvious that the overall level of internal homogeneity is bound to decrease as the size of the areal unit increases, the matching of CD dwelling profiles limited the risk of aggregating CDs with very dissimilar characteristics.[6] It may be noted that even after aggregation the areal units used in this study are no larger than census tracts in many American cities. These 611 aggregated CDs (hereafter called ACDs) provide the main basis for subsequent analysis of the residential differentiation of population categories in Melbourne.

Quantitative studies of ethnic concentration have generally been concerned with at least three questions. What are the patterns of residential distribution among various ethnic groups? To what extent are these patterns similar or dissimilar? And to what extent do these various patterns represent differing degrees of residential concentration? The first question can usually be answered quite directly by calculating for each area the percentage of its population accounted for by a given ethnic group, ranking these values according to magnitude, and mapping them in selected class-intervals. The resultant areal pattern can then be described. The second question has sometimes been answered in terms of indexes of dissimilarity.[7] In this study ecological correlations have been preferred, mainly because they are amenable to further statistical analysis (such as principal component analysis). The statistical meaning of an ecological correlation of this type is now well understood. Being specific to the areal case it provides a precise statement of the degree to which areal distributions of *group* characteristics are related.[8] Unless otherwise stated all correlations cited in this paper are Pearsonian product-moment correlation coefficients. The third question, the degree of residential concentration, has been investigated in many ways. As the Duncans[9] and more recently the Taeubers[10] have shown, measures of ethnic concentration commonly derive from the concentration curve, which gives the Gini index of concentration. This is the measure of ethnic concentration[11] adopted in this paper. In addition to the values of the Gini index, the concentration curve for each ethnic group is also shown. The Gini index has a potential range of zero (no concentration) to unity (complete concentration).

Changes in ethnic concentration, 1954 to 1961

Since the end of the Second World War Melbourne's population has increased by over 50 per cent. Of this increase almost exactly half was due directly to the arrival of overseas-born settlers. Over this period, as Table 17.1 shows, Melbourne's ethnic composition changed substantially.

Table 17.1 Ethnic composition of Melbourne, 1947, 1954 and 1961 (major birthplaces only)

| | Percentages | | |
Birthplace	1947	1954	1961
Australia	89·79	82·84	76·75
New Zealand	0·69	0·56	0·47
United Kingdom	7·15	8·01	8·13
Germany	0·27	0·88	1·51
Greece	0·16	0·37	1·51
Italy	0·35	1·96	3·86
Malta	0·04	0·40	0·87
Netherlands	0·04	0·47	1·12
Poland	0·14	1·13	1·06
Other	1·37	3·38	4·72
Total population	100·00	100·00	100·00
Number (000s)	1,226	1,524	1,912

In 1947 Melbourne was in ethnic terms very homogeneous, with 98 per cent of its population born in Australia, the United Kingdom, or New Zealand. By 1961 this figure had fallen to 85 per cent, as a result of heavy immigration from southern, and to a lesser degree northern and central, European countries. This change is even more striking when expressed in absolute numbers. For example, at the end of the Second World War Melbourne's southern European population numbered little more than 4,000 persons: in 1961 it numbered almost 120,000 persons.

Both in its relative size and in its composition Melbourne's foreign-born population differed importantly from the Australian norm. Melbourne accounted for only 17 per cent of Australia's total population, but for 25 per cent of all the foreign-born in Australia, 44 per cent of Maltese 38 per cent of Greeks, 33 per cent of Poles, and 32 per cent of Italians. More than one in four of Australia's postwar settlers lived in Melbourne in 1961. In an earlier study of ethnic concentrations in Australia's four largest metropolitan areas, Zubrzycki[12] showed that by 1954 marked ethnic concentrations had emerged in Melbourne, particularly among southern Europeans in the inner suburbs of the city. Table 17.2 gives Gini indexes of concentration for Local Government Areas in 1954 and 1961, and for ACDs in 1961. As expected the Gini indexes based on the smaller areal units are uniformly larger. But it is interesting that the increases in the index values (cols 3 and 4) vary from 14 per cent to 39 per cent, reflecting differences in patterns of residential distribution not detected when the larger areal units are used.

Table 17.2 generally confirms Zubrzycki's results and the same rank ordering of the eight groups by degree of residential concentration emerges. There are some slight deviations in relative values, mainly because of differences in the construction of Zubrzycki's index and the index adopted in this paper. In 1954 the Maltese, Italians and Greeks were clearly the most concentrated ethnic groups; the British and the New Zealanders were the least concentrated, followed by the Germans, with the Dutch and the Poles occupying a position intermediate between the Germans and the Greeks. In 1961 the position was very similar. Ignoring small movements in the index values, between 1954 and 1961 only one major change occurred in the rank order of the eight groups according to their degree of residential concentration. Although the Gini indexes for the two most densely con-

Table 17.2 Gini indexes of concentration for selected birthplaces by Local Government Areas and aggregated Collectors' Districts, Melbourne, 1954 and 1961, and median group residence in 1961

1	2	3	4	5
	Gini indexes			Median group residence —in years in
Birthplace	1954	1961	1961	1961
New Zealand	0·203	0·261	0·370	20·0
United Kingdom	0·138	0·167	0·212	11·6
Germany	0·356	0·322	0·431	7·2
Greece	0·542	0·635	0·726	5·2
Italy	0·553	0·542	0·637	6·5
Malta	0·654	0·648	0·768	6·4
Netherlands	0·478	0·495	0·600	5·9
Poland	0·476	0·477	0·595	10·4
No. of areal units	41*	46*	611†	

* Local Government Areas.
† Aggregated Collector's Districts.

centrated groups in 1954 (the Maltese and Italians) registered marginal decreases during the intercensal period, among the Greeks the degree of residential concentration increased sharply, accompanied by a very rapid growth in numbers. By 1961 there were in Melbourne 28,917 Greeks, compared with only 5,597 in 1954. As Table 17.1 suggests, the Greek population increased at a much more rapid rate than any other major ethnic group between the two census dates. The degree of concentration also increased slightly among the New Zealanders and British, but nonetheless remained at relatively low levels. The Germans registered a small decrease in concentration over the period.

Unlike some other indexes, the Gini index does not measure variations in the relative size of ethnic groups. It measures the *degree* of concentration without regard to the variable size of the groups involved. Variations in group size are obviously important sociologically, however, and need to be taken into account in interpreting the index values. Even though the Greeks were the only group to record a sharp increase in residential concentration between 1954 and 1961, clearly the social impact and 'visibility' of Melbourne's ethnic minorities was much greater in 1961 than it had been in 1954. As Table 17.1 shows, most of the groups increased at a much more rapid rate than the population as a whole. To take only one example, Melbourne's southern European population increased almost threefold, from 41,552 to 119,270 persons, compared with the overall rate of population increase of only 25 per cent.

Notwithstanding the usefulness of summary indexes of concentration, the concentration curves communicate a more graphic sense of the implications of residential concentration (Fig. 17.1). These show, for example, that among the two most concentrated groups (Maltese and Greeks) half their number lived in areas which contained only seven per cent of the rest of Melbourne's population. Similar values can be read off the curves for the other groups. Converting the curves to dissimilarity indexes (that is, the maximum vertical distance between the diagonal and the curve), we can say that for the Maltese to have a residential distribution that did not differ from the rest of the population, 60 per cent of them would have to change their ACD of residence. The comparable figures for other groups were: Greeks 57 per cent, Italians 50 per cent, Dutch 46 per cent, Poles 45 per cent, Germans 31 per cent, New Zealanders 26 per cent, and British 15 per cent.

Melbourne's major ethnic groups not only showed different degrees of concentration. They had different residential patterns as well. Maps showing the location of densest areas of concentration were prepared for each group. However, for reasons of space they have not been reproduced here. The following general comments are restricted to the ecological correlations given in Table 17.3. These measure the extent to which the residential distributions of the various groups are associated, but do not

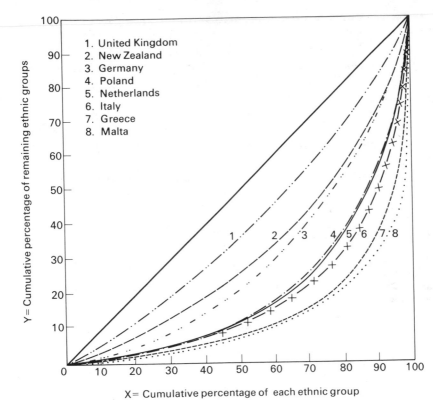

Fig. 17.1 Concentration curves of the residential distribution of ethnic groups in 611 ACDS, Melbourne 1961.

in themselves indicate anything about location within the city. Where locational references are made they are based on the aforementioned distribution maps.

Without examining in detail the full significance of these correlations it can be suggested that in 1961 three general patterns of ethnic concentration could be distinguished in Melbourne. The first, and most marked, was among the southern European groups, which were heavily concentrated in Melbourne's 'zone of transition' in the inner industrial suburbs settled in the late nineteenth and early twentieth century and characterized today by decaying housing, declining population, and increasing industrial and commercial land uses. Although the competition among Italian and Greek immigrants for residences in this zone has led to a partial partitioning of these inner suburbs between these two groups, the extent to which the residential distributions of the Italians, Greeks, and Maltese overlapped is well illustrated by the moderate to high ecological correlations of +0·679, +0·598, and +0·530. A second pattern, which emerges less clearly from Table 17.3, could be distinguished among Polish and other central

291

and eastern European Jews, in suburbs east and southeast of the city center. This is partly reflected in an ecological correlation of $+0.588$ between the German and Polish distributions. In 1961, 38·1 per cent of Poles and 9·4 per cent of Germans returned themselves as Hebrews, compared with only 1·5 per cent of Melbourne's population as a whole. Moreover, as indicated below, a number of these 'Germans' were in fact the children born to Polish refugees in Germany. The weaker positive correlations between the Polish distribution and those of the Greeks, Italians, and Maltese reflect the process of ecological invasion and succession by southern Europeans in

Table 17.3 Ecological correlations between the residential distributions of eight birthplace groups, Melbourne 1961

Birthplace (%)	Birthplace							
	1	2	3	4	5	6	7	8
(1) New Zealand-born	1·000	0·191	−0·044	−0·135	−0·291	−0·536	−0·26	0·010
(2) United Kingdom-born		1·000	0·274	−0·419	−0·479	−0·301	0·530	−0·121
(3) German-born			1·000	0·178	0·159	0·211	0·446	0·588
(4) Greek-born				1·000	0·679	0·530	−0·299	0·443
(5) Italian-born					1·000	0·598	−0·212	0·359
(6) Maltese-born						1·000	−0·135	0·294
(7) Netherlands-born							1·000	−0·030
(8) Polish-born								1·000

some areas of former Jewish concentration. The third pattern can be termed a northwestern European concentration and was located mainly on the western and eastern rural-urban fringe of the metropolis. It is reflected in the moderate associations between the Dutch and German $(+0.446)$ and the Dutch and British distributions $(+0.530)$. A fuller account of these concentrations, including a detailed discussion of their occupational and religious composition is in the course of preparation.

Residential concentration and assimilation

Recent studies of residential concentration among immigrants have emphasized its importance as an indicator, and a major determinant, of assimilation.[13] Concentration serves to reinforce the differences between groups by heightening their 'visibility', and through the spatial proximity afforded to group members provides a means whereby distinctive cultural patterns and group affiliations can be maintained.

The preceding analysis indicates that in 1961 clearly defined ethnic concentrations existed in Melbourne. The degree of residential concentration among all six non-British groups considered was moderate to high, reflecting in part the comparative recency of large-scale non-British immigration in Australia. These concentrations were more marked among the southern European groups, with the Dutch and Poles showing somewhat lower degrees of concentration and less clustering as well.[14] The low index value for the Germans requires some comment, since it partly reflects the internal heterogeneity of that birthplace group rather than a more rapid rate of assimilation. Although a detailed cross-tabulation of birthplace by nationality is not available for 1954 or 1961, Zubrzycki's work on the records of the International Refugee Organization indicates that perhaps half Australia's net permanent intake of 54,039 German-born persons between 1947 and 1954, a period which covers the arrival of 170,700 displaced persons from the refugee camps of Europe, consisted of nationals of countries other than Germany.[15] These were mainly the children of Polish, Ukrainian, Yugoslav, and Baltic persons interned in Germany during World War II.

Assimilation, as a process in time, is partly a function of the number of years an immigrant group has been in the country of resettlement. Can differences in the degree of residential concentration be explained in terms of differences in length of residence amongst the groups considered? To test this possibility the index values of residential concentration for the eight birthplaces in 1961 were correlated with their median period of residence in Australia. The groups differed considerably in terms of median residence, from just over 20 years for the New Zealand-born to 5·2 years for the Greek-born. The indexes of concentration and median residence correlated negatively to a moderate degree ($-0·640$), indicating that the most concentrated groups tended also to be the most recently arrived groups. However, less than half (41 per cent) of the variation in residential concentration could be explained by differences in median group residence. We now examine to what extent differences in residential concentration are associated with other factors, such as differences in occupational composition, marriage patterns, and rates of naturalization.

Occupational concentration

Unpublished statistics showing the detailed occupations of foreign-born males in Melbourne are available for 1961. For the purposes of the present analysis these occupations were regrouped into a shorter list of 100 occupational categories,[16] from which Gini indexes of occupational concentration were calculated.

As Table 17.4 shows, the ordering of the eight birthplace groups according to their degree of occupational concentration closely parallels the pattern which emerged from the analysis of residential concentration. The British-born were the most dispersed in occupational terms, followed by the New Zealanders, Dutch, Germans, and Poles. The three southern European groups again had the highest degree of concentration. The simple cor-

Table 17.4   Gini indexes of occupational concentration
for selected birthplaces, Melbourne 1961

1 Birthplace	2 Gini index	3 No. of male workers
New Zealand	0·297	3,181
United Kingdom	0·186	60,557
Germany	0·377	10,714
Greece	0·614	13,300
Italy	0·552	34,803
Malta	0·541	7,294
Netherlands	0·309	8,859
Poland	0·412	10,619

relations between, (1) residential concentration, (2) occupational concentration, and (3) median group residence were

$$r_{12} + 0·877, r_{13} = -0·640, \text{ and}$$
$$r_{23} = -0·573.$$

After controlling for the effect of differences in median group residence, a first-order partial correlation coefficient of $r_{12.3} = +0·810$ was derived indicating that a high positive association between residential concentration and occupational concentration existed independently of the effect of length of residence. Taking residential concentration as the dependent variable, it can be suggested that a large part of the differing degree of residential concentration among these immigrant groups in Melbourne in 1961 can be seen as a function of differences in occupational composition independently of differences in median group residence.

Intermarriage

Although the propensity of persons of a given birthplace to select marriage partners from the same birthplace is influenced by a number of factors (including the sex ratio, the availability of marriageable persons of the same ethnic stock, and the possibility of re-immigration to the country of origin to find a bride),[17] it seems reasonable to use the rate of ethnic inmarriage as an indicator of assimilation. Marriage statistics relating the respective birthplaces of grooms and brides are not available for Melbourne but are available for the State of Victoria as a whole. Since in 1961 Melbourne accounted for 77 per cent of the State's total population for the eight birthplaces under analysis, the use of State statistics of inter-marriage probably introduces very little distortion, at least for the present purposes. A further problem is that for the years up to 1961 the Victorian statistics do not provide separate figures for persons born in New Zealand or Poland. Such figures are available for Australia as a whole and Table 17.5 compares the Victorian and national statistics of inmarriage for the three-year period

1959 to 1961. When cols 3 and 6 and cols 4 and 7 of Table 17.5 were compared, it was found that while the Australian inmarriage rates were generally lower than those for Victoria,[18] the *relative magnitudes* of the two pairs of figures were virtually identical. The correlation coefficient between the Victorian and total Australian inmarriage rates for the six birthplaces of Table 17.5 was $+0.995$ for grooms and $+0.997$ for brides. Because such very high correlations existed between the two series and because the national figures distinguished both New Zealanders and Poles, the national figures have been used in the following analysis as if they were the Victorian figures.

Table 17.5 Number and percentage of inmarriages among eight birthplace groups, Victoria and Australia 1959–1961

1	2 Victoria	3	4	5 Australia	6	7
Birthplace	No. of inmarriages	% of grooms inmarried	% of brides inmarried	No. of inmarriages	% of grooms inmarried	% of brides inmarried
New Zealand	NA	NA	NA	95	7·6	9·2
United Kingdom	967	24·5	27·8	3,018	22·1	26·2
Germany	549	48·5	48·7	1,226	41·3	42·2
Greece	2,516	92·2	89·8	5,534	89·1	89·9
Italy	3,145	78·8	93·4	7,047	70·4	92·7
Malta	347	54·7	73·1	693	51·6	69·6
Netherlands	486	43·4	51·0	1,190	38·1	47·3
Poland	NA	NA	NA	863	47·7	65·5

Source: Commonwealth Bureau of Census and Statistics, Victorian Office, *Demographic Statistics*, 1959 to 1961; and Commonwealth Bureau of Census and Statistics, *Demography Bulletin*, 1959 to 1961.

The broad pattern which emerges from the inmarriage rates again tends to confirm the patterns already discussed. The rate of inmarriage was higher among the southern Europeans than among the Dutch, Germans, or Poles, and was lowest among the British and New Zealanders. The lower rate of inmarriage among the Maltese compared with the Greeks and Italians is interesting, and probably results from the fact that the Maltese are British subjects and usually speak English on arrival. This presumably increases their ability to mix with native Australians. The German and Polish inmarriage rates are probably artificially low, for the reasons given in discussing differences in the degree of residential concentration.

The correlations between the Gini indexes of residential concentration and the male and female inmarriage rates were quite high ($+0.769$ and $+0.823$ respectively). However, the rates of inmarriage were also quite strongly related to differences in median group residence (-0.778 and -0.768 respectively), indicating that the groups with the highest inmarriage rates tended to be those with the lowest median residence. After controlling for period of residence, first-order partial correlation co-efficients between residential concentration and rates of inmarriage of + 0·562 and + 0·673 were derived. While these coefficients are substantially lower than the simple correlations and can be described as only moderately strong, they do support the previous findings and show that a high degree of residential concentration tends to be associated with a high degree of inmarriage. This association is also consistent with findings that residential propinquity is a determining factor in the choice of a marriage partner.[19]

Naturalization

Persons born in countries outside Australia or other Commonwealth countries may acquire citizenship by naturalization subject to a residence qualification (normally five years), to having an adequate knowledge of the responsibilities and privileges of citizenship, and to taking an oath of allegiance to the British Crown. It is a reasonable assumption that the naturalization of a non-British subject, involving a change in political allegiance and national identification, indicates that at least a minimal amount of assimilation has occurred. Naturalization is probably not, however, an entirely adequate indicator of assimilation, since it involves primarily a politico-legal action which has different implications for each alien group.

Only five of the eight groups considered previously consist of alien nationals. Since neither the 1954 or 1961 censuses cross-classified birth-place by nationality, an indirect method of measuring the rate of naturalization for each group has to be adopted. Again, State figures of naturalization are used in the absence of separate statistics for Melbourne. Table 17.6 relates the number of aliens resident in Victoria at the time of the 1961

Table 17.6 Estimated number of persons naturalized between July 1952 and June 1961 in Victoria compared with the number of unnaturalized aliens resident in Victoria at the 1961 census for five nationality groups.

1 Former or present nationality	2 Est. no. of persons naturalized June 1952 to July 1961*	3 Unnaturalized aliens 1961†	4 3 as a % of 2 and 3
Dutch	9,734	14,866	60·4
German	5,845	9,817	62·7
Greek	3,973	13,137	76·8
Italian	18,625	38,239	67·2
Polish	15,561	5,180	25·0

* The number of naturalization certificates issued in Victoria is shown in the *Victorian Year Books*. From 1956 onward unpublished figures of persons affected by such certificates are available from the Department of Immigration. The ratio of persons per certificate for each nationality from January 1956 to June 1961 was used to derive an estimate of persons naturalized during the earlier period July 1952 to December 1955. Only 10 per cent of the certificates considered were issued during this earlier period.
† Excluding aliens with less than five years residence in Australia.

census who had been in Australia for more than five but less than fourteen years (i.e. postwar alien settlers who presumably could have become naturalized but had not), to the number of aliens who had been naturalized in the nine-year period July 1952 to June 1961. It is assumed that all the naturalizations which took place in this period involved postwar settlers, and in the absence of relevant satistics no account could be taken of mortality, internal migration, or the emigration of naturalized persons. It is unlikely, however, that possible differences in the levels of any or all of those factors would have been of sufficient magnitude to vitiate the analysis presented below. By summing columns 2 and 3 of Table 17.6, a population at risk to naturalization in the post-1947 period was derived and column 4 shows the percentage of unnaturalized aliens who in 1961 had satisfied the residence qualifications for naturalization.

The percentage of unnaturalized aliens varied from a comparatively low figure of 25 per cent unnaturalized for the Poles to a high figure of 78 per cent among the Greeks. However, the percentage of unnaturalized aliens was very strongly associated with differences in median group residence[20] (a simple correlation of -0.956). Thus, differences in these percentages could be explained very largely by differences in length of residence. Groups with the highest percentage unnaturalized were those with shorter periods of residence in Australia. By contrast the relationship between residential concentration for the five comparable birthplace groups and percentage unnaturalized, although positive, was quite weak ($+0.247$), and after controlling for period of residence this relationship changed to a weak negative correlation (-0.290). This relationship is not in the hypothesized direction, and although the number of groups considered is very small, it seems that only a small proportion of the variation in residential concentration can be explained by differences in rates of naturalization. This finding is not too surprising, however, and in one of the few Australian studies which has explored the behaviorial correlates of naturalization Zubrzycki found no consistent relationship between percentage naturalized and patterns of social participation for eight European birthplace groups, and concluded that although further analysis was required naturalization did not seem to be a reliable indicator of social participation.[21] It can be suggested that while naturalization may be a very significant event in the life of an individual immigrant, it may have few important behavioral implications beyond its direct political consequences.

Discussion and conclusions

The cultural origins of Australia's postwar immigrants have been more diverse than in any other period of her history, with the exception of the gold rushes of the 1850s. Although some groups, such as the British and

New Zealanders, have cultural backgrounds similar to those out of which modern Australia has grown, others represent cultural streams which have had relatively little impact in Australia until the last fifteen years. These immigrant groups differ among themselves, and from the native-born population, in terms of the range of skills they bring (or do not bring) with them, in their educational levels, religious composition, language, customs, and even physical characteristics. Moreover, native-born Australians tend to rank invidiously the different immigrant groups according to how acceptable they see these settlers in the 'Australian way of life'.[22] It is not surprising, therefore, that immigrants from different countries adapt differentially to the Australian social environment and differ in their rates of assimilation.

In this paper census data have been used to show that in 1954 and 1961 Melbourne contained some substantial immigrant concentrations. Between 1954 and 1961, a period in which most groups increased rapidly in size, the degree of residential concentration remained relatively stable, except among the Greeks, who recorded a sharp increase. The southern European groups were more concentrated than the Dutch or the Poles, and more clustered as well. (This can be established from maps showing the residential distribution of each group but not presented in this paper.) The heterogeneous composition of the German-born obscured their position in this broad ranking. The British and the New Zealanders showed the lowest degrees of residential concentration.

Some of this variation in the degree of residential concentration could be explained in terms of differences in length of residence among the groups concerned. Thus, the most concentrated groups tended also to be the most recently arrived groups. However, the analysis of two other possible indicators of assimilation – occupational concentration and inmarriage rates – indicated that the extent of residential concentration among these immigrant groups was related independently of differences in median group residence to differences in occupational composition and to differences in the propensity to marry persons from the same country of birth. Thus the eight birth-place groups considered can be systematically differentiated in terms of these three indicators of assimilation, even after the effect of differences in median period of residence has been taken into account. A fourth indicator of assimilation, the rate of naturalization, was found to be almost entirely a function of differences in median group residence, and differences in the naturalization rate failed to confirm the previous results. As a possible explanation of this inconsistency it was suggested that naturalization may have few important behavioral implications beyond its immediate political consequences.

The process of assimilation in Australia, and particularly the emergence of ethnic residential concentrations, must be viewed against Australia's background of recent large-scale immigration and rapidly changing ethnic composition. Although Melbourne and other parts of Australia are still predominantly 'British' in culture and in population, in the last fifteen years Melbourne's foreign-born population of non-British origin has increased sevenfold. In 1961, 51 per cent of this non-British population had been in Australia for less than seven years, and another 35 per cent had arrived during the preceding seven years. Studies of intergroup relationships among immigrants from different birthplaces have yet to be conducted in an Australian metropolis. General observations, however, suggest that Melbourne's ethnic concentrations have largely arisen out of the positive desire among recent immigrants with different cultures to create familiar surroundings through which established modes of interaction can be maintained. Present indications, imprecise as they are, suggest that over time these ethnic groups will become more dispersed in Melbourne's residential, occupational, and social structure, although the findings of the present study indicate that the rate of this dispersal will differ from one immigrant group to another.

Notes and References

Revised and extended version of a paper delivered to Section P of the 38th Congress of the Australian and New Zealand Association for the Advancement of Science, 1965.

1. For recent discussions of the relevant literature see James M. Beshers, *Urban Social Structure*, Glencoe: The Free Press, 1962, and the readings edited by George A. Theodorson, *Studies in Human Ecology*, Evanston, Row, Peterson, 1961.
2. Robert Park, *Human Communities: The City and Human Ecology*, Glencoe, The Free Press, 1952, 177.
3. For example, Stanley Lieberson, *Ethnic Patterns in American Cities*, Free Press of Glencoe, 1963, and Jerzy Zubrzycki, *Immigrants in Australia: a demographic survey based on the 1954 Census,* Melbourne University Press, 1960.
4. Differences in CD size could have been overcome by weighting observations according to population size. This would have left an important, but often neglected, question of the meaningfulness of rates based on small populations. Frank Alexander Ross, 'Ecology and the statistical method', *Am. J. Sociol.*, **38**, (Jan. 1933), 507–32; Robert E. Chaddock, 'Significance of infant mortality rates for small geographic areas', *J. Am. Stat. Ass.*, **29**, (Sept. 1934), 243–9.
5. The population size of CDs was correlated with seventy socioeconomic, demographic, and ethnic variables. The highest correlation observed was − 0·081. The average of all seventy correlation coefficients (ignoring sign) was 0·028.

6. A detailed analysis of the internal variation among the constituent CDs of each new areal unit has been made according to the three measures included in the profiles. In 55 per cent of the new areas the proportion of private houses in each CD varied by less than 10 per cent. The corresponding figures for owner-occupancy and period of building were 59 per cent and 54 per cent respectively. If a maximum variation of 15 per cent in each measure is permitted, these figures are raised to 74, 73 and 64 per cent respectively. Given the small average size of the original CDs these figures are reassuringly high.

7. For example, Otis Dudley Duncan and Stanley Lieberson, 'Ethnic segregation and assimilation', *Am. J. Sociol.*, **64**, (Jan. 1959), 364–74 [7].

8. W. S. Robinson, 'Ecological correlation and the behavior of individuals', *Am. Sociol. Rev.*, **15**, (June 1950), 351–7.

9. O. D. Duncan and B. Duncan, 'A methodological analysis of segregation indexes' *Am. Sociol. Rev.*, **20**, (April 1955), 210–17 [2].

10. Karl E. Taeuber and Alma Taeuber, *Negroes in Cities: residential segregation and neighborhood change*, Chicago, Aldine Publishing Co. 1965, pp. 195–245.

11. My use of 'concentration' where many use 'segregation' and some 'isolation' is not perverse. It rests on two considerations. (1) Residential 'concentration' is not equivalent to residential 'segregation'. Two ethnic groups may show different degrees of concentration but may be equally segregated from some other group. I use Gini indexes to measure concentration as such and reserve ecological correlations to measure the degree of similarity or dissimilarity between the residential distributions of various ethnic groups. (2) 'Segregation' and 'isolation' have much stronger behavioral implications than 'concentration'. While such implications are often soundly based (otherwise one would hesitate to undertake this sort of analysis at all), a more neutral term such as concentration may be initially preferred, particularly when discussing immigrant as against racial residential patterns.

12. Zubrzycki, *op. cit.*, 79–85.

13. Lieberson, *op. cit.*, esp. 3–13.

14. For reasons of space no account of the residential patterns of ethnic concentration is attempted here.

15. Zubrzycki, *op. cit.*, 51–7.

16. For an account of this classification, see Leonard Broom, F. Lancaster Jones, and Jerzy Zubrzycki, 'An occupational classification of the Australian workforce', *Australian and New Zealand Journal of Sociology*, **8**, (Oct. 1965), Supplement.

17. C. A. Price and J. Zubrzycki, 'The use of inter-marriage statistics as an index of assimilation', *Population Studies*, **16**, (July 1962), 58–69; and 'Immigrant marriage patterns in Australia', *Population Studies*, **16**, (Nov. 1962), 123–33.

18. This presumably reflects the fact that immigrants from these birthplaces were relatively over-represented in Victoria and this probably provided more opportunity for inmarriage.

19. It is assumed that the State figures can be applied to Melbourne. Obviously if

there is a high rate of inmarriage in the State as a whole, the major contribution to such a rate almost certainly comes from Melbourne.

20. Median group residence for alien immigrants arriving in Australia between 1947 and 1956 was calculated for each national group. However, as this series correlated strongly with median group residence for the comparable birthplace groups ($r = +0.893$), the birthplace figures were used.

21. Jerzy Zubrzycki, *Settlers of the Latrobe Valley: A Sociological Study of Immigrants in the Brown Coal Industry of Australia*, Canberra: Australian National University, 1964, 156–8.

22. See O. S. Oeser and S. B. Hammond, eds, *Social Structure and Personality in a City*, London: Routledge & Kegan Paul, 1954, 51–65.

R. J. Stimson

18 Patterns of immigrant settlement in Melbourne, 1947–61*

Introduction

Between 1947 and 1961 the population of Australia increased by 2·9 million, 41·8 per cent of this increase being directly due to immigration. If the indirect effects of immigration are considered, immigrants and the children born to them in Australia accounted for 50·3 per cent of this population increase.[1] It is understandable that the one million immigrant settlers who arrived in Australia during the period under review have attracted the attention of researchers in many disciplines. However, few geographers have been concerned with analysing the distributional aspects of immigrants within a large metropolis, and studies enquiring into the spatial aspects of immigrant settlement are limited to those by Rose,[2] Woolmington[3] and Scott.[4] Sociologists and demographers have been most active in this field, although their concern has been primarily with non-spatial aspects of immigrant settlement, which has received attention in the work of Zubrzycki,[5] Hempel,[6] and Jones.[7] This paper is concerned with analysing changes in the pattern of distribution of European immigrants within the Melbourne metropolitan area between 1947 and 1961.

The term European-born immigrants is intended to include United Kingdom and Republic of Ireland born persons (who will be referred to as UK-born immigrants). Where it is intended to refer to non-British European immigrants the term Continental European born immigrants is used, and an immigrant is regarded as a person defined by the Australian census as born outside Australia. Analysis of immigrant group distributions undertaken in this paper is based on Population by Birthplace data for Local Government Areas in the Melbourne Metropolitan Area at the 1947, 1954 and 1961 censuses.

* Reprinted from *Tijdschrift voor Economische en Sociale Geografie*, **61** (1970), 114–26.

Melbourne as a centre of European immigrant settlement

Since 1947 Melbourne has emerged as the major centre of immigrant settlement in Australia. In 1947 only 130,000 persons of overseas birth lived in Melbourne, these representing 10·25 per cent of the total population, a proportion which was only marginally above the Australian average of 9·8 per cent. Table 18.1 indicates how the number of overseas born persons had increased to 261,470 or 17·15 per cent of the total population in 1954, and to 444,479 or 23·25 per cent of the total population in 1961. The relative importance of the immigrant population was greater in Melbourne than it was for Australia as a whole in both 1954 and 1961 when immigrants formed respectively only 14·31 per cent and 16·93 per cent of the Australian population. In 1954 only 27,082 and in 1961 only 41,966 immigrants living in Melbourne were non-European born immigrants.

Melbourne, then, had become a metropolis in which about one-quarter of its population were immigrants, and, as Table 18.2 shows, in 1961 43·29 per cent of immigrants had arrived since 1954 and 77·76 per cent had arrived since 1947, compared with the respective figures for Australia as a whole of 34·60 per cent and 70·37 per cent. In Table 18.1 it is seen that the rapid increase in immigrant settlement during the period 1947 to 1961 was in fact a radical departure from the traditional pattern of immigration to Australia since between 1954 and 1961 82 per cent of immigrants settling in Melbourne were of Continental European origin, with particular emphasis being on Southern European immigrants. From Table 18.1 it is evident that by 1961 Melbourne, with only 16·81 per cent of the total population of Australia, had considerably more than its share of most immigrant groups. This was particularly so for immigrants from Malta, Greece, Poland, and Italy, and to a lesser extent for those from the Netherlands and the UK.

Immigration and the growth of Melbourne, 1947–61

Immigrant settlement of the magnitude outlined above, plus the immediate post-war large natural population increase and drift to the cities, has greatly influenced the growth pattern of the larger urban centres in Australia. The impact of immigrant settlement on to the population growth rate of Melbourne as a whole and more especially on that of its suburbs illustrates this point well.

For the metropolitan area there was an increase of 18·8 per cent in the total population and of 105 per cent in the European born population between 1947 and 1954. For the 1954–61 intercensal period the increase in the total population was 25 per cent and for the European born population was 72 per cent. However, within the metropolitan area there was considerable variation in the rate of increase for these populations during the

Table 18.1 Birthplace of population

Birthplace of population	1954					1961				
	Australia		Melbourne			Australia		Melbourne		
	Number	% of total population	Number	% of total Melbourne population	% of total birthplace nos in Australia	Number	% of total population	Number	% of total Melbourne population	% of total birthplace nos in Australia
Australia	7,700,064	85·68	1,262,641	82·84	16·40	8,729,014	83·07	1,467,416	76·75	16·81
Europe:										
UK & Rep. of Ireland	664,205	7·39	122,109	8·01	18·38	755,576	7·19	155,537	8·14	20·59
Germany	65,422	0·73	13,366	0·88	20·43	109,310	1·04	28,880	1·51	26·42
Greece	25,862	0·29	5,597	0·37	21·64	77,356	0·74	28,917	1·51	37·38
Italy	119,897	1·33	29,890	1·96	24·93	227,689	2·17	73,752	3·86	32·39
Malta	19,988	0·22	6,065	0·40	30·34	39,370	0·37	16,601	0·89	42·17
Netherlands	52,035	0·58	7,210	0·47	13·86	102,178	0·97	21,389	1·12	20·93
Poland	56,594	0·63	17,176	1·13	30·35	60,044	0·57	20,273	1·06	33·76
Other Europe	151,061	1·68	32,975	2·16	21·83	224,744	2·14	57,164	2·99	25·44
Total Europe	1,155,064	12·85	234,388	15·38	20·29	1,596,267	15·19	402,513	21·05	25·22
Foreign, non-European	131,402	1·46	27,082	1·78	20·61	182,905	1·74	41,966	2·19	22·94
Total overseas	1,286,466	14·31	261,470	17·15	20·32	1,779,172	16·93	444,479	23·25	24·98
Total population	8,986,530	100·00	1,524,111	100·00	16·96	10,508,186	100·00	1,911,895	100·00	18·19

Table 18.2 Period of residence of overseas-born population

| | 1954 | | | | | | 1961 | | | | | |
| | Australia | | | Melbourne | | | Australia | | | Melbourne | | |
	Number	% of Australian total overseas-born	% of total Australian population	Number	% of Melbourne total overseas-born	% Australian total for each period of residence group	Number	% of Australian total overseas-born	% of total Australian population	Number	% of Melbourne total overseas-born	% Australian total for each period of residence group
Under 1 year	82,271	6·51	0·92	16,547	6·33	20·12	123,516	6·94	1·18	30·798	6·93	24·93
Under 7 years	664,689	51·67	7·40	148,087	56·64	22·28	651,645	34·60	6·20	190,717	43·29	29·27
Under 14 years, 1961							1,252,086	70·37	11·83	345,647	77·76	27·61
Over 7 years, 1954	599,645	46·61	6·67	109,345	41·82	18·24						
Over 14 years, 1961							489,966	27·54	4·66	91,168	20·52	18·61
Not stated	22,132	1·72	0·25	4,038	1·54	18·24	37,120	2·09	0·34			
Total overseas-born	1,286,466	100·00	14·32	261,460	100·00	20·32	1,779,172	100·00	16·93	444,479	100·00	24·98

two intercensal periods under review. Figure 18.1 indicates the Local Government Areas (LGAs) comprising the 1961 Melbourne Metropolitan Area, and the spatial patterns of increases in the total population and European born population of the LGAs in Melbourne for the 1947–54 and 1954–61 intercensal periods are shown in Figs 18.2 to 5. One of the difficulties in using the LGA as a basis of comparing spatial patterns is that the number of LGAs in the Melbourne Metropolitan Area increased from forty-one to forty-six between 1954 and 1961. This increase in the number of LGAs plus the changes in the boundaries of LGAs in the 1947–54 and 1954–61 intercensal periods renders Figs 18.2 to 5 not strictly comparable. However, where a boundary change between two censuses was too great for statistical adjustment to be made the word 'Redefined' appears in the relevant LGA. As can be seen from Figs 18.1 to 5, Melbourne has expanded outwards from the CBD, which is situated roughly in the centre of the LGA of Melbourne City, in an unbalanced manner, the growth being in favour of the east and the southeast along Port Phillip Bay.

Between 1947 and 1954 the areas of greatest increase in total population were the outer western and northwestern suburbs extending from Sunshine to Broadmeadows, and a solid belt stretching from Heidelberg in the outer northeast through Doncaster-Templestowe, Nunawading, Ringwood, Oakleigh, Waverley, and Moorabbin to Dandenong in the outer southeast. Both these areas experienced an increase of over 50 per cent. As indicated in Fig. 18.2, apart from these rapidly developing residential and industrial suburbs growth elsewhere was relatively slow, with a distinct belt of actual population decline occurring in the inner city LGAs and the near eastern and southeastern suburbs. Figure 18.3 shows that the pattern of increase for European immigrants was similar, with greatest increases occurring in the outer western and northwestern fringe suburbs (over 500 per cent) and to a slightly less extent in the outer eastern and southeastern suburbs. But there was also considerable increase in the inner suburbs where up to 75 per cent growth was the rule. The lowest increase in European immigrant population was in the near eastern and southeastern middle to high status residential areas stretching from Camberwell to Sandringham. These patterns of growth in total and European born populations in general continued during the 1954–61 intercensal period when again the outer suburbs showed the greatest increase in total population. Figure 18.4 indicates how the fringe suburbs between Altona and Broadmeadows on the western side of Melbourne and those between Lilydale and Frankston on the eastern and southeastern fringe recorded increases of over 50 per cent, while the eastern suburbs between Doncaster-Templestowe and Waverley, an area which also had rapid growth in the 1947–54 period, had an increase in total population of over 100 per cent. The inner suburbs continued to experience population decline between 1954 and 1961, this being in excess of 10 per cent in Melbourne and South

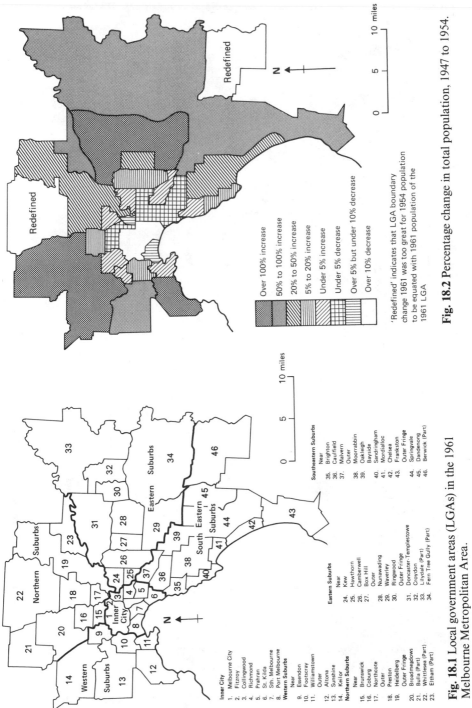

Fig. 18.2 Percentage change in total population, 1947 to 1954.

Over 100% increase

50% to 100% increase

20% to 50% increase

5% to 20% increase

Under 5% increase

Under 5% decrease

Over 5% but under 10% decrease

Over 10% decrease

'Redefined' indicates that LGA boundary change 1961 was too great for 1954 population to be equated with 1961 population of the 1961 LGA.

Fig. 18.1 Local government areas (LGAs) in the 1961 Melbourne Metropolitan Area.

Inner City
1. Melbourne City
2. Fitzroy
3. Collingwood
4. Richmond
5. Prahran
6. St. Kilda
7. Sth. Melbourne
8. Port Melbourne

Western Suburbs
Near
9. Essendon
10. Footscray
11. Williamstown
Outer
12. Altona
13. Sunshine
14. Keilor

Northern Suburbs
Near
15. Brunswick
16. Coburg
17. Northcote
18. Preston
19. Heidelberg
Outer Fringe
20. Broadmeadows
21. Bulla (Part)
22. Whittlesea (Part)
23. Eltham (Part)

Eastern Suburbs
Near
24. Kew
25. Camberwell
26. Box Hill
27. Hawthorn
Outer
28. Nunawading
29. Ringwood
Outer Fringe
30. Croydon
31. Doncaster-Templestowe
32. Lilydale (Part)
33. Fern Tree Gully (Part)
34. Berwick (Part)

Southeastern Suburbs
Near
35. Brighton
36. Caulfield
37. Malvern
Outer
38. Moorabbin
39. Oakleigh
40. Sandringham
41. Mordialloc
42. Chelsea
43. Frankston
Outer Fringe
44. Springvale
45. Dandenong
46. Berwick (Part)
39. Bayside

307

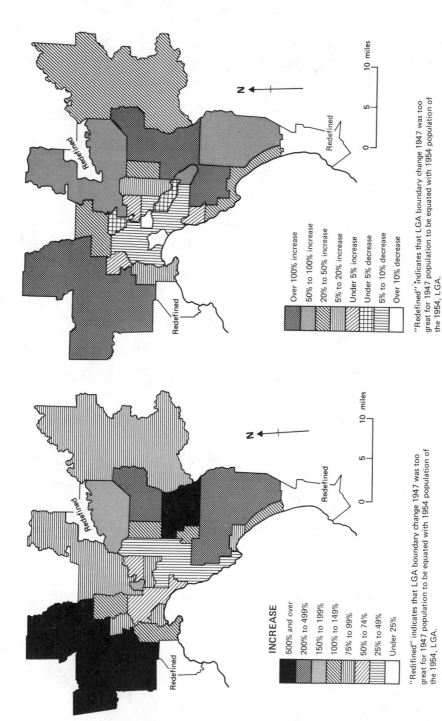

"Redefined" indicates that LGA boundary change 1947 was too great for 1947 population to be equated with 1954 population of the 1954, LGA.

Fig. 18.3 Percentage change in European-born population of LGAs, 1947 to 1954.

"Redefined" indicates that LGA boundary change 1947 was too great for 1947 population to be equated with 1954 population of the 1954, LGA.

Fig. 18.4 Percentage change in total population, 1954 to 1961.

INCREASE

500% and over
200% to 499%
150% to 199%
100% to 149%
75% to 99%
50% to 74%
25% to 49%
Under 25%

Over 100% increase
50% to 100% increase
20% to 50% increase
5% to 20% increase
Under 5% increase
Under 5% decrease
5% to 10% decrease
Over 10% decrease

Melbourne LGAs, but the extent of the area of decline had not increased. The rate of decline had decreased in some LGAs, notably Richmond, Collingwood, Fitzroy, Brunswick and Northcote. An explanation of this trend is evident from Fig. 18.5 which indicates an increase of more than 50 per cent in the European born population of inner city LGAs. However, the pattern in Fig. 18.5 remains little changed from that in Fig. 18.3 with the exception of the decline in the rate of increase of the European immigrant population in the outer western and northwestern suburbs and the higher rates of increase in the outer eastern suburbs, notably the fringe areas of Doncaster-Templestowe, Croydon, Lilydale, Oakleigh, Springvale and Dandenong. These outer southeastern LGAs continued to register above 150 per cent increase in European born population, but the rate of increase had slackened in the Moorabbin area. Once again the Camberwell to Sandringham belt in the near east and southeast had an increase of under 50 per cent for European immigrants. It is obvious from Figs 18.2 to 5 that

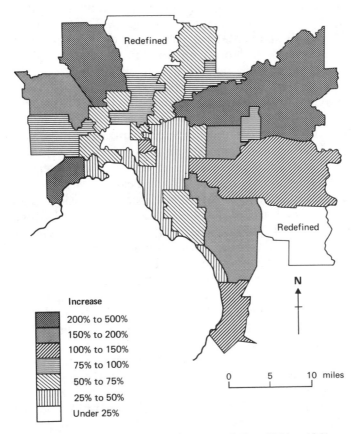

Fig. 18.5 Percentage increase in European-born population, 1954 to 1961.

between 1947 and 1961 the influx of European settlers had a profound effect on the pattern of growth rates of suburbs within Melbourne and on the direction of expansion of the metropolitan area. There have been two obvious effects; first, the contribution of immigrants to the rapid 1947–54 growth of the outer western suburbs and the growth of the outer south-eastern suburbs, especially in the 1954–61 period; and, second, the slowing down effect of European immigration on the rate of depopulation in the inner city area, where the combined influence of continued immigration and post-1961 developments in high density housing could well reverse this trend.

Distribution patterns of immigrant groups

The tendency for immigrant groups to become areally concentrated and segregated from the remainder of the population is a common pheno-menon in the 'western' city and within Melbourne, as elsewhere, immigrant groups displayed considerable variation in the extent to which they had become concentrated in specific areas of the city. The extent of variation between LGAs in the percentage of their population that came from a particular birthplace is evident from an analysis of Table 18.3, which shows how the gap between the LGA with the highest percentage of its population from a particular birthplace category and the LGA with the lowest percentage of its population from that birthplace category tended to increase for most of the European birthplace groups during the period 1947–61. The distribution of percentage concentration of each birthplace category in the LGAs comprising the metropolitan area were analysed for the 1947, 1954 and 1961 censuses. The distributions were in general markedly positively skewed according to the Pearsonian skewness measure (Sk). This was particularly so for Maltese, Greek, Yugoslavian and Ukrai-nian born immigrants, and slightly less so for Italian, USSR, Czecho-slovakian, Netherlands, Hungarian, Austrian and German born immigrants. The UK, Latvian and Lithuanian born immigrants had the least positively skewed distributions (see Table 18.4).

In order to analyse changes in the distributional pattern of immigrant concentrations within the metropolitan area of Melbourne the percentage of the LGA's population born in the countries of birth listed in Table 18.3 was calculated for each of the 1947, 1954 and 1961 censuses. This percen-tage was then converted into an index of concentration (Ic) so that direct comparison could be made of the degree of concentration of an immigrant group between LGAs at the same census and for the one LGA between censuses. The index is a ratio between the number of a birthplace group expressed as a percentage of the population of an LGA and the number of that birthplace group expressed as a percentage of the population of the metropolitan area. Ic values were used for mapping variations in the

Table 18.3 Proportion of Melbourne's population from specific birthplaces, 1947, 1954 and 1961

Birthplace	1947			1954			1961		
	% of Melbourne area total population	% for lowest ranking LGA	% for highest ranking LGA	% of MMA total population	% for lowest ranking LGA	% for highest ranking LGA	% of MMA total population	% for Lowest ranking LGA	% for highest ranking LGA
Total foreign-born	10·25	6·76	16·33	17·16	10·22	37·70	23·25	14·03	45·13
Total UK & European-born	8·90	5·91	14·07	15·38	9·23	35·36	21·05	11·85	42·91
UK & Republic of Ireland-born	7·21	5·04	9·97	8·01	4·82	18·45	8·14	3·49	18·87
Netherlands	0·04	0·00	0·13	0·47	0·10	9·14	1·12	0·25	7·86
Germany	0·27	0·02	1·40	0·88	0·25	5·59	1·51	0·34	6·45
Austria	0·12	0·00	0·77	0·21	0·04	0·92	0·37	0·00	1·43
Hungary				0·22	0·03	0·78	0·47	0·00	2·93
Czechoslovakia	0·30	0·00	1·86	0·03	0·02	1·07	0·19	0·00	1·07
Poland				1·13	0·08	5·36	1·06	0·10	5·64
Latvia				0·27	0·02	0·80	0·24	0·04	0·48
Lithuania				0·14	0·00	0·70	0·11	0·00	0·26
Ukraine				0·21	0·00	2·77	0·18	0·00	1·04
USSR	0·09	0·00	0·50	0·18	0·04	0·79	0·19	0·02	0·70
Yugoslavia	0·02	0·00	0·28	0·25	0·03	1·49	0·64	0·00	2·84
Malta	0·04	0·01	0·30	0·40	0·00	2·33	0·87	0·00	5·13
Greece	0·16	0·04	0·81	0·37	0·00	3·22	1·51	0·02	10·93
Italy	0·36	0·08	1·61	1·96	0·21	12·23	3·86	0·00	18·65
Other European-born	0·32	0·68	0·81	0·47	0·21	1·23	0·61	0·17	1·87
Foreign, non-European-born	1·35		2·51	1·78	0·04	5·43	2·19	0·86	6·24

311

Table 18.4 **Pearsonian skewness measures (Sk) of distribution of birthplace groups**

Birthplace	Sk 1954	1961
Total UK and European	0·927	0·328
UK & Republic of Ireland	0·341	0·486
Netherlands	1·375	0·720
Germany	0·950	0·830
Austria	0·938	0·889
Hungary	0·563	0·783
Czechoslovakia	0·947	0·882
Poland	0·893	0·636
Latvia	0·000	0·545
Lithuania	0·750	0·000
Ukraine	0·941	1·125
USSR	1·125	0·923
Yugoslavia	0·794	1·304
Malta	1·655	1·658
Italy	1·123	0·878
Greece	1·291	1·125
Other European	1·000	0·909
Foreign, non-European	0·888	0·647

Table 18.5 **Index of residential segregation (Is) for birthplace groups**

Birthplace	Is (percentage) 1954	1961
Total UK and European	14·65	18·49
UK & Republic of Ireland	9·63	10·97
Netherlands	37·46	37·87
Germany	25·93	23·70
Austria	27·34	25·48
Hungary	22·66	30·90
Czechoslovakia	30·63	29·62
Poland	35·22	34·93
Latvia	20·16	19·15
Lithuania	25·92	22·96
Ukraine	48·41	46·05
USSR	27·67	27·04
Yugoslavia	35·78	35·49
Malta	53·07	52·17
Greece	41·54	50·35
Italy	44·81	41·51
Other Europe	17·73	20·06
Foreign, non-European	17·08	15·06

relative concentration of immigrant groups within the metropolitan area of Melbourne for the three censuses. The map legends indicate, in addition to the Ic value for each LGA, the possible range for the percentage of

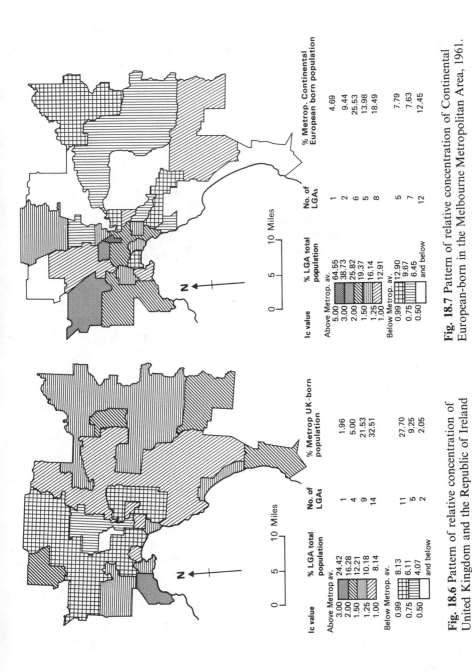

Fig. 18.6 Pattern of relative concentration of United Kingdom and the Republic of Ireland born in the Melbourne Metropolitan Area, 1961.

Fig. 18.7 Pattern of relative concentration of Continental European-born in the Melbourne Metropolitan Area, 1961.

LGA population from a birthplace group, the actual number of LGAs thus classified, and the actual percentage of the total number of immigrants in the metropolitan area from a birthplace group within the LGA thus classified. The 1961 areal patterns for immigrants born in the UK, Continental European countries, the Netherlands, Germany, Poland, Malta, Greece and Italy are given in Figs 18.6 to 13, while Fig. 18.14 indicates those LGAs which had average and above (i.e. an Ic of unity or above) concentration of immigrant groups which were absolutely less numerous than those from the countries just mentioned.

The extent to which immigrant groups are residentially segregated from the remainder of the population is another aspect worthy of consideration when discussing distribution and concentration of immigrant groups within a city. Indices of segregation (Is) for European immigrant groups in Melbourne for 1954 and 1961 are given in Table 18.5. This index is widely used to measure the extent of areal differentiation between population sub-groups in respect to their residential segregation from the population of which they are a part. The index is computed from the expression

$$Is = \frac{\frac{1}{2} \sum_{i=1}^{k} \left| x_i - y_i \right|}{1 - \dfrac{\Sigma x_{ai}}{\Sigma y_{ai}}},$$

where:

x_i = % of a birthplace group in the i'th LGA
y_i = % of the total population in the i'th LGA
Σx_{ai} = total number of a birthplace group in the metropolitan area.
Σy_{ai} = total population of the metropolitan area.
k = number of LGAs in the metropolitan area.

The following generalizations regarding patterns of distribution of immigrant groups in Melbourne over the period 1947 to 1961 may be drawn from the data in Tables 18.3 to 5 and from the patterns in Figs 18.6 to 14.

1. UK born immigrants increased in number from 92,000 in 1947 to 155,500 in 1961. Figure 18.6 shows that in 1961 the areas of greatest relative concentration were the outer eastern, northeastern and bayside suburbs, plus the western-northwestern suburbs which were the really dominant areas of concentration in earlier years. Clearly UK-born immigrants lacked the inclination to settle in the inner suburbs which attracted Southern European immigrants in particular. UK-born immigrants have greatest socio-economic affinity with the Australian born population and their distribution pattern reflects the tendency for Australian born to settle in outer suburban locations. The distribution of UK-born immigrants was

314

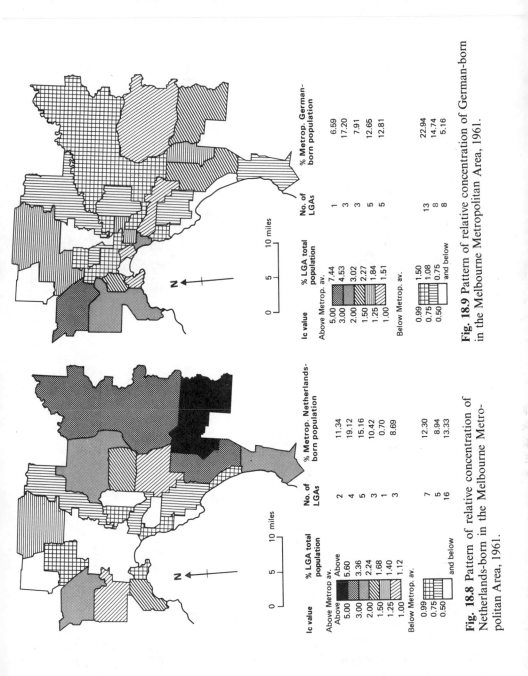

Ic value	% LGA total population	No. of LGAs	% Metrop. German-born population
Above Metrop. av.			
5.00	7.44	1	6.59
3.00	4.53	3	17.20
2.00	3.02	3	7.91
1.50	2.27	5	12.65
1.25	1.84	5	12.81
1.00	1.51		
Below Metrop. av.			
0.99	1.50	13	22.94
0.75	1.08	8	14.74
0.50	0.75	8	5.16
	and below		

Fig. 18.9 Pattern of relative concentration of German-born in the Melbourne Metropolitan Area, 1961.

Ic value	% LGA total population	No. of LGAs	% Metrop. Netherlands-born population
Above Metrop. av.			
Above 5.00	5.60	2	11.34
3.00	3.36	4	19.12
2.00	2.24	5	15.16
1.50	1.68	3	10.42
1.25	1.40	1	0.70
1.00	1.12	3	8.69
Below Metrop. av.			
0.99		7	12.30
0.75		5	8.94
0.50 and below		16	13.33

Fig. 18.8 Pattern of relative concentration of Netherlands-born in the Melbourne Metropolitan Area, 1961.

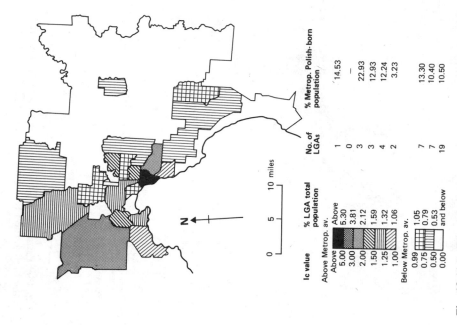

Ic value	% LGA total population	No. of LGAs	% Metrop. Polish-born population
Above Metrop. av.			
Above 5.00	Above 5.30	1	14.53
3.00	3.81	0	–
2.00	2.12	3	22.93
1.50	1.59	3	12.93
1.25	1.32	4	12.24
1.00	1.06	2	3.23
Below Metrop. av.			
0.99	1.05	7	13.30
0.75	0.79	7	10.40
0.50	0.53	19	10.50
0.00	and below		

Fig. 18.11 Pattern of relative concentration of Maltese-born in the Melbourne Metropolitan Area, 1961.

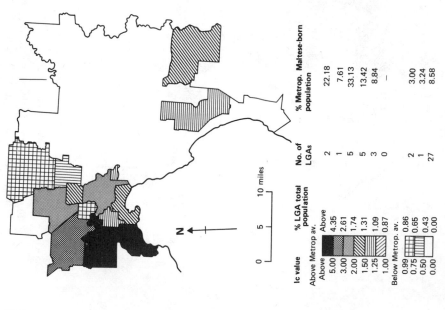

Ic value	% LGA total population	No. of LGAs	% Metrop. Maltese-born population
Above Metrop. av.			
Above 5.00	Above 4.35	2	22.18
3.00	2.61	1	7.61
2.00	1.74	5	33.13
1.50	1.31	5	13.42
1.25	1.09	3	8.84
1.00	0.87	0	–
Below Metrop. av.			
0.99	0.86	2	3.00
0.75	0.65	1	3.24
0.50	0.43	27	8.58
0.00	0.00		

Fig. 18.10 Pattern of relative concentration of Polish-born in the Melbourne Metropolitan Area, 1961.

the least skewed of any group and they were least residentially segregated.

2. Figure 18.7 shows how Continental European-born immigrants had developed three major areas of concentration; firstly the inner city area, where mainly Southern Europeans settled; secondly the outer western-northwestern suburbs, where many of the central and eastern European immigrants, who were largely refugee settlers, were located; and thirdly the outer eastern and southeastern suburbs which attracted Netherlands born, and to a lesser extent German born immigrants.

3. The patterns of concentration of the major birthplace groups making up the heterogeneous Continental European-born immigrant group are shown in Figs. 18.8 to 13. Analysis of these patterns reveals startling contrasts between the groups. Netherlands-born immigrants obviously preferred the outer eastern-southeastern rural-urban fringe suburbs and assiduously avoided inner city suburbs (Fig. 18.8). Their distribution in 1961 was highly positively skewed and their degree of residential segregation was higher than that for all but the Southern European immigrants. In previous years Dutch immigrants were also markedly concentrated in the outer western suburbs. The outer western suburbs had high concentrations of German immigrants (Fig. 18.9), but by 1961 there was considerable strengthening of concentrations in the near southeastern and outer eastern-southeastern suburbs. Similarly, Polish-born immigrants[8] by 1961 had become concentrated less in the western suburbs and more in the inner and near southeastern and eastern suburbs (Fig. 18.10), although the former areas remained the points of highest relative concentration. In contrast to these patterns, Southern European immigrants displayed preference for the lower rent inner and near city suburbs. Maltese immigrants were highly concentrated in relatively few LGAs in the inner city and western suburbs (Fig. 18.11). Greek immigrants were also concentrated in a well defined belt of inner city and near northern and western suburbs (Fig. 18.12), while by 1961 Italian immigrants (Fig. 18.13) had shown signs of dispersing from the inner city area to the adjacent near northern and western LGAs, and even into the outer southeastern industrial suburbs of Springvale – Dandenong. However, the Southern European immigrants tended to display greatest residential segregation and were concentrated in well defined areas, this being a reflection of the continuing operation of the 'chain migration'[9] process which has characterized the migration of Southern European peoples throughout the 'new world' countries.

4. The areas of above average concentration for the eight remaining Continental European birth plan groups for which LGA data is available for 1961 are shown on Fig. 18.14. It is evident that again the inner and western, and to a lesser extent the northern LGAs on the one hand, and the near southeastern LGAs on the other hand, had the highest concentration of these immigrant groups.

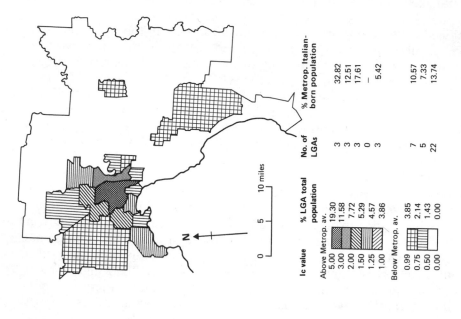

Fig. 18.13 Pattern of relative concentration of Italian-born in the Melbourne Metropolitan Area, 1961.

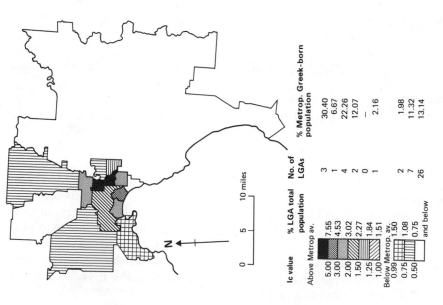

Fig. 18.12 Pattern of relative concentration of Greek-born in the Melbourne Metropolitan Area, 1961.

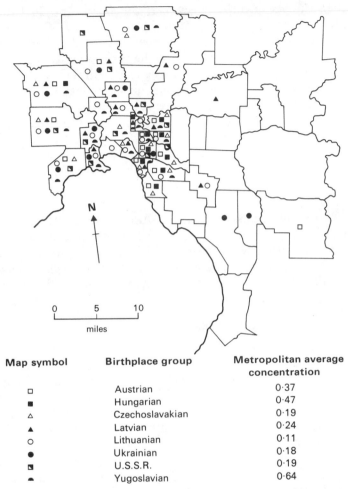

Map symbol	Birthplace group	Metropolitan average concentration
□	Austrian	0·37
■	Hungarian	0·47
△	Czechoslavakian	0·19
▲	Latvian	0·24
○	Lithuanian	0·11
●	Ukrainian	0·18
◩	U.S.S.R.	0·19
◢	Yugoslavian	0·64

Fig. 18.14 LGAs above metropolitan average concentration of minor European birthplace groups, 1961.

Over the period 1954–61 there was a marked shift in emphasis away from the western suburbs to the near southeastern and northern LGAs with the rapidly developing industrial outer southeastern suburbs of Springvale, Oakleigh and Dandenong attracting increasing numbers of immigrants.

Ecological correlation between birthplace groups

Analysis of the patterns of concentration of European immigrant groups based on mapped Ic values reveals that some LGAs continually recur as being either the focal point or part of the area of greatest concentration of individual birthplace groups. However, the maps and Ic values do not tell us more than whether a particular LGA or sector of the metropolitan area is outstanding for or lacking in concentration of an immigrant group. To ascertain the degree of similarity of the rank position of LGAs for the percentage of their population born in each birthplace group, ecological correlations, using the Kendall Tied Rank Correlation Coefficient, were calculated between pairs of all the European immigrant groups studied. In this way the degree of areal association between the immigrant groups, based on the relative rank of LGAs, could be measured. Table 18.6 lists correlation coefficients between two immigrant groups where they are significant at the 0·05 level. From Table 18.6 it is evident, as one would expect, that there was significant correlation between most immigrant groups.

1. There was a high negative relationship between the Australian-born population and the overall European-born immigrant population, but the negative correlation was greatest with the Southern European groups, particularly the Maltese, Yugoslavians, and to a lesser extent with the Central and Eastern European groups. There was not a significant positive correlation between the Australian-born population and the UK-born immigrants.

2. UK-born immigrants had a high positive correlation with Netherlands born throughout the period under review, but there was no positive correlation significant at the 0·05 level with any other individual immigrant group. However, there was significant correlation with the Italians, Greeks, Maltese and Yugoslavians in 1961. With the central and eastern European groups the UK-born had negative correlation up to 1954, but only in 1961 was this negative correlation significant at the 0·05 level with Poles, Latvians, Lithuanians, Ukrainians and USSR-born.

3. Netherlands-born immigrants also failed in 1961 to have positive correlation significant at the 0·05 level with all but German and UK-born immigrants. In fact correlations were disappointing for the Netherlands-born immigrants despite their tendency to become concentrated in the eastern and southeastern fringe areas by 1961, but it needs to be realized that the whole eastern-southeastern sector of Melbourne had attracted Dutch migrants between 1954 and 1961, and it was really only the inner city LGAs that were avoided by them. Thus there were high negative correlations with those groups which were highly concentrated in the inner and western LGA, especially with Greek-born immigrants.

4. In contrast the German born immigrants had significant positive areal relationship with all but the Southern European groups. There was indeed high positive correlation with Austrian, Czechoslovakian, and Hungarian immigrants in particular and to a lesser extent with Polish, Lithuanians, Ukrainian, Yugoslavian and USSR-born immigrants.

5. Likewise Polish-born immigrants had highly significant positive cor-

Note: The correlation coefficients in the matrix are Kendall tied rank coefficients. Only coefficients significant at the 0·05 level are shown. An asterisk indicates coefficients significant at the 0·01 level where the coefficient between a pair of birthplaces was not significant. At the 0·05 level the plus (+) sign indicates that it was positive and the minus sign (−) indicates that it was negative.

Birthplace groups as % of total population of LGAs

Birthplace	Year	Australian-born	Total foreign-born	Total UK and European-born	UK and Republic of Ireland	Netherlands-born	German-born	Austrian-born	Hungarian-born	Czechoslovakian-born	Polish-born	Latvian-born	Lithuanian-born	Ukranian-born	USSR-born	Yugoslavian-born	Greek-born	Italian-born	Maltese-born	Other European-born
Total foreign-born	1947	−0·989*																		
	1954	−1·000*																		
	1961	−1·000*																		
Total UK and European-born	1947	−0·886*	0·898*																	
	1954	−0·871*	0·871*																	
	1961	−0·944*	0·944*																	
UK and Republic of Ireland	1947	−0·587*	0·599*	0·684*																
	1954	+	+	+																
	1961	+	+	+																
Netherlands-born	1947	−0·411*	0·405*	0·399*	0·551*															
	1954	+	+	+	0·491*															
	1961	+	+	−																
German-born	1947	−0·408*	0·403*	0·368*	+	0·385*														
	1954	−0·566*	0·566*	0·554*	+	+														
	1961	−0·431*	0·431*	0·402*	+	0·338*														
Austrian-born	1947	−0·382*	0·371*	0·313*	+	0·414*	0·659*													
	1954	−0·327*	0·327*	0·261	−	−	0·429*													
	1961	−0·392*	0·392*	0·352*	−	−	0·559*													
Hungarian-born	1954	−0·366*	0·366*	0·320*	−	−	0·424*	0·585*												
	1961	−0·361*	0·361*	0·336*	−	−	0·387*	0·654*												
Czechoslovakian-born	1954	−0·307*	0·307*	0·300*	−	−0·229	0·405*	0·605*	0·580*											
	1961	−0·282	0·282	0·249	−	−	0·412	0·648*	0·702*											
Polish-born	1947	−	+	+	+	0·326*	0·495*	0·504*												
	1954	−0·483*	0·483*	0·485*	+	−	0·527*	0·488*	0·454*	0·615*										
	1961	−0·370*	0·370*	0·366*	+	−0·219	0·322*	0·541*	0·463*	0·465*										
Latvian-born	1954	−0·451*	0·451*	0·459*	−0·215		0·402*	0·232	0·245	0·276*	0·451*									
	1961	−	+	+	−0·235		0·220	0·242		0·281	0·390*									
Lithuanian-born	1954	−0·437*	0·437*	0·434*	−		0·432*	0·315*	0·320*		0·529*	0·488*								
	1961	−0·394*	0·394*	0·396*	−0·245		0·338*	0·383*	0·402*	0·241	0·441*	0·365*								
Ukranian-born	1954	−0·476*	0·476*	0·493*	−		0·437*			0·241	0·485*	0·663*	0·537*							
	1961	−0·338	0·338	0·348*	−0·252		0·346*				0·363*	0·433*	0·517*							
USSR-born	1947	−0·345*	0·335*	0·302*	+	0·337*	0·440*	0·519*			0·573									
	1954	−0·483*	0·483*	0·490*	−	−	0·541*	0·424*	0·390*	0·493*	0·722*	0·539*	0·476*	0·427*						
	1961	−0·379*	0·379*	0·383*	−0·226	−	0·323*	0·464*	0·364*	0·384*	0·760*	0·462*	0·439*	0·442*						
Yugoslavian-born	1947	−	+	+			0·371*	0·239			0·257				0·390*					
	1954	−0·439*	0·439*	0·495*	−0·234		0·311	0·419*	0·254		0·551*	0·515*	0·666*	0·622*	0·463*					
	1961	−0·546*	0·546*	0·542*	−0·426*				0·457*		0·530*	0·421*	0·591*	0·536*	0·587*					
Greek-born	1947	+	−	−	−0·322*			0·276			0·445*		0·505*		0·344*	0·241				
	1954	−0·300*	0·300*	0·298*	−0·373*			0·268	0·323*		0·490*	0·262	0·439*	0·332*	0·378*	0·529*				
	1961	−0·446*	0·446*	0·456*	−0·382*	−0·259	0·259		0·330*	0·257	0·443*	0·260	0·498*	0·313	0·393*	0·592*				
Italian-born	1947	−	+	+	−0·371*		+	+	+		+					0·235				
	1954	−0·244	0·244	0·276	−0·485*	−0·293*	+	0·212		0·298*	0·285*	0·298	0·329*	0·368*	0·249	0·410*	0·534*			
	1961	−0·439*	0·439*	0·452*		−0·281*				0·278*	0·288*		0·433*	0·489*	0·320	0·611*	0·568*			
Maltese-born	1947	−	+	+	−										+					
	1954	−0·351*	0·351*	0·378*	−0·273*		0·234		0·366*		0·483*	0·290*	0·529*	0·432*	0·376*	0·483*	0·644*	0·534*		
	1961	−0·545*	0·545*	0·547*	−0·249	0·234	+		+		0·337*	0·278*	0·485*	0·561*	0·328*	0·558*	0·558*	0·568*		
Other European-born	1947	−0·300*	0·294*	0·242	−		0·397*	0·351*		0·313*	0·490*	0·439*	0·529*	0·405*	0·644*	0·251	0·272	0·230	0·227	
	1954	−0·468*	0·468*	0·441*	−		0·415*	0·537*	0·234	0·566*	0·556*	0·498*	0·556*	0·429*	0·554*	0·339*	0·424*	0·376*		
	1961	−0·508*	0·508*	0·487*	−0·204	0·325*	0·341*	0·545*	0·251	0·532*	0·492*	0·417*	0·298*	0·472*	0·511*	0·593*	0·377*	0·358*		
Foreign non-European-born	1947	−0·511*	0·499*	0·397*	−	−0·325*	0·465*	0·639*	0·324*		0·290*	0·310*	0·456*	0·280	0·405*	0·251	0·259		0·357*	
	1954	−0·280	0·280	+	−	+	0·536*	0·578*	0·510*	0·489*	0·556*	0·566*	0·417*	0·298*	0·429*	0·339*	0·429*	0·357*	0·339*	
	1961	−0·229	0·229	0·229	−0·245	+	0·325*		0·489*	0·245	0·532*	0·307*			0·472*	0·377*	0·358*	0·322*		

321

relation with other Central and Eastern European groups. This was also true with Southern Europeans, which is a little surprising.

6. The Greek, Maltese and Italian immigrants all had positive correlation, significant at the 0·01 level, with each other and with Ukrainian and Yugoslavian born immigrants. There was also positive correlation with most of the other Continental European immigrant groups, but the degree of positive association varied considerably over the period 1947 to 1961.

7. In general the degree of positive correlation between the Austrian, Hungarian, Czechoslovakian, Polish and USSR-born tended to increase between 1954 and 1961.

From an analysis of the correlation matrix in Table 18.6 it appears that there was in fact close positive areal relationship between those immigrant groups for which there appeared to be from analysis of the patterns in Figs 18.6 to 14. Indeed there was considerable strengthening or weakening of some of these relationships during the period under review.

Conclusion

That there is a tendency for immigrant groups to concentrate in well defined areas of a large city and for immigrant groups to be residentially segregated from the population as a whole has been verified by this study of immigrant settlement patterns in Melbourne over the 1947 to 1961 period of record immigrant intake. It has also been demonstrated that the degree of concentration and residential segregation of immigrant groups is variable, with the United Kingdom-born immigrants displaying greatest areal dispersion and having the closest, if not significant, areal association with the Australian-born population, a finding which would be expected for that immigrant group possessing greatest socio-economic affinity with the locally-born population. But the declining relative importance of British immigration to Australia in the period 1947 to 1961 has had a profound effect on the growth and character of the metropolitan area. The diversity of ethnic groups participating in this migrant influx has compounded the complexity of spatial arrangements of and interactions between the components of an increasingly heterogeneous urban population. However, it would appear that (1) there has been a change in emphasis from the western and inner city suburbs to the northern and near eastern-southeastern suburbs of Melbourne as the main areas of Continental European immigrant concentration; (2) the development of industrial activity in the other southeastern suburbs attracted increasing numbers of immigrant settlers, both UK- and Continental European-born; (3) the Southern Europeans should become more dispersed as the pressure on accommodation in the cheap-rent-old-inner-mixed-residential-industrial suburbs becomes more acute; (4) the St Kilda–Prahran–Caulfield–Hawthorn–Kew area has become a focus for many of the central and Eastern

European refugee settlers who initially were located more in the western suburbs; and (5) Dutch immigrants more than any other group show a distinct preference for areas on the east and southeastern fringe and the middle class suburbs between the fringe and the older near-east and southern suburbs.

While the pattern up to 1961 had been one of overwhelming concentration of immigrant groups in the inner city suburbs and those west of the line stretching from Whittlesea to St Kilda, the unbalanced growth of Melbourne in favour of an east and southeastern direction must surely mean that immigrants too will settle in increasing numbers in such areas. But this may well be a process slower than the natural growth of the city as immigrants tend to occupy those areas vacated as the locally born population moves out to the new suburbs. The Southern European groups in particular will occupy these areas as they had, at least up to 1961, occupied the vacated inner city residential areas. It is difficult to envisage a significant breakdown in the degree of concentration and residential segregation of Southern Europeans, providing they continue to migrate in large numbers. In this way one can observe the ecological processes of invasion and succession occurring in Melbourne whereby the Southern European immigrant groups gradually diffuse into and then consolidate in the older residential areas of incipient population decline. High density housing redevelopment programmes will, however, upset this trend. The outer suburbs, too, will become increasingly the home of Southern European immigrants, but they will most probably be the long-established immigrants. They will look to the newer industrial suburbs which will also be those most likely to attract the British, Dutch and German-born immigrants. The British, Dutch and Germans should continue to be the most dispersed and least residentially segregated, and may thus be the quickest to assimilate. Finally, as the influx of Polish, Czechoslovakian, Hungarian, Austrian, and USSR-born immigrants had been over by 1961 they will become less readily identifiable within Melbourne except for those who have been absorbed into the area of marked Jewish concentration in the St Kilda–Prahran–Caulfield area.

Further study of the distribution patterns of immigrants settlement in Australian cities is needed, preferably using the census collectors district as the mapping unit so that subtle changes in and consolidation of patterns of concentration can be traced at regular intervals. It is only now becoming possible to establish whether or not there are definite trends in the tendency of immigrant groups in Australian cities to diffuse, whether they maintain established concentrations, or whether they establish new areas of concentration.

R. J. Stimson

Notes and References

The author wishes to thank Professor M. McCaskill and Dr R. L. Heathcote of the School of Social Sciences, The Flinders University of South Australia, for their suggestions and comments in the later stages of preparing this article.

1. W. D. Borrie, *Report of the Committee of Economic Enquiry*, i, 1966, CBCS, 74.
2. A. J. Rose, 'The geographical pattern of European immigration in Australia', *Geogrl. Rev.*, **48**, (1958).
3. E. R. Woolmington, 'The distribution of immigrants in the Newcastle region of NSW', *Australian Geographer*, **7**, (1958), 85–96.
4. P. Scott, 'Population structure of Australian cities', *Geogrl J.*, **131**, (1965), 463–81.
5. J. Zubrzycki, 'Ethnic segregation in Australian cities', *in*: Proceedings, International Population Conference, Vienna 1959, and *Immigrants in Australia*, Melbourne University Press, 1960.
6. J. A. Hempel, *Italians in Queensland*, Canberra, 1960; *Dutch Migrants in Queensland*, Canberra, 1960.
7. F. L. Jones, 'Ethnic concentration and assimilation: an Australian case study', unpublished paper, ANU Dept. of Sociology, 1965.
8. Possibly many more persons could be classified as Poles, Czechs and Austrians since many refugee settlers of these nationalities were born in Germany during and after World War II.
9. The importance of 'chain migration' of Southern Europeans to Australia over the last century has been discussed fully in C. A. Price, *Southern Europeans in Australia*, Oxford University Press, 1963.

Other Literature

BORRIE, W. D., and SPENCER, G., *Australia's Population Structure and Growth*, CEDA, 1965.

DUNCAN, O. D. and DUNCAN, B., A methodological analysis of segregation indexes, *Am. Sociol. Rev.*, **20**, (1955), 210–17 [2].

JUPP, J., *Arrivals and Departures*, Cheshire-Lansdowne 1966.

PRICE, C. A., 'Overseas migration to and from Australia, 1947–1961', *Australian Outlook*, **16**, (1962).

STIMSON, R. J., 'Distributional aspects of immigrant settlement in Melbourne, 1947–1961: a quantitative analysis', unpublished Litt B thesis, University of New England, 1967.

TIMMS, D. 'Quantitative techniques in urban social geography', in R. J. CHORLEY and P. HAGGETT, eds., *Frontiers in Geographical Teaching*, London, Methuen, 1965.

I.H. Burnley

19 European immigration and settlement patterns in metropolitan Sydney 1947-1966*

Between 1947 and 1966 the population of Australia increased by 3·97 million, of which 1·39 million or 34·9 per cent was directly due to immigration. Yet, few geographers have been concerned with the analysis of the spatial distribution of immigrants within a large Australian metropolis; studies are limited to five papers (Rose, 1958), (Woolmington, 1958), (Scott, 1965), (Lee, 1970), (Stimson, 1970). Sociologists and demographers have studied aspects of the settlement of immigrants earlier in the post-war period. Zubrzycki discussed patterns of distribution of immigrants in the major cities at the 1954 census (Zubrzycki, 1960), while Jones included a chapter on residential patterns of the major immigrant groups in his study of the social areas of Melbourne (Jones, 1969). This paper compares and contrasts the distribution patterns of the eight largest overseas-born groups in Sydney in the 1947–66 period. The study of immigrant distributions undertaken in this paper is based on Population by Birthplace data for Local Government Areas 1947–66 and by Collector's District for the 1966 Census.

Immigration and growth of the Sydney Metropolitan Area

Although Sydney is the largest metropolitan area in Australia, with a population of 2,446,345 in 1966, it is the second centre of immigrant settlement in Australia, for between 1947 and 1966, the overseas-born increased by 329,320 in Sydney and by 409,724 in metropolitan Melbourne. The number of overseas-born in both metropolitan areas in 1966 were very similar (543,000 persons) but the Sydney overseas-born included a much higher number of pre-1947 immigrants, most of whom were born in the United Kingdom and Ireland. Thus in 1966, there were 412,440

* Reprinted from *Australian Geographical Studies*, **10** (1972) 61–78.

I. H. Burnley

post-1947 arrivals in Sydney compared with 457,856 in Melbourne. Whereas the overseas-born constituted 12·80 per cent of metropolitan Sydney's population in 1947, by 1966 the percentage had increased to 22·10 while the overseas-born increase accounted for 42·28 per cent of total metropolitan population growth.

Immigration to Sydney has been of such volume since 1947 that it has profoundly affected population composition within the city. Five areal categories can be delineated in terms of population growth, change and

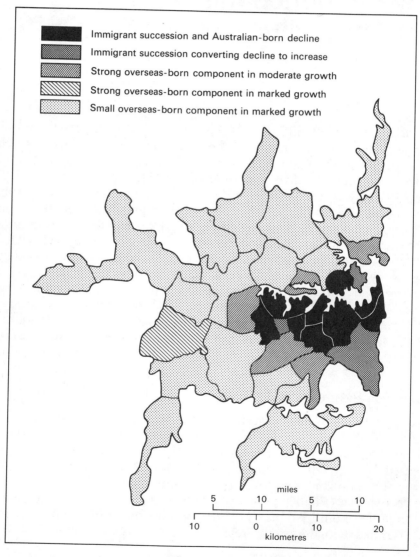

Fig. 19.1 Immigration and growth, Sydney, 1947–66.

the impact of immigration for the period under study. Regrettably, Local Government Areas had to be used rather than the more reliable aggregated Collector's Districts because birthplace statistics by CD were not available for censuses prior to 1961. The five categories, shown in Fig. 19.1 were:

1. An inner area with a steeply declining Australian-born population but with substantial 'replacement' by immigrants, although this ecological succession (Burgess, 1924) did not fully eliminate total decline.
2. Areas adjacent to category 1, with a moderately declining Australian-born population but with an overseas-born increase offsetting this decline and resulting in a total population increase.
3. Areas of moderate Australian-born and total population increase where immigration has contributed substantially to the total population increase in districts of mainly pre-war residential development.
4. Areas on the metropolitan periphery with marked population increase in post-war developed suburbs but where the role of immigration in growth has been substantially less than for the whole metropolitan area.
5. Areas of strong overseas-born contribution to rapid population growth in industrial suburbs near the western urban perimeter.

Inner areas of total population decline

Inner Sydney, in common with other Australian inner city areas, experienced a sharp decline in Australian, United Kingdom and New Zealand-born population but with an overseas-born increase offsetting this decline by 209,830 in the 1947–66 period, a decrease of 31·5 per cent. The total population declined at a much lesser rate, for the overseas-born increase in these areas was 96,765 or 46·1 per cent of the Australian-born decline. The impact of the overseas-born in replacing the declining host society population is actually understated in that children born to immigrants in Australia are included in the Australian-born figures. The Australian-born decline was the result of invasion of non-residential land uses into former residential areas, mortality in an ageing population and movement out to newer suburbs.

Table 19.1 indicates that the southern European birthplace groups constituted the greater part of the overseas-born increase in the inner LGAs of Sydney, Marrickville, Leichhardt and Drummoyne compared with 31·97 per cent of the overseas-born increase in metropolitan Sydney. Greeks, Italians and Maltese together accounted for 67, 72 and 74 per cent of the foreign-born increase in Marrickville, Leichhardt and Drummoyne respectively. But in Waverley and Woollahra, which were much higher in social status than those LGAs, the southern European contribution to the overseas-born increase was well below the metropolitan average. The foreign-born increase in these areas of more moderate

Table 19.1 Population change in areas of Australian-born and total population decline in Metropolitan Sydney, 1947–66

LGA	Sydney	Marrickville	Leichhardt	Drummoyne	Ashfield	Strathfield	Concord	North Sydney	Waverley	Woollahra
Southern European percentage in overseas-born increase	56·30	67·12	71·90	74·29	43·40	28·34	44·15	15·11	17·20	10·58
Total overseas-born increase	29,762	19,852	11,167	4,505	7,278	2,737	3,230	4,765	8,950	4,519
Total Australian-born and other birthplaces undergoing decline	−84,474	−31,808	−22,098	−6,860	−10,106	−3,899	−5,594	−13,395	−20,143	−11,453
Per cent decline	−41·54	−36·31	−32·04	−21·06	−22·95	−14·20	−19·20	−26·24	−28·54	−22·62
Total population per cent decline	−25·58	−13·48	−15·56	−7·14	−6·32	−4·17	−8·04	−14·29	−14·96	−12·78
Overseas-born increase as per cent Australian born and other decrease	35·23	62·41	50·53	65·57	72·02	70·19	57·74	35·57	44·43	39·45

Source: Census of the Commonwealth of Australia, 1947 and 1966.

Australian-born decline consisted of migrants from many areas of Europe, more especially persons of Jewish origin from central and east Europe.

Areas of declining Australian-born population but total increase due to immigration

Fringeing the inner suburbs of Australian-born decrease and ecological succession were areas of moderately declining Australian-born population but with immigrant succession resulting in total population increase (see Fig. 19.1). These areas were Mosman, Burwood, Randwick and Botany. Many factors were involved, such as partitioning of older homes into smaller units and possibly a higher density due to larger family size, including extended families with southern Europeans in Botany, Randwick and Burwood (Table 19.2). Certainly Greek, Italian and Maltese heads of households had more persons per dwelling unit in metropolitan Sydney (4·80, 4·09 and 4·66 respectively) than the Australian-born (3·29) in 1966, (as ascertained from unpublished cross tabulations of birthplace of household head by persons per room and number of rooms, (1966 Census)). In contrast to the inner suburbs of total population decline, the United Kingdom and Irish-born were significant in the overseas-born increase, especially in the north shore LGA, Mosman.

Table 19.2 Population change in areas of Australian-born decline with total population increase, Sydney, 1966

	LGA			
	Mosman	*Botany*	*Randwick*	*Burwood*
Southern European percentage in overseas-born increase	10·04	41·64	31·03	34·31
Total overseas-born increase	2,233	6,548	16,104	5,244
Total Australian-born and other birthplaces undergoing decline	−1,669	−1,862	−3,401	−3,750
Per cent decline	−7·16	−6·33	−3·79	−13·81
Total population per cent increase	+2·05	+17·28	+12·59	+4·92

Source: Census of the Commonwealth of Australia, 1947 and 1966.

Areas of moderate population increase where immigration has contributed substantially to growth

These were LGAs fringeing the two categories of inner suburbs already described (Fig. 19.1) which have grown slowly since 1947 with population

Table 19.3 Overseas-born component of total population increase in outer areas, Sydney, 1966

LGAs	Areas of moderate total population increase (below 40 per cent) : mainly pre-war residential development			LGAs	Areas of marked population increase (over 80 per cent) : mainly post-war residential development		
	Southern European per cent of overseas-born increase	Total overseas-born increase	Overseas-born percentage of total increase		Southern European per cent of overseas-born increase	Total overseas-born increase	Overseas-born percentage of total increase
Canterbury	49·21	12,777	77·88	Parramatta	22·11	11,252	23·29
Rockdale	47·51	7,076	96·79	Blacktown	20·12	19,813	23·78
Auburn	40·12	3,794	58·39	Fairfield	24·94	25,400	35·79
Hunter's Hill	20·25	976	35·67	Holroyd	44·58	10,237	24·55
Lane Cove	10·25	2,204	41·65	Bankstown	16·57	23,739	20·24
Manly	9·24	3,175	67·76	Ryde	29·07	7,235	17·78
				Other Metropolitan	11·59	85,408	20·01

Source: Census of the Commonwealth of Australia, 1947 and 1966.

increases below 40 per cent and in which residential development occurred mainly before World War II. In Canterbury, Rockdale and Auburn, all southern LGAs, southern Europeans were important in the overseas-born increase (Table 19.3) but in the North Shore LGAs of Manly and Lane Cove, United Kingdom and Irish-born were important whereas the role of the southern European groups was insignificant. The movement of southern Europeans into Canterbury, Rockdale and Auburn occurred mainly in the 1961–66 period and reflects in part movement out from the core areas of initial settlement into contiguous areas of better housing.

Outer areas of rapid population growth

In these LGAs near the urban periphery, total population increase was greater than 80 per cent between 1947–66 and most housing was erected in this period. The overseas-born contributed 24·4 per cent of the 872,080 total increase in these rapidly growing areas, a proportion considerably lower than the overseas-born contribution to metropolitan Sydney's 1947–66 population growth of 42 per cent.

The role of the overseas-born was less important in the non-industrial commuter suburbs, but more important in industrial Fairfield near the western urban perimeter (Fig. 19.1). In Fairfield, United Kingdom and Italian-born were important in growth while, in neighbouring Holroyd, United Kingdom, Italian and Maltese-born contributed substantially to the overseas-born increase.

Distribution patterns and relative concentration of immigrant groups

The tendency for immigrant groups to become areally concentrated and segregated from the host population has been well documented in America (Handlin, 1951), (Lieberson, 1963), (Duncan, 1959). The latter authors developed a relative concentration measure, the Index of Dissimilarity, which has been used in New Zealand (Burnley, 1970), (Trlin, 1971), in Melbourne, Australia (Jones, 1967), and Queensland (Timms, 1969). This measure is used here and maps of relative concentration derived from the index are presented to ascertain whether the distributional patterns of the eight major birthplace groups conform to the traditional ecological model (Burgess, 1924), and to the patterns described for Melbourne by Stimson and Jones.

Table 19.4 summarizes degree of residential concentration and dissimilarity of the various overseas-born immigrant groups in metropolitan Sydney, 1966. Index numbers have been calculated so that 100 indicates maximum dissimilarity in distribution and zero indicates complete similarity with the Australian-born distribution by LGAs. These indexes represent the percentage of a given birthplace group that would have to

Table 19.4 **Indexes of dissimilarity between selected overseas-born birthplace groups and The Australian-born in Metropolitan Sydney, 1966**

United Kingdom and Ireland	8·33	Yugoslavia	31·10
Germany	25·01	Greece	53·37
Netherlands	29·02	Italy	31·65
Poland	33·79	Malta	48·68

Source: Census of the Commonwealth of Australia, 1966.

redistribute itself to have the same per cent distribution by LGAs as the Australian-born population.

The indexes for each birthplace group were calculated by using the formula:

$$\frac{\Sigma\ |\ x-y\ |}{2}/1-p$$

where x is the percentage of the Australian-born in a local government area and y the corresponding percentage of the given birthplace in the area; and p is the proportion of the whole birthplace group in the population of the entire metropolitan area.

It can be seen that the United Kingdom and Ireland-born were the least dissimilar and the Greek and Maltese-born the most dissimilar or concentrated. The Dutch, Polish, Yugoslav and Italian-born were moderately concentrated. The rank ordering of birthplace groups in degree of concentration, although not identical, was similar to those in Melbourne and Queensland.

Figures 19.2 and 3 indicate the per cent overconcentration of immigrant groups in 1966, which is the percentage of the total birthplace group in metropolitan Sydney which is in a LGA in excess of the 'expected' percentage if the distribution of the immigrant population and the Australian-born were the same.

The high concentration of Greeks in the inner City, especially Sydney LGA and Marrickville, is apparent in Fig. 19.2A with the highest per cent overconcentration of any birthplace group in any LGA. Seventy-five per cent of the 41,800 Greek-born in metropolitan Sydney were resident in the four adjacent inner LGAs of Sydney, Leichhardt, Marrickville and Botany. The Maltese-born were also strongly concentrated in Sydney LGA and less so in neighbouring Leichhardt, Marrickville and Botany but the major concentration was in the outer western LGAs of Holroyd in particular, and also Blacktown and Fairfield where 8,000 of metropolitan Sydney's 19,600 Maltese resided in 1966 (Fig. 19.2B).

The Italian-born were concentrated in Leichhardt, Drummoyne and Ashfield west of the areas of Greek settlement and in northern Marrickville. Thirty-eight per cent of the 53,500 Italians in metropolitan Sydney

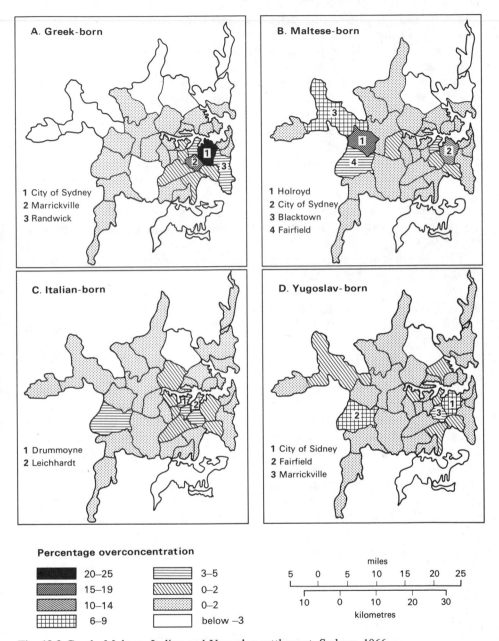

Fig. 19.2 Greek, Maltese, Italian and Yugoslav settlement, Sydney, 1966.

(Fig. 19.2C) were resident in Sydney LGA and these inner suburbs while another concentration occurred in Fairfield. The Yugoslav-born were concentrated in the inner LGAs of Sydney and Marrickville, and also in the outer industrial area of Fairfield. Lesser concentrations were also found in the other inner LGAs of Leichhardt, Marrickville, Botany and Kogarah, the north shore LGA Willoughby and industrial Blacktown (Fig. 19.2D).

Sydney's 13,490 Polish-born, on the other hand did not concentrate unduly in the inner LGAs but settled more in the outer western LGAs of Blacktown, Fairfield and Bankstown and in the eastern Woollahra and Waverley localities (Fig. 19.3A). The German-born population of 21,600 in 1966 was concentrated in Blacktown, Fairfield and Bankstown, with lesser representation in Liverpool and Campbelltown LGAs on the south-western urban periphery. There was also relative concentration in Sydney's eastern suburbs and in the inner LGAs of Sydney and Marrickville (Fig. 19.3B). In contrast, the 16,900 Netherlands-born avoided the inner and western suburbs, settling in new housing areas, more especially in War-ringah in the northeast, Blacktown in the west and Sutherland in the south (Fig. 19.3C).

The United Kingdom and Ireland-born population was relatively dispersed in 1966, but areas most favoured were the eastern north shore LGAs, the eastern LGAs, Fairfield and Liverpool in the southwest and again Sutherland. During the period 1947–66, the United Kingdom and Ireland-born population declined in the inner LGAs despite heavy con-tinued immigration and by 1966 the 211,500 British, while represented in every LGA, were relatively more numerous on the north shore and the urban periphery (Fig. 19.3D).

It has been shown how by 1966 the distributions of the eight major overseas-born groups in Sydney varied considerably. These variations are reflected in Table 19.5 in which indexes of dissimilarity between groups are shown. Although it might be expected that groups with similar occu-pational structures would settle in the same areas because of the city's residential stratification system, there were considerable variations between southern European groups, despite similar occupational structures (Table 19.7). The distributions of the northwest European populations were more similar than those of the southern communities. The Polish and

Table 19.5 Indexes of dissimilarity between major birthplace groups, Metropolitan Sydney, 1966

	British Isles	Germany	Netherlands	Poland	Yugoslavia	Greece	Italy	Malta
United Kingdom and Ireland	—							
Germany	22·65	—						
Netherlands	27·02	29·62	—					
Poland	32·80	17·11	38·95	—				
Yugoslavia	31·25	27·27	41·70	31·17	—			
Greece	54·06	54·07	65·62	57·55	38·46	—		
Italy	33·33	32·83	44·16	38·18	22·68	43·07	—	
Malta	48·18	39·25	48·68	39·64	29·59	44·73	43·04	—

Source: 1966 Census.

334

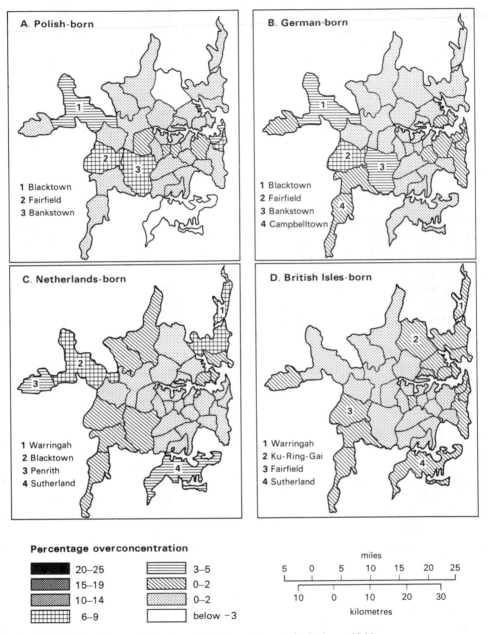

Fig. 19.3 Polish, German, Dutch and British settlement in Sydney, 1966.

German-born patterns may be closer because many ethnically Polish children were born to Displaced Persons in Germany and although resident with their Polish-*born* families were classified as persons born in Germany.

335

The Dutch and Polish-born were more segregated from the Greek population than from the host society or total population.

Chain migration and settlement evolution

The southern European communities in Sydney began to grow as early as 1900 by the process of chain migration, which has been defined as a movement of people from particular villages or regions to a new country from which immigrants assist relatives to migrate (Price, 1963). Through time, numbers of persons from particular localities and linked through kinship ties evolve settlements in the new country. Such persons have been referred to in the United States as 'urban villagers' (Gans, 1962). Jones has described chain migration and settlement formation with southern Italians in Carlton, Melbourne (Jones, 1962) while in New Zealand, recent studies have described ethnic concentrations in which village or region of origin were significant factors in separate settlement formation or neighbourhood groupings (Burnley, 1969; Trlin, 1970).

By using a sample of naturalization papers 1900–47, it is evident that in Sydney LGA a pre-war Darlington concentration originated in the Valtellina, Lombardy, while those south of the CBD and in King Street, Newtown and in Surry Hills came from the island of Salina off the Sicilian coast. The nucleus of the main present-day Italian concentration in metropolitan Sydney, between Parramatta Road, Balmain and Hill Streets, Leichhardt began to form before World War I with immigrants from the Lipari Islands, Sicily, and Vicenza and Udine in north Italy. In the rural urban fringe areas of Penrith, Fairfield and Holroyd, settlers from Sicily and Reggio Calabria became fruit growers and market gardeners.

The location of these early concentrations influenced the place of settlement of the much greater number of post-war Italian migrants. Between 1947 and 1954 Italians settled mainly in the areas of pre-war concentration in both inner and outer suburbs. Between 1954 and 1961 these areas continued to gain large numbers of Italians but major increases also occurred in Marrickville while between 1961 and 1966 the Italian population of Sydney LGA dropped from 6,100 to 5,100 and increased only slightly in Leichhardt and Marrickville while the major increases were now further out in Drummoyne, Ashfield and Canterbury, and in outer Fairfield. The traditional chain migrations continued as well as a new growth in chain movements from the Italian south, recent migrants often joining relatives who had already moved from old settlement areas.

Greek settlement before 1947 was also concentrated south of the CBD in Sydney LGA where migrants from Castellorizo and Kythera were grouped in George Street, Redfern and King Street, Newtown while other nucleations of settlers from Cephalonia, Arcadia, Ithaca, Samos and Smyrna settled in these areas and in Darlinghurst. Post-war, these chain migrations continued, while persons from Levkas formed a sub-concentration in Redfern (Jakubowicz, 1969) and new migrants from Crete, the Peloponnesos and Macedonia contributed to the growth of concentrations in Redfern, Newtown and Erskineville in Sydney LGA and in adjacent Enmore in Marrickville LGA, as evidenced from a field survey involving case studies of migrant families and their social networks including place of residence of kinfolk and associates. Another grouping of migrants from Castellorizo developed in Randwick.

The Greek population of Sydney LGA increased rapidly from 1,240 persons in 1947 to 8,650 in 1961 after which the increase continued (in contrast to the Italian decline), although over two-thirds of the 1961–66 increase of 3,800 consisted of females, joining males who had settled there earlier. The major increase between 1961–66 was of almost 6,000 persons in Marrickville while strong increases took place in Randwick after 1954 and in Canterbury after 1961. Whereas invasion of Italians into other inner LGAs to the west occurred particularly after 1961, the Greeks tended to move into southwest and southeastern inner suburbs.

Almost 50 per cent of the Greeks in Sydney in 1966 arrived in Australia after 1961 compared with only 22 per cent of Italians; this recency of arrival in part accounts for the higher degree of concentration of the Greeks as well as the increasing numbers in Sydney LGA with initial location there with relatives before moving out to other settlement areas (Table 19.6).

Before World War II small groups of Maltese had formed concentrations in Surry Hills within Sydney LGA and in the western urban fringe areas of Holroyd, Blacktown and Fairfield where market gardening and fruit farming were the main economic activity. Post-war, chain migration to these outer suburbs and Sydney LGA continued but in contrast to the Greeks and Italians, the inner city settlement was secondary to that in the western urban fringe. The Maltese increase in these outer areas from 460

Table 19.6 Period of residence of selected birthplace groups in Metropolitan Sydney, 1966

Birthplace	Under 5 years	5–12 years	12–19 years	Over 19 years	Not stated	Total No.	Per cent
United Kingdom and Ireland	27·78	17·32	16·79	35·98	2·11	202,081	99·98
Italy	22·69	40·07	27·04	8·12	2·06	53,520	99·98
Greece	47·30	34·52	9·80	5·63	2·73	41,824	99·98
Malta	28·35	28·08	36·51	4·40	2·63	19,628	99·97
Yugoslavia	34·99	37·43	20·89	3·92	2·75	17,953	99·98
Poland	8·38	13·45	67·79	8·79	1·55	13,493	99·96
Germany	15·41	33·95	39·21	9·65	1·76	22,350	99·98
Netherlands	13·24	42·22	41·17	2·20	1·14	16,902	99·99

Source: Unpublished Crosstabulation, 1966 Census. Figures in the first five columns are percentages.

persons in 1947 to 7,700 in 1966 could not be absorbed into the old market garden enclaves although the post-war arrivals settled in adjacent old established and recently developed residential areas; in 1966 only 3·1 per cent of the 8,698 gainfully employed Maltese males in metropolitan Sydney were farmers or farm workers. Despite the fact that 28 per cent of the Maltese in Sydney in 1966 arrived after 1961 (Table 19.6), the Maltese population in Sydney LGA fell from its peak of 4,000 in 1961. It increased considerably however in Fairfield, and to a lesser extent in the inner LGAs of Leichhardt, Marrickville, Canterbury and Randwick with invasion from Sydney LGA.

The southern European populations formed distinct concentrations within their principal LGAs of settlement. In Marrickville and Sydney LGAs, Greeks constituted between 30 and 35 per cent of the total population of four Collectors Districts in 1966 and between 20 and 30 per cent of an additional twenty CDs, compared with the Greek component of 1·71 per cent of the metropolitan population. Collectors Districts are the smallest units for which birthplace data were available at the 1966 Census; their average population size was approximately 900 in the inner suburbs and 1,000 persons in the outer suburbs. In Leichhardt, Drummoyne and Fairfield LGAs, Italians formed 20 to 30 per cent of the population of fourteen CDs compared with 2·19 per cent of the metropolitan population while the Maltese-born constituted over 30 per cent of one CD in Holroyd LGA and between 20 and 30 per cent of seven others in Holroyd and Sydney LGA. With the exception of the Italians in Drummoyne, these concentrations formed from nuclei established by chain migration before World War II. By contrast, Germans, Poles, and Dutch although concentrating in particular LGAs as noted earlier did not exceed 10 per cent of any CD population. Although size of a total immigrant population affects the proportion likely to be found in any CD the southern European concentrations undoubtedly resulted from chain migration and its associated neighbourhood formation.

Socio-economic factors in the evolution of immigrant distributional patterns

The occupational and economic circumstances of migrants on arrival affects the location of ethnic populations in the metropolitan system of residential differentiation and stratification. Chain migration of southern Europeans often means a financial burden to families paying their own or relatives' travel costs and this is reinforced by a disproportionate number of southern Europeans and Yugoslavs being unskilled workers on arrival (Price, 1969). Indeed in 1966, 43 per cent of Greek males in Sydney were unskilled manual or service workers, as were 33 and 36 per cent of the Italians and Maltese, compared with 25 per cent of the Polish and only 14 and 15 per cent of the Dutch and Australian-born respectively (Table 19.7).

Only 12 per cent of Italians and 8 and 12 per cent of Maltese and Greeks were in white collar occupations compared with much higher percentages of northwest Europeans and 40 per cent of the Australian-born. In consequence, southern Europeans, Yugoslavs and Poles had limited choice

Table 19.7 Male occupations of selected immigrant groups in Metropolitan Sydney, 1966

	United Kingdom and Ireland	Germany	Netherlands	Poland	Yugoslavia	Greece	Italy	Malta	Australia
Professional	10·1	8·6	8·6	7·4	2·6	0·7	1·4	1·4	9·9
Managerial	10·0	8·4	10·4	9·8	3·2	10·1	8·3	1·3	10·3
Clerical	15·2	10·5	11·9	3·9	2·5	1·4	2·4	5·4	19·1
Skilled manual	27·8	42·1	35·4	26·1	33·6	17·5	30·1	24·3	23·4
Semi-skilled manual	19·5	17·0	18·6	26·6	25·0	26·6	22·6	28·7	21·5
Unskilled manual and service	17·1	13·2	14·4	25·9	31·5	43·5	33·7	35·8	15·3
Graziers	0·0	0·0	0·0	0·0	0·0	0·0	0·0	0·0	0·1
Farmers	0·1	0·1	0·4	0·2	1·4	0·1	1·1	2·2	0·2
Farm workers	0·2	0·1	0·3	0·1	0·2	0·1	0·4	0·9	0·2
Total number	17,313	9,342	7,860	7,120	9,298	18,423	24,730	8,698	517,918
Per cent	100·0	100·0	100·0	100·0	100·0	100·0	100·0	100·0	100·0

Source: 1966 Census, Unpublished Crosstabulations, ANU Sociology Department Occupational Code.

of residence and could only rent or purchase low cost housing in inner suburbs or outer western industrial areas.

One index of housing cost is the average rent for private homes in various LGAs of the metropolitan area. The rent variations are an indication of socio-economic status variations within the urban area. Thus average private home rents in 1966 ranged from lows of 6 and 7 dollars in the inner Sydney and Leichhardt LGAs to intermediate levels of 8–9 dollars in the surrounding LGAs and in the western LGAs Fairfield, Blacktown and Holroyd and higher values of 12–13 dollars in most North Shore LGAs with peaks of 14 dollars in Woollahra and 18 dollars in Kuringai. It can be seen from Table 19.8 that the percentages of southern European birthplaces in the population were strongly negatively correlated with rank order average rents while lesser negative correlations occurred with the Polish and German-born. Thus immigrant groups with large unskilled occupation percentages and low white-collar proportions settled in low rent, low cost housing areas. The negative German-born figure is surprising considering the occupational structure shown in Table 19.7 but it may be that migrant aspirations are a factor here, with Germans preferring to rent their homes more than any of the other groups or the Australian-born and preferring modest rentals in order to save and possibly intending to return to their homeland. The British Isles and Netherlands-born were positively correlated, both groups preferring intermediate to high rent residential areas.

Despite the low occupational status of the southern European groups, they were home owners rather than renters, even with the recency of arrival of significant proportions of their populations particularly the Greeks (Table 19.6). Thus 82 per cent of Italian household heads and 73 and 76 per cent of Greeks and Maltese were owners and buyers in 1966 compared with 64 per cent of both the British Isles and Netherlands-born and 70 per cent of the Australian-born, as ascertained from unpublished cross-

Table 19.8 **Rank order correlation between immigrant group distributions and average rent levels for private houses by local government areas, 1966**

United Kingdom and Ireland	+0·40	Yugoslavia	−0·56
Germany	−0·31	Italy	−0·52
Netherlands	+0·45	Greece	−0·60
Poland	−0·34	Malta	−0·67

Source: Birthplace data by LGA, 1966 Census; unpublished tabulations of average rent by LGA, 1966 Census.
Spearman's Co-efficient of Rank Correlation was the measure used.

tabulations of nature of occupancy of private dwellings by birthplace of household head. Almost 79 per cent of the Poles were owners and buyers, most of whom arrived in Australia in 1949–51 and thus in 1966 had been longer in Australia than the southern Europeans (Table 19.6). Although the southern Europeans and Displaced Person Poles started with occupational and economic disadvantages, home ownership has been within their reach; for immigrants with limited education, and occupational prospects, home ownership may be an emotional necessity.

Conclusion

The impact of immigration on metropolitan Sydney's population growth has been profound in the 1947–66 era. In particular, immigration partially arrested the marked decline in population in the inner suburbs, converted adjacent LGAs of population decline into areas of population increase, contributed strongly to population increase in moderately growing outer suburbs of pre-war residential development, and in rapidly growing western industrial areas of the urban periphery. In so far as the impact of immigration on population growth and change followed a concentric pattern, the Burgess model is applicable to postwar Sydney with population succession occurring in the inner suburbs and progressively moving outwards and with Italians and Maltese attaining numerical peaks in Sydney LGA in 1961 with a latter decline but with major increases in adjacent suburbs. Since 1966 new Turkish and Yugoslav migrants have begun to form concentrations in Sydney LGA. However, the direct formation of outer concentrations in western low to medium rent industrial suburbs with Italians, Maltese, Poles and Germans contradicts the Burgess system in which first settlement occurs in the inner city and new arrivals enter through the immigrant receiving areas and progressively diffuse outwards. A multiple nuclei system combined with the concentric zone model may be the actual pattern.

The chain migration phenomenon has been important in the localisation of Greek, Italian and Maltese settlement and also requires modification of the Burgess theory in two ways. First, neighbourhoods of persons from particular localities of origin have survived and grown over a considerable time interval in areas where migrants could purchase their own homes relatively cheaply as in southern Leichhardt, Redfern, Surry Hills, Marrickville in the inner city and Fairfield and Holroyd in the outer suburbs. In the 1961–66 period Italian-born numbers declined in Sydney LGA and northern Leichhardt yet in the old neighbourhoods, as indicated by comparing CD populations at both censuses, Italian numbers and proportions of the population increased. This survival of old neighbourhood concentrations has been noted in Carlton, Melbourne (Jones, 1962) and New York (Glazer and Moynihan, 1963). Second, recent chain migrants joining relatives who have sponsored or nominated them may avoid the inner suburbs by settling with their kinfolk who had already moved out from the first settlement areas to adjacent or even outer suburbs.

Finally, the patterns of migrant settlement in Sydney resemble those in Melbourne (Stimson, 1970; Jones, 1969) with inner city southern

341

European concentrations, and lesser concentrations of eastern Europeans of refugee origin in western industrial suburbs along with Maltese, Italians and Germans. The Netherlands-born concentrated in higher rent and status outer suburbs on the urban periphery and Poles and Germans of Jewish origin settled in higher status eastern suburban areas of Waverley and Woollahra, the equivalent of Melbourne's St Kilda and Caulfield. Factors affecting residence patterns have been low socio-economic status of southern Europeans, Yugoslavs and Poles, chain migration with southern Europeans, higher occupational status of British and Netherlands-born although even British and Netherlands-born of low occupational status avoided the inner suburbs.

Notes and References

Burgess, E. W. (1924) 'The growth of the city: an introduction to a research project', *Publ., Am. Sociol. Soc.*, 85–97.

Burnley, I. H. (1969) 'The Greek, Italian and Polish communities in New Zealand', unpublished PhD thesis, Victoria University of Wellington.

Burnley, I. H. (1970) 'The Greeks', in K. Thomson and A. D. Trlin, eds, *Immigrants in New Zealand*, Massey University, pp. 100–24.

Duncan, O. D., and Lieberson, S. (1959) 'Ethnic segregation and assimilation', *Am. J. Sociol.*, **64**, 364–74 [7].

Gans, H. J. (1962) *The Urban Villagers*, Free Press of Glencoe.

Handlin, O. (1951) *The Uprooted*, Boston, Little Brown.

Jakubowicz, A. (1969) 'Changing patterns of community organisation', unpublished honours thesis, University of Sydney.

Jones, F. (1962) 'The Italian population of Carlton', unpublished PhD thesis, Australian National University.

Jones, F. L. (1967) 'Ethnic concentration and assimilation: an Australian case study', *Social Forces*, **45**, 3 [17].

Jones, F. L. (1969) *Dimensions of Urban Social Structure*, Canberra: Australian National University Press.

Lee, T. R. (1970) 'The role of the ethnic community as a reception area for Italian immigrants in Melbourne, Australia', *International Migration*, **8**, nos. 1/2, 50–63.

Lieberson, S. (1963) *Ethnic Patterns in American Cities*, Free Press of Glencoe.

Price, C. A. (1963) *Southern Europeans in Australia*, Oxford University Press.

Price, C. A. (1969) 'International migration – Australia and New Zealand, 1947–1968', *International Union for the Scientific Study of Population General Conference*, 9.1.12.

Riis, J. (1898) *Out of Mulberry Street, Stories of Tenement Life in New York*, New York.

Rose, A. J. (1958) 'The geographical pattern of European immigration in Australia',

Geogrl Rev., **48**, 512–27.

Scott, P. (1965) 'Population structure of Australian cities', *Geogrl J.*, **131**, 463–81.

Stimson, R. J. (1970) 'Patterns of European immigrant settlement in Melbourne, 1947–1966', *Tijdschrift Voor Econ. En Soc. Geographie.*

Timms, D. W. G. (1969) 'The dissimilarity between overseas born and Australian born in Queensland: dimensions of assimilation', *Sociology and Social Research*, **53**, 363–74 [20].

Trlin, A. D. (1970) 'The Yugoslavs', in Thomson and Trlin, eds, *Immigrants in New Zealand.*

Woolmington, E. R. (1958) 'The distribution of immigrants in the Newcastle region of N.S.W.', *Australian Geographer*, **7**, 85–96.

Zubrzycki, J. (1960) *Immigrants in Australia*, Melbourne University Press.

D. W. G. Timms

20 The dissimilarity between overseas-born and Australian-born in Queensland: dimensions of assimilation*

Assimilation and dissimilarity

Analyses of the assimilation of migrant populations have been bedevilled by ambiguities in definition. In the present essay assimilation is taken to be a function of the degree of dissimilarity which exists between the members of migrant populations and those of the receiving society. A concept of assimilation in these terms applies to patterns rather than to processes, and is concerned with aggregates rather than with individuals.[1]

As Price has intimated, it is common assumption of statistical studies that 'the less an ethnic group differs ... from the dominant group, the more nearly "assimilated" it is'.[2] Lieberson, adopting the assumption as the basis of his empirical study of the patterns of assimilation in ten American cities, believes that it has 'a somewhat awkward implication if carried to its logical conclusion: to wit, all differences between ethnic populations and the (dominant) population indicate lack of assimilation'.[3] In the opinion of the present writer all such differences are indeed indicators of a lack of assimilation. The fact that such differences are of long standing, are associated with no apparent prejudices, or are even a 'condition of declining prejudice and discrimination, of increasing acceptance into the social groups of the receiving population',[4] is believed to be irrelevant. In the present conception, if it be the case that knowledge of a particular population's ethnic background is in itself sufficient to allow the prediction of differences in social characteristics between its members and those of the host society in which it is located, then that population is not fully assimilated.[5]

The question of the existence and the extent of differences in social characteristics between the members of the receiving society and those of its various immigrant populations is conceptually and empirically distinct

* Reprinted from *Sociology and Social Research*, **53**, no. 3 (April 1969), 363–74.

from that concerning the attitudes of acceptance and rejection which the populations hold for each other. Although it is likely that there will generally be a positive correlation between the existence of differences and the existence of hostile attitudes it should not be assumed that the relationship is inevitable. The existence of dissimilarity, or a belief in its existence, may well be a necessary condition for the existence of prejudice and discrimination, but it is unlikely in itself to be a sufficient condition. The relationship between dissimilarity and other aspects of intergroup relations should be subject to empirical investigation rather than *a priori* assumption.

The measurement of dissimilarity

A considerable literature has developed concerning the definition and the measurement of similarity and difference. In the present context three separate measures are used: the Index of Dissimilarity (ID), the Social Distance Index, and the Index of Perceived Dissimilarity.

The ID is a measure of net displacement and may be simply interpreted as showing the minimum percentages of one population which would have to change its given categorical location in order to reproduce the percentage distribution of the population used as a standard. Although most commonly used in connection with studies of a real differentiation the ID is readily generalizable to the nonspatial case. An ID of zero indicates that the two populations concerned have identical distribution patterns, an ID of 100 indicates maximum dissimilarity.[6]

The social distance quotient is generated by the conventional Bogardus Social Distance Scale and consists of the arithmetic averages of nearest-relationship responses.[7] The most intimate relationship allowed, marriage into the family, is given an arbitrary scale value of one, the most distant relationship, exclusion from Australia, has an arbitrary scale value of seven.

The index of perceived dissimilarity represents the average response of subjects when asked to estimate the difference existing between pairs of populations in terms of an unmarked five-inch scale anchored by statements of 'very similar' at one end and 'very different' at the other. The index is tabulated in terms of percentage maximum dissimilarity. A zero score would indicate an average judgment of great similarity between the populations concerned, a score of 100 would indicate a judgment of maximum difference.

Areas of differences

Although it has been argued that any differences between a migrant population and members of the host society may be taken as evidence of a lack of assimilation, it is clear that not all differences between sets of people are of equal significance. The choice of substantive areas in any particular study of the dissimilarity between populations must reflect the theoretical perspective adopted by the investigator and the data which is available.

The empirical focus of the present study is the pattern of dissimilarity between the Australian-born residents of Queensland and members of the eight largest migrant populations in the State. Three main aspects of the situation have been sampled: the difference between each of the overseas-born groups and the Australian-born in terms of their dispersion over the residential, occupational, and religious structures of Queensland, the marriage patterns which each group exhibits, and the perceived dissimilarity of each set of migrants as viewed from an Australian-born perspective. For purposes of exposition the key variable is taken to be marriage.

Marital assimilation is a function of the extent to which knowledge of the ethnic background of a given set of individuals predicts to that of their spouses. Assimilation may be said to have taken place fully when knowledge of a migrant group's ethnic background gives no more information about its pattern of marriage choices than does knowledge of the general community in which it is located. Under these circumstances the pattern of marriage choices amongst the birthplace groups will be identical and the index of marital dissimilarity will be zero. The existence of full marital assimilation is a *sine qua non* for the disappearance of dissimilarity between migrant and host populations. As Gordon states:

> Once marital assimilation . . . takes place fully, the minority group loses its ethnic identity in the larger host or core society and identificational assimilation takes place. Prejudice and discrimination are no longer a problem since eventually the descendants of the original minority group become indistinguishable, and since primary group relationships tend to build up an 'in-group' feeling which encloses all members of the group.[8]

One may thus hypothesize a close relationship between the degree of marital assimilation exhibited by a given group and the extent to which that group is perceived as being 'different' by members of the host society. At the same time, the more different the migrant population is perceived to be the less attractive will be primary interaction with its members and the greater the reluctance to admit these latter into such intimate and status-equalizing relationships as marriage and friendship.[9] Thus, both perceived dissimilarity and marital dissimilarity should show a high positive correlation with subjective social distance.

The development of full marital assimilation demands the chance of contact between the populations concerned. It is primarily in this connection that significance is believed to attach to the dispersion of migrant and host populations in the residential, occupational, and religious structures of the community.

It is a widely-held proposition that there is a close relationship between residential propinquity and the probability of marriage.[10] It has even been suggested that residential location may be manipulated by parents in order to ensure that their children are likely to meet potential marriage partners from the 'right' social categories.[11] More generally it may be postulated that the more dissimilar the residential distribution of two populations, the less similar will be their patterns of social contact, and the more dissimilar will be their patterns of marriage choice.

As a result of the occupational differentiation between men and women in Western society it is unlikely that propinquity at the work-place is as significant as propinquity in residence in the development of strong intersex relationships. On the other hand, occupation provides one of the most important single clues to socioeconomic rank in urban-industrial society. Since a strong association may be shown to exist between similarity in socioeconomic rank and the desirability of intimate social interaction it may be posited that if migrant populations differ significantly from the host population in terms of their occupational characteristics then they will also differ in terms of their attractiveness as marriage partners.[12] The more different the occupational composition of two or more groups the more different will be their pattern of marriage choices.

The relationship between religious differences and patterns of marriage choice will vary in strength with the degree of religious commitment in the groups concerned and with the size of the institutionalized barriers which face interfaith marriages. In general, however, the greater the dissimilarity in the religious composition of two or more populations the less desirable will be marriages between them and the greater will be the dissimilarity in their choice of marriage partners.

No attempt is made in the present argument to delineate a simple directional or causal chain connecting the three aspects of social dissimilarity. It is clear that considerable feedback exists in the system. It may, however, be postulated that a close association will exist between all three areas of dissimilarity. Knowledge of the degree of dissimilarity exhibited by a specified migrant population in one area should be highly predictive to its degree of assimilation in other areas. The basic hypothesis for test is that there will be a high positive correlation between the various aspects of dissimilarity across migrant populations.

Data

Three main sources of data are utilized: the Queensland reports of the 1961 Census of the Commonwealth of Australia, marriage-by-birthplace records for the years 1960–62 kept by the Queensland office of the Commonwealth Bureau of Census and Statistics, and the responses of a probability sample of Australian-born residents of Brisbane interviewed in December, 1967.[13] It should be noted that differences in the temporal and geographical referents of the data make it dangerous to claim more than suggestive value for the interpretation given to their interrelationships.

Results

The dissimilarity of the overseas-born and the Australian-born
Descriptive data on the dissimilarity between each of the migrant populations and the Australian-born residents of Queensland is given in Table 20.1. Columns 1 to 3 of the table show the indexes of residential, occupational, and religious dissimilarity for each migrant population in 1961. Columns 4 and 5 give the indexes of marital dissimilarity, first for brides and then for grooms,[14] and cols 6 and 7 show the index of perceived dissimilarity and the social distance quotient of each group in 1967.

The residential patterning of the overseas-born in Brisbane is virtually identical with that which has been reported for other Australian cities.[15] The United Kingdom-born differ least in residential patterning from the Australian-born, the Southern Europeans differ the most. Only 10 per cent of the United Kingdom-born would have to move to other Census collectors' districts in order to reproduce the residential pattern of the Australian-born residents of Brisbane. In contrast, 76 per cent of the Yugoslavs, 68 per cent of the Greeks, and 60 per cent of the Italians would need to move in order to reproduce the Australian-born pattern. The New

Table 20.1   The dissimilarity between Australian-born and overseas-born residents of Queensland

Group	Indexes of dissimilarity, 1961					Perceived soc. dist.	
	Res. 1	Occ. 2	Rel. 3	Mar. (b) 4	Mar. (g) 5	Diss., 1967 6	Ind., 1967 7
New Zealand	32	17	9	29	10	17	1·1
United Kingdom	10	6	13	21	17	22	1·2
Netherlands	43	13	22	43	32	51	1·7
Germany	38	25	25	49	34	57	1·8
Poland	48	29	33	65	53	67	2·3
Italy	60	24	39	88	52	75	2·4
Yugoslavia	77	29	30	85	50	76	2·5
Greece	68	43	42	81	66	76	2·4

Sources: Residential distribution: Collector's District tabulation *Census of the Commonwealth of Australia, 1961.*
Occupational and religious distributions: *Queensland, Census of the Commonwealth of Australia, 1961,* vol. iii.
Marriage-by-birthplace distribution: m/s data for 1960–62, Bureau of Census and Statistics, Brisbane, Queensland.
Perceived dissimilarity and social distance: interviews with a probability sample of 301 Australian-born residents of Brisbane, December, 1967.
Base categories for computation of indexes of dissimilarity: Residential: 554 Census CD's Brisbane Met. Area. Occupational: 7 major occupational categories. Religious: 20 religious categories. Marital: 14 birthplace categories.

Zealand-born,[16] the Dutch, the Germans, and the Poles occupy intermediate positions in terms of their residential dissimilarity from the Australian-born.

The occupational differences between each of the migrant groups and the Australian-born population of Queensland are generally of a similar pattern to those revealed in the residential data.[17] The polar positions of dissimilarity are occupied by the United Kingdom-born and the Greek-born. In order to show the same percentage distribution over the seven major occupational categories used in the computation of the index of occupational dissimilarity as the Australian-born population more than 42 per cent of the employed Greeks would have to change their jobs compared with less than 6 per cent of the United Kingdom-born.[18] The Dutch and the New Zealand-born differ from the Australian-born occupational pattern to only a slight degree while the German, Polish, Italian, and Yugoslav populations, in order of increasing differences, exhibit a moderate index of occupational dissimilarity.

The pattern of differences revealed by the index of religious dissimilarity closely resembles that given by each of the other indexes of structural dissimilarity. The New Zealand-born and the United Kingdom-born reveal the least degree of religious dissimilarity to the Australian-born residents of Queensland, the Greek-born reveal the highest degree of religious dissimilarity. The Roman Catholic populations reveal a surprisingly high index of religious dissimilarity, but it should be remembered that, in contrast to the Greeks, migrants from Italy or Poland have a ready-made native institution to enter. The religious isolation of the Greek-born from the host society is, therefore, more pronounced than the raw index of religious dissimilarity might indicate.[19]

Differences in cultural constraints and in the size of population at risk amongst males and females caution a dual consideration of the patterns of marital dissimilarity between the various overseas-born populations and the Australian-born residents of Queensland.

The tendency for females to practise endogamy is reflected in the generally higher values of marital dissimilarity for brides than for grooms. The very high index values amongst Italian, Yugoslav, and Greek brides is primarily a function of the high proportion of migrant girls from these countries who marry grooms from their own group.[20] In order to reproduce the marriage-by-birthplace pattern exhibited by Australian-born brides more than four-fifths of those coming from Italy, Yugoslavia, and Greece would have to change their husbands for others of other ethnic background. Only approximately one-quarter of the New Zealand and United Kingdom brides would have to follow their example. The German and Dutch group occupy an intermediate position.[21]

The pattern of marital dissimilarity for grooms is somewhat different from that evidenced by brides. The index values are lower[22] and the

349

division into British, Northern European, and Southern European categories, so evident in the case of the bridal series, is not as clearly apparent British and Northern European categories may still be distinguished, but the Poles fall into a new Roman Catholic set with Italians and the Yugoslavs, while the Greeks are out on their own. Two-thirds of the Greek-born grooms would have to exchange their brides for others with different ethnic backgrounds in order to reproduce the bride-by-birthplace pattern exhibited by Australian-born grooms. Less than one-tenth of the New Zealand-born grooms and one-fifth of the United Kingdom-born would need to make similar exchanges.

The patterns revealed by the various indexes of structural and marital dissimilarity are closely paralleled by those produced in the course of a series of interviews with Australian-born residents of Brisbane designed to illustrate the subjective social distance at which the various migrant populations are kept. The index of perceived dissimilarity shows the New Zealand-born and the United Kingdom-born as differing but little from the Australian base; the Dutch and the Germans are seen as occupying positions close together in the middle of the scale; the Italians, Yugoslavs, and Greeks are seen as clustering in a relatively extreme position. The Poles are intermediate between the German-Dutch and the Italian-Yugoslav groups. The social distance indices show the same general pattern. The New Zealanders and the United Kingdom-born score close

Table 20.2 Intercorrelation of measures of dissimilarity between the Australian-born and overseas-born residents of Queensland

Measures	a	b	c	d	e	f	g
a Residential dissimilarity	—	0·80	0·80	0·93	0·83	0·88	0·90
b Occupational dissimilarity	0·80	—	0·82	0·79	0·86	0·78	0·79
c Religious dissimilarity	0·80	0·82	—	0·92	0·98	0·95	0·94
d Marital dissimilarity (brides)	0·93	0·79	0·92	—	0·91	0·95	0·97
e Marital dissimilarity (grooms)	0·83	0·86	0·98	0·91	—	0·95	0·96
f Perceived dissimilarity	0·88	0·78	0·95	0·95	0·95	—	0·99
g Social distance index	0·90	0·79	0·94	0·97	0·96	0·99	—

All coefficients significant at better than the 0·02 level.

to the theoretical minimum, the Dutch and the Germans exhibit middle-of-the-range scores, the Poles, Greeks, Italians, and Yugoslavs have relatively high scores. More than 95 per cent of the respondents checked the nearest relationship, marriage, in the case of New Zealand and United Kingdom migrants. This percentage fell to less than 75 in the case of migrants from Southern and Eastern Europe.

The interrelationship of the measures of dissimilarity

The zero-order correlation coefficients between each pair of dissimilarity

indexes are shown in Table 20.2. The general hypothesis of a close association between each aspect of a migrant group's dissimilarity to the host
population predicts that all coefficients in the table shall be positive in sign
and significantly greater than zero. The results are clearly in agreement
with this pattern.

All the coefficients appearing in the table are significant at better than
the 0·02 level. The hypothesis of a close correspondence between the
positions of the migrant populations on each index of dissimilarity to the
Australian-born population of Queensland receives considerable support.
A group's dissimilarity in one sphere, whether it be structural, behavioral,
or attitudinal, is closely paralleled by its dissimilarity in other spheres.

Assimilation and length of residence

It is frequently assumed that the degree of assimilation characteristic of
a given set of migrants is a function of the average length of their residence
in the host society. Jones has found a moderate degree of correlation
between the index of residential concentration and the median length of
residence of migrant populations in Melbourne and similar findings have
been reported for the United States by Lieberson.[23] In order to assess the
strength of the relationship in Queensland each of the indexes of dissimilarity was compared with data on the proportion of each migrant
group which had been resident in Australia for less than five years and for
more than fifteen years.[24] No significant relationship could be found in
either case. It apparently makes little sense to discuss assimilation in
Queensland in terms of an old/new distinction among migrant populations.

Conclusion

It is clear that the major hypothesis about the inter-relationship of the
various measures of the dissimilarity of migrant groups from the Australian-
born members of the host society is supported. There is a high degree of
correlation across the birthplace groups between the indexes of residential,
occupational, religious, and marital dissimilarity and of perceived dissimilarity and social distance. A group's position on one index predicts
highly to its position on the others.

The migrant populations are not evenly spaced along the dimensions
of dissimilarity from the host society. Three distinct clusters of populations may be discerned: a New Zealand-United Kingdom set, occupying
a position at the most assimilated end of the scales, a moderately assimilated
set containing the Dutch and the German-born, and a least assimilated
set containing migrants from Italy, Yugoslavia, and Greece, with the
Polish-born as peripheral members. The similarity of the ranking with that
reported in American studies is remarkable.[25]

Notes and References

1. For a discussion of the confusion and the variations in the interpretation of the concept of assimilation see Milton M. Gordon, *Assimilation in American Life: the role of race, religion, and national origins,* New York: Oxford University Press, 1964, especially chapter iii, and Charles A. Price, *The Study of Assimilation,* mimeo., Canberra: Australian National University, 1967.

2. Price, *op. cit.,* 20.

3. Stanley Lieberson, *Ethnic Patterns in American Cities,* New York: The Free Press, a division of The Macmillan Co., 1963, 12.

4. Price, *op. cit.,* p. 21.

5. Cf. Lieberson, *op. cit.,* p. 10.

6. A good discussion of the various indexes used to measure the dissimilarity between populations is to be found in Karl E. Taeuber and Alma F. Taeuber, *Negoes in Cities: residential segregation and neighborhood change,* Chicago: Aldine Publishing Co., 1965, Appendix A. The Index of Dissimilarity has been used in several studies of structural differentiation, e.g. Taeuber and Taeuber, *op. cit.*; Otis D. Duncan and Beverly Duncan, 'Residential segregation and occupational stratification', *Am. J. Sociol.,* **60,** (Mar. 1955), 493–503 [3]; Eugene S. Uyeki, 'Residential distribution and stratification', *Am. J. Sociol.,* **69,** (Mar. 1964), 491–8 [4]; Leonard Broom and Jack P. Gibbs, 'Social differentiation and status interrelations: the Maori-Pakeha case', *Am. Sociol. Rev.,* **29,** (April 1964), 258–65.

7. For references see Delbert C. Miller, *Handbook of Research Design and Social Measurement,* New York: McKay Social Science Series, 1964, pp. 143–50.

8. Gordon, *op. cit.,* p. 80.

9. On marriage as a status-equalizing process see James M. Beshers, 'Urban social structure as a single hierarchy', *Social Forces,* **41,** (Mar. 1963), 233–8.

10. See Alvin M. Katz and Reuben Hill, 'Residential propinquity and marital selection: a review of theory, method, and fact', *Marriage and Family Living,* **20,** (Feb. 1958), 27–35.

11. James M. Beshers, *Urban Social Structure,* New York: The Free Press, a division of The Macmillan Co., 1962, pp. 105–7. On the general relationship between social distance and physical distance see Arnold S. Feldman and Charles Tilly, 'The interaction of social and physical space', *Am. Sociol. Rev.,* **25,** (Dec. 1960), 877–84 [5].

12. See Edward O. Laumann, *Prestige and Association in an Urban Community: an analysis of an urban stratification system,* Indianapolis, Bobbs-Merrill, 1966.

13. The sample was of a multistage cluster design. N = 301.

14. The index of marital dissimilarity for brides reflects the birthplace of their grooms; the index of dissimilarity for grooms reflects the ethnic origins of their brides.

15. For example, Jerzy Zubrzycki, *Immigrants in Australia: a demographic*

survey based on the 1954 Census, Melbourne University Press, 1960, pp. 79–85; F. Lancaster Jones, 'Ethnic concentration and assimilation; an Australian case study', Australian National University, 1967 [17].

16. The index of residential dissimilarity for the New Zealand-born is considerably higher than expected. On further analysis this appears to be the result of the peculiar nature of New Zealand settlement in Queensland. More than one-quarter of the New Zealand-born resident in Queensland in 1961 had been in Australia for less than a year. The majority of these were probably visitors rather than intending settlers and were geographically concentrated in inner-city boarding-house districts.

17. Again the index of dissimilarity for the New Zealand-born is higher than had been anticipated. In this case the most likely explanation involves an interaction effect between the occupational characteristics of the New Zealand-born population and the constitution of the 'core society' in Queensland. It is implicit in the paper that the dominant or core population in Queensland, the base for any study of assimilation in the State, consists of the Australian-born. This is only true, however, in a very crude sense. Any more detailed examination of the assimilation situation must take account of the considerable variation in ethnic background which exists within the Australian-born category. It may well be that, as in the United States, the true core society for the measurement of assimilation should be not the total local-born population but only that part of it which derives from Anglo-Saxon Protestant stock. If data were available on this basis it is highly probable that the index of occupational dissimilarity for the New Zealand-born would be considerably reduced. Their major deviation from the occupational characteristics of the Australian-born population of Queensland involves a relative over-concentration in high status occupational categories. It is likely that the Anglo-Saxon Protestant members of the local-born population would show a similar profile.

18. Further consideration of the occupational and employment characteristics of the various migrant populations highlights the exceptional position of the Greek-born. More than one-quarter of the Greeks are categorized as employers, twice as many as among the Italians and three times as many as among the Australian-born. Virtually none of the Greek-born are categorized as professionals.

19. The fact that the Greek-born migrants have had to set up their own Church organization has also enabled them to develop a range of parochial schools and other Church-related activities which is unmatched by any of the other groups considered here.

20. Less than 8 per cent of the Italian-born brides, less than 12 per cent of the Yugoslav, and 15 per cent of the Greek-born married grooms born in Australia. Eighty-eight per cent of the grooms of Italian-born brides were themselves born in Italy. It should be noted that even these figures exaggerate the extent of intermarriage since they fail to take into account the varied ethnic

background of the Australian-born population. Presumably, a sizeable proportion of the Southern European-Australian-born intermarriages in fact involves marriages between first and second generation migrants from the same ethnic background. See Charles A. Price, *Southern Europeans in Australia*, Australian National University Press, 1963.

21. Marriage-by-birthplace data for 1966 indicate that the German and Dutch groups have become indistinguishable in marriage patterns from those comprising the British group. The index of marital dissimilarity for Greek brides actually increased during the period (p. 0.01).

22. This may be seen as at least in part a function of the sex ratio amongst the migrant populations. Uncorrected sex ratios per 100 males in each group in 1961 were as follows: Australian-born 107; New Zealand-born 89; United Kingdom-born 95; Netherlands-born 81; German-born 107; Italian-born 74; Polish-born 65; Yugoslav-born 57; Greek-born 71.

23. Jones, *op. cit.*; Lieberson, *op. cit.*

24. Data from *Census of the Commonwealth of Australia, 1961*, vol. iii, *Queensland*.

25. For example, James M. Beshers, Edward O. Laumann, and Benjamin S. Bradshaw, 'Ethnic congregation-segregation, assimilation, and stratification', *Social Forces*, **42**, (May 1964), 482–9.

D.T. Rowland

21 Maori migration to Auckland*

Since the early 1940s Maori urbanization in New Zealand has been steadily gaining momentum. In 1945 only 9 per cent of the Maori population lived in cities and boroughs. By 1961 the proportion had reached 33·3 per cent and at the 1966 census it was 49·5 per cent. Two factors are responsible for this trend of accelerating urbanization: first, the volume of rural-urban migration has expanded greatly, and, secondly, the movement of young people has lowered the natural growth potential of rural areas while heightening that of urban areas. The 'new Maori migration' is having a significant impact on urban population characteristics, particularly in Auckland, the most cosmopolitan city in New Zealand. Cityward migration continues to be the main component of the growth of Auckland's Maori population, despite the mounting importance of natural increase. The discussion which follows is concerned with evaluating the volume and composition of the Maori migration stream and showing some of its effects on the population geography of Auckland.

Maori population growth

Auckland has always been the main urban centre for Maoris. In 1966, 34 per cent of all Maoris in New Zealand cities and boroughs were in Auckland.[1] Its total Maori population of 33,926 was nearly five times larger than that of Rotorua (7,445) and more than three times larger than the combined Maori population of Wellington and Hutt urban areas (10,500). Because Auckland is the most important commercial and manufacturing centre in New Zealand, it has been able to attract and absorb an increasing proportion of the country's population, both Maori and non-Maori. However, Auckland is the main centre for Maoris not only on account of the economic

* Reprinted from *New Zealand Geographer*, **27**, no. 1 (April 1971) 21–37.

and social opportunities it has to offer, but also because it is favourably situated in relation to the country's Maori-populated areas, especially those of the Far North.

A number of measures of the growth of the Maori population of Auckland are given in Table 21.1. These figures show the trend of accelerating growth, which has become especially marked during the 1960s, and also the tendency for Auckland to have a rising proportion of non-Europeans in its total population. An average of about 2,800 Maoris were added to Auckland's population each year between 1961 and 1966, which is nearly four

Table 21.1 Maori population growth in Auckland

Year	Totals	Per cent total population of Auckland	Per cent increase	Annual growth Average number	Rate per cent*
1945	5,187	1·8	—	—	—
1951	7,621	2·3	46·9	405	8·0
1956	11,361	3·0	49·1	748	8·2
1961	19,847	4·4	74·7	1,697	11·8
1966	33,926	6·2	70·9	2,816	11·3

* Annual growth rate calculated using the 'compound interest' formula.

Source: New Zealand Census of Population and Dwellings, 1966, i, 16.

times the annual numerical increase for 1951–1956. The growth rate similarly shows the recent surge in population expansion, the slight decline in the 1961–66 rate simply being due to the greater absolute numbers. The most portentous data in Table 21.1 are those showing the relative size of the Maori population. Maoris as a proportion of Auckland's total population increased from 1·8 per cent in 1945 to 6·2 per cent in 1966. These figures indicate the rapidity of Maori population growth compared with non-Maori and emphasize Auckland's future as an increasingly multi-racial centre.

The rapid expansion of the numbers of Maoris in Auckland is attributable to an unusual combination of the three determinants of population growth: mortality, fertility and migration. New Zealand's Maori population has one of the lowest mortality rates in the world, a high birth rate (38·70 per 1,000 in 1966), and possibly one of the highest rates of rural–urban migration. Maoris in New Zealand as a whole have a lower mortality rate than non-Maoris on account of their younger age structure. In 1966 the crude death rate for Maoris was 6·37 per thousand compared with 8·86 for the total population. Though no data are available on rural–urban differentials in Maori mortality, it is probably true that the mortality rate for Maoris who have their homes in Auckland is at least as low as the national average.[2] This is because Auckland is relatively well provided with medical services and also because the Auckland Maoris have a youthful age structure. Mortality is thus operating as only a very moderate restraint on the growth of Auckland's Maori population.

The contribution of fertility to population growth has been increasing slowly since 1951. In the intercensal period 1951–56 natural increase accounted for about a quarter of the total growth in the number of Maoris in

Table 21.2   Components of Maori population growth in Auckland

Period	Increase	Net in-migration Number	Percentage	Natural increase Number	Percentage
1951–1956	3,740	2,771	74·1	969	25·9
1956–1961	8,486	5,717	67·4	2,769	32·6
1961–1966	14,079	8,820	62·5	5,259	37·5

Source: New Zealand Population Census, 1966, i, 16; and migration estimates based on census survival ratios.

Auckland, while between 1961 and 1966 it contributed about a third (Table 21.2). Although these proportions are small compared with the contribution of migration, the fertility of Auckland Maoris is non the less high, and it is even higher than might be expected in an urban situation. The general fertility rate shows that Maoris in Auckland have a high level of fertility, similar to that of the national Maori population (Table 21.3). A factor strengthening the significance of high fertility is the youthfulness of the age structure. In Auckland 43·1 per cent of the Maori population are in the reproductive age groups (15–44) and 47·8 per cent are in the pre-reproductive age groups. The corresponding figures for Auckland's total population are 41·0 and 29·9 per cent. The age structure, together with the general absence of family planning (Pool, 1964, p. 404), promises that the natural growth rate will be sustained at a level higher than for the non-Maori population.

As already indicated, migration is by far the most important factor in Maori population growth in Auckland. Between 1951 and 1966 the Maori population grew by 26,305, and about two-thirds of this increase was attributable to migration. Table 21.2 shows that the net inward migration, that is the excess of arrivals in Auckland over departures,

Table 21.3   General fertility rates 1966*

	Maori	Total Population
New Zealand	201·0	114·4
Auckland Urban Area	202·3	108·0

* The general fertility rate is the number of births per thousand women aged 15–44.

Source: New Zealand Population Census, 1966 and New Zealand Vital Statistics, 1966.

357

has continued to expand numerically from 2,771 in 1951–56 to 8,820 in 1961–66, though its relative contribution to population growth fell by 13 per cent over the same period (1951–66). This decline has been caused by the cumulative effect of migration expanding the reproductive age groups, which has inevitably increased the relative contribution of natural growth.

Age structure of migrants

City living and its associated economic and social benefits have proved most attractive to Maoris aged 15–24; that is, people whose occupations are not yet finalized and whose hopes for personal and material success outweigh the less tangible ties with the land and the home community. Data on the age structure of Maoris migrating to Auckland were obtained using Pool's (1966) 'census survival ratio' formula. The method consists of comparing the growth of population cohorts with their expected natural decline. The difference between the actual and 'expected' populations is the net inward migration, the excess of arrivals in Auckland over departures.[3]

Between 1961 and 1966, 40 per cent of the Maoris migrating to the eighteen 'urban areas' had their destinations in Auckland. Maoris moving to Auckland during this five-year period totalled 8,820. Their age structure in 1966 is shown in Fig. 21.1. The pyramid is heavily weighted in the young age groups. People aged 15–19 years are the most mobile and account for 21 per cent of the total migrants. There are also extremely large numbers of 'passive' migrants under the age of 14 (44 per cent of the total), indicating that the migration stream to Auckland is composed of families as well as un-

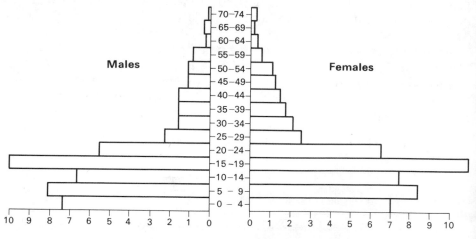

Fig. 21.1 Age structure of rural–urban migrants in Auckland 1966.

married people aged 15–24. The necessity to migrate becomes stronger when children have to be provided for and their education and employment prospects need to be taken into consideration. Thus people who may not have had sufficient reason or initiative to move when they were single are being motivated to move for their families' sake. This explains the presence of significant numbers of migrants over the age of twenty-five (Table 21.4). Among the older age groups, cityward migration is probably due to medical reasons or a wish to be with children or grandchildren.

Maoris coming to Auckland in the period 1956–61 had a similar age structure to those arriving in 1961–66, but the migration stream during the late 1950s appears to have contained a higher proportion of young single people (Table 21.4). The data suggest that young adults were even more predominant in the early 1950s, a characteristic which was found also by Butterworth (1967, 26) in his analysis of the age structure of Maoris

Table 21.4 Estimated age distribution of Maoris migrating to Auckland

Migration period Year of age estimate	1951–56 1956		1956–61 1961		1961–66 1966	
Age group	M	F	M	F	M	F
0– 4	230	216	441	436	641	616
5– 9	134	70	382	420	713	744
10–14	136	189	312	344	579	652
15–19	536	487	634	627	884	959
20–24	303	224	362	396	488	561
25–29	− 28	20	169	189	208	221
30–34	− 3	20	149	139	137	185
35–39	31	27	95	100	140	150
40–44	1	46	76	83	137	131
45–49	9	21	62	76	110	106
50–54	20	30	50	58	104	101
55–59	20	5	30	7	75	45
60–64	13	7	10	28	22	30
65–69	− 13	4	6	8	23	8
70–74	− 1	− 5	4	7	6	14
75–79	8	10	8	6	16	2
80–84	1	0	3	− 4	4	2
85–89	3	0	4	0	0	6
Totals	1400	1371	2797	2920	4287	4533
Grand totals	2771		5717		8820	

Source: Statistics calculated using Pool's (1966, pp. 92–3) formulae for estimating Maori migration from census survival ratios.

moving to all urban areas. Precise comparisons of the figures for the three periods cannot be made, however, because the migration data are merely estimates whose accuracy depends upon the quality of the census data and the validity of the statistical assumptions, both of which become increasingly precarious as smaller populations are considered.

More reliable comparisons can be made between the age-sex structure of migrants to Auckland and migrants to all the statistical urban areas (Table 21.5). The two sets of data show that females predominate slightly in the migration stream to Auckland, whereas males predominate in the migration stream to all the urban areas combined. Employment opportunities for Maori women are more restricted than those for men, and the excess of females migrating to Auckland is most likely a reflection of the greater availability there of jobs in light industry and domestic service. The presence of hospital facilities in Auckland must also help to cause the excess of females.

Table 21.5   Estimated age distribution in 1966 of Maoris migrating to Auckland and to the eighteen urban areas combined 1961–66

| | Numbers | | | | Rates* | | | |
| | Urban areas | | Auckland | | Urban areas | | Auckland | |
Age group†	M	F	M	F	M	F	M	F
0– 4	1,549	1,488	641	615	181	180	177	178
5– 9	1,848	1,938	713	744	284	293	262	274
10–14	1,420	1,764	579	652	302	359	301	343
15–19	2,166	2,239	884	959	505	487	507	515
20–24	1,287	1,057	488	561	341	271	317	337
25–29	750	505	208	221	213	146	150	151
30–39	991	918	277	335	213	195	149	172
40–49	662	614	247	237	254	230	231	218
50–59	406	325	179	146	259	222	273	233
60–69	118	139	45	38	165	208	161	167
70–79	54	33	22	17	248	177	282	246
Totals	11,251	11,020	4,283	4,525	274	266	252	266
Grand totals	22,271		8,808		270		260	

$$* \text{ Migration rate} = \frac{\text{total migrants aged x}}{\text{total population aged x}} \cdot \frac{1000}{1}$$

† Ten-year age groups have been used in part since a complete breakdown by five-year age groups was not given in the 1961 census.

Source: Statistics calculated using Pool's (1966, pp. 92–3) formulae for estimating Maori migration from census survival ratios.

Apart from the slight difference in the sex ratios, Auckland's migration stream resembles the total rural–urban migration stream. The age structures of the migrants are similar and the migration rates also display parallel tendencies. The migration rates confirm the relative importance of people aged 15–19 years, their rate being 511 per thousand in Auckland (Table 21·5). The 20–24 age group ranks second among the active migrants with a rate of 320, followed by the 70–79 age group (264) and the 50–59 group (253). Maoris aged 25–39 have comparatively low migration rates (150–

160), which supports the hypothesis that economic circumstances and the lack of employment and educational opportunities put pressure on people to migrate as their families grow larger and some of their children near secondary school age. These pressures are least significant among people aged 25–29, and consequently their migration rate is lowest of all. Furthermore, it may be observed that the migration rates of children are lowest at ages 0–4 and highest at 10–14, which again is evidence that Maori migration is sometimes motivated by the requirements of growing families.[4]

Origins and destinations

Maori migration to Auckland has been stimulated particularly by hopes for economic and social advantages (Metge, 1964, 130). These motives are understandable in view of the economic backwardness and physical isolation of many of the places from which they have come. Joan Metge (1964, 124) found that the largest proportion of the Maoris in her sample were originally from the Far North, and the present research on the origin of Auckland-bound migrants during the 1960s shows that the northernmost counties of the North Island continue to be the principal source areas.

Data on internal migration are not provided by the population census and the analysis here is based mainly on information extracted from the Maori electoral rolls for 1960, 1963 and 1966. The procedure used was to compare the addresses of Maoris at different dates and record any change of address which occurred during a three year interval.[5] The electoral rolls offered a convenient means of obtaining a complete coverage of all places of origin and destination. In addition, they contained data on occupations, marital status (for females only) and tribal membership. Another feature commending the use of the electoral rolls was that they enabled the study to be restricted to movements which occurred during the 1960s, which was valuable because origins and destinations in particular have probably changed through time. Finally, all Maoris listed on the rolls were theoretically of half or more Maori descent, which meant that the universe of migrants was directly comparable with the Maori population enumerated in the census. Against these advantages, however, must be set the disadvantages of electoral rolls as sources of migration data. First, only people over twenty-one were listed and the movements of the younger age groups have had to be inferred from the population census. Secondly, there is evidence that people listed on the Maori rolls are not all of half or more Maori descent and, conversely, that many Maoris who should be listed on Maori electoral rolls are on European rolls instead.[6] It is also likely that large numbers of Maoris do not enrol at all.[7] Thirdly, there is the possibility that a migrant has moved twice in three years but only one move has been detected from the electoral rolls.

Scrutiny of the electoral rolls yielded information on 590 adult Maori

361

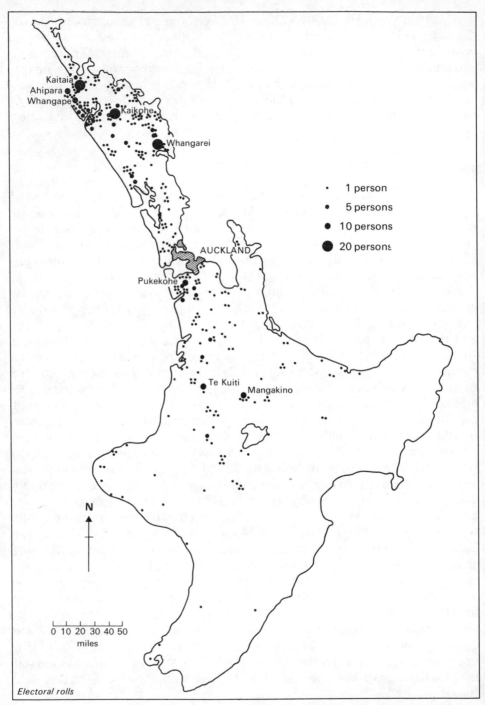

Fig. 21.2 Origin of adult Maoris migrating to Auckland 1960–66. Total sample 590.

cityward migrants, 317 males and 273 females. This represented approximately 20 per cent of the total migrants over twenty-one who moved to Auckland between 1960 and 1966. Since the study of the electoral rolls was fairly comprehensive it can be assumed that at least 50 per cent of the adult Maoris moving to Auckland failed to enrol as Maori electors either at their place of origin or at their destination in Auckland. The places of origin of the migrants are shown in Fig. 21.2. Forty-nine per cent of the migrants in the sample came from the northernmost counties of Mangonui, Hokianga, Bay of Islands and Whangarei, with the towns of Kaitaia, Kaikohe and Whangarei accounting for a third of this total. Sixty-four per cent of the migrants came from Northland as a whole, and in this region the frequency of migration generally rose with increasing distance from Auckland. This is because Maori population numbers are greatest in the less developed Far North. In Northland it is apparent that many Maoris are coming from isolated areas lacking opportunities for full and lucrative employment, Hokianga and Mangonui counties in particular having high outward migration in relation to the size of their Maori populations.

South of Auckland, Maoris are also coming from areas where employment opportunities are not favourable, the main places of origin being Pukekohe, Te Kuiti and Mangakino, which together accounted for about 7 per cent of the migrants. However, only 36 per cent of all the migrants came from places south of Auckland. This low incidence of migration is due to the greater development of cities in the central North Island than in Northland, and also to the presence of hydro-electric construction towns such as Turangi, and towns associated with the forestry industry, such as Kawerau and Murupara, which provide employment opportunities for the unskilled Maori labour force. Maori land development in the central North Island may also be of some significance in curtailing rural–urban movement.[8] In the south, Auckland appears to exert its greatest attraction in Maori-populated areas closest to the city (Fig. 21.2), and its influence further afield is probably due to the fact that it is the largest city in New Zealand and offers the widest variety of employment and social opportunities. This influence has not been sufficient to attract significant numbers from the eastern and southern parts of the North Island, because of the distance involved and the alternative attractions of Wellington and Lower Hutt. Thus the growth of the Maori population of Auckland by migration during the 1960s was due especially to the city's favourable location in relation to the Maori-populated areas of Northland, and the lack of urban centres in the north, apart from Whangarei, which could compete with Auckland in attracting the migrants.

Since the majority of Maoris migrating to Auckland are coming from Northland it is to be expected that the northern tribes predominate in the migration stream. The Ngapuhi tribe from the Far North is best represented and accounted for nearly 47 per cent of the Maoris in the sample. Three

363

other tribes from the north – Te Aupouri, Te Rarawa and Ngati Whatua – accounted for a further 16 per cent of the migrants. Also well represented were three southern tribes – Ngati Maniapoto, Waikato and Te Arawa – who comprised 11 per cent of the total. Another fifty-eight tribes and sub-tribes were present in the sample, mainly from south of Auckland, though the number of migrants in each was below ten.

Upon arrival in Auckland, the Maoris in the sample took up residence in almost every statistical subdivision of the urban area (Fig. 21.3). Otara, Mangere and Papakura were the most important destinations in terms of absolute numbers and altogether 43 per cent of the migrants had destinations in south Auckland, that is, the area from Otahuhu south. Second in importance as an area of inward migration was the inner city,[9] which accommodated 15·4 per cent of the migrants, and this area was followed by the central suburbs (12·4 per cent) and the western suburbs (9·7 per cent) (Fig. 21.3, inset). The dominance of Auckland's newly developed outer suburbs is most striking and suggests that large numbers of cityward migrants stay with relatives upon arrival.[10] This view is borne out by the fact that between 1966 and 1969, 40 per cent of the Maori families in Auckland who applied for Department of Maori Affairs housing loans stated, as one of their reasons for wishing to move, that they were over-crowding the home of relatives or friends.[11] Some cityward migrants obtain new houses of their own immediately, through the Maori Affairs relocation scheme (Butterworth, 1967, p. 38), or through private arrangements, but they would only comprise a small proportion of the total. Others obtain flats or boarding house accommodation in the outer suburbs, especially near employment centres, but it is probably more common for adult Maoris initially to share a dwelling with relatives or friends who preceded them to the city.

In order to gain an indication of the relative importance of different areas as destinations for Maori migrants, migration rates were calculated using the electoral roll data. High rates of inward migration – 50 per 1,000 or more – were characteristic of most parts of south Auckland as well as East Coast Bays, Avondale and Henderson. Elsewhere comparable rates occurred only in Ponsonby and Newton in the inner city area. It is clear that in both relative and absolute terms the newly developed parts of Auckland are by far the most significant destinations of adult cityward migrants. The high rates of migration to the inner city areas can be attributed partly to the hospitality of the permanent Maori residents, but more particularly to the availability of temporary accommodation. The inner city is most attractive to unmarried people who are less particular about their environment and can overcome the frequent problem of high rentals by sharing expenses with others. In the remainder of the city, migration rates generally ranged from 20 to 49 per 1,000, indicating that most parts of Auckland have a significant function as receiving areas for migrants. Places with cityward

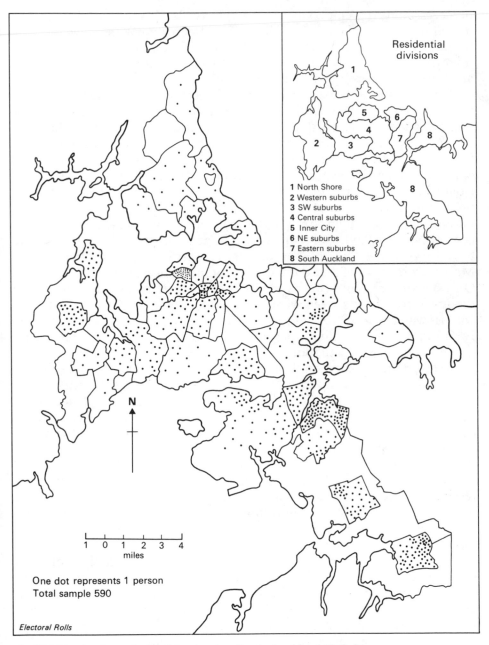

Fig. 21.3 Destinations of adult Maoris migrating to Auckland 1960–66.

migration rates below 10 per 1,000 have very small total populations, showing that the areas are unsuited to the requirements of Maoris in terms

365

of accessibility to employment and the availability of suitable accommodation. This explanation applies to Westmere and Waterview, and also to the northeastern suburbs such as Mission Bay and Kohimarama. A low migration rate was recorded for Freeman's Bay, but it seems to be due to addresses being wrongly given as Ponsonby or Grey Lynn.

Some variations in the choice of destination occurred depending on the areas from which the migrants came. Ninety-three per cent of the people migrating from areas south of Auckland went to destinations in the outer suburbs, especially south Auckland, while only 50 per cent of the Maoris from Northland took up residence in the outer suburbs. While there is no concrete evidence to explain this situation it is likely that Maoris from the isolated parts of Northland are less aware of the better environment of the outer suburbs, as well as of the opportunities to obtain State rental dwellings or housing loans, than are Maoris from more progressive areas in the central North Island. Consequently, a large number of the former group tend to gravitate towards boarding house areas, while the majority of Maoris from south of Auckland find accommodation in the outer suburbs. Only one of the twenty-two migrants from Whangarei took up residence in the inner city while sixteen went to the outer suburbs. This suggests that Maoris who are accustomed to urban living exercise greater selectivity than rural Maoris when seeking a place to live. Nevertheless, further research is needed to clarify the situation.

No direct information on the movements of younger active migrants has been obtained and their destinations have had to be inferred from population census data on ages. The areal distribution of the age structures of Maoris in Auckland is relatively simple. The statistical areas comprising the inner city and the central suburbs are characterized by waisted 'migrant' age structures, while the outer suburbs have broad-based 'youthful' population pyramids.[12] The surplus of people aged 15–29 in the older parts of Auckland shows that the inner city and the central suburbs are the main receiving areas for young unmarried migrants. Inclusion of these people would therefore boost the migration rates for the inner city and central suburbs and would have little effect on those for the outer suburbs. Variations in the 'migrant' structures occur especially according to the presence or absence of institutional influences. The total Maori populations of many of the older areas are small and consequently the presence of hostels, and welfare, penal and military institutions have had exaggerated effects on the age structures, while the outer suburbs have broad-based 'youthful' popula-all have striking 'migrant' age structures, but the total Maori populations of these areas in 1966 ranged only between 498 and 68.

In summary, the migration stream to Auckland is composed principally of parents with children, about three-quarters of whom take up residence in the outer suburbs. The single people and the couples without children, who comprise about 30 per cent of the total migration stream, tend to take up residence mainly in the inner city and the central suburbs. Variations in the destinations of cityward migrants may be attributed particularly to differences in life cycle stage and knowledge of urban life.

Occupations of migrants

Economic circumstances encourage or precipitate cityward migration, but the electoral rolls showed that after the migrants reached Auckland few of them entered occupations which required more skills or more knowledge than their former occupations. At their places of origin the most frequent occupations of males were labouring, representing 43 per cent of the total, and farming, farm labouring and forestry which accounted for another 18 per cent. There were relatively few white-collar workers, and occupations requiring some form of manual skill were also under-represented apart from driving (7 per cent) and carpentry (4 per cent). Maori women had the choice of stating their marital status or their occupations when they enrolled as electors. Only 13 of the 273 female migrants were listed as gainfully employed, mainly in factory work, domestic service or teaching. About 90 per cent of the adult Maori females were already married when they moved to Auckland and it is likely that a very high proportion of the Maori males were also married.

Upon arrival in Auckland, 91 (28 per cent) of the males changed their occupations. Thirty-two of them, especially farmers, became labourers, seventeen became truck drivers and bus operators, while the majority of the remainder became factory workers, carpenters, and welders. Although some Maoris entered more skilled occupations an equal proportion obtained less exacting employment, particularly those who had previously been classified as professional workers. Thus, while the migrants may be earning better pay and have more secure employment than formerly, their overall level of accomplishment has not improved. This is not true of some of the younger migrants, however, since Maoris who come to Auckland soon after leaving school are able to accept low wages while they receive trade training as apprentices and as students at the technical colleges. Of the female migrants, only 13 per cent were listed as gainfully employed in Auckland, mainly as factory workers. Twelve women previously engaged in 'domestic duties' took jobs in Auckland. There were twenty-three 'pensioners', invalids, and widows in the whole sample, which indicates that older Maoris migrate to be with younger relatives, while others come to Auckland on account of its medical services or because of the facilities it offers for training the physically handicapped, such as the Blind Institute.

Distribution of Maoris in Auckland

The present distribution of Maoris in Auckland strongly reflects their low

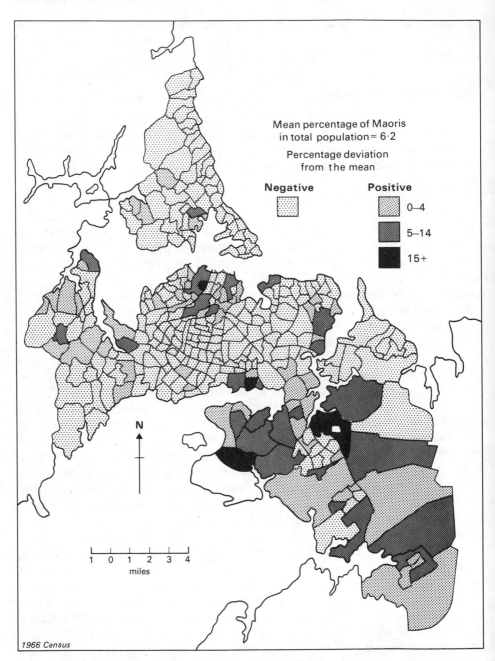

Fig. 21.4 Maori population distribution in Auckland 1966.

socio-economic status. Maoris are over-represented in inner city areas characterized by residential deterioration, and in parts of the outer suburbs where there has been large scale development of relatively low cost houses and State flats. Cityward migration has increased the numbers of Maoris living in both the inner city and the outer suburbs, while intra-city migration, which is mainly a centrifugal movement, has tended to reduce the numbers of Maoris living in the inner city.

In 1966, 6·2 per cent of Auckland's population were Maoris, but the new suburbs of low cost housing, such as Glen Innes, Otara and Mangere, contained disproportionate Maori numbers (Fig. 21.4). In Otara, for example, 27·3 per cent of the population were Maoris. The over-representation of Maoris in some of the newer parts of Auckland is attributable mainly to their economic status and cultural background. Because of low incomes, high dependency ratios or a lack of experience in managing household finances, Maoris are usually unable to obtain houses of their own without State assistance, and rarely can they afford more than a basic utilitarian dwelling. Consequently, Maori householders are obliged to live in new suburbs where State houses and flats, Maori Affairs houses and group houses are found in association, often to the near exclusion of privately built dwellings.[13] The concentration of Maoris in these areas is aggravated substantially by the fact that the hospitality of Maori residents has made them important receiving areas for cityward migrants (Fig. 21.3). In contrast to the situation in the outer suburbs, Maoris are markedly under-represented in the central suburbs of Auckland. This pattern is attributable partly to the recency of Maori urbanization: the central suburbs area was mostly built up before Maori urbanization gained momentum and Maoris have not had many opportunities to obtain housing there. Also partly responsible for the under-representation of Maoris in the central suburbs was a legal restraint which, until 1969, prevented capitalization of the family benefit for the purchase of existing dwellings. Since capitalization is indispensable to most Maoris attempting to raise a housing deposit (Schwimmer, 1968, p. 33) they have been compelled to purchase a new house in the outer suburbs. Maoris may have also deliberately avoided renting houses in the central suburbs because of the difficulty of commuting from this area to the industrial centre of southeastern Auckland. In the old residential areas adjacent to the central business district, such as Freeman's Bay, Ponsonby and Newton, Maoris are over-represented on the same scale as in parts of the outer suburbs (Fig. 21.4). These inner city areas function particularly as receiving centres for cityward migrants and other footloose elements in the Maori population, though they probably also have significant numbers of permanent Maori residents. Many Maoris coming to Auckland seem to prefer to live where other Maoris have lived and for this reason they have favoured inner city areas more than the less familiar central suburbs (Metge, 1964, p. 142). Thus despite the inner city's decaying residential environment and its distance from the main industrial employment centre, the area maintains its attraction to Maoris who are less selective, less knowledgeable, or who desire to be independent of others.

Conclusion

Maori migration to Auckland in the 1960s was primarily a movement of young families coming from isolated rural areas or small towns. In the city Maori families aspired to achieve material success comparable to that of most Europeans, such aspirations being reflected particularly in the shift of population away from the blighted areas to the new suburbs. In seeking to improve their living standards, however, the majority of Maoris were handicapped by their rural background, which had not equipped them with sufficient education or occupational skills to enable them to compete for jobs and housing on equal terms with Europeans in Auckland. Because of their low income and lack of experience in urban living the Maoris' choice of a place to live was largely restricted to areas of low cost housing. The volume of cityward migration in the 1960s was such that Maoris were apparently the fastest growing component of the low income group in Auckland, and as a result they became over-represented in the poorest of the new housing estates. Thus, to some extent, socio-economic segregation has had a similar effect to racial segregation. The number of Maoris migrating to Auckland shows no signs of diminishing and the problems arising from their newness to city life may be expected to persist. Maoris will continue to concentrate in particular areas as long as their educational standards prevent them achieving greater material success and as long as low cost housing is developed in nucleations rather than being dispersed.

Notes and References

1. 'Auckland' refers to the Auckland Urban Area as defined by the Department of Statistics. The boundaries of the Urban Area were extended in 1966 to include all the former Manukau County. However, in this paper the 1961 boundaries have been followed as closely as possible for mapping and analysis since they correspond more to the built-up area than do the 1966 boundaries.
2. The *New Zealand Vital Statistics* publication contains data on Maori fertility by residence of mothers, but no information is available on deaths by domicile for the Maori population.
3. In his description of the method for calculating Maori migration, Pool (1966, 96) advised against applying it to individual urban areas, because minor inaccuracies in census data could produce misleading migration figures for a small population. The Auckland Urban Area's Maori population in 1966, however, was large enough to justify the use of Pool's formulae, and the results compare favourably with the figures for the eighteen urban areas combined (Table 21.5). The migration figures for 1961 appear satisfactory also,

but the 1956 figures are probably less realistic on account of the small size of Auckland's Maori population at that time (Table 21.4).

4. More detailed discussions of the reasons for Maori migration to cities are given by McEwan (in Brookes and Kawharu, 1967, pp. 75–7) and Metge (1964, pp. 127–31).

5. Electoral rolls were also used by Anderson (1964) in a study of migration to and from Palmerston North.

6. All people of more than half Maori descent are required by law to be on the Maori electoral rolls. Those of half Maori descent may choose to enrol either as Maoris or as Europeans, while people of less than half Maori descent must enrol as Europeans. The member of parliament for Northern Maori estimated in 1967 that more than 5,000 Maoris living in his electorate were illegally on the European rolls (Hansard 1967, 353, 3269).

7. The 1969 Maori electoral rolls contain far fewer names than the 1966 rolls. The fall has been attributed both to the transference of Maoris to European constituencies and to a lack of appreciation of the need to re-enrol at each election.

8. McCreary (in Schwimmer, 1968, p. 196) emphasized the importance of migration between rural areas in satisfying the employment needs of Maoris. His study of outward migration from a community in the central North Island showed that short distance moves predominated.

9. To simplify the description of population distribution patterns the statistical areas of Auckland were grouped into a number of 'residential divisions' shown in the inset on Fig. 21.3. The groupings are as follows:
    i. Inner City: Freeman's Bay, Auckland Central, Ponsonby, Grey Lynn, Newton, Parnell, Herne Bay, Grafton, Arch Hill, Eden Terrace and Newmarket.
    ii. Central Suburbs: Waterview, Pt Chevalier, Westmere, Mt Albert, Mt Eden, Epsom, Remuera, Ellerslie, One Tree Hill, Onehunga.
    iii. Northeastern Suburbs: Meadowbank, Orakei, Mission Bay, Kohimarama, St Heliers, Glendowie.
    iv. Outer Suburbs: the remainder of the Urban Area.

10. Metge (1964) makes frequent reference to Maori traditions of hospitality which oblige Maori householders, both in the central city and in the suburbs, to accommodate homeless relatives on a short or long-term basis.

11. Department of Maori Affairs housing records, from the form 'Submission to sell a house', April 1966 to April 1969 inclusive. For the sake of comparability of data the study was restricted to families in which both husband and wife were of at least quarter Maori descent and one of them was at least a half blood.

12. A similar situation was observed by Pool (1961, p. 63) in his analysis of Maori age structures in Auckland in 1956.

13. The concentration of Maoris in particular suburbs of Auckland does not seem to be attributable to a desire for communal living, particularly in view of the

multi-tribal nature of the population. A survey carried out by Jane Ritchie (1961) in Wellington suggested that Maori families prefer to live scattered amongst non-Maori families.

References

Anderson, A. G. (1964) 'Aspects of population change in Palmerston North', *New Zealand Geographer*, **20**, 165–79.

Brookes, R. H. and Kawharu, I. H., eds (1967), *Administration in New Zealand's Multi-Racial Society*, New Zealand Institute of Public Administration.

Butterworth, G. V. (1967) *The Maori in the New Zealand Economy*, Department of Industries and Commerce, Wellington.

Hansard (1967) *Parliamentary Debates*, Wellington: Government Printer.

Metge, J. (1964) *A New Maori Migration*, London: University of London Press.

Pool, I. (1961) 'Maoris in Auckland: a population study', *Journal of the Polynesian Society*, **71**, 43–66.

Pool, I. (1964) 'The Maori population', PhD thesis, Australian National University.

Pool, I. (1966) 'The rural-urban migration of Maoris: a demographic analysis', *Pacific Viewpoint*, **7**, 88–96.

Ritchie, J. (1961) 'Together or apart. A note on urban Maori residential preferences', *Journal of the Polynesian Society*, **70**, 194–9.

Schwimmer, E. (ed.) 1968: *The Maori People in the Nineteen-Sixties*, Auckland: Blackwood and Janet Paul.

C.G.Clarke

22 Residential segregation and intermarriage in San Fernando, Trinidad*

For more than a decade the image of Trinidad society projected by the government has been one of racial and religious harmony. This is expressed by the saying 'All o' we is one', and also by the national anthem, which assures the listener that 'Here ev'ry creed and race find an equal place'. But the very emphasis on equality and harmony draws attention to social divisions within the island. Differences of race, color, class, and culture are significant in Trinidad, and each factor defines important elements in the population. The principal feature of the social structure is the dichotomy between Creole and East Indian.

The term 'Creole' has a particular meaning in Trinidad. It excludes the East Indian population, together with the small Syrian, Portuguese, Chinese, and Carib minorities. Creoles may be white, brown, or black, and genotype correlates with socioeconomic status. Stratification of the Creole segment was established during slavery, and the whites remain the social arbiters. Soon after emancipation in 1834 Indian indentured laborers were brought in to work on the sugar estates. This influx continued until 1917. Their descendants, known as East Indians, now equal just under 40 per cent of the island's population. The East Indian element is itself highly segmented and comprises Hindus, Muslims, and Christians.

The present study examines selected patterns of association among the Creoles and East Indians in San Fernando, the second largest town in Trinidad. The major racial and religious components of the population are identified, and their distributions and spatial associations are considered. A sample of households drawn from the major racial and cultural groupings is then analyzed to assess the frequency of intermarriage and the homogeneity of domestic units. By concentrating on segregation and intermarriage, two widely used indices of intergroup association, it has been

* Reprinted from *The Geographical Review*, **61**, no. 2 (1971), 198–218.

possible to achieve certain measures of social interaction in the ecological, or public, domain and in the domestic, or private, domain.

San Fernando

The town of San Fernando lies on the Gulf of Paria some thirty-five miles south of Port of Spain. It occupies a spectacular site on the flanks of Naparima Hill, and its streets curve out toward the canefields or drop steeply to the sea, either directly or from a smaller ridge called Spring Vale

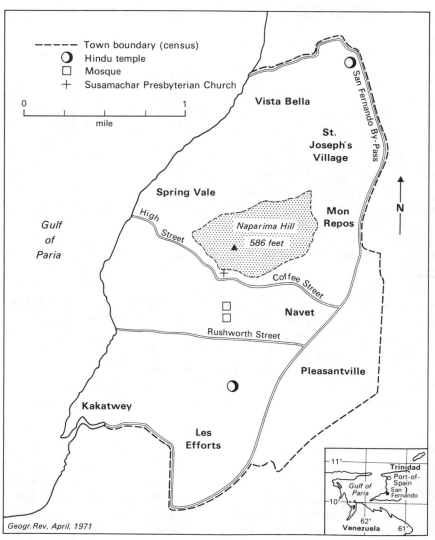

Fig. 22.1 San Fernando, Trinidad.

(Fig. 22.1). In 1960 San Fernando had a population of almost 40,000, and it was the only major settlement whose social structure reflected the national situation, albeit with distortions. The population of the town splits into a neat division in which Creoles account for more than 70 per cent of the inhabitants, and East Indians for just over a quarter (Table 22.1). The Creole population comprises three major elements, whites (3 per cent of the town's inhabitants), Negroes (47 per cent), and a mixed group (21 per cent). The mixed, or colored, group is composed predominantly of mulattoes, though it also contains the offspring of miscegenation between

Table 22.1 **Race and religion in San Fernando**

Race	Total and % by race	Religion Anglican	Methodist	Presbyterian	Roman Catholic	Hindu	Muslim	Other*
Negro	18,784	8,639	878	37	7,199	6	11	2,014
	46·9	*45·8*	*4·7*	*0·2*	*38·2*	*0·03*	*0·06*	*10·7*
White	1,306	422	21	64	649	0	0	150
	3·3	*32·5*	*1·6*	*4·9*	*50·0*	*0·0*	*0·0*	*11·6*
Portuguese	140	1	0	7	131	0	0	1
	0·4	*0·7*	*0·0*	*5·0*	*93·0*	*0·0*	*0·0*	*0·7*
East Indian	10,296	366	10	3,379	848	3,011	2,282	400
	25·7	*3·6*	*0·1*	*32·8*	*8·2*	*29·2*	*22·1*	*3·9*
Chinese	705	166	0	11	473	1	0	54
	1·8	*23·2*	*0·0*	*1·5*	*66·2*	*0·1*	*0·0*	*7·6*
Mixed	8,283	1,949	134	344	5,400	26	24	406
	20·7	*23·5*	*1·6*	*4·2*	*65·1*	*0·3*	*0·3*	*4·9*
Carib	12	6	0	1	5	0	0	0
	0·0	*50·0*	*0·0*	*8·3*	*41·7*	*0·0*	*0·0*	*0·0*
Syrians	152	10	0	0	135	0	0	7
	0·4	*6·6*	*0·0*	*0·0*	*88·8*	*0·0*	*0·0*	*4·6*
Other	146	17	0	0	109	0	1	19
	0·4	*11·5*	*0·0*	*0·0*	*74·1*	*0·0*	*0·01*	*12·9*
Not Stated	6	3	0	0	0	3	0	0
	0·0	*50·0*	*0·0*	*0·0*	*0·0*	*50·0*	*0·0*	*0·0*
Total	39,830	11,579	1,043	3,843	14,949	3,047	2,318	3,051
	100·0							

Source: Trinidad and Tobago Population Census, 1960, vol. 3, Part D, Table 10.

* The 'other religion' category consists of Christian religious groups not listed separately in the table, of other non-Christians, and of those not stated or with no religion.

Negroes or mulattoes on the one hand and Chinese, Syrians, Portuguese, or Caribs on the other. In addition, this group includes a small number of people of part Indian origin known locally as *douglas*.[1]

Not only are the Creoles numerically dominant in San Fernando; they are also proportionally more numerous in the town than in the island as a whole. Most of them are either Anglican or Roman Catholic, and San Fernando may with some justification be described as a Creole and

Catholic town (Table 22.1). No member of the white population and only a few Negroes and mulattoes are adherents of Hinduism or Islam; Hindus and Muslims are almost exclusively East Indian. The distinction between Creole and East Indian is therefore reinforced by religious differences. Moreover, most of the East Indian converts are Presbyterian, and nearly all Presbyterians are East Indian. Presbyterian East Indians comprise 8·5 per cent of the town's population and outnumber Hindus (7·6 per cent) and Muslims (5·8 per cent), though the converse is true for Trinidad as a whole.

The size of the Presbyterian population of the town is partly explained by the fact that Susamachar Church in San Fernando was established as the headquarters of the Canadian Mission during the second half of the nineteenth century. Proselytization proceeded at a rapid rate both in San Fernando and on the surrounding sugar plantations, where East Indians comprised the labor force. Conversion provided a major avenue for acculturation and social mobility among the East Indians and contributed indirectly to their migration to the town. In recent years the economic prosperity of San Fernando has further stimulated urban growth and social change. In addition to its status as the industrial capital of Trinidad, the town is the major service center for the southern part of the island, and its hinterland embraces sugar plantations, oilfields, and oil refineries.

Residential patterns

Maps have been prepared to show the distribution of the major racial and religious groups, using as a basis the forty-seven enumeration districts[2] into which the town was divided for the 1960 census (Figs. 22.2–8). For each group, there are nodes of concentration in which the group in question is over-represented compared with its proportional contribution to the total population of the town. These nodes are surrounded by areas where the group is underrepresented. Although each group evinces spatially separate nodes or sets of nodes, only rarely – except in the case of the large Negro population of the town. These nodes are surrounded by areas where the half the inhabitants in the area of greatest concentration. It is easy enough to describe the government housing schemes at Navet and Pleasantville as Negro areas; to think of St Joseph's Village and Spring Vale as white enclaves (Fig. 22.3); to locate many of San Fernando's 'old' colored families (Fig. 22.4), whose fretwork verandas overlook the Gulf of Paria from the lower slopes of Naparima Hill; or to point to the concentration of East Indians (Fig. 22.5) on the northern and southern peripheries of the town. But the fact remains that in only four enumeration districts, 8 per cent of the total, do the white, mixed, or East Indian populations, taken separately, comprise more than half the inhabitants.

The absolute size of each group is, of course, an important factor. Negroes, who account for 47 per cent of the population of San Fernando,

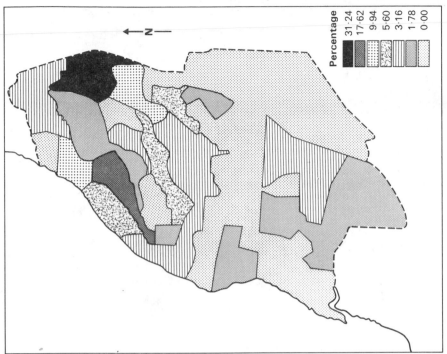

Georgr. Rev. April, 1971

Fig. 22.2 San Fernando: Negro population, 1960.

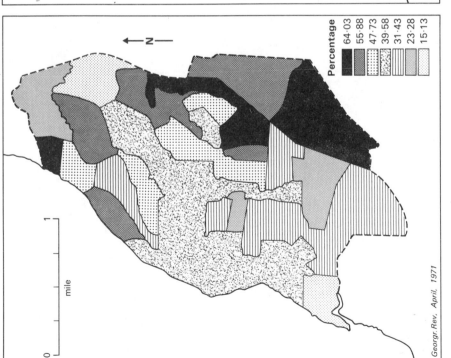

Fig. 22.3 San Fernando: white population, 1960.

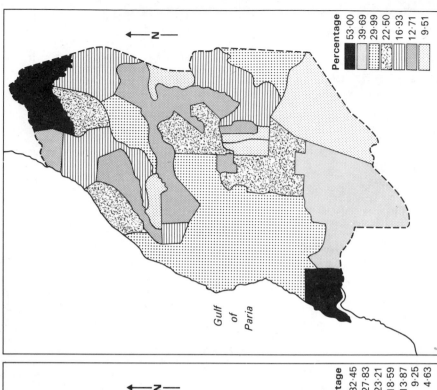

Fig. 22.5 San Fernando: East Indian population, 1960.

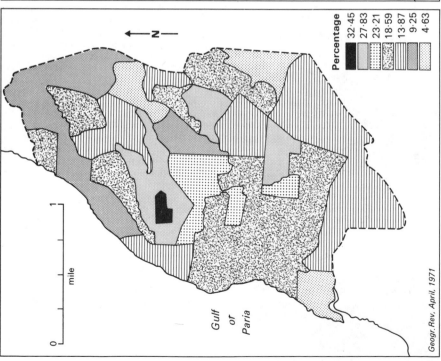

Fig. 22.4 San Fernando: mixed population, 1960.

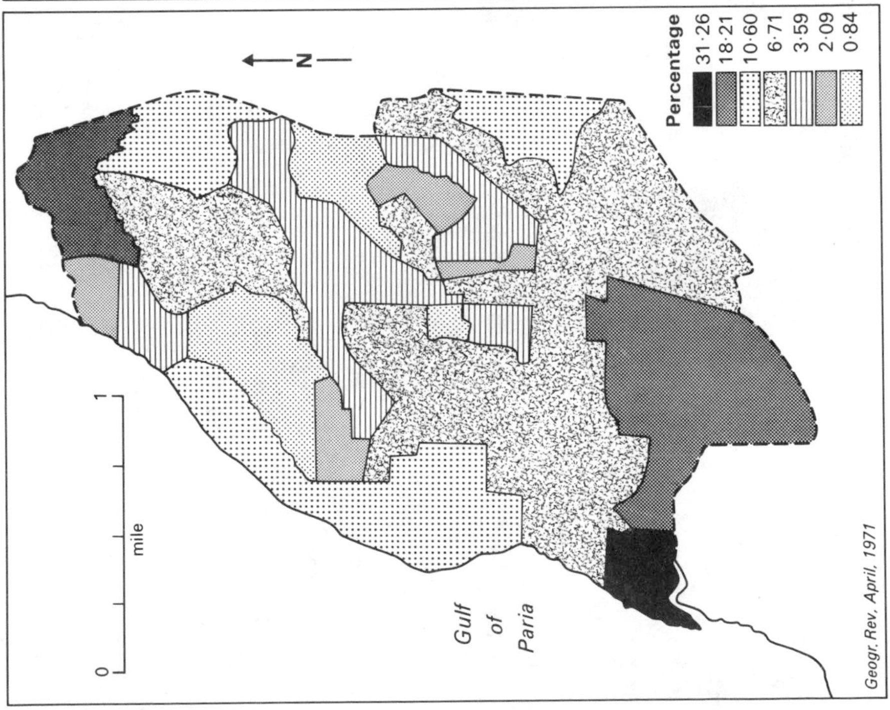

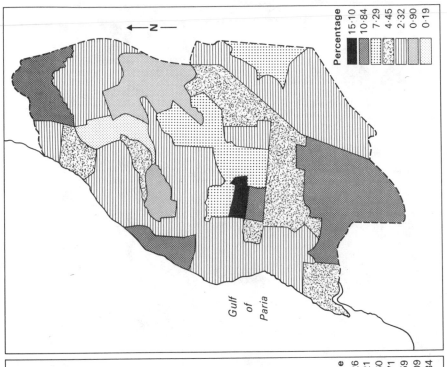

Fig. 22.7 San Fernando: Muslims, 1960.

Fig. 22.6 San Fernando: Hindu population, 1960.

Geogr. Rev, April, 1971

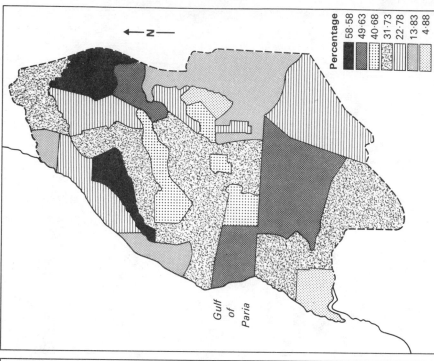

Fig. 22.9 San Fernando: males in non-manual occupations, 1960. Expressed as percentage of males in labor force

Percentage
58·58
49·63
40·68
31·73
22·78
13·83
4·88

Gulf
of
Paria

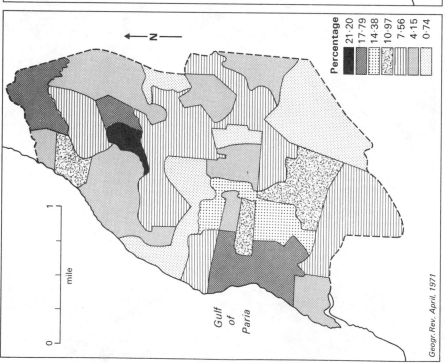

Fig. 22.8 San Fernando: Presbyterians, 1960.

Percentage
21·20
17·79
14·38
10·97
7·56
4·15
0·74

Gulf
of
Paria

Geogr. Rev. April, 1971

are the only racial element to achieve overall numerical dominance throughout several adjacent districts. Although Negroes account for more than half the population in two-fifths of the census areas, they exceed 70 per cent only in two. At the other extreme Hindus (Fig. 22.6) form a majority of the population in one enumeration district, and Muslims (Fig. 22.7) and Presbyterians (Fig. 22.8) are everywhere overshadowed by the larger groups. Nevertheless, the areas of relative concentration are important for the religious organization of the East Indians: the two Hindu nodes, at the northern and southern ends of the town respectively, support temples, and the major Muslim district possesses two mosques (Fig. 22.1). The failure of the minority groups to concentrate has an important corollary. With the exception of the small population of whites, who are absent from one-quarter of the districts, the remaining groups are represented in each census area. A major consequence of these distributions is that although Creoles dominate all but two enumeration districts, the locations of Creoles and of East Indians are polarized rather than segregated.

Indices of dissimilarity

This generalization can be examined by calculating the index of dissimilarity between Creoles and East Indians, using the enumeration-district data from the census. Whereas the maps of the racial and religious groups are based on the percentage of the population of each enumeration district who are, say, white or Hindu, the index incorporates the percentage distribution of each group by area.[3] The index of dissimilarity between Creoles and East Indians is 27 (Table 22.2), which means that 27 per cent of the East Indian population would have to change their residence to reproduce the percentage distribution recorded by the Creoles and vice versa. Although the index relates only to the proportion and not to the absolute size of the groups, it nevertheless provides a useful summary of a complex spatial relationship. Moreover, in this instance it substantiates the conclusion drawn from the maps that Creoles and East Indians are only weakly segregated.

It may be argued that the analysis so far has been tied to a specific areal base – the enumeration district – and that a change in the scale of the analysis would lead to different results. To test this the electoral rolls were searched for the addresses of East Indians. Universal adult suffrage exists in Trinidad, and an examination of voters' photographs in the electoral register for San Fernando showed that it was possible to identify East Indians accurately by their names. The rolls indicate that even where East Indians comprise more than 25 per cent of the population it is impossible to find streets that are devoid of Creoles.

Although spatial associations may be inferred from the maps, these, too, are easier to assess initially from indices of dissimilarity (Table 22.2). The

C. G. Clarke

Table 22.2 Indices of dissimilarity for racial and religious groups in San Fernando*

Group	Mixed	Negro	Hindu	Muslim	Presbyterian	East Indian
Creole			33·7	34·2	27·9	27·0
White	59·5	57·6	61·0	63·8	59·0	59·2
Mixed		21·6	31·5	30·5	24·2	22·4
Negro			32·2	34·5	27·4	27·2
Hindu				30·3	28·0	
Muslim					30·5	

* The information about the Creoles has been built up from the tabulations for the white, mixed, and Negro groups. This analysis omits the data for the Chinese and other races. No separate enumeration district material was published for the Portuguese, Caribs, and Syrians.

whites are highly segregated from all the other groups but are closer to the Negroes (57·6) than to the East Indians (59·2) or the mixed (59·5). Among the East Indians, the distribution of whites is more nearly approximated by the Presbyterians (59·0) than by the Hindus (61·0) and the Muslims (63·8). These racial and religious groups are much more highly segregated from the whites than they are from one another. The high index of dissimilarity between whites and Hindus is expressed cartographically by the enclaves of whites at St. Joseph's Village and Spring Vale (Fig. 22.3) and by the concentration of Hindus in the squatter camp at Kakatwey (Fig. 22.6). All the nonwhite groups are interrelated by indices of dissimilarity ranging from 21·6 to 34·5, or almost half those recorded for the whites. This exemplifies the isolation of the white population and hints at their social supremacy at the time of Trinidad's independence in 1962.

It is clear that the Negro and mixed populations are closer to one another in distribution than they are to either the entire East Indian population or to any one of the East Indian groups. In every instance the mixed population is closer than the Negroes to the Hindus, Muslims, or Presbyterians, though both Creole groups record low indices of dissimilarity with the Presbyterians. Although the Negroes are closer in distribution to the Hindus than to the Muslims, the mixed group is closer to the Muslims than to the Hindus. When it is remembered that the Negro and mixed populations account for about 95 per cent of the Creole inhabitants of San Fernando, it is hardly surprising that the index of dissimilarity with Creoles of all colors increases from 27·9 for Presbyterians to 33·7 and 34·2 for Hindus and Muslims respectively. In no case are the indices large.

So far as the East Indian groups are concerned, the indices of dissimilarity for Hindus and Muslims, taken separately, are greater with the Creoles than with any one East Indian element. The bifurcation between adherents of the Eastern religions and the Creoles, in terms of spatial associations, is quite marked. Furthermore, Muslims are closer to Hindus (30·3) than to Presbyterians (30·5), while Hindus are closer to Presbyterians (28·0) than to Muslims (30·3). The anomalous position of the Presbyterians within

382

the East Indian population is further emphasized in the indices they record with the mixed group (24·2) and the Negroes (27·4); these are smaller than those achieved with the Hindus (28·0) and the Muslims (30·5). However, Muslims are virtually equidistant spatially between Hindus (30·3) and Presbyterians (30·5).

The socioeconomic basis for these spatial patterns and associations deserves brief attention. The 1960 census of Trinidad published no cross-tabulations between race and occupation. To remedy this situation for San Fernando, indices of dissimilarity have been calculated between males in nonmanual occupations and the membership of the various racial and religious groups: the higher the index of dissimilarity, the greater the divergence of the category in question from the spatial pattern of white-collar workers and the lower its socioeconomic status. The two major groups, Creoles (19·2) and East Indians (17·5), achieve similar indices, though Creoles record a slightly lower socioeconomic status. Within the Creole population, the mixed group (14·0) ranks above the Negroes (21·5). It is pointless to compute the index for the whites because they are so highly segregated. But map evidence (Fig. 22.9) shows that the principal white enclaves record the highest proportions of males in nonmanual occupations. Among the East Indians, the Presbyterians (20·0) rank above the Hindus (27·5) and the Muslims (27·6).

The data on race, religion, and occupation depict a Creole population among whom whites, coloreds, and Negroes rank in decreasing order of socioeconomic status and in increasing order of numerical size and an East Indian population of approximately equal status that comprises a relatively high-ranking stratum of Presbyterians and low-ranking groups of Hindus and Muslims. Although the Hindus and Muslims in general occupy the lowest socioeconomic position in the town, the Presbyterians rank above the Negroes. The success of the Presbyterians in obtaining white-collar jobs highlights the importance of conversion as a factor in East Indian social mobility, and it is largely through the achievements of members of this group that East Indians rank marginally above the Creoles. In most cases racial and religious groups that are adjacent to one another in the socioeconomic scale are also close to one another spatially. Similar socioeconomic scores imply similar jobs and equal opportunities to obtain housing.

Spatial patterns

By no means all of the spatial patterns are explicable entirely in economic terms, nor is it always clear whether the patterns of association are causal or coincidental. Cultural factors undoubtedly play a part; for example, it seems that the greater spatial proximity between Hindu and Presbyterian than between Hindu and Muslim is attributable partly to antipathy between members of the two Eastern religious groups and above all to the fact that Christian converts have been derived principally from Hinduism. Many Presbyterians retain cultural practices of Hindu origin, and links with Hindus are frequently maintained.

People of mixed descent are closer to Hindus, Muslims, and Presbyterians than Negroes are. This is largely explained by the high proportion of Negroes who live in government housing schemes; all the other groups are virtually confined to the private sector. It is much more difficult to explain why Negroes more closely reproduce the distribution of Hindus than of Muslims, or why the mixed group are closer to Muslims than to Hindus. Perhaps chance factors are at work in situations like these where the interrelationship is of minor social importance. The equidistance of Muslims from Presbyterians and Hindus may represent the operation of stochastic processes or may even indicate that the Muslims occupy an intermediate position between poles of repulsion created by the socioeconomic distance of the Presbyterians and the antipathy of the Hindus.

It is interesting to speculate on the nature of spatial relationships, but it is also important to remember that the East Indian religious groups are to a marked degree organized internally. The presence of religious institutions in San Fernando is both influenced by and influences the location of considerable numbers of Hindus, Muslims, and Presbyterians. These groups are essentially self-centered, and their relationships with 'out' groups must be to some extent coincidental. A further factor should also be borne in mind: the East Indian suburbs on the northern and southern extremities of the town were less than five years old in 1960. They resulted from the rapid increase in the East Indian population of San Fernando and from the growing demand for homes in 'Indian' areas developed by East Indian realtors. This pattern of suburban growth was influenced by the increasing tension between East Indians and Creoles, which in turn reflected the deep involvement of race in the politics of Trinidad. These suburbs contain large numbers of socially mobile Hindus, Muslims, and Presbyterians, and their growth has also affected measures of intergroup associations among the East Indians. However, the fact that they developed at the same time as the government housing schemes has helped to increase segregation between Creoles and East Indians in recent years.

The spatial analysis indicates that there is considerable racial and religious integration at the ecological level of enquiry, underlain by socioeconomic factors. From this can be built a continuum that provides an adequate summary of the sociospatial situation in San Fernando. In the continuum the whites constitute a segregated minority located at the apex of the social scale and at a spatial and socioeconomic distance from all the other racial and religious groups. The Negro and mixed groups are closer to one another than to any other category and, numerically, comprise the greater part of Creole society. Hindus and Muslims form a distinct element and generally rank at the bottom of the social scale. Between them and the Creoles, but closer to the Creoles, are the Christian East Indians. They stand closer to the Hindus than to the Muslims in this continuum but are by no means completely acculturated to the Creole host community.

Household data

A further objective of this study is to examine patterns of intermarriage and to determine the racial and cultural composition of households sampled from each of the principal groups in the population. To facilitate the investigation several alterations of the social continuum were effected. Since Creole–East Indian relations are of primary importance in San Fernando, the Creoles were brought together as a single group. However, the dougla population was removed from the mixed group and treated as a separate element; since they are the product of mating between Creoles and East Indians, this seemed an essential step. The Hindu and Muslim groups were retained as categories for analysis, but the population of Presbyterian East Indians was expanded to include all Christians of Indian origin. Finally, for purposes of comparison with the urban East Indian groups, the Hindu population of Débé, a village some six miles to the southeast of San Fernando, was added to the continuum. Débé is almost entirely East Indian, and four-fifths of its population are Hindu. Economically, the village depends on the sugar industry and on the cultivation of pumpkins, rice, and other food crops. It is possible to rank the members of this continuum in approximate order of social and cultural proximity, using the Creoles as the starting point and moving farther away from them with each successive group: Creoles, douglas, Christian East Indians, Hindus, Muslims, Débé Hindus.

A list of adults of both sexes was obtained from the electoral roll for San Fernando. The East Indians were distinguished from the Creoles on the basis of their names, and a sample of individuals was selected at random from each group. The East Indian sample was divided into three components – Hindu, Muslim, and Christian – and these can be treated as independent samples. Similarly, a random sample was drawn from the Hindu population of Débé. Information on the dougla population of San Fernando came to light only as the questionnaire survey among the sample populations proceeded. Dougla respondents were collected from surveys among both East Indians and Creoles, and the replies they gave are possibly not fully representative of the dougla population. However, since the douglas are an important element in the racial composition of the town, and since it is impossible to secure more satisfactory information about them, this survey material has been used in the analysis; due regard was given both to the means by which the dougla respondents were obtained and to the small size of the group covered in the survey.

In addition to the information collected about each individual, questions were also asked about the household in which the respondent resided. The information for the household samples has been analyzed in three ways: to consider endogamy and exogamy for household heads, using race and religion as the criteria; to examine the race and religion of dependants of the head of the household, where the head and spouse are of the same race and same religion; and to discover the race and religion of dependants where the household head has no spouse present. The measures of endogamy and exogamy are made with reference to three racial groups (Creole, East Indian, and dougla) and three religious groups (Christian, Hindu, and Muslim). Consequently, a Creole head who marries a Christian East Indian forms a union that is racially exogamous but from the point of view of religion is endogamous. The term 'marriage' presents certain problems. As used here it includes consensual cohabitation, or concubinage, as well as legal and customary marriage. Visiting relationships are not considered directly in this study, though they may be important wherever the household head is without a resident spouse. The incidence of households of this kind is particularly high among Creoles, and in this respect they are significantly different, statistically, from the East Indians (see chi-square tests, Table 22.3).[4]

Racial and religious exogamy

The evidence relating to intermarriage between persons of different races indicates the marginality of exogamy, even when the upper limits of the sample errors for each group are taken into account. Among all unions household headship is usually invested in males, and the 'difference' in the marriage partner recorded in the tables almost invariably refers to females. Racial exogamy is particularly low for Hindus (3·1 per cent) and for Muslims (1·8 per cent), probably owing to parental influence over the choice of marriage partners. Intermarriage is conspicuously absent among the Hindus in Débé, where endogamy is the rule. This is attributable to the conservative values of rural Hindus,[5] to the overall homogeneity of the village, and to the preponderance of Hindus within it.

Creoles record the highest rates of exogamy (11·9 per cent) but are closely followed by the Christian East Indians (10·7 per cent), from whom they cannot be distinguished, statistically, in this respect. Parental control over children's behavior is known to be less strong among these two groups. The mixed racial origin of the douglas is neatly demonstrated by the sample data: exogamy exceeds endogamy. Furthermore, except for three Spanish or Portuguese spouses, the non-dougla mates comprise five East Indians and six Negroes – that is, the pattern of exogamy is divided equally between the two major groups from which the douglas have been derived.

The characteristics of the exogamous mates of Creoles and East Indians

Table 22.3   The household mix in the San Fernando and Débé samples

Household head	Race of household head					
	Creole	Hindu	Muslim	Christian East Indian	Dougla	Débé Hindu
*With no spouse present**						
Total households in samples	217	154	132	244	28	80
No spouse present – number	74	25	19	57	4	8
– percentage	*34·1*	*16·2*	*14·4*	*23·4*	*14·3*	*10·0*
±2 S.E. %(∴ at 95% level of probability)	6·3	6·0	6·0	5·3	13·2	6·6
With resident spouse of different race†						
Total households	143	129	113	187	24	72
Spouse of different race – number	17	4	2	20	14	0
– percentage	*11·9*	*3·1*	*1·8*	*10·7*	*58·3*	*0·0*
±2 S.E. %	5·3	2·8	2·4	4·4	6·3	—
With resident spouse of different religion††						
Total households	143	129	113	187	24	72
Spouse of different religion – number	1	18	13	15	1	2
– percentage	*0·7*	*14·0*	*11·5*	*8·0*	*4·2*	*2·8*
±2 S.E. %	1·4	6·1	6·0	3·9	8·1	3·9
With resident spouse of same race ‡						
Total households	126	125	111	167	10	72
Dependant of different race – number	3	1	3	5	3	2
– percentage	*2·4*	*0·8*	*2·7*	*3·0*	*30·0*	*2·8*
±2 S.E. %	2·8	1·8	3·0	2·4	9·2	3·9
With resident spouse of same religion □						
Total households	142	111	100	172	23	70
Dependant of different religion						
– number	0	19	10	11	0	5
– percentage	*0·0*	*17·1*	*10·0*	*6·4*	*0·0*	*7·1*
±2 S.E. %	—	7·0	6·3	4·8	—	5·2
With no spouse present △						
Total households	74	25	19	57	4	8
Dependant of different race – number	10	2	3	5	2	0
– percentage	*13·5*	*8·0*	*15·8*	*8·8*	*50·0*	*0·0*
±2 S.E. %	7·7	10·7	16·6	7·4	50·0	—
With no spouse present						
Total households	74	25	19	57	4	8
Dependant of different religion						
– number	0	1	9	5	0	1
– percentage	*0·0*	*4·0*	*47·4*	*8·8*	*0·0*	*12·5*
±2 S.E. %	—	7·7	22·9	7·4	—	23·4

* Total $\chi^2 = 32·72$; d.f. = 5; p < 0·001, where d.f. = degrees of freedom, and p = probability value
  Christian East Indian-Hindu $\chi^2 = 2·5$; d.f. = 1; p > 0·05
  Christian East Indian-Creole $\chi^2 = 6·0$; d.f. = 1; p < 0·01
† Christian East Indian-Creole $\chi^2 = 0·026$; d.f. = 1; p > 0·40
‡ Total $\chi^2 = 22·18$; d.f. = 5; p > 0·05
  Hindu-Christian East Indian $\chi^2 = 2·27$; d.f. = 1; p > 0·05
Total $\chi^2 = 26·42$; d.f. = 5; p < 0·001
  Hindu-Muslim $\chi^2 = 0·39$; d.f. = 1; p > 0·25
□ Hindu-Muslim-Christian East Indian $\chi^2 = 6·92$; d.f. = 2; p < 0·05
△ Creole-Hindu-Muslim-Christian East Indian $\chi^2 = 1·20$; d.f. = 3; p > 0·70

throw further light on the nature of intergroup relations. Among the seventeen non-Creole spouses married to Creoles, eleven are East Indian and six dougla. The majority of these unions are legal; consensual cohabitation is outnumbered by seven to ten. The four cases of exogamous Hindu heads record one white, one dougla, and two colored; all these unions are legal. Both the exogamous unions entered into by Muslim heads are with douglas, one legal and the other not. Four of the spouses of Christian East Indians are douglas, and the remaining sixteen have Creole mates. Seventeen of these unions are legal. Racial exogamy in San Fernando seems to be associated with marriage rather than with concubinage; intermarriage may be infrequent, but it is certainly not clandestine. Only among Creoles is exogamy associated with consensual unions. However, this is probably to be expected, since copious evidence shows that concubinage is widespread throughout the Creole societies of the Caribbean.[6] Endogamy, therefore, is the norm, except for douglas. Despite their small numbers, douglas figure prominently in the exogamous unions of all other groups.

Unions contracted across religious lines are just as infrequent, though there are significant differences among the various racial and religious groups in this respect. In San Fernando religious exogamy is highest for Hindus (14·0 per cent), Muslims (11·5 per cent), and Christians (8·0 per cent), and lowest for douglas (4·2 per cent) and Creoles (0·7 per cent). Such marriages are usually legal. The difference in frequency for Hindus and Christians is not significant at the 95 per cent level. Although it is more common for Creoles and douglas to marry out of race than out of religion, the converse is true among Hindus and Muslims. East Indian Christians again occupy an intermediate position in the system, though they record slightly higher rates of racial than of religious exogamy. The opposite holds among the Hindus at Débé (2·8 per cent), where the heterogeneity of the community is expressed (though weakly) in religious terms.

Whenever Creoles marry out of race they almost invariably unite with Christians, whether douglas or East Indians: no Creole head of household has a Hindu spouse and only one spouse is Muslim. Christian East Indians, in turn, are more than twice as likely to marry Hindus as Muslims, and this emphasizes the close links between Hindus and Christians – forged, paradoxically, through conversion. Children of mixed marriages in San Fernando are likely to adopt their mother's religion if she is Christian and less likely if she is Hindu or Muslim.

Race and religion of dependants

Generally speaking, when the household head and spouse are of the same race the dependants in the sample are identical to them. Only small numbers of these dependants are racially distinct from the head, and the difference between the groups, as measured by chi-square, is due principally to the dougla households. In none of the other groups do more than 3 per cent of the households contain persons of a race different from that of the head and spouse: douglas are prominent among these dependents. Hindu households are notably homogeneous, though not significantly different from those with Muslim heads. Only one Hindu household contains a non-Indian child; although he is an adopted son of Negro and white parentage, he has been brought up as an orthodox Hindu. In none of the three Creole households in question are the non-Creole dependants related by blood to either the head or the spouse.

The variation in the frequency of household heads having dependants of another religion is much greater. Creoles and douglas do not enter in, and the rate increases from Christian East Indians (6·4 per cent) and Muslims (10·0 per cent) to Hindus (17·1 per cent), with the Débé sample (7·1 per cent) falling between the Christian and Muslim categories. The difference between East Indian groups in San Fernando is statistically significant. Most of the dependants who occur in this analysis are in-laws of the household head. Among the Hindus, however, sixteen of the nineteen cases concern children who have been converted to Christianity.

Where the household head has no spouse present, the percentage of households with dependants of another race is greater than where there is a spouse for all groups except the Hindus at Débé. The rate increases from Hindus in Débé (0·0 per cent) to douglas (50·0 per cent). The evidence is scanty, the sample errors are large, and no statistically valid distinction can be made between the Creole, Hindu, Muslim, and Christian East Indian groups. The data may imply that households increase in heterogeneity under conditions of family breakdown; alternatively, they may indicate that interracial unions are more brittle than endogamous ones.

The presence or absence of the spouse of the household head has a less clear-cut impact on the religious affiliation of dependants. For Muslims, Christian East Indians, and Débé Hindus the frequency of households having dependants of a different religion increases when there is no spouse, but this circumstance has the opposite effect of the rate for Hindus. Moreover, Creoles and douglas record a zero frequency, as they also do wherever spouses are present. Again, the number of cases is small, and the sample errors are large. All nine Muslim households with dependants of a different religion owe their heterogeneity to conversion or to extremely complex family structures. Among Christian East Indians, however, most of the dependents are Hindu kinsmen. Although conversion contributes to the heterogeneity of households, the breakdown of the family, as measured by the absence of a spouse, possibly facilitates the formation of complex domestic units. This process is discernible among strongly paternalistic groups, especially the Muslims. The greater the authoritarianism within the family, the more drastic the consequences of any form of family breakdown.

Interpretation of the data

The household data reveal that the Creoles and the East Indians – Hindu, Muslim, and Christian – are all endogamous with respect to both racial and religious criteria. Although it is often claimed by East Indians, and especially by the Hindus, that Creoles are bent on assimilating them through inter-marriage, there is little evidence to support this. Creole heads who form unions with East Indians usually choose Christians, and they engage no more frequently in marriage with other races than their Christian East Indian counterparts. Indeed, Creole heads are less likely to cohabit with Hindu and Muslim spouses than Hindu and Muslim heads with Creole spouses. This possibly reflects the protected position of Indian women in the non-Christian religious groups. Hindu and Muslim heads are more likely to marry out of religion than out of race, and they constitute the bastions of racial endogamy. Conversely, the Christian East Indians are more likely to marry out of race than out of religion and so, too, are the douglas. These two groups form potential brokers in this socially polarized situation though their immediate roles are weak.

The sample material also demonstrates the homogeneity of most household groups and in so doing conforms to the social continuum: even the heterogeneity that exists in domestic groups among the douglas is consistent with it. Christian East Indians and douglas form links in the continuum, as their exogamous records suggest, while Hindus stand closer to the Creoles and Christians than the Muslims do. Intermarriage between Muslims and Creoles is virtually nonexistent. Hindus in Débé represent the ultraconservative end of the East Indian spectrum. Racial endogamy is complete, and religious endogamy is marked. This rural sample provides a yardstick for measuring the greater exogamy of Hindus in particular, and of East Indians in general, in San Fernando. A number of households in the town contain all three racial elements, or all three religious groupings, or mixtures of both.

Although the patterns of intergroup association established by the spatial and household analyses are similar, each analysis indicates different degrees of association among the major racial and religious groupings. The spatial data, underlain as they generally are by economic factors, suggest the absence of marked segregation, except for the whites. Conversely, the household samples reveal endogamous units that constitute separate social and cultural cells in the structure of San Fernando's society. A part of the residual between these two measures of association is explained by the scale of the settlement under study. It is likely that spatial separation and segregation are associated with size, and that small compact towns such as San Fernando tend to record low indices of dissimilarity. Furthermore, the history of the town scarcely encourages segregation. Representatives of all the groups have been resident in San Fernando for at least half a century; the new East Indian suburbs and the concentration of Negroes in the government housing schemes are the closest local approximation to ghettos. It must also be remembered that the household analysis disregards the importance of more restricted forms of endogamy and that no attempt has been made to subdivide the Christians by denomination. The preponderance of Presbyterians among the Christian East Indians in San Fernando undoubtedly inhibits contacts with Creoles belonging to other denominations.

Above all, the data depict different degrees of association at the spatial level in the public domain and at the domestic level in the private domain. The comparative prosperity of Trinidad in general, and of San Fernando in particular, is largely responsible for the high degree of spatial association, while the cultural values of the household units are reflected in endogamy and social separation. It may be argued that the relatively high degree of association in the public domain is more important, and that the choice of a marriage partner is a private concern. However, the Eastern religions, to take an extreme example, apply a brake on racial exogamy, and endogamy forms the basis for the segmentation of the community. Nevertheless, this does not imply that the Hindus and Muslims are not an integral part of Trinidad society. There are many other mechanisms for integrating them into the urban structure of San Fernando and the polity of Trinidad.

The major problem stems from the fact that the principal endogamous segments – Creoles, Hindus, Muslims, and Christian East Indians – exist as categories that can be, and are, organized and manipulated by politicians. It is most unfortunate that national politics excite intersegmental friction, especially between Creoles and Hindus, and that political activities have immediate racial and cultural implications, impinge on the pattern of urban development in San Fernando, and possibly inhibit intermarriage still further. The lack of intermarriage is a critical index in San Fernando, not because intermarriage is in itself a good thing (in many complex societies it may be irrelevant), but because the endogamous segments provide the social and cultural basis on which manipulators can work and on which political parties are built.

Notes and References

An earlier version of this paper was read at the twenty-eighth annual meeting of the Society for Applied Anthropology, held in Mexico City, 9–15 April 1969. The study is based on fieldwork carried out in Trinidad in 1964, with the support of the Research Institute for the Study of Man, New York.

1. *Dougla* is the Hindi word for bastard.
2. The urban area comprises forty-five enumeration districts listed under San

391

Fernando in the 1960 census (district number forty-eight is omitted because it is a hospital) (*Trinidad and Tobago Population Census* 1960, vol. 1, Part B). In addition, there are Victoria Naparima ninety-two and ninety-three, with a total population of 2,096. These two districts were not treated as part of San Fernando for the purpose of the cross tabulation that appears in Table 22.1, but they are important suburbs and have been included in the map analysis, the indices of dissimilarity, and the sample selection of households.

3. For a detailed discussion of the calculation and use of indices of dissimilarity, see Stanley Lieberson, *Ethnic Patterns in American Cities*, Free Press of Glencoe, 1963, 30–40.

4. Table 22.3 contains data for independent samples. Chi-square has been used to test the significance of the difference between three or more samples and between selected pairs of samples. Where three or more samples are examined together, the average rate of, say, exogamy is calculated and used to compute the expected frequency; the null hypotheses that are tested state that the conditions being examined are distributed at random among the samples. The tests carried out on selected pairs of samples employ 2×2 contingency tables, and the null hypotheses argue that there is no significant difference between the values recorded in the two populations. This set of calculations incorporates corrections for continuity.

5. For a description of rural Hindus, see Arthur Niehoff and Juanita Niehoff, 'East Indians in the West Indies', *Milwaukee Public Museum Publs. in Anthropology, no. 6*, 1960; Morton Klass, *East Indians in Trinidad* (New York and London, 1961).

6. M. G. Smith, *West Indian Family Structure*, Seattle, 1962, provides detailed documentation for several diverse communities.

Part VI

Distance, segregation and marriage

Ruby Jo Reeves Kennedy

23 Premarital residential propinquity and ethnic endogamy*

Propinquity of residence appears to be an increasingly important determinant in the selection of marriage partners in New Haven. In 1931 almost two-thirds of all New Haven residents getting married in that city lived within twenty blocks of one another.[1] A similarly high degree of closely propinquitous addresses (63·19 per cent) was true of Philadelphians marrying in Philadelphia in that same year.[2] In 1940 this phenomenon was even more pronounced in New Haven. More than three-fourths of its residents marrying in the city lived within twenty blocks of one another, an increase of 12 per cent over 1931 (see Table 23.1).

The trend to increased propinquity was marked in every distance category. There was even an increase in marriages of persons living at the same address. Correspondingly, there was a decided decline in marriages

Table 23.1 Distribution of marriages by residential propinquity before marriage in New Haven in 1931 and 1940

Number of blocks apart	Number of cases		Per cent	
	1931	1940	1931	1940
Within twenty	480	892	64·43	76·31
Over twenty	265	277	35·57	23·69
Total	745	1,169	100·00	100·00

of persons living more than twenty blocks apart (from 35·37 to 23·69 per cent) (see Table 23.2).

* Reprinted from *American Journal of Sociology*, **48**, no. 5 (1943), 580–4.

Table 23.2 Cumulative percentage distribution of residential propinquity before marriage in New Haven in 1931 and 1940*

Number of blocks apart	Per cent	
	1931	1940
Same address	9·05	9·92
Within five	33·30	35·79
Within ten	55·44	55·48
Within twenty	64·43	76·31
Over twenty	35·57	23·69
Total	100·00	100·00

* The percentages are cumulative up to the twenty-block range. Cases where one of the contracting parties was not a resident of New Haven have been eliminated from this study.

From Table 23.3 it is readily apparent that through the years certain groups (e.g. Italians, Negroes) have remained highly propinquitous in their mate selection. Others, previously less so, showed a sharp increase in propinquitous marriage between 1931 and 1940. The degree of residential proximity and its tendency to increase differ among the groups, as shown in Table 23.3. Particularly marked was the trend toward propinquitous marriage among Negroes and British-Americans within the five-block range, among Poles, Irish, British-Americans, and Germans within the ten-block distance; and among Jews, Irish, British-Americans, and Germans within twenty blocks. That the Italians do not figure in this ranking of high propinquity trends is due not to a lessening of propinquitous marriages among them but rather to their already pronounced rate in 1931. The over-all picture of increasing propinquity appears clearly in the decline of marriages between persons living more than twenty blocks apart for every group except the Negroes. The Negro irregularity is due to the recent scattering of small segments of the colored population to two or three new zones of residence far removed from their main Negro area. The general pattern of lessening distance between premarital abodes is further emphasized by the appreciable tendency, in every group except the Irish, toward marriages between persons living five or fewer blocks apart. Their 13 per cent increase of marriages within ten or fewer blocks, however, brings the Irish into line with the general trend (see Table 23.3).

Since marriage on a neighborhood basis (within twenty blocks) is on the increase among nearly all groups in New Haven's population, the question arises: Is the increase in propinquitous marriage due to ethnic-endogamy? The best way of securing an answer is to examine the distribution of 'in' and 'out'[3] marriages for each nationality and racial group in the various distance ranges.

Table 23.3 Premarital residential propinquity for each ethnic group in New Haven in 1931 and 1940*

| | Number of blocks apart | | | | | | | |
| | Within Five | | Within ten | | Within twenty | | Over twenty | |
Groups	1931	1940	1931	1940	1931	1940	1931	1940
Negro	57·14	70·35	82·86	74·06	96·30	88·88	3·70	11·12
Jewish	29·58	33·93	54·93	62·49	76·06	89·28	23·94	10·72
Italian	33·75	36·21	53·09	57·12	70·37	76·31	29·63	23·69
Polish	31·59	32·90	37·85	52·64	57·89	68·43	42·11	31·57
Irish	25·74	24·04	36·03	49·62	56·51	69·00	43·49	31·00
British–American	21·85	36·04	37·82	56·20	57·98	69·55	42·02	30·45
German	25·40	31·48	33·33	50·00	50·79	72·21	49·21	27·79
Total	33·30	35·79	55·44	55·48	64·43	76·31	35·57	23·69

* Only major groups are included. Those having fewer than twenty marriages were omitted since generalizations based on such limited numbers would be weak.

While two-thirds of all the marriages in New Haven in 1940 were 'in' unions, Negroes, Jews, and Italians – with 94·4, 90·1, and 85·5 per cent, respectively – led all other groups (see first two rows in Table 23.4). This strong pattern of 'in' marriage reflects the special solidarity existing in these three groups, which is accentuated by the fact that each forms its own area of residence, within which selection of marriage partners is more common than among the other groups (see Table 23.4).

We may take 66·7 per cent as the normal standard of measurement for 'in' marriage, since it indicates the over-all behavior of the entire community. We may then compare the conformity of each group with reference to it, and thus determine the relationship which propinquity bears to this as well as to the 'out' marriage standard of 33·3 per cent. Clearly, there is a high correlation between 'in' marriage and premarital distances of twenty blocks or less. Correspondingly, 'out' exceed 'in' marriages when more than twenty blocks separate premarital addresses of spouses. The Irish are the only exception; and explanation for this irregularity is offered below.

The ethnic groups in which the proportion of 'in' unions exceeds the 66·7 norm (Negroes, Jews, and Italians) rank highest in propinquitous marriages of less than twenty blocks; while groups whose 'out' marriage rate exceeds the general standard of 33·3 per cent (Poles, Irish, British-Americans, and Germans) have much higher proportions of unions between persons living more than twenty blocks apart (see Tables 23.3 and 4). Here, then, are three factors creating geographical boundaries within which mate selection ordinarily occurs: (1) a divergent and clannish religion in the case of the Jews, (2) race in the case of the Negroes, and (3) a

Table 23.4   Premarital residential propinquity for 'in' and 'out' marriages of each ethnic group in New Haven in 1940*

	Total	Negro	Jewish	Italian	Polish	Irish	British–American	German
Per cent 'In'	66·7	94·4	90·1	85·5	56·5	58·8	48·5	37·8
Per cent 'Out'	33·3	5·6	8·9	14·5	43·5	41·2	51·5	72·2
Blocks apart:								
Five								
'In'	36·7	70·6	32·7	37·8	32·6	18·2	36·8	20·0
'Out'	34·3	66·7	36·4	26·7	33·3	30·2	35·3	35·9
Ten								
'In'	57·8	74·5	63·4	58·4	65·1	40·9	52·6	53·3
'Out'	51·4	66·7	54·5	49·2	36·4	58·7	50·9	48·7
Twenty								
'In'	78·3	90·2	89·1	80·1	74·4	60·6	70·6	73·3
'Out'	73·3	66·7	81·8	74·6	60·6	77·8	68·6	71·8
Over twenty								
'In'	21·7	9·8	10·9	19·9	25·6	39·4	29·4	26·7
'Out'	26·7	33·3	18·2	25·4	39·4	22·2	31·4	28·2

* The percentages in this table indicate the proportions of all 'in' and 'out' marriages, respectively, which fall within each of the distance ranges. The percentages are cumulative up to the twenty-block range.

high degree of ethnocentrism, cultural peculiarities, and persistent Old World folkways among the Italians, owing in part to their relatively large numbers.[4] These factors operate to isolate these three groups geographically and maritally; each lives in its own area and marries within that area. However, the increasing tendency of other groups, formerly less propinquitous – the Poles, Irish, Germans, and British-Americans – in the direction of propinquitous marriage, further suggests a gradually increasing tightening of all social, and hence residential, barriers between the various nationality groups in the city. This is even further corroborated by the fact that the Irish, who registered a decrease in very propinquitous marriages (within five blocks) in 1940, are much more likely to go beyond twenty blocks for their mates if they are also Irish than if they are not. It seems clear, therefore, that cultural, especially religious, ties still hold, even in long-distance marriages, among the Irish. This is not true, however, of any of the other groups, for in each of them greater residential distance is much more likely to accompany 'out' than 'in' marriage (see Table 23.4).

To test further the possibility that there is in New Haven an increasing tendency toward the development of segregated communities based upon ethnic, racial, and religious characteristics, the addresses of couples were analyzed according to the ecological units or 'natural areas' into which the city of New Haven has been divided. The method by which these areas were derived and a description of their predominant traits have been reported elsewhere.[5] Twenty-two residential areas have been distinguished.

Table 23.5 shows the distribution of marriages according to premarital residence of 1,112 couples, or 2,224 individuals. This is a smaller number of cases than that upon which the foregoing statements have been based. For the ensuing ecological analysis, the total of 1,169 couples married in New Haven in 1940 had to be reduced by the elimination of thirty-nine instances where one or both of the contracting parties did not dwell in areas predominantly residential and of eighteen cases where either bride or groom was residing in a given area solely because of employment there as a servant.

The relationship between ecological residence and marriage selection may be observed more readily by classifying the twenty-two areas into three major groups as follows ('predominant' is taken to mean more than one-half):

A. Predominantly foreign-born; Catholic; laborers and artisans – low income: Areas III, IV, V, VI, XII, XIII.
B. Predominantly mixed nativity; mixed religion; laborers, artisans, office workers, dealers, and proprietors – low to median income; which may be subdivided as follows:
   1. Predominantly mixed nativity; Catholic; laborers, artisans, and office workers – low income: Areas VII, X, XI, XIX, XXII.
   2. Predominantly mixed nativity; mixed religion; artisans, office workers, dealers, and proprietors – median income: Areas II, XV, XVI, XVIII, XXI.
   3. Predominantly mixed nativity: Protestant; artisans, office workers, dealers, and proprietors – median income: Areas VIII, XIV, XX.
C. Predominantly native American; Protestant; professionals, business executives, office workers – high income: Areas I, XVII.

One of the most interesting situations disclosed by this analysis is that in 42·8 per cent of the cases the marriage-contracting parties lived in the same area (see Table 23.5). This is especially significant in view of the small size of most of the areas. They range in maximum extent from four to thirty-two blocks, averaging about eleven blocks. Only two areas show a maximum distance range of twenty or more blocks. If to these cases are added those of individuals marrying within like areas (30 per cent), then nearly three-fourths (72·8 per cent) of all persons marrying within the city chose mates residing in similar types of neighborhood. Very little intermarriage (5·7 per cent) occurred between areas markedly dissimilar in social, economic, and cultural traits.

Contrasting these facts with those disclosed for 1931, we find that almost no change occurred in the proportions of marriages involving parties from the same area (43·4 per cent in 1931) and from like areas (30·4 per cent in 1931) (see Table 23.5). On the other hand, the slight decrease in percentage (from 22·5 in 1931 to 21·5 in 1940) of marriages between persons from related areas is accounted for in part by the increase of marriages

399

between persons residing in dissimilar areas (from 3·7 in 1931 to 7·5 per cent in 1940) (see Table 23.5). For instance, in the areas inhabited predominantly by the foreign-born who are Catholics, laborers, and artisans having low incomes (major group A: Areas III, IV, V, VI, XII, and XIII) there has been a marked increase of marriages involving dissimilar areas (see Table 23.5). Likewise, in areas populated predominantly by native

Table 23.5 Percentage distribution of individuals marrying in New Haven in 1931 and 1940, by premarital residence according to type of Area

| | Area types | | | | | | | |
| | In same* | | In like† | | In related‡ | | In dissimilar # | |
Areas	1931	1940	1931	1940	1931	1940	1931	1940
I	50·0	37·5	8·3	12·5	41·7	25·0	—	25·0
II	18·2	24·3	54·6	43·9	13·6	9·8	13·6	22·0
III	45·0	26·2	32·5	50·0	22·5	13·1	—	10·7
IV	44·0	51·7	39·0	32·4	17·0	13·1	—	2·8
V	49·2	30·8	45·9	56·0	4·9	12·1	—	1·1
VI	43·9	42·7	31·6	32·6	23·2	20·2	1·3	4·5
VII	38·0	34·4	27·6	22·6	31·1	43·0	3·2	—
VIII	36·3	29·1	22·7	40·0	—	—	41·0	30·9
IX	—	33·3	26·6	29·2	66·7	37·5	6·7	—
X	10·5	42·9	42·1	30·4	42·1	25·0	5·3	1·7
XI	32·0	33·3	40·0	15·3	24·0	51·4	4·0	—
XII	60·2	56·4	16·8	18·3	22·6	21·6	0·4	3·7
XIII	34·7	8·3	52·2	41·7	13·1	41·7	—	8·3
XIV	32·5	34·8	40·5	37·7	2·7	—	24·3	27·5
XV	52·0	48·2	25·9	25·7	20·2	25·6	1·9	0·5
XVI	32·6	32·8	32·6	35·3	25·5	27·9	9·3	4·0
XVII	29·6	11·1	3·7	11·1	55·6	5·6	11·1	72·2
XVIII	36·4	22·2	27·2	22·2	36·4	50·0	—	5·6
XIX	—	—	50·0	100·0	50·0	—	—	—
XX	—	37·5	50·0	43·8	—	6·2	50·0	12·5
XXI	25·0	39·6	42·8	34·0	32·2	23·6	—	2·8
XXII	13·3	20·7	60·0	51·7	20·0	27·6	6·7	—
Total	43·4	42·8	30·4	30·0	22·5	21·5	3·7	5·7

* Both parties before marriage lived in the same one of the twenty-two areas.
† Both parties before marriage lived in areas that fall in the same major grouping, e.g., both in Group A.
‡ The two parties before marriage resided in areas falling in different, yet closely related, major groups.
# One of the contracting parties lived in an area falling in a major group least related to the area where the other party resided.

Americans who are Protestants employed as professionals, business executives, or office workers earning high incomes (major group C: Areas I and XVII), there has been an increase in the number of marriages involving dissimilar areas (see Table 23.5). On the other hand, in sections populated largely by Catholics of mixed nativity who are laborers, artisans, or office workers having low incomes (major group B, 1: Areas VII, IX, X, XI, XIX, and XX), there has been a pronounced decrease in marriages between persons from dissimilar areas (see Table 23.5). Over-all, however, very little change has occurred between 1931 and 1940, and the conclusions of the former year still apply in New Haven:

> Analysis of all the marriage licenses . . . has shown . . . that in the vast majority of cases marriage is an in-group affair, that is, the two contracting parties tend to be of the same race, nationality, religion, and socio-economic status. Urban ecological studies have disclosed that the population tends to be segregated spatially according to the same traits. Thus the coincidence of these two tendencies goes far to explain the factor of residential propinquity in marriage selection.[6]

A special analysis of the sixty-three marriages in 1940 between parties residing in dissimilar ecological areas of the city shows that more than half (58·8 per cent) were 'in' unions. In some groups an even higher proportion of the marriages involving dissimilar areas were of this type. This was true for all the Jewish marriages, 80 per cent of the Italian, and 77 per cent of the British-American. This indicates that the 2 per cent increase of marriages between partners residing in dissimilar ecological areas does not imply a corresponding increase of marriages between different ethnic, racial, and religious groups. Rather does it suggest a gradual change in the character of the areas, which is only to be expected in view of the sharp decline in the foreign-born population and the recent development of rehousing projects in several areas. The facts at hand point to shiftings in the location of homogeneous communities rather than to their disappearance and an increasingly firm integration of each on ethnic, religious, and racial lines as disclosed by the rising trend toward 'neighborhood' marriages.

Notes and References

1. Maurice R. Davie and Ruby Jo Reeves Kennedy, 'Propinquity of residence before marriage', *Am. J. Sociol.*, **44**, (Jan. 1939), 510–17.
2. James H. S. Bossard, 'Residential propinquity as a factor in marriage selection', *Am. J. Sociol.*, **38**, (Sept. 1932), 219–24.
3. 'In' marriage refers to a union between two persons of the same ethnic stock, whereas 'out' marriage implies a crossing of ethnic lines. Exceptions are the Jews, among whom religion rather than nationality is the criterion, and the Negroes, among whom race is the distinguishing feature.
4. Italians comprise about 40 per cent of all persons of foreign white stock in New Haven.
5. M. R. Davie, 'The pattern of urban growth', *Studies in the Science of Society*, ed. G. P. Murdock, 1937, 133–61.
6. Davie and Reeves, *op. cit.*, 517.

M. R. Koller

24 Residential propinquity of white mates at marriage in relation to age and occupation of males, Columbus, Ohio 1938 and 1946 *

Pioneer work by James Bossard in Philadelphia, 1931, suggested that residential propinquity of mates at the time of marriage is a factor in mate selection. Dr Bossard examined five thousand consecutive marriage licenses in which one or both of the applicants were residents of Philadelphia. The study found that one out of four couples lived within two city blocks of each other; one third of the couples lived within five blocks or less of each other. In an apt statement, Dr Bossard concludes: 'Cupid may have wings, but apparently they are not adapted for long flights.'[1] Follow-up studies by Maurice R. Davie and Ruby Reeves in New Haven, Connecticut, 1931; Dr W. A. Anderson in Genessee County, New York, 1934, and Carmella Frell in Warren, Ohio, 1947 confirmed Dr Bossard's original hypothesis.

It was the purpose of the present study to apply more rigorous techniques to determine the validity of residential propinquity as a factor in mate selection in Columbus, Ohio.

The first refinement of Bossard's study was to shift the years of study away from the 'Depression' of the early thirties. The possibility that the economic conditions of 1931 were responsible for Dr Bossard's findings had to be eliminated. By selecting 1938 as a year well removed from the trough of the economic cycle and yet not a year closely connected with World War II and 1946 as the post-war year, this possibility was eliminated. The war years themselves were not used, since residence was often waived as a licensing requirement. If a high degree of residential propinquity showed itself in these years, then its long run effect could be presumed.

The second change from Bossard's study was to discard information relating to Negroes as far as possible. Dr Bossard had included them in

* Reprinted from *American Sociological Review*, **13** (1948), 613–16.

his study, admitting that one-ninth of the city's population was Negro. The elimination of Negroes from our sample was done because Negroes do not have the freedom to move about a city compared to whites and hence are forced to live in segregated areas.

A third refinement was to employ the standard city block equal to one-eighth of a mile as the unit of measurement rather than to count individual city blocks 'as if' they were equal. City blocks vary in length within cities and between cities. The use of the standard city block enables future studies to secure comparative data upon which we shall finally base our conclusions concerning the importance of residential propinquity as a factor in mate selection.

Dr Bossard's study dealt with the first five months of the year and did not deal with those people who married in the last seven months of the year. To make sure that all couples in all twelve months would have a chance to be selected for study, a sampling technique of selecting the first fifty couples each month, starting with the first of the month and an additional fifty couples starting with the fifteenth of the month, or one hundred couples per month was employed.

A fifth refinement was to study solely the couples who were both residents of the city of Columbus, Ohio, and adjacent incorporated suburbs. A pilot study preliminary to defining the universe was run to determine how many of the couples marrying in Franklin County, the county in which Columbus is located, were both residents of the city. Over 70 per cent of those applying for a marriage license at the Franklin County Courthouse were both city residents. It was therefore decided to study only those couples who were both city residents rather than mix an urban and a rural study of distance between the homes of couples about to be married.

Lastly, Dr Bossard's work was carried a bit further by investigating two factors which might possibly help explain whatever residential propinquity was found. These were the age and occupation of the male. The age of the man was used because there is the greater probability of accuracy with men due to the alleged tendency of women to under- or over-state their age. Occupation for men was regarded as more important since the occupation of the woman tends either to end with marriage or is less permanent.

Summarizing the hypotheses implemented by the study:

1. Residential propinquity is a factor in mate selection for white mates who were both residents of the city of Columbus, Ohio, 1938 and 1946.
2. Residential propinquity is in part a function of (*a*) age and (*b*) occupation of males in Columbus, Ohio, 1938 and 1946.

It was possible to succeed in the original plan to take 1,200 cases in 1946 as there were adequate numbers. In 1938, however, the numbers were considerably smaller and therefore the sampling in 1938 yielded only 1,132 cases. The total cases handled by the study amounted to 2,332 cases.

Questions arise as to the adequacy and representativeness of the sample. With approximately 200 couples marrying each month the sampling amounted to close to a 50 per cent sample of the total universe. Dr Perry Denune has run studies in the past on Franklin County marriages in which he took only the first forty cases per month starting with the first of each month. He then has made studies of the entire universe and in plotting their curves finds that his sample of forty closely parallels that of the total universe. The sample, then, of 100 cases per month and spread over the month would seem quite adequate and give every opportunity for the major characteristics of the universe to manifest themselves.

The residences of both the male and female on each license were pinpointed on a large map of Columbus from the Office of the City Engineer. The closest possible distance in standard city blocks was desired. In the face of obstacles such as rivers, railroad tracks, golf courses, large estates, undeveloped areas, and large state institutions it was necessary to measure around them. For example, a couple whose residences faced each other across the river could not be measured in city blocks directly across the river but rather around the river to the nearest bridge and thence to the residence of the individual concerned.

The assembled data indicated very clearly that the refinements of Dr Bossard's study when applied to Columbus, Ohio, for 1938 and 1946 sustained Dr Bossard's original findings. The men tended to select women in the city who lived near the men's homes. Criticism that Bossard's study might have been influenced by the 'Depression', by the inclusion of Negroes, by the treatment of all city blocks as equal, or by the sampling technique is not supported by this study in Columbus. In 51 per cent of the 1,132 cases studied in Columbus, Ohio, 1938, the men selected a girl living within twelve standard city blocks. In 1946, 50 per cent of 1,200 men selected a girl living within fifteen standard city blocks. Combining the cases of 1938 and 1946, a total of 1,205 or 51 per cent of 2,332 cases chose a mate living within fourteen standard city blocks.

Analysis of the frequency distributions found for both years into quartiles yields the following table.

Residential propinquity of mates in standard
city blocks in Columbus, Ohio, 1938, 1946,
and total, by quartiles.

Quartiles	1938	1946	Total
Q 1	2·85	3·43	3·14
Q 2	11·75	14·69	13·33
Q 3	31·00	31·53	31·72
Q	14·08	14·05	14·29

There appears to be little difference in the degree of residential propinquity in the samples for 1938 and 1946. In both years one-fourth of all the white mates lived about three standard city blocks apart. In both years three-fourths of all the cases lived within thirty-one standard city blocks of each other. In 1938, half the couples were about twelve standard city blocks apart whereas in 1946 half the couples were about fifteen standard city blocks apart. The semi-interquartile range remained about fourteen standard city blocks for both years.

The potential criticism, that residential propinquity as found by this study might be nothing more than the operation of chance due to the selected nature of the sample universe, needs to be answered. Would any group of women and men with the common characteristics of being white, both city residents, and marriage license applicants in a given year on the basis of chance also select each other as future mates? If a close degree of residential propinquity was found for people who had these characteristics and yet had not selected each other as mates, the operation of the residential propinquity factor by sheer chance would be established.

The case records used in the study were thoroughly shuffled and 200 cases were taken at random for each year. By plotting the residence of the male of the first card and the residence of the female on the second card, 100 men and 100 women who did not select each other as mates and yet who possessed the three common characteristics mentioned above were measured relative to their degree of residential propinquity. The degree of residential propinquity of these 'chance couples' varied markedly from the degree of residential propinquity found for those couples who had actually selected each other as future mates. One-fourth of the 'chance couples' lived within seventeen standard city blocks whereas one-fourth of the actual couples lived within three standard city blocks of each other's homes. The median for the chance sample was about twenty-nine blocks whereas for the couples who selected each other the median was about thirteen blocks. The upper quartile for the chance sample was about forty-three blocks whereas the couples about to be married had an upper quartile of thirty-two blocks. These findings indicate that something other than chance explains the close degree of residential propinquity found between the couples studied.

Analysis of the frequency distributions of the various age groups and occupations of the men studied in 1938 and 1946 indicates possible factors operative in the degree of residential propinquity.

Rank order of medians of age groups by
standard city blocks, 1938 and 1946

1938	Age group	Median
	24–27	16·21
	32–35	15·00

	28–31	14·83
	20–23	10·64
	Over 35	6·66
1946	*Age group*	*Median*
	24–27	18·00
	20–23	15·30
	28–31	13·88
	32–35	13·25
	Over 35	7·83

Dividing the frequency distributions for age groups in quartiles reveals again the close degree of residential propinquity for each age group for each year . . . the results varying with each age group. The age group 24–27 consistently demonstrated the greatest distance in standard city blocks. The age group over 35 consistently demonstrated the closest degree of residential propinquity. The group 28 to 31 consistently remained in the middle between the age group 24–27 and the age group over 35. Other age groups were erratic in their behavior. Age appears to be partially related to the degree of residential propinquity but no generalization would be correct unless it was qualified by stating the age group concerned and the time span involved. Critical ratios of 3·880 and 3·414 were found between the age groups 24 to 27 and the group over 35 for 1938 and 1946 respectively. In 1938 a critical ratio of 2·626 was found between the age group 28 to 31 and the over 35 group. In 1946 a critical ratio of 2·670 was found between the age group 20 to 23 and the over 35 group. In other words, the differences between these groups were significant differences. Differences between other age groups yielded no significant differences.

Rank order of medians of occupational groups by
standard city blocks, 1938 and 1946

1938	*Occupational group*	*Median*
	Clerical and sales	17·38
	Professional and	
	managerial	15·94
	Skilled	10·30
	Semi-skilled	9·33
	Service	8·63
	Unskilled	2·83
1946	*Occupational group*	*Median*
	Professional and	
	managerial	18·50
	Clerical and sales	15·25
	Skilled	13·90
	Service	13·33

Semi-skilled	11·17
Unskilled	4·79

A similar study of the occupations of the males yielded more significant data. In general, the higher a man ranged on the occupational scale the greater the distance in standard city blocks in which he selected his future mate. The lower the occupational position, the greater the degree of residential propinquity found. Professional and managerial men had a median frequency of about sixteen to eighteen standard city blocks between themselves and their future wives whereas the unskilled men married girls living within three to five standard city blocks.

The findings of this study sustain the original hypothesis, namely that residential propinquity is a factor in mate selection for white mates who were both city residents of Columbus, Ohio, 1938 and 1946 and that residential propinquity is explainable, in part, as a function of (*a*) age and (*b*) occupation of males in Columbus, Ohio, 1938 and 1946. Generalizations applied to age and occupational groups are not wholly correct unless one specifies which age group or which occupational group in a given year he means.

What interpretation should be given these findings? What social inference can we find here? If our findings are correct, then some of Bossard's original ideas that there are 'social types in urban communities' who tend to marry may be correct. It is further suggested that because residential propinquity is operative in the city, the parents of boys and girls of marriageable age have unconsciously helped select their son's or daughter's mates by choosing to live in a given urban area. There appears to be a stronger than fifty-fifty chance that a young boy or girl in the city will marry someone living very close to his residence. Here, we might have a predictive device of great value.

We must be very cautious, however, before we generalize too freely about residential propinquity. Thus far the studies have dealt with marriage license applications. The findings must be supplemented by additional research, such as interviews, to determine if the residency reported in the documents are more apparent than real. More research using similar methods to this one should be undertaken to check these findings in Columbus. More researches using different methods are also welcomed as they might reveal discrepancies that cannot appear in a statistical study.

With Bossard then, we repeat, 'Yes, Cupid has wings but he doesn't fly very far. And even with five per cent bus fare, he still prefers to remain close to home.'

M. R. Koller

Notes and References

* Paper read before the annual meeting of the Ohio Valley Sociological Society, Columbus, Ohio, 24 April, 1948.
1. J. H. S. Bossard, *Marriage and Family*, University of Pennsylvania Press, 1940, ch. 4, 'Residential propinquity as a factor in marriage', pp. 79–92.

W. R. Catton, Jr. and R. J. Smircich

25 A comparison of mathematical models for the effect of residential propinquity on mate selection*

The idea that mate selection involves a 'propinquity factor' is well established in the sociology of family behavior. Evidence to support this idea usually takes the form of a frequency distribution or cumulative percentages of marriages in some community, classified by the distance separating bride's residence from groom's residence just prior to marriage.[1]

Table 25.1 Distribution of a one-month sample of Seattle marriage license applications by distance between groom's residence and bride's residence*

— Distance†	Number of couples	Cumulative percentage
Miles		
0·00 to 0·49	81	19·61
0·50 to 0·99	34	27·82
1·00 to 1·49	31	35·32
1·50 to 1·99	31	42·82
2·00 to 2·49	25	48·87
2·50 to 2·99	23	54·44
3·00 to 3·99	42	65·14
4·00 to 4·99	30	72·40
5·00 to 5·99	25	78·45
6·00 to 7·99	30	85·71
8·00 to 9·99	21	90·79
10·00 to 15·99	20	95·63
16·00 and over	20	100·00

* Seattle residents only.
† Zone widths vary so that no zone frequency is less than 20.

* Reprinted from *American Sociological Review*, **29** (1964) 522–9.

Almost no attempts have been made, however, to fit these distributions with a mathematical model.[2] Several hypothetical explanations for the regularity have been suggested, but not in precise quantitative terms.[3]

These crude procedures understate the extent to which mate selection is limited by residential propinquity. This can be readily seen in a sample of Seattle marriages. In the first column of Table 25.1, the frequency distribution is similar to those obtained in previous studies elsewhere. When these figures are converted to cumulative percentages, as shown in the second column, it is clear that a majority of grooms were residing within three miles of their brides at the time they applied for marriage licenses. This is as far as most propinquity studies have carried the analysis and interpretation of their data. In what follows, we will show that the effects of propinquity are more dramatic than has been apparent from the usual *treatment of the data*, but less dramatic than the usual *interpretation* implies. Because the usual treatment doesn't carry the analysis far enough, some theoretical implications of the propinquity pattern have been overlooked.

The prevalent normative interpretation

Sociological literature on marriage and the family contains abundant references to 'assortative mating', and to norms of endogamy and exogamy. A wealth of evidence supports the conclusion that marriages are predominantly homogamous with respect to the many dimensions of population heterogeneity. In keeping with a prevalent assumption,[4] sociologists are in the habit of explaining this homogamy as the result of norms. The propinquity studies, however, may indicate that the norms arise from the fact of homogamy rather than vice versa.[5]

Propinquity is treated differently in different family textbooks. The variety of treatment suggests some uncertainty in sociological thought as to the true relations between norms and behavior. Fairly clear distinctions can be made among the following five types of response to the findings on propinquity in mate selection. Each type is represented in one or more currently used textbooks on the family.

Type I – propinquity not mentioned. Some texts give no information on propinquity as such, and describe mate selection in terms of such factors as Oedipal conflicts, the search for a parent substitute, cultural and legal influences, rules of endogamy and exogamy, family influences, an Ego ideal, neurosis, and complementary personality needs.[6] In short, selective mating is explained voluntaristically, normatively, or social-psychologically.

Type II – propinquity as merely reflecting homogamy. Some texts 'explain away' the propinquity findings as a mere artifact of residential segregation combined with normative pressures for like to marry like.[7] In this view, physical distance has no independent effect on mate selection, either in terms of time and energy costs, or even in terms of intervening courtship opportunities.

Type III – propinquity as opportunity. Physical proximity is seen as simply a permissive factor, making interaction possible. Actual selection of a mate is more dependent on social nearness than on physical nearness, in this view.[8] Emphasis is still on normative factors in mate selection, though their operation is seen as circumscribed by non-normative facts of life.

Type IV – propinquity as powerful but so obvious it requires apology. Though the exact mathematical characteristics of the distance gradient are by no means self-evident, some authors appear apprehensive that the student may find unimpressive the proposition that A's probability of marrying B decreases as the distance between their homes increases.[9] Obviousness is somehow assumed to be inversely correlated with importance.

Type V – propinquity as accounting for homogamy. Few, if any, textbooks go quite this far, though some hint at this conclusion.[10]

Some texts mention the tendency to marry someone living nearby as a special case of the tendency for like to marry like.[11] Example: 'Residential propinquity is an ecological form of homogamy.'[12] To say that it is a 'form' of homogamy is not the same as saying either that it is a cause or that it is a result of homogamy. Kirkpatrick avoids the very term 'propinquity', and refers instead to 'locality homogamy', meaning 'similarity in location of residence prior to marriage.'[13] This seems almost a reversal of the usual drive to convert qualitative variables into quantitative ones.

Types I through V roughly constitute a scale of the causal importance attributed to propinquity, running from least to most. The notion of 'locality homogamy' is ambiguous with regard to this scale. Depending on interpretation, authors using such phrases might have intended something like either Type II or Type V, or they might even have in mind a legitimate combination of the two, where propinquity and homogamy are conceived as mutually interdependent.

The lack of consensus among sociologists as to the role of propinquity is interesting. Without proof that our interpretation is correct, it may nevertheless be instructive to suggest that this lack of consensus arises from the conflicting commitments incumbent upon all sociologists. Presumably committed to a concern for empirical fact, sociologists also happen to be committed to the prediction and explanation of behavior *in terms of norms*. Conflict between these two commitments is not apparent to most of us. But so far we have not fully reconciled the facts of propinquitous mate selection with theories attributing causal influence chiefly to folkways and mores. If we are unable to decide whether homogamy explains propinquity, or explains it away, or is explained by it, and if we are tempted by the conclusion that homogamy and propinquity are mutually reinforcing, we owe it to scientific clarity at least to take this position explicit rather than adopt it inadvertently by resorting to ambiguous or vague terminology.

The distance gradient for marriage rates

The usual propinquity study overlooks the fact that for a given groom more potential brides generally reside at a greater distance from his residence than at a lesser distance – as a manifestation of a simple geometric principle. That is, for concentric zones of constant width, the area of the zone will increase in direct proportion with increases in the radius of the zone's inner boundary. If the population of potential brides were evenly distributed over the land, then the number of potential brides residing at a given distance from a given groom would vary directly with that distance. In such circumstances, even a rectangular distribution of actual marriages by distance would indicate a propinquity factor in mate selection, since this distribution would involve diminishing marriage *rates* with increasing distance. The observed decrease in the *number* of marriages as distance increases, then, implies an even more powerful effect of the propinquity factor than has been supposed. Since the number of potentially available brides would not remain constant but actually would increase with distance, marriage *rates* should show an even steeper distance gradient than is apparent in the usual frequency or percentage table.

In real communities, of course, brides are not evenly distributed in space, any more than are other categories of population. Moreover, cities have edges, which further limits the applicability of this simple geometric principle. For Seattle in particular, the shape of the city is quite irregular, and therefore it cannot be assumed that the number of potential brides available is a simple linear function of distance.

From marriage license data, however, it is possible to get an empirical estimate of the mean number of potential brides available at various distances from each groom. In our sample of Seattle marriages, the addresses given in the marriage license applications for August, 1961, were plotted on a city map, and the frequency distribution given in Table 25.1 was compiled. Then the map was photographed. A transparent overlay was made, with concentric circles at one-half scale mile intervals. For each of the 413 grooms in turn, this overlay was centered on his residence (on the photograph) and a frequency distribution of brides by half-mile concentric zones was tabulated. These 413 frequency distributions were added together, and the mean number of brides available at each distance was computed.

Table 25.2 (col 1) shows that up to a distance of about four miles the mean number of brides in the sample residing a given distance from a sample groom tends to increase with distance (as the simple geometric model implied). Beyond four miles this number begins to decline again, although this decline is partially concealed by our combining zones to maintain adequate marriage frequencies at the larger distances. The decline may be attributed to an 'edge effect' – the fact that our sample was limited to residents of Seattle.[14] This arbitrary limitation does not greatly distort reality, however, as the markedly lower population density of the open country outside the city would produce such an 'edge effect' anyway.

Comparison of the first and second columns of Table 25.2 shows that frequency of marriage by zones tends to decrease with increasing distance *in spite* of this pattern of distribution of available brides by distance. In the third column each zone's marriage *rate* is given. These rates decrease monotonically as distance increases. Moreover, they fall away sharply from the initial high figure for the innermost zone. Even if we were to regard as spurious every one of the forty-five cases in which the same address was given by both bride and groom, and exclude these from our sample, the rate in the first half mile would still be 17·16, which is over twice the rate for the second half mile.

Thus, the probability that a given groom will marry a given potential

Table 25.2 Seattle marriage data, observed and expected, by pre-marital residential propinquity

	Data			Stouffer model		Zipf model		
	1	*2*	*4*	*4*	*5*	*6*	*7*	*8*
				Ratio of				
	Mean		*Marriage*	*brides*				
	number		*rate:*	*at a*	*Expected*			*Expected*
	of		*marriages*	*given*	*number*		*Ratio*	*number*
	brides	*Ob-*	*per*	*distance*	*of*		*of*	*of*
	avail-	*served*	*1,000*	*to all*	*marriages*	*Median*	*col.*	*marriages*
	able	*number*	*avail-*	*brides*	*(Col. 4*	*dis-*	*1 to*	*(Col. 7*
	per	*of*	*able*	*at lesser*	*×*	*tances*	*col.*	*×*
Distance	*groom*	*marriages*	*brides*	*distance*	*51·23)*		*6*	*3·08)*
Miles								
0·00 to 0·49	5·08	81	38·61			0·35	14·51	45
0·50 to 0·99	10·99	34	7·49	2·16	111	0·79	13·91	43
1·00 to 1·49	14·62	31	5·13	0·91	47	1·28	11·42	35
1·50 to 1·99	17·14	31	4·38	0·56	29	1·77	9·68	30
2·00 to 2·49	20·20	25	3·00	0·42	22	2·26	8·94	28
2·50 to 2·99	21·81	23	2·55	0·32	16	2·76	7·90	24
3·00 to 3·99	48·49	42	2·10	0·54	28	3·54	13·70	42
4·00 to 4·99	41·67	30	1·74	0·30	15	4·53	9·20	28
5·00 to 5·99	40·06	25	1·51	0·22	11	5·52	7·26	22
6·00 to 7·99	64·68	30	1·12	0·29	15	7·07	9·15	28
8·00 to 9·99	47·37	21	1·07	0·17	9	9·00	5·26	16
10·00 to 15·99	66·99	20	0·72	0·20	10	13·34	5·02	15
16·00 and over	13·90	20	3·48	0·03	2			

bride decreases as the distance between their premarital residences increases – the decrease being very rapid at first but diminishing as distance increases. The effect is stronger than might be supposed if analysis were carried no farther than calculation of cumulative percentages as in Table 25.1.

The intervening opportunities model

Years ago, Stouffer suggested that his hypothesis of intervening opportunities, which he proposed as a migration model, might 'illuminate' the relation between residential propinquity and mate selection.[15] His hypothesis states that 'the number of persons going a given distance is directly proportional to the number of opportunities at that distance and inversely proportional to the number of intervening opportunities'.[16] Rephrased to apply to mate selection, it might read as follows: the number of marriages to persons who resided a given distance away just prior to marriage is directly proportional to the number of potential spouses residing at that distance and inversely proportional to the number residing at shorter distances.[17]

The fourth column of Table 25.2 gives these *opportunity ratios*, computed from the data in the first column, and the fifth column gives marriage frequencies proportional to these ratios, as expected by the Stouffer model. (No opportunity ratio, and hence no expected frequency, can be calculated for the innermost zone.) The discrepancies between the observed data and the model are not random. When each observed frequency is divided by the corresponding expected frequency, there is a marked tendency for the quotient to increase with distance. In other words, the intervening opportunities hypothesis underestimates the number of marriages that occur at the greater distances. It exaggerates the steepness of the distance gradient.

The inverse distance model

Bassett has suggested that Stouffer's model could be improved by applying the intervening opportunities hypothesis to *perceived* rather than actual opportunities.[18] It has also been suggested that the probability of marrying a given person varies with opportunities for intimate interaction, and those opportunities in turn vary inversely with distance.[19] Thus a potential bride may have less potential as her remoteness from a given groom increases, *regardless of intervening brides*. A simple modification of Zipf's P_1P_2/D model describes this pattern. According to Zipf's model,[20] the amount of interaction between two social entities is proportional to the product of their populations and inversely proportional to the intervening distance. That is, $I = kP_1P_2/D$. But this could be rewritten: $I/P_1 = kP_2/D$.

Where P_1 is a sample of grooms and P_2 is the corresponding sample of brides, this equation would stipulate that the percentage of grooms marrying brides residing at a given distance is proportional to the number of brides at that distance and inversely proportional to the distance. This differs from the Stouffer model only in substituting intervening distance for intervening opportunities.

The sixth column of Table 25.2 gives the median distance for each of the zones – i.e. the distance that bisects the zone into inner and outer halves of equal area and (approximately) equal population. The seventh column gives the ratios of the means in column one and these distances. Proportional to these ratios, the zone marriage frequencies expected by the Zipf model are in the eighth column. No expected frequency can be calculated for the open-ended outermost zone, since no exact median distance can be specified. Both the first and last zones were therefore ignored in computing coefficients of agreement between expected and observed marriage frequencies. For the Zipf model, the coefficient of agreement is 0·93, compared with 0·60 for the Stouffer model, and the ratios of observed frequencies to expected frequencies are more nearly constant for the Zipf model.

Though not included in our computation of the agreement coefficient, an expected frequency for the open-ended outermost zone was obtained from the Stouffer model. It is only one-tenth the observed frequency. Similarly, an expected frequency for the innermost zone (not used in computing the agreement coefficient) was obtained from the Zipf model. It is a little more than one-half the observed frequency. Moreover, had we excluded from our sample the forty-five couples who gave the same address for bride and groom, this disproportion for the first zone would have been negligible.[21]

These results tentatively suggest, then, that the effect of propinquity on mate selection can be quantitatively described by Zipf's P_1P_2/D model. In addition, Stouffer's attempt to provide a theoretical explanation for the occurrence of distance gradients in human interaction apparently requires further elucidation. Rephrased to apply to mate selection, his model took a very plausible form; yet it did not fit the data. Why not?

In this connection, note that in the simple case where population is assumed to be evenly distributed over a plane, with no edges, the number of intervening opportunities would increase in proportion to the square of the distance. In the limiting case, then, the two models differ only in the exponent assigned to the distance factor: Zipf's model relates marriage frequencies to the inverse first power of intervening distance, while Stouffer's model would relate them to the inverse second power of distance. Neither of these models says anything about *normative* aspects of mate selection, though. The 'norm interaction' theory proposed by Katz and Hill suggests that normative selectivity in marrying is compounded with spatial (or opportunity) selectivity. To the extent that ethnic, religious, class, and other social differences tend to be reflected in residential segregation, the Katz-Hill theory implies that mate selection should exhibit a distance gradient as a function of intervening opportunities *and* as a function of residential segregation. Thus, the Katz-Hill model requires a distance exponent *at least as high or higher than* that involved in the intervening opportunities model. But our data fit even the intervening opportunities model less closely than they fit the simple P_1P_2/D model, and would therefore depart still farther from the kind of pattern predicted by the Katz-Hill 'norm interaction' theory.

Implications and interpretations

Distance gradients in patterns of human interaction may be plausibly interpreted as representing economy of time and energy, rather than either competition between distant and intervening opportunities, or response to norms reflected in ecological segregation. This is not to say that human beings always economize with regard to time and energy in all their interactions. But since marriage rates seem to decline more nearly as a function of distance than as a function of intervening opportunities, we may infer that the number of *meaningful* 'opportunities' for a person seeking a mate may be quite small. As the array of potential spouses physically present in the environment increases beyond a small number, the additional ones do not really constitute additional 'degrees of freedom' in mate selection. The average person, no matter how many potential spouses may be 'available' to him in terms of physical location and normative considerations of exogamy and endogamy, can be intimately acquainted with only a few of them. The probability that a given person of the opposite sex will be included in that small number apparently depends on the time and energy costs of crossing the intervening distance to engage in interaction rather than on intervening opportunities to interact with other similar persons.

But what about normative pressures? These may be less important than sociologists have supposed, and cultural variability with respect to marriage mores may be less significant than it seems. American students, taking a course in marriage and the family, sometimes react ethnocentrically when they learn of such exotic mate selection practices as go-betweens, family-arranged marriages, etc. On the other hand, the sociologist may sometimes overemphasize the cultural relativity of marriage norms by exaggerating the extent of cultural variability. Taking arranged marriage as one extreme and the American image of unrestricted individualism and romantic love as the other extreme, the range of variation in degrees of freedom in mate selection *appears* to be from one to infinity. The propinquity studies suggest that the actual range from one cultural extreme to the other may be only from one to about half a dozen or so.

As to the five scaled types of textbook interpretation of propinquity in mate selection, our findings suggest that Type V merits more serious consideration than it has heretofore received. It is possible that propinquity produces a substantial degree of homogamy, and that the familiarity of homogamous marriages gives rise to homogamy norms. The inference that non-homogamous marriages are rare because they are taboo may be less accurate than the inference that the taboos are enforceable precisely because the non-homogamous marriages are rare. At a still higher level of abstraction, we might say that a norm (in any realm) is enforceable only to the extent that it prescribes behavior which is likely for other reasons and prohibits behavior which is unlikely for other reasons. We suggest that these are fundamental notions to which sociological research should be specifically addressed.

Notes and References

1. The typical propinquity study has followed the pattern set by James H. S. Bossard, 'Residential propinquity as a factor in marriage selection', *Am. J. Sociol.*, **38** (Sept. 1932), 219–222.
2. For a summary of the various propinquity studies, see Alvin M. Katz and Reuben Hill, 'Residential propinquity and marital selection: a review of theory, method, and fact', *Marriage and Family Living*, **20**, (Feb. 1958), 27–35.
3. *Ibid.*
4. Probably most sociologists today would agree that 'norms help to make human behavior predictable'. See Francis E. Merrill, *Society and Culture*, Englewood Cliffs: Prentice-Hall, 1957, p. 94. Some go farther, however. For example, Hare says '. . . there is no basis for *organized* interaction in a group until some agreement' is reached about [norms and goals]'. (A. Paul Hare, *Handbook of Small Group Research*, Free Press of Glencoe, 1962, p. 24). In a similar vein, Landis has asserted, 'Without authority there can be no order in human society, in fact, no society. . . . Without it the whims and fancies of every person or group would have free reign, and group living would become impossible' (Paul H. Landis, *Social Control*, (rev. edn.), Chicago: Lippincott, 1956, p. 14).
5. It has been argued long ago that '. . . nations have always had that system of morals which justified their current rules of life. Moral theories no more make customs than do our ideas about the constitution of matter make the properties of bodies' (Jacques Rueff, *From the Physical to the Social Sciences*, trans. Herman Green, Baltimore: Johns Hopkins Press, 1929, p. 81).
6. See, for example, William F. Kenkel, *The Family in Perspective*, New York: Appleton-Century-Crofts, 1960, and Ruth Shonle Cavan, *The American Family*, 3rd edn., New York: Thomas Y. Crowell, 1963.
7. See Andrew G. Truxal and Francis E. Merrill, *Marriage and the Family in*

American Culture, New York: Prentice-Hall, 1953, 181, and Floyd M. Martinson, *Marriage and the American Ideal*, New York: Dodd, Mead, 1960, pp. 115–30.

8. See Sister Frances Jerome Woods, *The American Family System*, New York: Harper, 1959, p. 349.

9. Such apologies appear in Robert F. Winch, *The Modern Family*, (rev. edn., New York: Holt, Rinehart and Winston, 1963, p. 322, and Ernest W. Burgess, Harvey J. Locke, and Mary Margaret Thomas, *The Family*, 3rd edn., New York: American Book Co., 1963, p. 253.

10. For example, William M. Kephart, in *The Family, Society, and the Individual*, Boston: Houghton Mifflin, 1961, pp. 268–70, attempts to determine whether divorce is less likely among propinquitous marriages (as among homogamous marriages) than among others. See especially the reasoning on p. 269.

11. See, for example, Robert R. Bell, *Marriage and Family Interaction*, Homewood, Ill.: Dorsey Press, 1963, pp. 132–3. Though he says it is not strictly a category of endogamy, Bell includes propinquity in his discussion of endogamy because 'it refers to "like marrying like".' He also notes that 'it states the obvious. . .'

12. Robert F. Winch, Robert McGinnis, and Herbert R. Barringer, eds., *Selected Studies in Marriage and the Family*, rev. edn., New York: Holt, Rinehart and Winston, 1962, p. 471.

13. Clifford Kirkpatrick, *The Family as Process and Institution*, 2nd edn., New York: Ronald, 1963, pp. 418–19. Kirkpatrick does not indicate that locality homogamy might account for other dimensions of homogamy, but he says: 'Katz and Hill are not content with the mere facts but attempt to find an explanation in terms of the probability of interaction in relation to opportunities of interaction at a given distance in turn related to intervening opportunities'. This suggests that locality homogamy needs to *be explained* rather than used *to explain* other aspects of homogamy.

14. A number of non-residents took out marriage licenses in Seattle during the sample period. There were fourteen couples in which one or both partners omitted the address and could not be included in our sample. There were 176 couples in which both bride and groom gave a non-Seattle address; in the majority of these the same town was listed by both bride and groom (in many instances it was some Seattle suburb), so only a minority represent clearly non-propinquitous marriages. In another 256 couples, one partner gave a Seattle address and the other a non-Seattle address. Of these, 167 involved Seattle brides and non-Seattle grooms, compared with eighty-nine involving Seattle grooms and non-Seattle brides. About half of the apparently non-Seattle grooms were servicemen, who might have been either of Seattle origin or 'residing' in Seattle under military auspices at the time. Thus, although as many couples were excluded from the sample by non-Seattle residence as were included within it, they hardly refute the principle of propinquitous mate selection. Neither the present study nor any previous propinquity study denies that occupational or educational propinquity, etc.,

may be as important as residential propinquity.

15. Samuel A. Stouffer, 'Intervening opportunities: a theory relating mobility and distance', *Am. Sociol. Rev.*, **5**, (Dec. 1940), 867.

16. *Ibid.*, 846.

17. A similar formulation in sociometric terms reads: 'The number of persons in a group, *m*, choosing another group, *n*, varies directly with the attraction of *n* and inversely with the sum of intervening attractions' (see Raymond E. Bassett, 'A note on Stouffer's theory', *Am. Sociol. Rev.*, **10**, June, 1954, 246).

18. *Ibid.*

19. Katz and Hill, *op. cit.*, 31.

20. George K. Zipf, 'The P_1P_2/D hypothesis: on the intercity movement of persons', *Am. Sociol. Rev.*, **11**, (Dec. 1946), 677–86.

21. These couples might reasonably be excluded on grounds that one member actually was not a resident of Seattle. The disproportion for the first zone would similarly disappear if we assumed that these forty-five couples had given their anticipated address rather than their actual premarital addresses, and that the latter were distributed among the various zones in proportion to the rest of the sample. Of course, some of them may actually have had the same street address because they were neighbors in the same apartment building. If we assumed that these forty-five couples were illicitly cohabiting prior to marriage, then the relevant distance data should have been derived from their pre-cohabitation addresses; these are not known but could be expected to have been distributed in proportion to the rest of the sample.

    Exclusion of some or all of the forty-five couples as 'spurious' on any of the grounds mentioned above would have tended to enlarge the ratios in column four of Table 25.2, affecting the ratios for the inner zones most strongly because the denominator would have been reduced proportionately more than for the more distant zones. Thus, exclusion of such couples from the sample would have further reduced the agreement between the Stouffer model and the observed marriage frequencies.

N.R.Ramsøy

26 Assortative mating and the structure of cities*

Sociological studies have made available a good deal of information about the following three features of social life in cities: a more or less marked residential segregation of diverse social groups, a tendency toward endogamy or homogamy in mate selection, and a tendency to choose a spouse who lives close by.

When taken in conjunction with one another, the three indicate a bent toward separateness of and cleavages among urban residents of distinctive social statuses. Furthermore, since the pattern includes marriage and the formation of new families, it implies a mechanism by which existing cleavages may perpetuate themselves. Residential segregation may be continued into the future, provided that newly married couples, many of whom have married endogamously and in their own neighborhood, settle in the area where they grew up. Endogamy may be maintained by the concentration in a particular neighborhood of young men and women of the same social background, their close proximity to one another heightening the chances of their becoming friends, intimates, and eventually spouses. And finally, segregation and endogamy may give added and independent impetus to the rather general tendency to interact with others who are nearby, rather than with others who are far away.

On the whole, research on the interlocking relationships among residential segregation, homogamy, and propinquity ought to provide solid evidence for the extent to which city people live in non-overlapping networks of interaction, each network having both a spatial and a social location in the structure of the city. However, the amount of reliable data confirming so significant a feature of urban life is surprisingly small; furthermore, it appears to this writer that none of the studies has so handled

* Reprinted from *American Sociological Review*, **31**, no. 6, (1966), 773–86.

its data as to present a definitive answer to the question of how the three parts of the pattern relate to one another.

In a review of some 14 studies of residential propinquity in mate selection, Katz and Hill[1] were able to find only one with so broad a scope as to include a systematic analysis of both residential segregation and endogamy as well as propinquity itself. Leaning heavily on this simple inquiry, the details of which are discussed below, Katz and Hill developed an argument about the interlocking character of the three tendencies not unlike that presented above.[2]

In one of the well-known series of investigations of social and spatial differentiation in New Haven, the most explicit statement and analysis may be found of the way in which propinquity, endogamy, and residential segregation relate to one another. Ruby Jo Reeves Kennedy,[3] responding to James Bossard's originating study of propinquity,[4] attempted to demonstrate that the apparent preference for a mate who lives close by could be explained by the joint effect of residential segregation and endogamy. She relied on a type of analysis that, at first glance, appears adequate to such a demonstration. Classifying marriages into those where bride and groom were of the same racial, religious, or ethnic origins, and those where they so differed, she computed the distance between home addresses of spouses in endogamous and exogamous marriages. Somewhat more of the exogamous couples, she found, lived at least twenty blocks apart.

The figures are as follows:

Distance between spouses' premarital addresses	Endogamous marriages	Exogamous marriages
No more than 5 blocks	36·7%	34·3%
5–10 blocks	21·1	17·1
10–20 blocks	20·5	21·9
More than 20 blocks	21·7	26·7
	100·0	100·0

(Adapted from Kennedy, *op. cit.*, Table 4, p. 582 [see Table 23.4, p. 398 above])

In another part of the same study, an ecological classification of New Haven is presented, from which it is clear that the city can be divided into small areas of unlike social composition. When brides and grooms were classified according to their residential areas, Kennedy found that many persons married within their residential area or, failing that, married into an area of similar social composition.[5]

Kennedy's summary of her inquiry is as follows [see p. 401 above]:

Analysis of all the marriage licenses . . . has shown . . . that in the vast majority of cases marriage is an in-group affair, that is, the two contracting parties tend to be of the same race, nationality, religion, and socio-economic status. Urban ecological studies have disclosed that the population tends to be segregated spatially according to the same traits. Thus the coincidence of these two tendencies goes far to explain the factor of residential propinquity in marriage selection.[6]

The concluding sentence in the citation implies that the tendency to pick a spouse living close by would disappear if we could 'think away' the spatial concentration of ethnic, racial, and religious groups. It is the contention of the present author that techniques of analysis can be constructed that correspond precisely to the act of 'thinking away' residential segregation. Since neither Kennedy nor any other student of mate selection has applied such research techniques, the status of the argument concerning the interrelations of propinquity, assortative mating, and residential segregation is more tentative than Kennedy suggests.

Compare, for example, the attitude of Sundal and McCormick.[7] They classified a sample of brides and grooms in Madison, Wisconsin, according to the ecological area where each lived, and found that 39 per cent of the couples lived in the same area, while only 10 per cent of the couples would have lived in the same area 'if mate selection were completely random with respect to ecological area'.[8] But Sundal and McCormick conclude with this reservation: 'We do not know to what extent this (over-selection) was due to nearness in the physical sense and to what extent to likeness in certain socio-economic respects.'[9]

In the analysis to follow, the separate and joint effects of 'nearness' and 'likeness' on mate selection will be investigated, using techniques that are nothing more than an extension of conventional contingency analysis. To anticipate, we shall construct an *expected* distribution of couples classified jointly according to degree of nearness and likeness, and compare the expected with the observed distribution of couples again classified jointly according to degree of nearness and of likeness.From the comparison, it is possible to evaluate the extent to which overselection of spouses living nearby occurs, *independent of the degree of likeness between spouses*, and to evaluate the extent to which overselection of spouses of the same social status occurs, *independent of how close to one another the spouses live*.

Before explaining the technique of analysis in detail, a new set of data based on marriage license applications will be presented. The evidence for assortative mating, residential segregation, and residential propinquity will then be discussed, taking them first one at a time, and then in their relations with one another.

Description of the data

All marriage license applications filed between January 1 and December 31,

1962, where one or both spouses lived in Oslo, Norway, are included in the study.[10]

In all, 5,161 marriage license applications were listed in 1962 where either the bride or groom or both parties lived in Oslo. The residential status of brides and grooms is shown in Table 26.1

Table 26.1   Residential status of brides and grooms at time of marriage: Oslo, 1962

Residential status	No.	Per cent
I. One spouse Oslo resident		
(a) Bride Oslo, groom suburb	381	7·4
(b) Bride Oslo, groom further from city	594	13·4
(c) Groom Oslo, bride suburb	274	5·3
(d) Groom Oslo, bride further from city	624	12·1
Sub-total	1,973	38·2
II. Both spouses Oslo residents		
(a) Lived at exactly same address	528	10·2
(b) One or both gave non-codable address	87	1·7
(c) Both lived at codable and distinct addresses	2,573	49·9
Sub-total	3,188	61·8
Total	5,161	100·0

In some 38 per cent of all marriages, only one of the partners lived in Oslo. While a good many of these cases (about one-third) involved no greater residential distance than that between the city and its suburbs, the rest brought together a man and a woman living so far apart that their current places of residence are a poor indication of the ecological context in which they became acquainted. For this reason, we follow the convention, established in earlier inquiries into propinquity and mate selection, of eliminating in-city/out-of-city marriages from systematic study of 'the distance factor'.[11]

On the whole, the proportion of in-city/out-of-city marriages is higher in Oslo than in American cities – or so it seems at first glance. Twenty per cent is the modal figure reported in studies conducted in Philadelphia, New Haven, Duluth, and Nashville.[12] But the chances are extremely high that there is no real difference in this respect between Americans and Norwegians seeking a spouse. Instead, the situation that varies is the command the researcher has over *all* the data necessary to establish the true proportion of marriages in which only one of the spouses lives in the 'home' community. In Norway, where one and the same published source lists every marriage license application, *no matter where it is filed*, we were in a position to find all such cases. In the United States no such central listing exists.

423

Thus the practice in American studies is to base one's investigations on the universe of marriages *filed* in one community rather than on the universe of marriages involving *residents* of the community.[13]

The effect of the difference in research practices was tested as follows: A hand tally was made, for a sample of the Oslo/out-of-Oslo marriages, of the place of filing the license application. The results, extrapolated to all 1,973 cases, are given in Table 26.2. Over 40 per cent of in-city/out-of-city licenses were filed elsewhere than in Oslo. All of these marriages would have been lost to sight had we been forced to confine the study to marriages filed in Oslo. And the estimated proportion of marriages between one resident of the city and one 'outsider' would then have been reduced to 26 per cent – a figure more in line with the typical American estimate than the true figure of 38 per cent. Note also that the bride's place of residence determines the place of marriage in the preponderance of cases where the marriage partners live in different communities – an observation which conforms with commonly held notions of marriage customs in Western societies.

Table 26.2 **Place of filing marriage license application, by bride's and groom's residential status: Oslo, 1962**

Place of filing	Bride resident of Oslo, groom elsewhere		Groom resident of Oslo, bride elsewhere		Total	
	No.	Per cent	No.	Per cent	No.	Per cent
Oslo	800	74·5	328	36·6	1,128	57·2
Elsewhere	275	25·5	570	63·4	845	42·8
	1,075	100·0	898	100·0	1,973	100·0

In all studies of residential propinquity in mate selection, a number of cases have turned up where the prospective bride and groom state on the marriage application that they live at exactly the same address. In the Oslo study there were 528 such cases, or more than one in ten of the total number of marriages.[14] To say the least, these couples have a considerable impact on the distribution of marriages by distance between bride's and groom's address. Other studies have turned up occasional bits of evidence supporting the common-sense notion that those who report the same home address began living together before marriage. If there is evidence supporting the possibility that these couples took up joint residence before marriage, then they should not be included in an analysis the purpose of which is to evaluate the effect of distance between residences on the *selection* of a spouse. Even with the limited amount of information about the couple and the marriage available in the Oslo study, it was possible to compare the same-address couples with all other couples in certain respects particularly crucial for establishing the possibility of premarital cohabitation.

The comparisons, given in Table 26.3, do suggest the wisdom of excluding same-address couples, since their residential propinquity appears to be less the *basis* of mate selection, than a *consequence* of it.

In Oslo, marriage by a minister is more common than marriage by a civil official. But not so among couples who stated on their marriage license

Table 26.3 Comparison of couples giving same premarital address with all other couples: Oslo, 1962

	Per cent of marriages solemnized by religious ceremony	Per cent of grooms in semi- and unskilled occupations	Per cent of brides not at work
Couples giving same address (N = 528)	31·1	50·6	30·4
All other couples (N = 4,633)	68·7	32·5	10·1
All couples (N = 5,161)	64·9	34·4	12·1

application that they lived at the same address. Without further data, it is difficult to conclude that such couples refrain from a religious marriage because of fear of rejection by the minister, or because their living together expresses their own rejection of religion, or because one or both of them have been previously married and divorced, a status leading to virtually automatic exclusion from religious solemnization of a subsequent marriage in the Norwegian state church. But whatever the connections may be, the prevailing civil marriage ceremonies of the same-address couples are decidedly atypical in Norwegian society and do indicate that many of these couples may have begun to live together before marriage.

The same possibility is suggested by the markedly weaker labor force participation of the brides in same-address marriages. Three of every ten of them do not work, possibly because they have children from previous marriages or from the marriage about to be legalized, while only one in ten of all other brides is without an occupation.

It would seem that the most circumspect way of dealing with the cases where the prospective bride and groom report the same home address is to eliminate them from those parts of the analysis concerned with evaluating the effect of distance on mate selection. Note that this is tantamount to assuming that the distribution of these couples by their places of residence *before* they began living together was identical with that of all other couples – perhaps the safest assumption to make in the absence of more information.[15]

Following this procedure, the estimate of the proportion of intra-city marriages in Oslo in 1962 declines from 61·8 per cent to 56·6 per cent (after eliminating same-address couples both from the total and from the intra-city marriages.) In the systematic analysis of distance between prospective spouses, only intra-city marriages will be considered for reasons stated earlier. A few of the intra-city marriages are left out because full street addresses were not given for both bride and groom. The analysis of intervening distance between spouses was carried out for 2,573 cases – 50 per cent of all the marriages in the full study.[16]

Occupational data were reported for 98 per cent of the men and 88 per cent of the women. The other women were typically reported to be 'At home' (*hjemmeværende*). The occupational titles given in the gazette listings were sufficiently informative to permit classification into over twenty detailed categories, reduced to six for present purposes.

In this study, occupational status is the only indicator of social position and the only basis for evaluating homogamy and residential segregation in Oslo. While this is a limitation set by the available data, Oslo is so homogeneous in the racial, religious, and ethnic composition of its population as to make the exclusion of the information about these statuses a minor shortcoming.[17]

Table 26.4 Occupation of bride according to occupation of groom, Oslo, 1962

Groom's occupation	*Bride's occupation*							
	Professional, univ. student	Semi-Prof. Tech., admin. skilled clerical	Routine Clerical	Sales	Manual, service	No occupation	Total	No. of grooms
Professional, univ. student	20·1%	48·4	19·3	2·2	4·9	5·1	100·0	816
Semi-prof., admin. sales	2·5%	42·1	29·3	7·2	10·2	8·7	100·0	1,047
Routine white collar	1·3%	25·6	35·7	9·4	19·9	8·1	100·0	694
Skilled manual and service	0·3%	20·5	32·2	9·5	25·0	12·5	100·0	727
Semi- and unskilled manual and service	0·6%	11·9	26·6	11·3	32·3	17·3	100·0	1,770
No occupation	0·9%	21·5	19·6	2·8	16·8	38·4	100·0	107
All occupations	4·1%	27·0	27·8	8·4	20·5	12·2	100·0	5,161
No. of brides	212	1,394	1,438	431	1,058	628		

Note: Frequencies in the underlined cells exceed the expected numbers.

Marriage and occupational status

The first stage of the analysis concerns the occupational statuses of brides and grooms, and particularly, whether there is evidence to support the idea that marriage is assortative with respect to occupation.

The tendency toward occupational homogamy is shown in Table 26.4. Marriage does in fact tend to unite men and women of the same or similar occupational status. The coefficient of contingency for this array is 0·476.

This is somewhat lower than Sundal and McCormick's occupational homogamy data, for which the coefficient of contingency was 0·66.[18] It was necessary to use a slightly different set of occupational categories for brides and for grooms. Nonetheless, marriages occur more frequently than expected in the cells along the leading diagonal of Table 26·4 as well as in a few adjacent cells, where bride's and groom's occupational status are either identical or nearly so. If mate selection had been random with respect to occupational status, only 18·3 per cent of the couples would have been of the same or most similar status, in contrast to the 29·8 per cent who in fact were so.

Table 26.5 gives the ratios of actual to expected frequencies of marriage, according to the degree of similarity in occupational statuses of bride and groom.

Table 26.5 **Ratio of actual to expected number of marriages, according to occupational similarity of bride and groom**

Degree of similarity in occupational status	Ratio of actual to expected number of marriages
Identical or most similar status	1·63
One occupational category distant	1·25
Two occupational categories distant	0·83
Three occupational categories distant	0·46
Four or five occupational categories distant	0·41

The probability of marriage between a male and a female drawn at random from the marrying population in Oslo varies directly with the similarity of their occupational statuses. It has long been an open question as to what is the most crucial social context of the behavior responsible for this frequently observed regularity. Is it the *workplace*, which brings together men and women doing the same type of work, is it the *family*, urging, manipulating, or encouraging its offspring to find a 'suitable', i.e., socially equal, mate, or is it the *neighborhood*, putting into daily contact persons belonging to the same socioeconomic stratum?

The data at our disposal do not provide the contextual information needed to identify the workplaces and family backgrounds of the brides and grooms. Accordingly the remainder of the analysis concentrates on the neighborhood context of mate selection, and the related variable of the distance between spouses' places of residence before their marriage.

Distance between spouses' residences before marriage.
In all previous studies of residential propinquity of brides and grooms, addresses of spouses were plotted on city maps, and the intervening distance measured either by counting the number of blocks one would have to travel to get from one address to the other or by computing the straight-

line distance in miles. In the present study the city map was not introduced until street addresses of brides and grooms had first been coded according to a standard ecological classification scheme[19] consisting of three hundred tracts, in turn reducible to sixty residential districts.[20]

The city map was used to measure the straight-line distance from the midpoint of every residential district to the midpoint of every other district. A matrix of mileage distances between all pairs of districts was constructed, resembling the charts of mileage between pairs of cities often found on auto road maps. The matrix was used first to read off the distance between the home addresses of each groom and his bride. Distances were grouped into half-mile intervals, to allow for the loss of accuracy sustained by treating all addresses within a district as if they were located at its midpoint. The number of couples who lived at successive half-miles from one another before marriage is shown in the first column of Table 26.6.

Next, the *random or expected* distribution of couples by premarital residential distance was derived, using the following procedure. The actual number of grooms living in each of the (56) residential districts was defined as the marginal distribution of the columns in a contingency table, and actual number of brides living in each district defined as the marginal distribution of the rows of the table. The cross-products or random frequencies were computed electronically. The mileage distances between the centers of all pairs of districts were read into the computer, which then assigned the values in each cell in the contingency table – each cell representing a unique combination of two districts – to the appropriate distance interval. The final output was the expected number of couples living at successive half-mile distances from one another, shown in the second column of Table 26.6.

In Table 26.6, the observed distribution shows the same tendency as in all other studies of residential propinquity of spouses. The greater the distance, the fewer the couples. Only the first frequency, i.e. the number of couples living within the one-half mile of one another, represents a departure from the otherwise regular decrease. This exception should be placed in relation to two decisions taken concerning the analysis. First, all couples who gave exactly the same home address were excluded. Had all of them been included, the first frequency would have been 795, rather than 267. had only half been included, the first frequency would have been 531. Second, the method of measuring map distances from midpoint to midpoint of brides' and grooms' residential districts, rather than from bride's house to groom's house, probably led to an underestimate of the number of couples living less than half a mile from one another and an overestimate of the number in the second interval.[21]

The expected frequency distribution of couples tends to increase with distance up to about two miles, then remains relatively constant for another mile and a half, and then drops off sharply and steadily beyond a distance of

Table 26.6 Observed and expected numbers of couples according to distance between residences before marriage: Oslo, 1962

Distance	1 Observed number of couples	2 Expected number of couples	Ratio of 1 to 2
Less than 0·50 miles	267	114·2	2·34
0·50–0·99 miles	427	203·0	2·10
1·00–1·49 miles	339	291·1	1·16
1·50–1·99 miles	319	305·9	1·04
2·00–2·49 miles	239	285·2	0·84
2·50–2·99 miles	220	279·1	0·79
3·00–3·49 miles	219	285·7	0·77
3·50–3·99 miles	153	229·4	0·67
4·00–4·49 miles	119	137·4	0·87
4·50–4·99 miles	83	141·9	0·59
5·00–5·49 miles	54	93·0	0·58
5·50–5·99 miles	46	60·2	0·76
6·00–6·49 miles	33	51·0	0·65
6·50–6·99 miles	23	38·3	0·60
7·00–7·49 miles	17	24·7	0·69
7·50–7·99 miles	6	15·7	0·38
8·00 miles or more	9	17·2	0·52
Total	2,573	2,573·0	

four miles. The curve departs radically from the model generally employed by students of the 'distance-interaction' hypothesis[22] who assume a *steadily increasing* frequency of expected pair interactions with increasing distance. But their assumption rests on another – a population *evenly* distributed in space. If population is evenly spaced, then with increasing distance from a given point, the ring circumscribed by all points equidistant from it grows even larger and thus includes more and more people. But the assumption is not appropriate for cities, which tend to be more densely settled, residentially, close to but not at their centers, than they are in the outskirts. So the curve of expected numbers of couples rises only for a limited distance within which the effect of the 'growing circle of equidistant points' is apparent, but then falls off as the thinner densities at the periphery begin to operate.

The only expected distance distribution to be found in earlier propinquity studies is that reported by Catton and Smircich,[23] who measured on a city map of Seattle the distance from the home address of every groom to that of every bride. This of course yields a random distribution, since it is based on the appropriate model of allowing every 'male address' an equal chance of being paired with every 'female address'. Catton and Smircich found the same trend in Seattle as shown here for Oslo. The expected number of couples in Seattle increased with distance up to about three miles, stayed at a plateau between three and five miles, and then fell off with distances beyond that point.[24]

The ratios of observed to expected number of marriages tend to decrease with increasing distance between bride's and groom's premarital residences. There is a decided tendency to overselect spouses from the available supply at close reach, and to underselect from those living further away. The trend is somewhat less regular and less marked – especially beyond a distance of about five miles – than the trend reported for Seattle, where the ratio of observed to expected was considerably higher than in Oslo at shorter distances, and considerably lower at longer distances.[25] The use of mid-points in measuring distances in Oslo may be responsible.

Nearness and likeness in mate selection

Marriages between persons of the same or similar occupational status occur more frequently than expected, and marriages between persons who live close to one another occur more frequently than expected. To what extent are these tendencies independent of one another, and to what extent are they dependent on still another structural feature of urban populations, namely residential segregation?

As a first step in answering the question, the following relatively simple issue will be examined: Is it the case that the more homogamous the marriage, the lesser the distance between spouses' premarital residences? To recall, this was the procedure adopted by Kennedy, who found a small positive correlation between endogamous and propinquitous marriages. Nearness and likeness, she suggested, overlapped one another as bases of mate selection. In Oslo, however, *there is no correlation at all between the degree of nearness and the degree of likeness of spouses* (see Table 26.7).

The median distance between residences of all couples in the Oslo marriage series was 1·9 miles. No matter how occupationally similar or how occupationally unlike the brides and grooms were, the same median distance between their places (i.e. districts) of residence holds, within a tenth of a mile. It is just as interesting to express the lack of a correlation by referring to the identical distributions across the rows in Table 26.7. Just over two-thirds of all couples who married in Oslo in 1962 were either of identical occupational status or no more than one occupational category 'distant' from one another; this proportion holds no matter whether the brides and grooms lived less than a mile from one another, or more than eight miles apart.

The absence of a correlation between degree of homogamy and degree of premarital residential propinquity goes against common-sense expectations. What type of urban ecological distribution underlies a situation in which, let us say, two doctors or two factory workers are no more likely to live near one another than do one doctor and one factory worker? Oslo, it would seem, is a city in which occupational status is not a relevant basis of residential concentration. Persons occupying socially distinct occupational statuses must be distributed more or less at random over the various

Table 26.7   Distribution of observed couples according to distance between residential districts and similarity in occupational statuses: Oslo, 1962

Distance between residential districts	*Similarity of bride's and groom's occupational status*					All couples	Per cent in first two columns
	Identical or most similar status	One occup. category distant	Two occup. categories distant	Three occup. cat. distant	Four or five occup. cat. distant		
0·00–0·99 miles	201	272	156	48	17	694	68·2
1·00–1·99 miles	198	253	131	48	28	658	68·5
2·00–2·99 miles	140	176	98	30	15	459	68·8
3·00–3·99 miles	103	132	95	28	14	372	63·2
4·00–4·99 miles	64	75	46	10	7	202	68·8
5·00–5·99 miles	38	31	24	6	1	100	69·0
6·00–6·99 miles	10	25	15	4	2	56	(62·5)
7·00–7·99 miles	9	7	4	1	2	23	(69·6)
8·00 miles or more	1	5	2	1	—	9	(66·7)
All distances	764	976	571	176	86	2,573	67·6
Distance quartiles (miles):							
Q_1	0·96	0·92	0·98	0·93	1·13	0·94	
Q_2	1·92	1·85	1·98	1·78	1·91	1·90	
Q_3	3·25	3·20	3·42	3·22	3·25	3·27	

neighborhoods of the city.

Yet the inference receives no support at all from the facts. Paradoxically, the (marrying) population of Oslo is just as residentially segregated on the basis of occupational status as the total active populations of other cities of comparable size. Wilkins' work on residential segregation in eight medium-sized American cities provides a satisfactory basis of comparison.[26] Using, as Wilkins did, the index of residential dissimilarity developed by the Duncans[27] to assess the degree of residential segregation, and comparing the bridegrooms of each occupational status with those of every other in their distribution over the set of residential districts, resulted in the matrix of dissimilarity indexes reported in Table 26.8.

That the data testify to residential segregation of diverse occupational statuses can hardly be doubted. Professionals resemble managers and salesmen most closely in where they live, skilled workers resemble semi-skilled and unskilled workers most closely, and so on. The range of dissimilarity values in Oslo is from 18·7 to 43·8 (not counting the small set of men outside the labor force). Wilkins found a range of 12 to 58 for an average of eight medium-sized American cities.[28] The discrepancy, in good part, is likely to be due to the greater heterogeneity of the American

431

Table 26.8 Indexes of dissimilarity in residential distribution among occupational statuses, bridegrooms, Oslo: 1962

Occupational status	Occupational status					
	1	2	3	4	5	6
(1) Professional, university student	—	22·6	35·8	42·0	43·6	(60·5)
(2) Semi-prof., admin., sales		—	21·7	28·2	28·1	(48·9)
(3) Routine white-collar			—	27·0	21·6	(45·9)
(4) Skilled manual and service				—	18·7	(38·2)
(5) Semi- and unskilled manual and service					—	(41·0)
(6) No occupation						—
Number of men	(417)	(538)	(336)	(412)	(820)	(50)

population as a whole, and the greater homogeneity of each of the American occupational status and residential status categories.

If Oslo is so well differentiated residentially according to occupational status, how then can it be that two persons doing the same kind of work who choose one another for marriage are no more likely to live close to one another than two persons of highly different occupational statuses. What accounts for the paradox?

The answer was suggested by the Duncans, who pointed out, over a decade ago, that residential *dissimilarity* and residential *distance* are by no means the same thing.[29] The members of two occupational statuses may be distributed quite dissimilarly over a set of neighborhoods, without there necessarily being a very large distance between them. This is a well-known configuration in American cities, where avenues and the streets crossing them may each be reserved for different and socially distant status groups – despite the fact that they can often see into one another's houses.

If residential segregation of diverse statuses is to play a part in explaining *propinquity* in mate selection, then it must do so not because men and women of the same social status live 'similarly' to one another, but because they live *close* to one another. To state the point more strictly as a hypothesis: 'The greater the social (occupational) distance between a male and a female in the marrying population, the greater the residential distance between them'.

The statistical model corresponding to the hypothesis involves the familiar urns and balls. Imagine one urn containing n balls, one for each male in the marrying population, each ball marked with a symbol identifying the male's occupational status and a symbol identifying his district of residence. Another urn contains an equal number of balls, one for each female, and each marked again with two symbols.

To test the hypothesis, every ball in the male urn is to be paired with every ball in the female urn, and the distance between residences and between occupations is to be noted for each pair. In practice – and the computer program was so written[30] – the males and females may first be sorted into categories homogeneous both in occupational status and district of residence, and the number of males in each category multiplied by the number of females in each to compute the cross-products.

By matching every male and female in the marrying population, it is possible to examine the *full set* of opportunities, i.e. available spouses, out of which marriage partners are selected. In particular the hypothesis raises the issue of whether there is a correlation between nearness and likeness in the full set of available spouses.

Table 26.9 shows that there is in fact only the faintest trace of a relation between residential distance and occupational similarity in the full set of male-female pairs that can be formed out of the marrying population. The coefficient of correlation for the array (in half-mile distance intervals) is +0·01. Despite the residential segregation of persons of diverse occupational statuses, a man and woman of the same occupational status live, on the average, less than one-tenth of a mile closer to one another than a man and woman of highly discrepant occupational statuses.

So two expectations are not upheld by the Oslo data: first, that homo-

Table 26.9   Distribution of random male-female pairs according to distance between residential districts and similarity in occupational statuses: Oslo, 1962

	Similarity of male's and female's occupational status						
Distance between residential districts	*Identical or most similar status*	*One occup. category distant*	*Two occup. categories distant*	*Three occup. cat. distant*	*Four or five occup. cat. distant*	*All couples*	*Per cent in first two columns*
0·00–0·99 miles	60·1	99·3	81·2	51·7	24·9	317·2	50·3
1·00–1·99 miles	111·1	183·6	153·8	100·6	47·9	597·0	49·4
2·00–2·99 miles	101·8	173·6	146·5	93·5	48·9	564·3	48·8
3·00–3·99 miles	92·8	156·5	134·3	87·3	44·2	515·1	48·4
4·00–4·99 miles	49·8	85·4	74·7	46·2	23·2	279·3	48·4
5·00–5·99 miles	27·7	46·9	40·2	25·7	12·7	153·2	48·6
6·00–6·99 miles	15·7	27·1	23·8	14·8	7·9	89·3	(47·9)
7·00–7·99 miles	7·2	12·3	10·7	6·6	3·6	40·4	(48·3)
8·00 miles or more	2·9	5·2	4·9	2·8	1·4	17·2	(47·1)
All distances	469·1	789·9	670·1	429·2	214·7	2,573·0	48·9
Distance quartiles (miles):							
Q_1	1·50	1·54	1·57	1·57	1·62	1·56	
Q_2	2·62	2·65	2·63	2·66	2·70	2·66	
Q_3	3·83	3·85	3·89	3·87	3·91	3·86	

gamy and propinquity are mutually interrelated; and second, that the 'explanation' lies in the 'geographical clustering of opportunities' implied by residential segregation. Instead, if the frequencies in Table 26.7 are taken as a set of observed values, and those in Table 26.9 as a set of expected values, it can be shown that the tendency toward homogamy, i.e., over-selection of spouses among those who are similar in social (occupational) status, is *independent* of the tendency toward propinquity, and vice versa.

As shown in Table 26.10, the ratios of observed to expected marriage frequencies tend to decline both across the rows and down the columns. Marriage is less probable with decreasing homogamy, no matter what the degree of propinquity, and with decreasing propinquity, no matter what the degree of homogamy.

Note that the procedure followed in the construction of the ratios of observed to expected marriage frequencies permits us to 'think away' or control for the supposed effect of residential segregation on mate selection. Let us imagine that nearness and likeness had been correlated among the observed couples – as Kennedy found. Let us further imagine that such a correlation had also been found in the marrying population as a whole: the closer together men and women lived, the more similar they were in occupational status. If Kennedy's final assertion were correct, we would then have found that the observed marriage frequencies by residential distance between partners were strictly proportional to the expected frequencies at each level of homogamy. In this way, segregation and homogamy would 'explain' propinquity.

Table 26.10   Ratios of observed to expected marriage frequencies, according to distance between residential districts and similarity in occupational statuses: Oslo, 1962

Distance between residential districts	Similarity in occupational status					
	Identical or most similar status	One occup. category distant	Two occup. categories distant	Three occup. cat. distant	Four or five occup. cat. distant	All couples
0·00–0·99 miles	3·34	2·74	1·92	0·93	0·68	2·19
1·00–1·99 miles	1·78	1·38	0·85	0·48	0·58	1·10
2·00–2·99 miles	1·38	1·01	0·67	0·32	0·31	0·81
3·00–3·99 miles	1·11	0·84	0·71	0·32	0·09	0·72
4·00–4·99 miles	1·29	0·88	0·62	0·22	0·30	0·72
5·00–5·99 miles	1·37	0·66	0·60	0·23	0·08	0·65
6·00–6·99 miles	0·64	0·92	0·63	0·27	0·25	0·63
7·00–7·99 miles	1·25	0·57	0·37	0·15	0·56	0·57
8·00 miles or more	0·34	0·96	0·41	0·36	0·00	0·52
All distances	1·63	1·24	0·85	0·41	0·40	

Discussion

The foregoing represents an intensive and strict analysis of the interrelations among three structural features of urban populations, all of which bear on the tendency toward closed social networks of interaction. People marry their equals in social status; they marry their neighbors; neighbors tend to be social equals.

So stated, the picture seems clear, persuasive and deserving of careful verification. But while the first two propositions stood up under successively more stringent analytic procedures, the third did not – at least, not in the ultimate form in which it was tested. If pairs of persons are drawn at random from the (marrying) population, the probability of their being social equals is virtually *independent* of the distance between their residences. When taken in conjunction with the marked residential segregation of persons in diverse occupational statuses, the failure to find similarity in occupational status associated with residential proximity represents an anomaly to be investigated in the course of the future.

Two lines of inquiry for such investigation may be mentioned here briefly. First, the map measurements used in the Oslo analysis to indicate distances between residences may have washed out whatever tendency in fact exists for neighbors to be social equals. The problem of measuring the distance between addresses of couples living in the same district was not fully resolved. Perhaps the most satisfactory technique for studying distance as strictly as has been attempted here is the following. A very finely meshed grid of coordinates may be superimposed on the city map so that any location may be identified as so many units north or south, east or west from a point of origin. Residential addresses may then be coded in the form of pairs of coordinates, and the distance between any two addresses can easily be reckoned by a computer programmed to apply the Pythagorean theorem to the problem. Provided the grid system is fine enough, neighbors can be identified more adequately than by the method followed in the present study of measuring distances from midpoint to midpoint of only fifty-six residential districts.

The second type of inquiry is of a different order. What we have labelled here as an anomaly may turn out to be a genuine discontinuity between ecological structure on the one hand, and the spatial or distance factor on the other. Social processes of growth, interaction, change, or stability in cities may express themselves in an ecological structure with clearly definable neighborhoods. But only under very special conditions, no more probable than others, would neighborhoods be so distributed spatially as to show social gradients corresponding with increasing distance in all directions. Theories of differentiation in land use or of the locations of diverse types of functions in the city by no means imply a simple transformation of distance into diversity or the reverse. Yet the assumption that such a

435

transformation can be made underlies the argument that the extraordinarily regular decline in the number of spouses chosen with ever increasing distance can be 'explained' away by the residential segregation of the population into distinct neighborhoods.

It now seems more fruitful to examine empirically the relationship between the ecological and the spatial distribution of diverse social elements in the population. The relationship is certain to vary from city to city. Oslo, for example, may be less smoothly graded spatially than most cities – although its population is ecologically differentiated.[31] In any event, the pattern of residential segregation as shown by indexes of dissimilarity can no longer be taken as prima facie evidence that the 'distance factor' in social interaction can be explained away.

To recall another unsettled issue raised by the analysis, nearly 40 per cent of the marriages in the Oslo series included one spouse whose reported place of residence was outside of the city. Many marriages represent the uniting of two persons one or both of whom were freed from their residential ties for some period between their meeting and the time of deciding to wed. The neatly declining curve relating residential distance to the probability of selecting a mate holds only for that part of the urban population for which place of residence and locus of interaction hang fairly well together – the stable part of the population, in other words. In addition, there are those who are on the way in, others on the way out. It seems likely that in-migrants to the city are especially likely to marry a non-resident, although the data on this point are scanty for the Oslo marriage series.[32] The relative frequency and distribution of marriages uniting a resident and a non-resident of the city deserve far more attention and integration into studies of urban mate selection than they have thus far received.

Mate selection in modern urban communities, when studied systematically and in detail, does not yield to any all-encompassing theory. An open marriage system, with endogamous, homogamous, and propinquitous tendencies, does not reduce to a set of closed networks of interaction. Instead, the intellectual stance with the greatest chance of advancing our understanding of such a system must include a good measure of curiosity about the character of the networks of interaction which provide the context of mate selection: their stability, extensiveness, openness, and correlation with other forms of social differentiation.

Notes and References

* The author wishes to acknowledge the support of Professor Sverre Holm and the Institute of Sociology of the University of Oslo and of the Norwegian Council for Research in the Sciences and Humanities (NAVF), which made possible the collection and processing of the data presented here. The analysis was developed and

executed by the members of a seminar in research methods at the University of California in Los Angeles. The members of the seminar, trainees in the program supported by the National Institute of General Medical Sciences, were Joan Gronner, Michael Silverstein, James Watson, and Robert Winslow, who willingly and competently mastered the difficulties of participating in a study of neither their own making nor culture. To the Institute and the director of its program in the Department of Sociology of UCLA, Charles R. Wright, I owe a debt for encouraging me to contribute to the training of students by sharing with them the uncertainties and gratifications of my own research in progess.

1. Alvin M. Katz and Reuben Hill, 'Residential propinquity and marital selection: a review of theory, method, and fact', *Marriage and Family Living*, **58**, (Feb. 1958), 27–35.
2. *Ibid.*, 32–3. Katz and Hill cast their ideas in more abstract terms. They suggest that prevailing norms concerning mate selection define suitable '*fields of eligibles*' (the term is Robert Winch's); in turn, the field of eligibles may be substituted for the concept of '*opportunities*', as Stouffer used that term in his work on distance and interaction. Finally, they ask rhetorically if residential segregation does not imply 'a geographical clustering of opportunities'.
3. Ruby Jo Reeves Kennedy, 'Premarital residential propinquity and ethnic endogamy', *Am. J. Sociol.*, **48**, (Mar. 1943), 580–84 [23].
4. James H. S. Bossard, 'Residential propinquity as a factor in marriage selection', *Am. J. Sociol.*, **38**, (Sept. 1932), 219–24.
5. Kennedy, *op. cit.*, Table 5, 583.
6. *Ibid.*, 584.
7. A. Philip Sundal and Thomas C. McCormick. 'Age at marriage and mate selection: Madison, Wisconsin, 1937–1943', *Am. Sociol. Rev.*, **16**, (Feb. 1951), 37–48.
8. *Ibid.*, 44.
9. *Ibid.*, 44–5.
10. The data were collected from the daily issues of *Norsk Lysingsblad*, the official government gazette. The information on each couple is less comprehensive than that filed in the Ministry of Church and Education, where age, birthplace, previous marital status, and other demographic facts about the applicants are recorded. But easy access to the gazette, and inclusion in the listings of home addresses and occupational statuses of bride and groom, led to the decision to examine these data.
11. They are included, however, in the analysis of assortative mating with respect to occupational status.
12. Katz and Hill, *op. cit.*, conclude their article with a numbered bibliography of studies on propinquity in mate selection. Reports on the cities listed above are to be found in studies 1, 2, 4, 5, 8, and 10 in the bibliography. See Katz and Hill, *op. cit.*, 34–5.
13. The problem of out-of-area marriages has been recognized by several other

researchers. Katz and Hill discuss it systematically, although, because of lack of data, they cannot estimate its relative effect. See Katz and Hill, *op. cit.*, 28–9.

14. This number does *not* include couples who, while living at the same house number, lived in apartments on different floors or with separate street entrances. It is common practice in Norway to specify addresses with a Roman number for floor and a letter for street entrance.

15. It might have been advantageous to exclude only a certain proportion of the same-address couples, since it is unlikely that all of them represent cases of premarital cohabitation. Katz and Hill propose such a solution. See Katz and Hill, *op. cit.*, 27–8.

16. The total sample and the half included in the analysis of residential distance were compared with respect to the few variables available for evaluating representativeness. The latter proved to be representative of the former in the occupational distributions of both males and females, and in the proportion of couples who applied to a civil, rather than religious instance, for permission to marry.

17. At the time of the 1960 census of population, 96·2 per cent of the inhabitants of Oslo were native-born. Half of the foreign-born were natives of Sweden, Denmark, Finland, or Iceland. Some 95·4 per cent of Oslo residents were members of the state church (Lutheran), and almost half of the non-members were identified with other Protestant denominations or sects. See Central Bureau of Statistics of Norway, *Population Census*, 1960, vol. VIII, Table 1, p. 12 and Table 5, pp. 34–9.

18. Sundal and McCormick, *op. cit.*, 44, Goodman and Kruskal's *gamma* was computed for the Oslo data; the value of the coefficient was 0·457.

19. The classification scheme was developed by Fridthiov Andhøy, an engineer, and is now used extensively by collectors and consumers of information about the city of Oslo, including the municipal office of statistics and the city planning division. Andhøy also provides a coded address book covering all house numbers in the city.

20. Since four districts are devoted exclusively to nonurban functions – chiefly farming and timber-cutting – the few persons in the marrying population who lived there were excluded.

21. Looking back on the procedures followed, it would probably have been a good idea to construct a spot map for the brides and grooms whose addresses fell within the same district, and to measure residential distance directly for them. Instead, a rough estimate was made of the *area* of each district in square miles and 'intra-district' distances were estimated, proportional to the area. Of the couples in which both bride and groom lived within the same district (almost 15 per cent of all couples) nearly 60 per cent were assigned to the distance interval 0·50–0·99 miles, and only 40 per cent to the first interval. It is likely that the method of grouping addresses led to an over-estimation of the residential distance between brides and grooms living within the same district, more often

than to an underestimation.

22. See, for example, George K. Zipf, 'The hypothesis of the "minimum equation" as a unifying social principle: with attempted synthesis', *Am. Sociol. Rev.*, **12**, (Dec. 1947), 627–50. See especially 646–7, where Zipf discusses the then available data on residential propinquity in mate selection.

23. William R. Catton, Jr. and R. J. Smircich, 'mathematical models for residential propinquity and mate selection', *Am. Sociol. Rev.*, **29**, (Aug. 1964), 525 [25].

24. Catton and Smircich, *op. cit.*, 525–6.

25. *Ibid.*, Table 2, 526.

26. Reported in Otis Dudley Duncan, 'Population distribution and community structure', *Cold Spring Harbor Symposia on Quantitative Biology*, **22**, (1957), 357–71.

27. Otis Dudley Duncan and Beverly Duncan, 'Residential distribution and occupational stratification', *Am. J. Sociol.*, **60**, (Mar. 1955), 493–503 [3].

28. Duncan, reference in fn. 26, Table 4, 361.

29. Otis Dudley Duncan and Beverly Duncan, 'A Methodological analysis of segregation indexes', *Am. Sociol. Rev.*, **20**, (April 1955), 210–17 [2].

30 Robert Winslow, a member of the seminar at UCLA, wrote the program.

31. Until recently, Oslo resembled most cities in having a regularly declining density of residential population with increasing distance from the city center. But after the building of many multi-storied housing developments in the outskirts, the curve relating density to distance now has an extra peak in the interval of 4–5 miles from the center. See Oslo Byplankontor, *Transportanalysen for Oslo-Omradet*, p. 39.

32. Women living in the city were more likely than men to marry non-residents. (See Table 26.1.) Women also outnumber men among migrants from other parts of Norway into Oslo – especially in the marriageable age groups. Of migrants into Oslo in 1961 who were 15–24 years of age, 63·5 per cent were women. See Municipal Office of Statistics of Oslo, *Statistical Yearbook*, 1961, Table 31, p. 28.

Index